28.79

THE EUROPEAN UNION SERIES

General Editors: Neill Nugent, William E. Paterson

The European Union series provides an authoritative library on the European Union, ranging from general introductory texts to definitive assessments of key institutions and actors, issues, policies and policy processes, and the role of member states.

Books in the series are written by leading scholars in their fields and reflect the most up-to-date research and debate. Particular attention is paid to accessibility and clear presentation for a wide audience of students, practitioners and interested general readers.

The series editors are **Neill Nugent**, Professor of Politics and Jean Monnet Professor of European Integration, Manchester Metropolitan University, and **William E. Paterson**, Founding Director of the Institute of German Studies, University of Birmingham and Chairman of the German British Forum. Their co-editor until his death in July 1999, **Vincent Wright**, was a Fellow of Nuffield College, Oxford University.

Feedback on the series and book proposals are always welcome and should be sent to Steven Kennedy, Palgrave Macmillan, Houndmills, Basingstoke, Hampshire RG21 6XS, UK, or by e-mail to s.kennedy@palgrave.com

---

General textbooks

Published

Desmond Dinan **Encyclopedia of the European Union**
[Rights: Europe only]

Desmond Dinan **Europe Recast: A History of European Union**
[Rights: Europe only]

Desmond Dinan **Ever Closer Union: An Introduction to European Integration (3rd edn)**
[Rights: Europe only]

Mette Eilstrup Sangiovanni (ed.) **Debates on European Integration: A Reader**

Simon Hix **The Political System of the European Union (2nd edn)**

Paul Magnette **What Is the European Union? Nature and Prospects**

John McCormick **Understanding the European Union: A Concise Introduction (4th edn)**

Brent F. Nelsen and Alexander Stubb **The European Union: Readings on the Theory and Practice of European Integration (3rd edn)**
[Rights: Europe only]

Neill Nugent (ed.) **European Union Enlargement**

Neill Nugent **The Government and Politics of the European Union (6th edn)**
[Rights: World excluding USA and dependencies and Canada]

John Peterson and Elizabeth Bomberg **Decision-Making In the European Union**

Ben Rosamond **Theories of European Integration**

Forthcoming

Laurie Buonanno and Neill Nugent **Policies and Policy Processes of the European Union**

David Howarth **The Political Economy of European Integration**

Series Standing Order (outside North America only)
ISBN 0–333–71695–7 hardback
ISBN 0–333–69352–3 paperback
Full details from www.palgrave.com

Visit Palgrave Macmillan's
EU Resource area at
www.palgrave.com/politics/eu/

The major institutions and actors

Published

Renaud Dehousse **The European Court of justice**

Justin Greenwood **Interest Representation in the European Union (2nd edn)**

Fiona Hayes-Renshaw and Helen Wallace **The Council of Ministers (2nd edn)**

Simon Hix and Christopher Lord **Political Parties in the European Union**

David Judge and David Earnshaw **The European Parliament (2nd edn)**

Neill Nugent **The European Commission**

Anne Stevens with Handley Stevens **Brussels Bureaucrats? The Administration of the European Union**

Forthcoming

Wolfgang Wessels **The European Council**

The main areas of policy

Published

Michelle Cini and Lee McGowan **Competition Policy In the European Union (2nd edn)**

Wyn Grant **The Common Agricultural Policy**

Martin Holland **The European Union and the Third World**

Jolyon Howorth **Security and Defence Policy in the European Union**

Stephan Keukeleire and Jennifer MacNaughtan **The Foreign Policy of the European Union**

Brigid Laffan **The Finances of the European Union**

Malcolm Levitt and Christopher Lord **The Political Economy of Monetary Union**

Janne Haaland Matláry **Energy Policy in the European Union**

John McCormick **Environmental Policy In the European Union**

John Peterson and Margaret Sharp **Technology Policy In the European Union**

Handley Stevens **Transport Policy in the European Union**

Forthcoming

Karen M. Anderson **Social Policy In the European Union**

Michelle Chang **Monetary Integration In the European Union**

Johanna Kantola **Gender and the European Union**

Bart Kerremans, David Allen and Geoffrey Edwards **The External Economic Relations of the European Union**

Jörg Monar **Justice and Home Affairs In the European Union**

John Vogler, Richard Whitman and Charlotte Bretherton **The External Policies of the European Union**

Also planned

Political Union

The member states and the Union

Published

Carlos Closa and Paul Heywood **Spain and the European Union**

Alain Guyomarch, Howard Machin and Ella Ritchie **France in the European Union**

Brigid Laffan and Jane O'Mahoney **Ireland and the European Union**

Forthcoming

Federiga Bindi **Italy and the European Union**

Simon Bulmer and William E. Paterson **Germany and the European Union**

Phil Daniels and Ella Ritchie **Britain and the European Union**

Brigid Laffan **The European Union and Its Member States**

Baldur Thorhallson **Small States in the European Union**

Issues

Published

Derek Beach **The Dynamic of European Integration: Why and When EU Institutions Matter**

Steven McGuire and Michael Smith **The European Union and the United States**

Forthcoming

Thomas Christiansen and Christine Reh **Constitutionalizing the European Union**

Robert Ladrech **Europeanization and National Politics**

The European Parliament

Second Edition

**David Judge
and
David Earnshaw**

First edition 2003
Second edition 2008

Palgrave Macmillan in the UK is an imprint of Macmillan Publishers Limited, registered in England, company number 785998, of Houndmills, Basingstoke, Hampshire RG21 6XS.

Palgrave Macmillan in the US is a division of St Martin's Press LLC, 175 Fifth Avenue, New York, NY 10010.

Palgrave Macmillan is the global academic imprint of the above companies and has companies and representatives throughout the world.

Palgrave® and Macmillan® are registered trademarks in the United States, the United Kingdom, Europe and other countries.

ISBN-13: 978–0–230–00141–1   hardback
ISBN-10: 0–230–00141–6   hardback
ISBN-13: 978–0–230–00142–8   paperback
ISBN-10: 0–230–00142–4   paperback

This book is printed on paper suitable for recycling and made from fully managed and sustained forest sources. Logging, pulping and manufacturing processes are expected to conform to the environmental regulations of the country of origin.

A catalogue record for this book is available from the British Library.

A catalog record for this book is available from the Library of Congress.

10 9 8 7 6 5 4 3 2 1
17 16 15 14 13 12 11 10 09 08

Printed and bound in China

Contents

List of Tables, Figures and Boxes   viii

List of Abbreviations   ix

Preface   xi

Introduction   1

   Structure of the Book   5
   Note on Referencing   7
   Note on Treaty Numbering   7

1   Locating the European Parliament   9

   The European Parliament as a Legislature   9
   'Universal' Functions: Policy Influence, Linkage
      and Legitimation   12
   'Parliamentary Model'   15
   Locating the European Parliament in the European Union's
      System of Governance   17
   Conclusion   24

**2   Historical Evolution: The European Parliament and
Ever Closer Union**   26

   Monnet's Ambiguous Institutional Legacy   26
   Common Assembly: Bridge to Federal Model?   28
   Members, Integrationist Aspirations and Interinstitutional
      Relations   30
   The Treaty of Rome and the Establishment of the European
      Economic Community   31
   Formal Structures and Informal Changes, 1957–79   35
   A Directly Elected Parliament: Small Steps and Large Strides,
      1979–87   38
   Formal Treaty Reforms   42
   Moving Beyond the SEA   46
   The Journey from Maastricht to Amsterdam   47
   The Amsterdam Treaty   51

The Road from Amsterdam to Nice   53
The Treaty of Nice   55
The Constitutional Treaty   57
The Lisbon Treaty: A Slight Detour on the Path Set by
    the Constitutional Treaty   62
Conclusion   66

3   **Linkage, Elections and Legitimacy**   **68**

The European Parliament and Direct Elections   68
2004 Elections   69
Turnout   76
Elections, Democracy and Legitimacy   80
Demos or Demoi?   82
Demos, Demoi and EU Governance   84
Conclusion   88

4   **Linkage, Representation and MEPs**   **90**

Microcosmic Representation   90
Territorial Representation   98
Functional/Interest Representation   101
Party Representation   108
The 'How' of Representation: Representative Style   111
Conclusion   111

5   **Party Groups in the European Parliament**   **113**

Development of Transnational Party Groups   113
Rules on Size and Formation   115
Parliamentary-specific Activities   116
Composition of Groups   124
National Party Delegations   134
Party Cohesion: National vs European Party Group?   135
Inter-Group Coalitions and Competition   140
Development of Left–Right Politics?   141
Roll-Call Votes in the EP: Finding What You Want To Find?   143
Conclusion   145

6   **Internal Organization**   **147**

Seat   148
Speaking in Tongues   154
Formal Parliamentary Leadership   158
The Presidency   159

The Vice-Presidents   162
Quaestors   162
The Bureau   163
Conference of Presidents   163
Conference of Committee Chairs and Conference of
   Delegation Chairs   165
Secretariat   166
Formal Organization: Committees   167
Temporary Committees/Committees of Inquiry   178
Conciliation Committee   181
Rules of Procedure   182
Intergroups   184
Plenary   185
Conclusion   186

7 **Formal Powers**   **188**

Legislative Powers   188
Budgetary Powers   198
Appointment and Dismissal   203
Appointments to Other EU Bodies   212
Power of Scrutiny   217
Judicial Review   225
Conclusion   226

8 **Influence and Decision-Making**   **229**

Assessing Legislative Influence   229
Rejection   237
Legislative Influence: Case Study   254
Influence over the Executive   267
Conclusion   271

9 **A Parliamentary Europe?**   **273**

Introduction   273
A Europe of Parliaments: The European Parliament and
   National Parliaments   274
Parliamentarization of the EU: Executive–Legislative Roles   284
Post-Parliamentarism: Alternative Conceptions of Governance   292
Parliamentarization: Addressing Post-Parliamentarism in a
   Semi-Parliamentary System?   298

References   300

Index   330

List of Tables, Figures and Boxes

Tables

3.1 2004 Electoral Systems and Turnout   71
4.1 Female representatives: European Parliament (2004) and
     national parliaments   96
4.2 Ratio of MEPs to population (2004 election)   99
5.1 Political groups by member state   125
6.1 Parliamentary committees and chairs, 2007   169
6.2 European Parliament committee reports, July 2004 to
     July 2007   170
7.1 Type of question by year   220
8.1 Codecision2 1996–2006: The European Parliament
     in conciliation   233

Figures

1.1 Policy-making and policy-influencing categorizations   14
7.1 Codecision2 procedure   190

Boxes

6.1 Functions of the President of the EP   161
6.2 Main duties of the Bureau   163
6.3 Main duties of the Conference of Presidents   164

List of Abbreviations

ACP-EU	Parliamentary Assembly of the African, Caribbean and Pacific regions and the EU
ALDE	Alliance of Liberals and Democrats for Europe
BEUC	Bureau Européen des Unions de Consommateurs
CAP	Common Agricultural Policy
CAT	Committee for Advanced Therapies
CDU	Christlich Demokratische Union
CFSP	Common Foreign and Security Policy
COREPER	Committee of Permanent Representatives
COSAC	Conference of European Affairs Committees
CRP	Committee on Rules of Procedure
Ebs	Europe by Satellite
EC	European Community
ECB	European Central Bank
ECOFIN	Economic and Financial Affairs Council
ECON	Economic and Monetary Affairs Committee
ECSC	European Coal and Steel Community
EDC	European Defence Community
EDD	Europe of Democracies and Diversities
EDF	European Development Fund
EDP	European Democratic Party
EEC	European Economic Community
EFA	Europe Free Alliance
ELDR	European Liberal, Democrat and Reform Party
EMI	European Monetary Institute
EMEA	European Medicines Agency
EMU	Economic and Monetary Union
EP	European Parliament
EPC	European Political Community
EPLP	European Parliamentary Labour Party
EPP	European People's Party
EPP-ED	European People's Party and European Democrats
EPU	European Political Union
ERC	Esquerra Republicana de Catalunya
EU	European Union
EUL	European United Left
FDP	Freie Demokratische Partei
GUE	Group of the European United Left

ID	Independence and Democracy Group
IGC	Intergovernmental Conference
IIA	Interinstitutional Agreement
IMCO	Internal Market and Consumer Protection Committee
ITRE	Industry, Research and Energy Committee
ITS	Identity, Tradition and Sovereignty Group
JPC	Joint Parliamentary Committee
LAUS	Laikos Orthodoxos Synayermos
LIBE	Civil Liberties, Justice and Home Affairs Committee
MEP	Member of the European Parliament
NGL	Nordic Green Left
NGOs	Non-governmental organizations
OJ	Official Journal of the European Union
ONP	Open Network Provision
OMC	Open Method of Coordination
ÖVP	Österreichische Volkspartei
PCP	Plaid Cymru
PSE	Party of European Socialists
QMV	Qualified majority voting
RPIE	Rassemblement pour la France et l'Indépendence de l'Europe
SEA	Single European Act
SNP	Scottish National Party
SPD	Socialdemokratische Partei Deutschlands
STV	Single Transferable Vote
TDI	Technical Group of Independent Members
TEU	Treaty on European Union
TFEU	Treaty on the Functioning of the European Union
UDF	Union pour la Démocratic Française
UEL	Union of European Left
UEN	Union for Europe of Nations
UKIP	United Kingdom Independence Party
VVD	Volkspartij voor Vrijheid en Democratie
WTO	World Trade Organization

Preface

The first edition of this book appeared in 2003 to favourable reviews. This is noted not simply to boost our egos but also to explain why the basic structure of this second edition remains the same as that of the first edition. Reviewers particularly praised the way the first edition sought to locate the study of the European Parliament within broader analytical frames provided by studies of legislatures and of European Union governance. Equally they recognized that our discussion of organization, powers and influence was 'clearly set down, readable and informative'. So with these endorsements ringing in our ears our intention remains the same: to provide a comprehensive insight into how the European Parliament works and analytical frames within which Parliament's fulfilment of its roles can be assessed.

If it is a truism that the European Union is in a state of almost perpetual institutional evolution (some would say 'permanent revolution') then it is even more of a truism that the European Parliament has been the institution most affected by these rapid changes. While the upside is that the study of the EP is never static, the downside is that it is often difficult to keep abreast of the changes taking place within the EP and in its interactions with other institutions and actors. What this edition provides, therefore, is a comprehensive updating of data and information to take account of: the 2004 elections and the elections in Bulgaria and Romania in 2007; internal organizational changes within the EP – to party groups, committees, rules of procedure, leadership structures; new interinstitutional agreements; and the major changes to the EP's formal powers and status incorporated in the Lisbon Treaty. This second edition also draws upon the significant analytical studies that have been published in recent years and which have added new perspectives and new controversies to the study of the EP. Indeed, the range and scope of academic writing on the EP continues to increase almost exponentially (as reflected in the 33 per cent increase in the references in this edition!).

To keep readers up-to-date in the intervening period before the 2009 elections, and immediately after the European elections, data and information about changes in the EP's membership and in the composition of party groups and committees will be provided on the Palgrave Macmillan website <http://www.palgrave.com/politics/eu>. Links to other useful sites will also be made available.

Just as the text of this second edition has grown in size and, we trust, in quality so too has the list of people who have helped the authors. Pride of place goes to the new addition of Nicolas Keir James Earnshaw Wood who has provided a 'second edition' to complement the 'first edition' of Toni Cowan Brown. Jo Wood and Lorraine, Ben and Hannah Judge have suffered in, relative, silence and remain convinced that a second edition of this book is one too many. On the contrary, Steven Kennedy and the Series editors Neill Nugent and Willie Paterson have remained convinced that a second edition was necessary and equally convinced that the authors could have produced the edition far more expeditiously and with far less prevarication. To all of the above: many thanks for sticking with us.

Thanks are also due to those MEPs who were good enough to share some of their time and thoughts with us during interviews in September 2005: John Bowis, Richard Corbett, Chris Davies, Karl-Heinz Florenz, Edit Herczog, Caroline Jackson, Peter Skinner, Alexander Stubb, Gary Titley, Graham Watson, (the late) Philip Whitehead and Terry Wynn. Equally this book has been enriched by both the direct and indirect advice and assistance offered by Frazer Clarke, Sir Ken Collins, Elisa Fenzi, Francis Jacobs, Peter Kerstens, David O'Leary, Niall O'Neill, Michael Shackleton, Sylwia Staszak, Luisa Strani, Anca Toma, and Martin Westlake.

In the first edition Fiona Macintyre demanded a sentence all to herself. In this edition, she demanded two – so here they are!

DAVID JUDGE
DAVID EARNSHAW

Introduction

One of the few things upon which both proponents and opponents of the European Union (EU) are able to agree is that the pace of European integration has been rapid and continuing. Whether it should be, or not, is what separates the two. In this process of change, the EU's institutions are, often simultaneously, both the propagators of change and the 'reapers' of this integrationist dynamic; and none more so than the European Parliament (EP). Indeed, of all the EU's institutions, the EP has come furthest and fastest in the enhancement of its role and powers since what was, in many respects, a 'standing start' after the first direct European elections in 1979.

Even since the first edition of this book appeared in 2003 the pace of change has been relentless. The European Union has grown from 15 to 27 member states and the European Parliament has increased its membership from 626 to 785. European elections were held in 25 member states in June 2004 and in a further two new member states in 2007 – in May in Bulgaria and in November in Romania. National elections have also been held in each member state in the intervening period and the composition of the Council has reflected changes in government in major states such as France, Germany, Italy, Poland and Spain. In addition, a new Commission came into office in 2004. Changes to the formal institutional status of the EP have been mapped out in two Intergovernmental Conferences (IGCs), in 2004 and 2007, and in successive treaties. The first, the Constitutional Treaty, was signed by the Heads of State and Government in Rome on 29 October 2004 and was effectively buried by the referendums in France and the Netherlands in 2005; and the second, the Reform Treaty, was signed in Lisbon on 13 December 2007 and was, before the uncertainties caused by the Irish referendum in June 2008, originally scheduled for ratification by 1 January 2009. Less formally, the EP has entered into a number of agreements – in the form of Interinstitutional Agreements, Framework Agreements, Declarations and Decisions – with the Council and Commission, both bilaterally and trilaterally, which have impacted upon the 'institutional balance' within the EU. These exogenous changes have been reflected in, and are also often prismatic reflections of, endogenous changes within the EP. Thus, one visible indicator of the rapidity of change is that, since the drafting of the first edition of this book, Parliament has completed a major revision of its entire Rules of Procedure, and has considered amendments to a further 26 of its individual Rules of Procedure since 2004.

Not only has the formal institutional position of the Parliament changed but its very physical presence has changed as well. Impressive new buildings have mushroomed in both Brussels and Strasbourg to accommodate the addition of 159 new Members of the European Parliament (MEPs) brought about by the enlargements of 2004 and 2007. Not surprisingly, therefore, enlargement has brought with it attendant changes to the working patterns and routines of the EP – from having to accommodate new members in its organizational structures, through to ensuring that MEPs can still communicate with each other across 506 possible language permutations in the 2004–2009 Parliament (up from 110 in the 1999–2004 Parliament). Equally, the dynamic of institutional change has been accelerated by the changed ideological, political and cultural profile of the post-enlargement EP.

In short, the European Parliament has changed dramatically in recent years. While there is manifest evidence of the quantity of change the important question, however, concerns the quality of change. This is a difficult question to answer. One answer is provided by the EP itself. In its resolution on the Treaty of Lisbon, adopted before the Irish referendum, Parliament noted that once that treaty comes into effect, EU laws will be 'subject to a level of parliamentary scrutiny that exists in no other supranational or international structure'; the EP will be coequal with the Council, with very few exceptions, in processing EU legislation; the 'electoral' dimension of the appointment of the Commission President will be enhanced; virtually all of the EU's expenditure will be subject to the approval of, and scrutiny by, the EP acting as an equal partner with the Council; European agencies will be subject to greater parliamentary scrutiny; and the EP, in the future, will be inextricably linked into the revision process of the treaties (Texts adopted 20 February 2008, P6_TA-PROV(2008)0055). This answer also finds support from one of the leading academic analysts of the EP, Simon Hix, in his assessment (with his co-authors) that, in 'a rather short space of time', the European Parliament has evolved into 'one of the most powerful elected assemblies in the world' (Hix *et al.* 2007:3).

As we will see, however, this is an answer that many academics, politicians and parliamentarians (especially beyond 'Brussels') still seek to qualify. In part, this reflects a fundamental paradox surrounding the EP that, despite its enhanced powers, many academics and, more importantly, European citizens, seem to be oblivious of such change. As Simon Taylor noted, 'While those on the inside need no convincing of the importance of the institution, it is a very different story outside the Brussels beltway and the Strasbourg *ceinture*' (*European Voice* 8 November 2007). In an attempt to address this paradox, the EP has adopted various strategies, among which was a relaunched 'communications strategy' agreed in October 2007. This was a strategy designed to convince voters, ahead of the 2009 elections, of the growing importance of the Parliament in influencing EU legislation and policies which directly affected their daily lives. But whether recourse to claims of significance based upon the EP's capacity to amend pieces of legislation that are often technical is sufficient to mobilize voters in the absence of the aggregation of political interests, in the form of transnational parties with structured relationships to a 'government', is an argument we will return to later in this book.

For the moment, however, if this initial overview of recent developments provides some brief insight into where the EP is now, it also raises a number of fundamental questions about how the EP reached this position. One of the purposes of this book, therefore, is to explain how the EP developed from being merely an advisory and consultative assembly into an institution that is 'a central, "mainstream" part of the Union's governing system' (Scully 2007:177). In this 'central' location it is important to understand how the European Parliament operates and how it interacts, and is interlinked, with other institutions. Obviously, many aspects of these interinstitutional relations are prescribed in formal treaty provisions, but a consistent theme throughout this book is that the influence of the EP can only be understood fully if the informal dimensions of its legislative and procedural activities are factored into an assessment of the EP's contribution to the EU's decision-making process. In other words, an understanding of the formal powers of the EP provides only a partial insight into the significance of the EP. What also has to be taken into account is how the EP organizes itself and how MEPs interact with each other internally – through party groups, national delegations, committees and authority hierarchies – and how they interact externally with other institutions, political actors and citizens. In this sense this book provides vital information about how the EP works; but it is equally concerned to provide some assessment of why the EP works in the way it does and how successful it is in doing what it does.

The starting-point of our assessment of the EP, therefore, is to see what analytical purchase existing models and categorizations of legislatures and legislative activity hold for the study of the European Parliament – an institution widely regarded as *sui generis*. Without giving the full answer away at this early stage, the short answer is that these models and classifications do, indeed, prove useful in structuring the analysis of the EP. Thus, a first step towards understanding the EP is to outline the characteristic features of legislatures and then to discover whether the EP conforms to those characteristics. In identifying three 'universal' functions of legislatures – legitimation, linkage and decision-making – this book assesses the relevance of these functions for the EP and the EU across time. In so doing, it becomes apparent that the balance between functions, and the relative emphasis placed upon the performance of these functions by the EP itself, has varied over time.

A further assumption driving this study is not only that the EP has to be understood as a legislature but also that it has to be understood as part of the wider system of EU governance. Where the EP is located conceptually within the EU's institutional structures has a bearing on how well it is perceived to play the roles ascribed to it as a legislature. To understand the EP's linkage functions, or its contribution to the legitimation of EU outputs, or to the EU's legislative process, requires some idea of how the EU as a political system is conceived in the first place.

In locating the EP within wider conceptions of the EU as a system of governance this book acknowledges that the Parliament is part of multiple, complex, interwoven and overlapping institutional networks. In other words, we agree with Peterson and Shackleton (2006:10) that 'the EU's institutions are inescapably interdependent'. Hence, a basic premise of this book is that the EP, as an institution, can be understood only in terms of its wider interinstitutional interactions. Unfortunately, what complicates this understanding in the case of the EU is that there are no singular institutional structures, only plural institutional forms. Thus, terms that have a certain precision in the context of member states acquire ambiguity in the context of the EU. For example, there is no single executive but rather a 'dual executive' of Commission and Council; nor is there a single legislature but a series of interconnected 'legislative bodies' – in so far as the European Parliament shares legislative functions with the Council and the Commission. From the outset, therefore, we have to recognize that the conceptualization of interinstitutional relations in the EU not only affects the assessment of the past and current performance of the EP but also conditions prognostications about a future 'parliamentarization' of the EU.

Indeed, the implementation of the Amsterdam Treaty, the Nice Treaty and the prospective Treaty of Lisbon have served to heighten beliefs in 'parliamentarization' and the enhancement of 'parliamentary democracy' in the EU. In examining such perceptions the need to recognize the *interconnectedness* of the defining elements of a 'parliamentary model' have to be explicitly acknowledged. As a minimum, criteria by which the process of 'parliamentarization' should be assessed have to be specified.

In raising fundamental questions – about the location of the EP within the comparative study of legislatures, about its location within notions of EU governance and about the parliamentarization of the EU's system of governance – we claim neither to treat these questions equally nor to answer them in the detail specialists of, for example, integration theories or democratic theories would like. What we do claim, however, is that these are important questions and should at least be raised by students of the European Parliament.

Similarly we raise some important issues surrounding the question of whether or not the EP is a 'proper' parliament. As the discussion about the location of the EP illustrates, it all depends how a 'parliament' is defined in the first place and what expectations are held of the role and functions of a parliament. In the case of the EP, not only is it relatively new, having been in existence for just over fifty years, but also it is chameleon-like in its capacity to adapt to constant change in the nature of treaty-defined institutional relations, of political constellations (of parties, states and civil societies), and of informal interinstitutional networks. What becomes evident fairly soon in any analysis of the EP is that global assessments of its powers, its legislative influence and its linkages with other groups and institutions are extremely easy to assert but difficult to substantiate in the face of such perpetual change. Indeed, a constant theme of our writing since the early 1990s has been that it is difficult to assess the EP, especially its legislative impact, in aggregate or absolute terms. In practice, assessments of the EP are contingent upon the following factors: the chronological period under study; the formal powers and scope of competencies held at that time; treaty-prescribed interinstitutional relations; informal modes of interinstitutional networking; the ideological and national configurations within the EP itself; relations with other EU institutions and member states; and the differentiated nature of EU policy sectors and networks. Certainly, if the Treaty of Lisbon is enacted, the EP would be a true co-legislator with the Council in most EU policy areas and so is in a radically different relationship to the Council and Commission than it was in the early 1990s, yet in a few areas it would remain in essentially an advisory capacity. Similarly, in its linkage and legitimating roles the EP is clearly in a different relationship both to the EU's dual executive and to citizens in member states from that before direct elections in 1979 (and in an altered relationship yet again after the low turnouts at the 1999 and 2004 elections), yet many disconnections remain in terms of public perceptions and knowledge of the EP.

Structure of the book

Locating the European Parliament within wider theories of legislatures and models of the EU's political system is of importance in understanding what role we would expect the EP to perform as a legislature and the broader political context within which it is expected to perform this role. To this end, Chapter 1 examines how the EP can be located within comparative typologies of legislatures, and identifies three universal functions – of legitimation, linkage and decision-making – performed by legislatures. In addition, Chapter 1 also outlines two basic models of governance which provide contextual background for later chapters.

Chapter 2 pursues the analytical prescriptions of Chapter 1 and considers the interinstitutional, contextual and interconnected dimensions of the historical development of the EP. In seeking to 'locate' the EP across time, both as a legislature and within the developing EU integrationist project, a useful historical perspective is provided from which the EP can be viewed in the early twenty-first century.

Chapters 3 and 4 examine the first two of the three 'universal' functions ascribed to legislatures – legitimation and linkage. Chapter 3 focuses upon the electoral linkage at the core of the process of representation and analyses the concepts of demos, legitimacy and democracy within the EU. Chapter 4 then extends the analysis of linkage by looking at how the EP acts as a representative body, and how it links citizens and decision-makers in the periods between elections.

Chapter 5 serves as a pivot in the study. It turns the analysis away from the broader issues of Chapter 4 – of linkage and the representative roles of political parties and the extent of transnational party competition – towards the examination of the role performed by party groups in the internal workings of the European Parliament. Not only do parties link the people to decision-makers but they also link, structure and regularize interactions between decision-makers themselves. Party groups in the EP work within an institutional context that has changed dramatically with successive treaty reforms and enhancements of the legislative role of the EP. Concomitantly, the extension of formal power has increased the importance of exerting institutional controls over the activities of party groups and their members. The identification of a dynamic relationship between the organization of the EP as an institution and the party system and party groups is then used to answer one of the central organizational questions confronting legislatures: how do elected representatives effectively and efficiently organize themselves in order to make collective decisions? In answering this question, Chapter 6 analyses the EP's rules and procedures, its formal institutional leadership positions, and the all-important internal division of labour in the form of its committees.

Chapters 7 and 8 echo the theme of Chapter 1 that any assessment of the EP's formal powers and legislative influence requires recognition of the interconnected, interinstitutional and contextual elements of the exercise of such powers. In this sense, Chapter 7 makes clear that a study of the powers of the EP is intrinsically comparative in nature: in relation to other institutions involved in the EU's legislative process, and in relation to the exercise of these powers across time.

Chapter 8 moves beyond the specification of formal powers to examine the actual influence wielded by the European Parliament towards the end of the first decade of the twenty-first century. In so doing, the chapter highlights another general theme of the book that the formal dimensions of the EP's influence have to be supplemented by recognition of the informal dimensions of its contribution to the EU's decision-making processes. Indeed, not only is this a historical phenomenon, as revealed in Chapter 2, but it also constitutes a future strategy for the development of the EP.

In 'looking to the future', Chapter 9 examines exactly what further 'parliamentarization' means and the forms that this process takes. If 'the future of Europe' is 'parliamentary', we need to understand what 'parliamentarization' entails and the extent to which the interinstitutional connections among the EU's institutions, and between national parliaments and the EP, contribute to such a process. Ultimately, representative democracy still provides the normative frame within which debate about governance in the EU is conducted – in which case an understanding of how the EP operates and interacts with other institutions and actors in a multi-level EU polity is vital. And for this reason, we stand by our initial claim that the EP has to be understood both as a legislature and as part of the wider system of EU governance.

Note on referencing

Given the complexities of the referencing of EU documents we have adopted the following conventions. Wherever possible:

- European Parliament committee reports are noted by PE number. (To ease identification in the references at the end of the book each report is listed numerically by PE number, rather than by PE number by year of publication.)
- Other European Parliament documents (Rules of Procedure, working papers, or information documents) are referenced under 'European Parliament', unless they have a specific author, in which case they are referenced under the author's name.
- European Parliament resolutions are referenced as they appear in the *Official Journal* of the European Union (OJ) C-series or, if not yet published in the *Official Journal,* the reference and date in Parliament's minutes is provided.
- European Commission documents are referenced by COM number.

The term European Union (EU) has been used wherever possible, unless its use is historically inaccurate.

Note on treaty numbering

On 13 December 2007 the Treaty of Lisbon was signed. The Treaty of Lisbon, or the Reform Treaty, comprises two substantive clauses amending respectively the Treaty on European Union (TEU) and the Treaty Establishing the European Community (the latter is re-named the Treaty on the Functioning of the European Union (TFEU)). The rejection of the Lisbon Treaty in the Irish Referendum of 12 June 2008 (when this book was at proof stage) raised doubts as to whether the Treaty would be ratified, and virtually guaranteed that its major provisions would not come into force in January 2009. The European Council, at its meeting in Brussels of 19 and 20 June, agreed that more time was needed to analyse the outcome of the Irish referendum and decided to revisit the issue at its next meeting in October 2008. In noting that 19 member states' parliaments had already ratified the Treaty, and that the ratification process continued in the other countries, the European Council also recalled that the objective of the Lisbon Treaty was to help an enlarged Union to act 'more effectively and more democratically'. Similarly, the President of the European Commission, José Manuel Barroso, in his speech to the European Parliament in Strasbourg on 18 June, maintained that: 'The Lisbon Treaty remains essential to help us respond to the challenges that Europe faces today'.

Given these statements we have chosen to retain, generally, consideration of the provisions of the Treaty and, more specifically, the 'post-Lisbon' numbering of treaty articles, except where it would have been historically inaccurate to do so – in which case the appropriate numbering at the specific time has been used. However, aware of the uncertainties surrounding ratification of the (consolidated) Lisbon Treaty, we have included, where appropriate in the text, dual references to the existing treaties and to the Lisbon Treaty. In addition, in the event of the non-ratification of the Treaty we have provided, on the companion website to this book, a comparative table which cross-references articles in the Lisbon Treaty with those in the Treaty on European Union and the Treaty Establishing the European Community. We also outline on this website the pre-Lisbon powers of the EP as specified under the existing treaties (see <http://www.palgrave.com/politics/eu>).

Chapter 1

Locating the European Parliament

Where is the European Parliament located? The answer seems to be obvious, at least in geographical terms: in Brussels, along with the other major institutions of the European Union – the Council of the European Union and the European Commission. However, as we will discover in the rest of this book, there are no simple answers as far as the EP is concerned. Certainly, there is an impressive parliamentary complex just off the rue Belliard in Brussels, strategically located across from the building which houses the Council of Ministers and close by the Commission buildings. Dominated by the Spaak and Spinelli Buildings the complex contains a futuristic debating chamber (hemicycle) and the offices of the 785 Members of the European Parliament (MEPs) and their staff. It is used for meetings of the Parliament's committees and for plenary part-sessions. However, this impressive complex is matched by another imposing set of buildings in the French city of Strasbourg, some 450 kilometres from Brussels. The Strasbourg complex comprises the Churchill, Weiss and Madariaga Buildings and accommodates MEPs and their staff during twelve weekly plenary sessions each year. So the answer to the original question is: Brussels *and* Strasbourg. Even this is only a partial answer, however, as the full answer is Brussels *and* Strasbourg *and* Luxembourg. Indeed, Luxembourg was the original home of the Parliament before direct elections in 1979, and is still the formal location of the Parliament's General Secretariat. Thus, even locating the European Parliament geographically is not a simple undertaking.

The European Parliament as a legislature

If there are problems locating the EP geographically it should come as no surprise, therefore, to find that trying to locate the EP institutionally is an even more daunting prospect. Yet it is a prospect that has to be addressed from the outset, because, very simply, where, how and why the EP is located first within comparative assessments of legislatures and second within the institutional structure of the European Union raises wider issues about democracy, legitimacy, accountability and responsiveness within the EU itself.

9

If we are to understand what the European Parliament 'does' and how well it 'does what it does' then we need to be clear about what our expectations of a parliament are in the first place. What this chapter seeks to do, therefore, is to raise the question of how we would go about making such an assessment. The answer we propose is to be found through 'locating' the EP within a broader study of legislatures. This perspective – on legislatures – prompts an examination of what functions the European Parliament performs, or is expected to perform. What we seek to do is to examine existing analytical maps in this chapter and then to use these conceptual 'coordinates' to enable the reader in subsequent chapters to locate the EP as a legislature and as part of the EU's political system. Unless we are clear at the outset what the models are, and where the EP is located in each, then we will be unclear what the criteria of assessment are and what expectations we should have of the European Parliament.

The 'sui generis' issue

Problems will always emerge in the study of the institutions of the European Union, the EP included, precisely because they have no exact counterparts in national political systems. This leads immediately to the *sui generis* issue of whether the European Union is unique in its institutional form and in its trajectory of development. Most concern with the *sui generis* issue, or the '$n = 1$' problem, has been expressed by theorists of regional integration (for an overview see Caporaso *et al.* 1997:1–5). However, the issue is of direct relevance to the EP because of the continuing belief that the European Parliament is unique and so 'defies easy categorization' (Corbett *et al.* 2007:2). But it is worth noting from the outset that this belief is not exclusive to analyses of the EP, for, as Norton (1990:9) notes, 'there is a tendency for scholars to view their particular legislature as *sui generis*'. The starting-point of any assessment of the EP, therefore, is to decide what are the characteristic features of legislatures and then to discover whether the EP conforms to those characteristics.

Characteristic features of legislatures

According to Philip Norton (1990:1), what legislatures have in common is that they are 'constitutionally designated institutions for giving assent to binding measures of public policy, that assent being given on behalf of a political community that extends beyond the government elite responsible for formulating those measures'. The value of Norton's definition is that it does not focus exclusively on 'law-making', but instead directs attention to the wider issues surrounding the 'giving of assent' in terms of legitimation, consent and authorization. The definition also recognizes that not all legislatures are directly elected. More particularly, it acts as an analytical pointer towards the multidirectional relationship between a legislature and its broader 'political community' as well as with its involvement with other policy-making institutions.

Implicit within Norton's definition, and in fact explicit in most discussions of what legislatures 'are', is some conception of what legislatures 'do'. In this respect, attention becomes focused on the functions of legislatures, with Robert Packenham (1970:523), for example, proclaiming that 'everyone who has written about legislatures is, explicitly or implicitly, a functionalist'. Packenham, himself, grouped the functions of legislatures into three main categories (based upon his study of the Brazilian legislature) – legitimation; recruitment and socialization of elites; and decisional or influence. Of these functions 'legitimation' was identified as of greatest significance in the political system; while 'decisional' functions – traditionally the primary functions associated with 'legislatures' – were deemed to be of least consequence for the political system as a whole.

Packenham's delineation of functions provided the starting-point for many subsequent studies (see, for example, Norton 1990), but its significance for present purposes is that it directs attention away from a preoccupation with 'law-making' and refocuses attention upon the broader roles of legislatures. What becomes clear, rapidly, in Packenham's specification and indeed in any other listing of functions, is that legislatures are not mono-functional bodies concerned exclusively with 'law-making'. In fact, as Packenham emphasizes, 'even if [a legislature] had no decision making power whatsoever, the functions which it performs would be significant' (1970:536).

From the outset, therefore, it needs to be recognized that legislatures are multifunctional institutions. The exact number of functions and their ranking in terms of importance naturally varies from author to author but it is possible to identify three key functions based loosely on the headings provided by Packenham. These are legitimation, linkage and decision-making. This precise listing of universal functions is provided by Copeland and Patterson (1994:154) and will be used throughout the rest of this book (see also Cotta 1974:208–16; Loewenberg and Patterson 1979:43–67). The general significance of this threefold classification of 'key functions' is that:

> a parliament's very reason for existence is found in them. Failure to fulfil these functions challenges the very basis for the existence of parliaments. A parliament without legitimacy may no longer be considered a parliament; a parliament that lacks any decision-making capacity hardly qualifies for the title; and an entity not formally linked to a broader population is no parliament. (Copeland and Patterson 1994:154)

The threefold classification of functions also points to the fact that parliaments perform their functions in relation to other political institutions and organizations, most particularly political executives in one direction and the electorate and civil society in the other. Thus, at the interstices of government and governance parliaments perform their common functions of legitimation, linkage and decision-making. What we intend to do, therefore, is concentrate upon the three 'universal' functions identified by Copeland and Patterson and assess the relevance of these functions for the EP and the EU across time. In so doing it will be apparent that the balance of importance between functions, and the relative emphasis placed upon the performance of these functions by the EP itself, has varied over time. The best we can do therefore is to follow Copeland and Patterson's (1994:153) advice and 'identify the major functions of parliaments that tend to be universal across both time and space, and [then] identify functions of particular relevance to a polity at a specific juncture in its history'.

'Universal' functions: policy influence, linkage and legitimation

Policy influence

> The simplest and most common comparative statements about legislatures . . . usually refer to the importance of the legislature in the policy-making process relative to the importance of non-legislative institutions, commonly those operating through the executive branch of government. (Mezey 1979:23)

Two typologies have dominated the comparative assessment of the policy impact of legislatures and their respective capacities to influence or to 'make' policy. The first was provided by Michael Mezey (1979); and the second was an explicit reworking of Mezey's model by Norton (1990). Despite recent questioning of the merits of these established typologies, and attempts to refine them through the incorporation of broader notions of 'legislative performance' alongside 'policy outputs' (see Arter 2006:462–82), Mezey and Norton still provide the most parsimonious frameworks for the classification of legislatures.

Michael Mezey: policy-making strength of legislatures

According to Michael Mezey a legislature can be placed into one of three discrete categories depending on the strength of its policymaking capacities (1979:26). 'Strong' legislatures can modify or reject executive proposals; legislatures with 'modest policymaking power' can modify but cannot reject policy proposals; and those legislatures that can neither modify nor reject policy proposals can be seen to have 'little or no policy-making power'.

In defining the policy-making strength of legislatures, Mezey drew both upon Blondel's (1973) notion of the constraints operating on a legislature, and on his earlier concept of 'viscosity' (Blondel 1970:80). For Blondel, 'viscosity' reflected the degree of freedom – or alternatively the compliantness – of a legislature in relation to the executive's processing of legislation. Mezey refined the notion of constraint to mean not simply the 'constraints placed on the legislature that prevent it from influencing the policy-making process, but rather the constraints that the legislature is capable of placing on the policy-related activities of the executive' (Mezey 1979:24–5). In other words, he takes as an indication of the policy role of a legislature the extent to which a legislature restricts the ability of the executive to make policy unilaterally. Ultimately, therefore, Mezey maintains that the 'saliency of the legislature's policy-making role, whether ultimately evaluated as positive or negative, stems at base from its capacity to restrict the process, because that capacity is what compels other institutions to deal with it when they seek to make policy' (Mezey 1979:25).

An equally important part of Mezey's argument, however, is that any evaluation of legislative influence has to deal with 'real rather than paper powers' (Mezey 1979:25). Moreover, any evaluation of the constraints imposed upon executive policy discretion should also include informal mechanisms (for example, private discussions or anticipated opposition) as well as formal procedures for legislative amendment.

Philip Norton: policy-making versus policy-influencing

Philip Norton (1990) refines Mezey's categorization to include the capacity of legislatures to 'formulate' or 'make' policy. This moves beyond Mezey's notion of constraint to take into account the ability of a legislature to substitute its own policy for that of the executive. The essential difference for Norton is between those legislatures that can initiate or formulate legislation and those that cannot. The capacity to 'generate alternative policies' (Norton 1990:179) distinguishes 'policy-making' from 'policy-influencing' legislatures.

In the rest of this book these categorizations will be used to locate the EP diachronically (across time), and in comparison with other parliaments. As we will see in later chapters, empirical investigation of the EP's role and functions produces different answers at different times to the question of where the EP is located. What we should be suspicious of from the outset, however, are global claims that the EP is 'not a proper parliament'. For the question of what defines a 'proper parliament' is itself a complex issue.

FIGURE 1.1   Policy-making and policy-influencing categorizations

Mezey	Norton
Strong policy-making power A legislature can: • modify or reject executive proposals	**Policy-making** A legislature is able to: • modify and reject measures put forward by government and • formulate and substitute policy for that proposed by government
Modest policy-making power A legislature can: • modify but cannot reject policy proposals	**Policy-influencing** A legislature is able to: • modify and reject measures put forward by government • but cannot substitute a policy of its own
Little or no policy-making power A legislature cannot: • modify or reject policy proposals	**Little or no policy impact** A legislature cannot: • modify or reject measures • generate and substitute policies of its own

Sources: Mezey (1979), Norton (1990).

Linkage

If the categorization of legislatures in terms of 'policy-making' or 'policy-influencing' is based upon an assessment of interinstitutional relations (primarily with executives), then, in turn, these relations are influenced by the linkage between a legislature and its wider political and societal environment. The inextricable connections between specific policy role and wider linkage is apparent in Copeland and Patterson's (1994:153) definition of a parliament as 'a group of individuals operating on behalf of others in a binding and legitimate manner and making decisions collectively but with formal equality'. The questions of exactly how, and in what respects, parliamentarians act 'on behalf of others' have been at the heart of representative theories and practice alike (see Judge 1999) and will be at the centre of the discussion in Chapters 3 and 4.

Legitimation

In Mezey's classificatory model a second dimension for distinguishing legislatures was the extent to which 'support' accrued to representative institutions. Support was taken to mean 'a set of attitudes that look to the legislature as a valued and popular political institution' (Mezey 1979:27). Support could be gauged by manifest indicators, such as institutional continuity, elite and public attitudes towards the institution itself, or satisfaction with the policy outputs of a legislature. Equally it could entail 'diffuse support' as part of an abstract 'cultural phenomenon nested within a set of supportive attitudes toward all of the political institutions that make up a political system' (Mezey 1979:31). In this sense the concept of diffuse support is inextricably linked to notions of legitimation. While this is not the place to examine these ideas in detail (see Chapters 3 and 4), the important point is that a parliament's role within a political system (and its location within a comparative categorization of legislatures) is influenced by the 'combination of policy powers and supportive orientations' (Scully 2000a:242). Certainly the role played by the European Parliament in the legitimation of the EU's political system is both important and extremely complex. This complexity is revealed in the discussion of the democratic and legitimacy deficits within the EU (see Chapter 3). For the time being, however, it is sufficient to note Scully's (2000a:244) cautionary statement that: 'A more powerful EP may indeed make the EU more democratic in a technical sense but it has thus far done little to accord the EU as a system of governance the legitimacy which democracy is normally seen to accord.' The location of the EP within the 'EU as a system of governance' will be examined below, but first one further classificatory system based upon 'systems of government' needs some discussion.

'Parliamentary model'

In addition to classification by functions, legislatures can also be differentiated in accordance with the characteristics of the wider political systems in which they perform their functions. One classic point of differentiation has been between 'parliamentary' and 'presidential' systems of government. These two models have been classified in accordance with different institutional configurations between the electorate, the legislature and the executive (Lijphart 1991; Judge 2008). In a parliamentary system there is a single direct act of delegation from the electorate to representatives in parliament. From this single act flows a sequential and serial process of delegation, whereby representatives in parliament then delegate the routines of decision-making to a related institution – the political executive – which acts as the agent of the 'principal' of parliament. In contrast, in a presidential system, citizens elect and directly authorize both a political executive and representatives in a legislature. In presidential systems, therefore, the electorate has two agents. Moreover, in presidential systems there is a separation of powers between the legislature and the executive; whereas in parliamentary systems there is a fundamental fusion of parliamentary and executive institutions.

Indeed, the significance of this distinction between parliamentary and presidential systems has become more pronounced in analyses of the EU since the implementation of the Amsterdam Treaty in 1999 and a heightened belief in the 'parliamentarization' of the EU and its movement towards a 'parliamentary model' (Dehousse 1998; Muntean 2000; Majone 2002). One problem common to such analyses, however, is that too often the criteria by which the process of 'parliamentarization' should be assessed are never fully specified. Moreover, there is a tendency to select individual characteristics of the 'parliamentary model' and to proclaim that because the EU displays individual elements of this model it is necessarily evolving towards a 'parliamentary democracy'. What we seek to argue in this book, however, is that a 'parliamentary model' is defined by the very *interconnectedness* of its defining elements. However, before developing this argument, a preliminary specification of what constitutes a 'parliamentary model' is required.

According to Loewenberg and Patterson (1979:56), 'the distinguishing characteristic of legislatures in parliamentary systems of government' is 'the overlap of executive and legislative leaders.' In a parliamentary system political executives are authorized by parliaments. Using the concept 'authorization' avoids using notions of the 'selection' or 'emergence' of executives from parliaments. In practice, few parliaments actively select leaders from their ranks. A basic feature of parliamentary systems remains however that there is a fusion of executive and legislative roles. Moreover, 'in a parliamentary system, the chief executive . . . and his or her cabinet are responsible to the legislature in the sense that they are dependent on the legislature's confidence and that they can be dismissed from office by a legislative vote of no confidence or censure' (Lijphart 1984:68). The logic of parliamentarism is that the executive should retain the confidence of the legislature because it derives both its legitimacy and its authority from the representative parliament. In this manner there is an intrinsic institutional interconnectedness between the executive and the legislature and the performance of the parliamentary functions of legitimation, linkage and decision-making.

An important corollary of this interconnectedness is the general belief that 'Parliaments are supposed to control the operation of the executive' (Dehousse 1998:598). The exact degree of control is determined, in turn, by the formal and informal constraints that the legislature is able to place upon the executive and vice versa (see Blondel 1973:45–54). These constraints may stem from formal, constitutionally prescribed powers, or from less formal practices, procedures and internal rules of a legislature itself.

In raising the concept of the 'parliamentary model' at this early stage all we seek to do is to reinforce Loewenberg and Patterson's (1979:65) dictum that 'In conceptualizing the activity of legislatures in functional terms, we are also calling attention to the relationship between what legislatures do and what is done by other structures in the political system.' What we are particularly concerned to emphasize in this book is that the study of the EP, or any other legislature for that matter, has to be: *interinstitutional* – to take account of its relation with other institutions; *contextual* – to take account of the systemic context in which it operates; and *interconnected* – to take account of the multifunctional nature of legislatures.

This is not to claim that all legislatures are unique and cannot be compared, only that there is a danger of extracting isolated variables from different systems and reconstituting or 'stacking them up' in any single legislature to conclude that because some common characteristics can be identified, the aggregate is necessarily a 'parliamentary system'. That the EP performs the defining parliamentary functions of legitimation, linkage and decision-making is not in dispute (though how well it performs these functions is more contentious). What is in dispute, however, is whether the EU's political system *as an entity* conforms to a 'parliamentary model'.

Locating the European Parliament in the European Union's system of governance

> Assessments of the role of the EP within the EU are shaped by conceptions of the EU as a system. The schools of thought [on the EU as a system] . . . orient us toward different approaches to the legitimacy of the EU . . . They represent useful points of reference for the ongoing debate about the place of the EP within the EU as a whole and its importance for the problem of legitimacy. (Wessels and Diedrichs 1999:135)

Not only does the EP have to be understood as a legislature but it also has to be understood as part of an institutional matrix. In other words, where the EP is located conceptually within the EU's institutional structures has a bearing on how well it is perceived to play the roles ascribed to it as a legislature. It is important, therefore, to keep in mind where the EP is located within broader conceptions of the EU as a political system when trying to assess its location within conceptions of it as a legislature. It makes little sense to make assessments of the EP's linkage functions, or its contribution to the legitimation of EU outputs (Chapters 3, 4 and 5), or to the EU's policy process (Chapters 7 and 8), unless we have a clear idea of what our expectations are of the EP in the first place. Do we expect it to display a direct electoral linkage between the represented and their representatives as in member states? Do we expect representatives at EU level to be authorized and account-able to an EU-wide electorate? Do we expect the existence of a European-wide 'people' or 'demos' in the first instance? Do we con-ceive of EU institutions in terms that are analogous to existing state-level institutions? Or is the EU's institutional matrix *sui generis*, so that it requires a new institutional vocabulary and new conceptualizations of legitimacy within the EU? Clearly detailed answers to these ques-tions lie beyond the immediate scope of the present book, but at the very least these questions should be borne in mind when reading the following chapters.

The danger in raising these questions at such an early stage, however, is that the reader may become swamped by the sheer range of models and theories (for example, intergovernmental, federal, cooperative federal, confederal consociationalism, regulatory state, multilevel gov-ernance, multitiered governance – for overviews see Rosamond 2000; Hooghe and Marks 2001; Weiner and Diez 2004; Pollack 2005; Rosamond 2007). What all these models and theories share, however, is a recognition that there is dispersion of formal authority among supranational, state and subnational governing institutions and that decision-making is not the sole preserve of elected representative insti-tutions at any single level. In fact, Hooghe and Marks provide a useful organizing frame for our discussion by identifying two main types of governance. 'Type I governance' is based upon federal conceptions and is characterized by dispersed decision-making among a limited number of governments operating at just a few levels. This type of governance is characterized by 'general-purpose, nonintersecting, and nested juris-dictions' (Hooghe and Marks 2003:237). 'Type II governance', on the other hand, is based on the proliferation of functionally specific juris-dictions and the organization of governance across a large number of levels. In this model 'formal government has shrunk' (Hooghe and Marks 2001:10) as 'self-rule' on the part of diverse groups and associ-ations has expanded. It is a vision of a decision-making process which is interconnected, non-state-centred, non-majoritarian, and with shared competences among a multiplicity of actors.

In accepting this basic bifurcation of models of governance our inten-tion here is simply to highlight the implications of these models for the conception of the EP. Hence, we do not intend to describe these models in detail, nor do we intend to make judgements upon their respective utility for understanding EU governance. Instead, our intention is far more restricted, and is simply focused upon locating the position of the EP within the institutional matrix identified in each type of governance.

Type I governance: the federal analogy

Hooghe and Marks (2003:236) identify federalism as the 'intellectual foundation for Type I governance'. Earlier, William Wallace (1996:445) had commended the appropriateness of the 'federal analogy' as a 'starting-point for understanding the institutions, politics and policy-making of the EU'. The use of the word 'analogy' is significant in that the EU should not be conceived of as an unambiguous federal system. Such a system is normally characterized by the existence of a sovereign state, with a constitutional division of powers between different levels of government; and with external sovereignty exercised at the higher level (see Burgess 2004, 2007). A bicameral legislature is a common characteristic of such a federal system, with representation in the upper chamber based upon lower levels of government (states). The relationship between the federal level of government and lower levels (states) is regulated through formal mechanisms for constitutional modification, often with a requirement for super-majorities; and through the existence of constitutional courts to adjudicate in disputes over the allocation and exercise of powers between different levels of government (see Elazar 1991:xv; Laffan 1992:7–9). It is not surprising to find therefore that those who actively promote a federalist vision for the EU's future largely subscribe to a model of 'a parliamentary Europe' or aspire to 'full parliamentarization' of the EU (see Abromeit 2002:20).

In analysing the EU's political system, a useful distinction may be drawn between a fully developed federation along the lines of a 'United States model'; a 'confederation' or a 'neo-federal model'; and a 'cooperative federal model'. Taking these models in turn, the United States of Europe variant stipulates a formal-legal division of responsibilities between supra-state/EU-level institutions and state/substate political institutions. An institutional sketch of this model would pencil in a separation of powers at the EU level with the Commission clearly identified as the executive branch, a directly elected EP serving as the first legislative chamber; and with the Council of Ministers acting as a second chamber in areas of concurrent competences between EU and member states (see Wessels 1996b:25–6). The European Court of Justice would serve as a constitutional court with major responsibilities in the adjudication of institutional disputes among the tiers of government and between EU institutions themselves. In this 'United States' model the basic source of legitimation would be a directly elected EP, with the EP serving as the formal linkage between the represented and 'their' government at the EU level. Through elections to a European Parliament the will of the 'European people' would be expressed and their contribution to EU decision-making would be 'unfiltered' (Wessels and Diedrichs 1997:3). There would be no doubt that 'the EP is regarded as the main legitimizing factor of the EU system' (Wessels and Diedrichs 1999:136). The preexisting states and substates, in turn, would have their own designated competences and, through their own democratic processes, would derive legitimation through 'traditional national sources'. They would, however, be 'of secondary importance' (Wessels 1996b:25).

Analysts who acknowledge that the EU has federal characteristics but is not a federal state have turned to concepts of 'confederalism', 'neo-federalism' or 'confederal consociationalism' to understand its institutional configuration. What each of these terms recognizes is a division of decision-making authority among different layers of government. Unlike federalism, where there is a central source of legitimacy grounded in an identifiable demos in a 'union', a confederation is based on the concept of 'dual legitimacy' where the nation states maintain their own democratic legitimacy and continue to claim political sovereignty while allowing a 'pooling of sovereignties' at the EU level. In such a system member states would seek mutual benefits through cooperation over common policies at a supranational level. Such a system would require neither a 'sense of community' among the peoples of the confederation nor the existence of a single demos. Moreover, the 'polycentric and multilogic pattern' of decision-making is associated with a large dose of intergovernmentalism (Chryssochoou 1997:530). In these circumstances, the EP would remain in a secondary relationship to the EU's dual executive institutions (most particularly the Council of Ministers), and national parliaments would share a similar subsidiary relationship to their own national executives. The result would be that 'the main source of democratic legitimacy for EU decisions [rested more] in the Council of Ministers' representation of national governments – in turn based on their respective national parliamentary structures – than on the powers of the EP as the natural exponent of representative democracy at the regional level' (Chryssochoou 1994:7). However, in the absence of a transnational demos there would be no effective mechanism for the direct democratic control of intergovernmental EU institutions, and in this lacuna are to be found the roots of the EU's 'crisis of legitimacy' and its various 'democratic deficits' (see Chapters 3 and 9).

Type II governance: 'multilevel'

According to Peterson and Bomberg (2000:25) multilevel governance has become 'a central point of consensus' among scholars of the EU. The initial premise of this model is that neither the concept of the nation state nor notions of international organizations capture the complexity of decision-making in the EU. The form of governance in the EU is thus both new and unique. What has emerged is a 'new, non-territorial form of governance' (Jachtenfuchs and Kohler-Koch 1997). It is *sui generis* in form, and decision-making is 'through a unique set of multi-level, non-hierarchical and regulatory institutions, and a hybrid mix of state and non-state actors' (Hix 1998a:39). To complicate matters still further the EU is a dynamic system subject to regular constitutional change and institutional innovation. Overall, therefore, 'because the EU as a political system is unique, it is an open process of trial and error to find out what kind of decision-making routines will develop and what will be the relative importance of individual institutions in the game' (Kohler-Koch 1997:3).

The 'multilevel governance' model acknowledges the continuing importance of state-level political systems, and that 'state arenas remain . . . the *most* important pieces of the European puzzle' (Marks *et al.* 1996:346, original emphasis), but it also recognizes that the state does not exercise a monopoly of decision-making competences. Instead, these competences are shared by institutions and policy actors at different levels rather than concentrated at the level of individual states. 'That is to say, supranational institutions – above all, the European Commission, the European Court, and the European Parliament – have independent influence in policy making that cannot be derived from their role as agents of state executives' (Marks *et al.* 1996:346). Moreover, an essential part of the 'multilevel governance' model is that states no longer provide the sole interface for national political actors – whether as individuals, groups, private and public organizations or parties – between state and supranational levels.

Another feature of this model is functional differentiation or policy segmentation (see, for example, Hix 1998a:39–41, Peterson and Bomberg 1999:22–8; Peterson 2004:119; Richardson 2006:9–14). Consequently, decision-making in any single policy field is likely to engage the activities of subnational, national and supranational agencies, institutions and non-governmental organizations. Moreover, decision-making comes to be structured around informal contacts, networks and norms, and no longer involves clear hierarchies of power and competences. In this sense, in its very complexity, and in its engagement of a myriad of functional and territorial constituencies at multiple levels, the system has been characterized as a system of 'governance' rather than simply of 'government' (see Kohler-Koch and Rittberger 2007:7–9).

Nonetheless, even within this model, formal institutions of politics and government – executive, legislative, judicial institutions and political parties, for example – continue to be of importance, but their significance has now to be understood in terms of their relations with wider forces of governance. When the specific location of the EP is considered in models of multilevel governance two contrasting visions, among many, can be perceived. One is a pessimistic vision of a 'post-parliamentary Europe'; the other is a more optimistic vision of 'a new kind of parliamentary system'.

Post-parliamentary Europe

Judge noted in 1999 that it is commonplace to argue that the position of parliamentary institutions in Western liberal democracies is undergoing systematic erosion in complex systems of governance (see Judge 1999:121–48). In the case of the EU this argument is encapsulated in Andersen and Burns's (1996:234) statement that:

> The EU is, then, a mix between international co-operation with nation state representatives as key actors and particular forms of governance with elaborate, specialised sub-governments, policy networks and lobbying . . . Parliament is only marginally important even on the formal level.

What is of particular concern for the EP in this model is a 'frustrating and delegitimising gap between representative democracy's responsibility and its lack of structural capability and control' (Andersen and Burns 1996:243). In this gap, alternative forms of legitimacy – of 'output legitimacy' – derived from effective and efficient sectoral policy-making and policy solutions, become of increased importance (see Höreth 1999:259–61; Lord and Beetham 2001:451–2). In one extreme view, 'governance' and 'output legitimacy' crowd out or supersede parliamentary institutions, and representative democracy more generally (Andersen and Burns 1996:242). In this manner, the importance of the EP is seen to be residualized and the EU's political system becomes characterized as 'post-parliamentary'.

The fusion model

An influential strand of multilevel governance analysis is that the institutional structure and the sources of legitimacy within the EU are not directly comparable either to national political systems or to a supranational model of a 'United States of Europe'. Instead, the EU comes to be conceived as a 'multi-level system of governance in which a direct representative element in the shape of the EP is having an important say, as part of a European legitimacy complementary to the national and functional one, but in which the sources and dimensions of legitimacy are progressively getting merged' (Wessels and Diedrichs 1997:9). What is seen to be emerging therefore is a new kind of political system with *sui generis* characteristics (see Wessels 1996a:68; Wessels and Rometsch 1996:364). In essence established perspectives of federalism or intergovernmentalism cannot capture the role of the EP adequately within the EU's novel political system. Instead the EU should be understood as a 'new kind of polity characterized by fusion' (Wessels and Diedrichs 1999:139). The word 'fusion' acknowledges the merging of instruments of governance among national, subnational and supranational actors and institutions. What results is a 'mixed polity' which shares political authority among several levels of governance and 'includes a multitude of different sources of direct and indirect, functional, legal and democratic legitimacy' (Wessels 1996a:59). It is within this context that the role of the EP is identified as departing from established parliamentary models and 'essentially renders the EU a new kind of parliamentary system' (Wessels and Diedrichs 1999:139).

Within this new system there is an assumption of joint decision-making by the European Parliament and the Council. The expectation is that the Commission would serve increasingly as the executive of the EU – with its head elected by both the EP and the European Council, and other Commissioners nominated by the head of the Commission and approved by the EP. Majority voting in all EU institutions would be the norm, with some mechanism to 'unblock' institutional impasses between the legislative institutions of equal status (the Council and the EP). Yet the EP remains 'neither the emergent legislature of a European superstate in the making nor a powerless institution at the center of an intergovernmental system' (Wessels and Diedrichs 1999:143). It occupies an intermediate and somewhat indeterminate institutional position. Indeed, in the multitudinous vertical and horizontal institutional transactions involved in the complex process of 'institutional fusion', the EU's decision-making process is 'hardly understandable' with the concomitant danger that 'its output lacks a deeper-going acceptance' (Wessels and Rometsch 1996:365). There is the danger that 'the ability of the public to identify outcomes with their sponsors and assign responsibility accordingly will diminish [as the] process of fusion progressively blurs the boundaries between the different actors and makes their roles functionally less distinguishable' (Wessels and Diedrichs 1999:149).

Ultimately, the logic of Wessels and Rometsch's argument leads – in one direction – to a call for the 'extended participation of national institutions – especially of national parliaments' (1996:365). But equally their logic leads, in another direction, to the conclusion that:

The EP's direct representative capacity will continue to play an important role in this system, potentially bolstering a European legitimacy . . . The EP will likely never become a central representative institution comparable to national parliaments. Nonetheless, the Parliament's further development will continue to have far reaching implications for EU legitimacy. (Wessels and Diedrichs 1999:149)

In this conception the EU is seen as a complex and highly differentiated institutional system which 'combines several levels of governance and a wide range of actors' and the result of which is a 'mixed polity' and an 'optimal form of government' (Wessels and Diedrichs 1997:8). Unlike the post-parliamentary variant of the new governance thesis, in this 'new kind of polity' the EP is an increasingly important component of the EU political system' (Wessels and Diedrichs 1999:148).

Conclusion

Locating the European Parliament within wider theories of legislatures and of the EU's political system is of importance in understanding what role we would expect the EP to perform as a legislature and the broader political context within which it is expected to perform this role. What is apparent from this preliminary review of theories is that the EP, in conformity with all legislatures, is a multifunctional organization; but unlike other legislatures it is a transnational body operating in a system of multilevel governance. This very multiplicity of roles and the multilevel context within which it operates should lead us to view global assessments of the EP and whether it is, or is not, a 'true' or 'proper' parliament (see, for example, Höreth 1999:253) with some caution. As the historical review of the EP's legislative powers in the next chapter reveals, the 'location' of the EP, in terms of policy influence, has changed over time. After the Treaties of Maastricht, Amsterdam, and Nice, the EP – with its capacity to 'modify and reject executive proposals' – can already be located in Mezey's category of legislatures with 'strong policy-making power'. The implementation of the Lisbon Treaty would simply reinforce this position. But even this location needs to be qualified by recognition that the policy influence of the EP should be disaggregated into its constituent elements. In other words, some acknowledgement has to be made that the EP will be more influential in some policy areas than in others, and will be more influential even within the same policy area at some times rather than others (see Judge *et al.* 1994).

If assessments of the policy influence of the EP vary across time and across substantive policy areas, then equally judgements of the efficacy of the EP's legitimating and linkage functions vary in accordance with which model of the EU's political system is utilized. Understanding the location of the EP in the respective models not only helps us to assess the EP's historical contribution, or lack of it, to the legitimation of the EU but also identifies prognostications as to the development of the EU as a political system and the EP's role in that process. Put very simply, different conceptions of what the EU is now, and what its future development entails, result in different assessments of what role the EP performs in the wider legitimation of the EU and what its future contribution to the 'democratization' of the EU will be. Whether this future is a 'parliamentary' one remains to be seen.

Chapter 2

Historical Evolution: The European Parliament and Ever Closer Union

Chapter 1 introduced a variety of models of legislative functions, and theories about the EU as a political system, with little attempt to locate the EP decisively in any single model or theory. Instead, the categories and variables that might be of use in undertaking such an exercise were simply identified and listed. The purpose of Chapter 1, therefore, was limited to making the analytical prescription that the study of the EP has to be: *interinstitutional* – to take account of its relation with other institutions; *contextual* – to take account of the systemic context in which it operates; and *interconnected* – to take account of the multi-functional nature of legislatures. The purpose of this chapter is to follow this prescription and examine how the location of the EP has varied across time in accordance with changes to its functional roles, its interinstitutional relations with the Commission and Council, and the systemic context in which it operates. It is important to deal with this cross-time analysis at the outset, both to provide a historical perspective on the development of the EP, and to provide a perspective from which the EP can be viewed in the early twenty-first century – without constantly having to refer back to the evolution of the EP in subsequent chapters.

Monnet's ambiguous institutional legacy

The origins of the EU are normally traced back to 1945, though ideas about European integration had persisted throughout the interwar period (see Urwin 1991:4–7; Dinan 1999:12–13). However, the prototype of the institutional structure of the EU is to be found in the European Coal and Steel Community (ECSC) which was established by the Treaty of Paris on 18 April 1951. The ECSC was the result of the initiative taken in May 1950 by Robert Schuman, the French Foreign Minister, when he proposed the pooling of the coal and steel resources of France and the Federal Republic of Germany specifically, and more generally other West European states which cared to join a new Coal and Steel Community. The details of the genesis of the Schuman Plan need not detain us here other than to note that the diplomatic ground-work and inspiration for this plan can be located in the French Modernization Plan of 1946, known as the Monnet Plan. Jean Monnet, the French Commissioner General with responsibility for for-mulating the 1946 Plan, is regarded as the 'architect of the European Community' (see Featherstone 1994:150; Holland 1994:9). Indeed, the enduring achievement of Monnet remains the institutional configura-tion of EU government.

The hallmark of Monnet's role in the drafting of the Treaty of Paris was the combination of pragmatism and idealism. From the outset Monnet was clear that 'Europe will not be built all at once, or as a single whole: it will be built by concrete achievements which first create *de facto* solidarity' (Monnet 1978:300). Nothing was more con-crete than the establishment of institutions. Indeed, for Monnet, insti-tutions were the key to successful integration: 'Only institutions grow wiser. They accumulate collective experience' (Monnet 1978:393; see Holland 1994:10; Featherstone 1994:159). If the enduring achieve-ment of Monnet remains the institutional configuration of EU govern-ment, there are many who are willing to argue that Monnet's was an ambiguous institutional legacy. On the one side an elitist technocratic model can be discerned, while on the other a federalist democratic vision can be identified.

Elitist/technocratic blueprint

The first institutional blueprint (or map) ascribed to Monnet is essen-tially an elitist, technocratic model (see Pryce and Wessels 1987:24; Featherstone 1994:150). Monnet's 'method' of institutional building is now commonly associated with 'neo-functionalist' theories of integra-tion (on neo-functionalism see Rosamond 2000:50–73; Cram 2001:55–60). From the outset a distinctive form of interest representa-tion – derived from an expectation of functional consultation, and gen-erating, in turn, an impetus for the creation of new networks focused upon the High Authority – came to be imprinted in the institutional structure of the new European Community. The objective of 'consulta-tion' was to cultivate a 'combination of benevolent technocrats and interest-propelled economic groups to build transnational coalitions in support of European policies and to undermine the scope for national policies' (Wallace 1993:300). The fact that the ECSC existed in a 'political vacuum' with no 'independent legitimacy or direct political authority' (Wallace 1993:300) assisted the growth of these coalitions. Given this technocratic vision, some commentators have been led to argue that there was no provision for a parliamentary assembly in Monnet's original plans (Milward 1984:409). In this view, an Assembly came as a late addition and was proposed shortly after the start of negotiations in order 'to blunt the technocratic edge of the Authority'.

An alternative view maintains that Monnet acknowledged the need for a Common Assembly even before negotiations on the ECSC began (see Westlake 1994a:71). By this view, while there is no doubt, as Monnet's own *Memoirs* makes clear, that his primary objective was to ensure that the vital first political step was taken by the setting up of the High Authority (Monnet 1978:324), it was also clear that the draft treaty discussed in Paris in June 1950 incorporated 'parliamentary control' in its design (see Oliver Harvey in Bullen and Pelly 1986:216). The need for a 'control body' mirrored the universal belief that the High Authority should be accountable for its actions if it was not to become a 'dictatorship of experts' (Spierenburg and Poidevin 1994:16). But exactly what form such control and accountability would take was the cause of considerable disputation among national delegations (see Rittberger 2005:78–107). In the end, Monnet's view prevailed that the High Authority should to be accountable to a 'rudimentary assembly' acting as a 'parliamentary control organ' (quoted in Rittberger 2005:99). What is not in doubt, equally, is that the Assembly was designed to operate at the peripheries of the grand European design. While the Common Assembly might have been the first transnational Assembly in Europe, it had no legislative powers and no direct democratic legitimacy derived from direct elections. In terms of Mezey's categorization, noted in Chapter 1, it was easily located at this time in the 'little or no policy-making' group of legislatures, and in Norton's terminology it had 'little or no policy impact'.

Common Assembly: bridge to federal model?

The Assembly's role was prescribed in Articles 20 to 25 of the Treaty of Paris. Articles 20 and 21 stated that the composition of the Assembly 'shall consist of the peoples of the States brought together in the Community . . . of delegates who shall be designated by the respective Parliaments'. Article 21(3) recorded that 'The Assembly shall draw up proposals for elections by direct universal suffrage in accordance with a uniform procedure in all Member States'. But it was to be the Council which was to 'make appropriate provisions' in accordance with the respective constitutional requirements of member states for the implementation of direct elections. The powers of the Assembly were specified in Article 24 and were essentially deliberative and supervisory.

The powers of the Common Assembly were thus closely circumscribed from the outset. In these circumstances, perhaps it is not surprising to find that the negotiations concerning the Assembly revolved around its composition rather than its powers, given that its powers were only minimally conceived. Equally unsurprising, perhaps, is that national interests predominated in these negotiations. Paramount importance was accorded to the defence of national interests in the treaty negotiations and the sovereignty of national parliaments was underscored throughout.

Locating the Assembly in the ECSC

Before moving on to consider the 1957 Treaty of Rome and later treaty revisions, it is advisable to reiterate the location of the EP in the institutional structure of the ECSC. The Common Assembly was neither directly elected nor directly capable of influencing or authorizing legislation. Instead, it was the Council that was to 'add to and endorse the decisions of the High Authority' (Hayes-Renshaw and Wallace 2006:7). In other words, it was the Council that was designed to play the legislative role normally ascribed to parliaments. Authorization of legislation was to be provided indirectly by ministers of elected national governments meeting in the Council. The outputs of the ECSC decision-making process would thus be legitimated indirectly by national governments, but would also derive their legitimacy in part from technocratic sources. 'Technocratic legitimation' was to derive from the ability of experts, operating in a supranational institution, the High Authority, to reach effective decisions that would promote the economic well-being of member states. While the emphasis was clearly upon 'output legitimation' there was, nonetheless, explicit recognition that '[i]n a world where government authority is derived from representative parliamentary assemblies, Europe cannot be built without such an assembly' (Monnet quoted in Rittberger 2005:99). Initially, however, the belief prevailed that 'effective problem solving' would slowly extend the legitimacy of the High Authority. The very name – High Authority – was a significant signal that this supranational agency would gradually extend its authority to undermine the independence (and legitimacy) of member nation states. The expectation was that supranational institutions would be surrounded by a plurality of groups, and that a variety of functional 'stakeholders' would thus emerge in the European policy arena.

Hence, the new Community placed the emphasis firmly upon a 'locking-in' (or *engrenage*) of interested organizations, whether national administrative agencies or functional groups, into the European dual executive structure of the High Authority and the Council, rather than upon securing the direct involvement of national publics through parliamentary representation. It was envisaged that the issue of popular consent and direct democratic legitimation could be postponed until national publics had experienced the benefits of integration.

Democratic participation through elected representative institutions was thus something for the future. In this context Article 21 of the Treaty of Paris, which provided for the possibility of direct elections, was not mere window-dressing. Moreover, Article 25 of the Treaty, seemingly innocuous at first sight, conferred upon the Assembly the right to adopt its own rules of procedure. This control over its own procedures was to prove vital to the evolution of the Assembly and later to the European Parliament.

That the EP did evolve into something far more far-reaching in practice was dependent not only upon its membership and its democratic aspirations but also upon the innate rivalry between supranational and intergovernmental organizations which became institutionalized at the heart of the emerging European Community. At this point the interinstitutional dimension of analysis of the EP needs to be remembered and it is to this that we now turn.

Members, integrationist aspirations and interinstitutional relations

The 78 members of the Common Assembly of the European Coal and Steel Community met collectively for the first time in Strasbourg on 10 September 1952. All members were nominated by their respective national parliaments, and as Wallace and Smith (1995:142) note the membership was partly self-selected, as 'the most enthusiastic for European cooperation were happy to volunteer, the most sceptical saw little point in coming forward'. One immediate practical manifestation of this 'Euro-enthusiasm' was the decision taken in June 1953 for members of the Assembly to sit according to political affiliation rather than by nationality. Transnational cooperation was reinforced in the decision to provide financial assistance to transnational party groups in the Assembly. From the beginning, therefore, there was an internal dynamic within the Assembly in favour of enhanced supranational cooperation generally, and the maximization of the role ascribed to the Common Assembly under the Treaty of Paris specifically. Moreover the Assembly rapidly established a subcommittee, chaired by Bernard Dehousse, to see how Article 21's provision for direct elections to the Assembly might be implemented (Herman 1980:14).

Given the majority predisposition within the Assembly in favour of the integrationist project, the High Authority rapidly recognized 'how attractive an alliance with the Common Assembly could be, in order to ensure that the two institutions, which were genuinely *communautaire*, were on the same side' (Albert Coppé, Member of High Authority, quoted in Wallace and Smith 1995:142). This attraction was reciprocated with the Assembly constantly urging the High Authority to expand its supranational initiatives (see Urwin 1991: 55–6). This mutually enhancing relationship was to remain a characteristic feature of Assembly and High Authority interactions (and later between the Commission and the European Parliament; see Westlake 1994b:225).

If the predisposition in favour of enhanced integration was evident both internally within the Assembly and externally in its relationship with the High Authority, this predisposition found almost immediate institutionalization. This came about through an invitation from the Council to the Common Assembly to convene a special committee to consider the feasibility of establishing a European Political Community (EPC). The Council's initiative was taken in the context of negotiations over the creation of a European Defence Community (EDC) which was to coexist with the ECSC. While the background to, and details of, the EDC – formalized in the Paris Treaty of 27 May 1952 – are not of concern here, the significant point is that the Common Assembly was asked to draft a blueprint for a future EPC to balance the functional ECSC and the military EDC. Thus, on *only its second day of existence* (11 September 1952) the Assembly created a working party to draft proposals for radical constitutional change. Even if the Council did not expect much to come of these proposals, nonetheless the Assembly's own expectations were raised. From the outset it was given a legitimate role in advancing further political integration.

A draft Treaty Establishing a Political Community was accepted by the Assembly on 10 March 1953 (for details see Urwin 1991:64–5; Nicoll and Salmon 2001:16–17). If the blueprint was more confederal than federal, nonetheless the experience of drafting a new constitutional settlement was 'inculcated in the European Parliament's collective memory' (Westlake 1994a:13). Despite the rejection of the EDC Treaty by the French National Assembly on 30 August 1954, the ECSC survived the wreckage, and, in the process, the Common Assembly had secured, almost by default, the acceptance of the six contracting governments to the principle of direct elections for a European representative institution.

The Treaty of Rome and the establishment of the European Economic Community

In effect the two Treaties of Rome of 1957, along with the Treaty of Paris of 1951, constituted the constitution of the European Communities. The institutional arrangements of the ECSC were consolidated and extended in the 1957 treaties. Reflected in the institutional design of the EEC and Euratom (and ultimately of the Merger Treaty of 1965) was the characteristic mix of the intergovernmental and supranational elements of the ECSC. A supranational body, the Commission, which was the equivalent of the ECSC's High Authority, was given the powers to: formulate recommendations for legislative proposals; 'participate in the shaping of measures taken by the Council'; implement decisions reached by Council; and generally to act as the 'guardian of the Treaty' by ensuring 'that the provisions of this Treaty and the measures taken by the institutions pursuant thereto are applied' (Article 155). To counterbalance this supranational body, a Council, consisting of a representative of each member state at ministerial level, was conferred with the 'power to take decisions' and was charged to ensure the coordination of the general economic policies of the member states (Article 145). The Council of the EEC thus had greater powers bestowed upon it in relation to the Commission than its predecessor in the ECSC. The EEC Treaty also institutionalized the representation of functional interests more explicitly through the creation of an Economic and Social Committee. This body was to have advisory status and for decades after the Treaty of Rome it insisted upon its co-equal status with the Parliamentary Assembly established for the EEC.

The Assembly's formal powers

The Parliamentary Assembly of the EEC was manifestly the child of the ECSC Assembly. The Articles of the Treaty of Rome pertaining to the Parliamentary Assembly were based on the corresponding Articles of the Treaty of Paris. Article 137 (1957) repeated the wording of Article 20 (1951) that the Assembly 'shall consist of representatives of the peoples of the States brought together in the Community' but added the word 'advisory' in the phrase 'to exercise the advisory and supervisory powers which are conferred upon it by this treaty'. In so doing, the Treaty of Rome acknowledged a marginal enhancement of the new Assembly's powers – an enhancement which was to prove significant in the long term.

The EEC Treaty introduced a formal right of parliamentary involvement in the Communities' legislative process. In 22 articles of the EEC Treaty and in 11 articles of the Euratom Treaty provision was made for the Assembly to be consulted on Commission proposals before adoption by the Council. Unlike the Economic and Social Committee, which also had rights of consultation but which was subject to a deadline imposed by Council for the submission of its opinions, the Assembly was not subject to Council deadlines. This difference was to prove of importance to the later expansion of parliamentary participation in the European policy process.

Once granted a formal role in the legislative process, no matter how limited in practice, parliamentarians sought the incremental expansion of that role through *informal* internal processes and external interinstitutional agreements. Perhaps because the Assembly was granted such a tangential role in the legislative process its *very* marginality invited its members to seek alternative, informal modes of influence. As we will see below, considerable institutional ingenuity and constitutional dexterity were deployed by members of the Assembly/Parliament in ensuring an incremental accretion of their influence. Such ingenuity and informal modes of influence were to prove a characteristic feature of the development of the European Parliament.

The formal powers of the Assembly over the Communities' budget was enhanced in Article 203 of the EEC Treaty and Article 177 of the Euratom Treaty. Under these provisions the Assembly effectively became a twin arm of the EEC's budgetary authority (Westlake 1994a:15). Article 144 of the EEC Treaty and Article 114 of the Euratom Treaty confirmed the right, granted initially under the ECSC Treaty, of the Assembly to censure and to force the resignation of the Commission as a body. However, the EEC and Euratom treaties extended this right of censure beyond consideration of the Commission's annual report to include, implicitly, all aspects of the Commission's activities. Although frequently dismissed as a 'nuclear weapon' or as a 'sledgehammer' – and, moreover, criticized as a weapon wrongly targeted on the Commission rather than the Council – the linked powers of censure and dismissal were to prove vital to the evolution of the EP (see Chapters 7 and 8). The very fact that the weapon existed was sufficient to ensure that both the Parliament and the Commission had a vested interest in securing interinstitutional cooperation rather than conflict. In this sense, the negative power of censure and dismissal helped to forge a constructive relationship between the Parliament and the Commission. As such it has played a central role in the political and constitutional development of the European Union.

Proposal for direct elections

The EEC Treaty, like the ECSC Treaty before it, provided for the introduction of direct elections. The Assembly itself was to draw up proposals for direct elections which were to be conducted under a 'uniform procedure in all member states'. This right of initiative, in the drafting of a legislative proposal on direct elections, was unique; in all other areas of Community law it was the Commission that enjoyed the formal right of initiative. In conferring this right upon the Assembly the treaties instilled a democratic dynamic in the constitutional arrangements of the Community. As long as there were no direct elections, and as long as there was no uniform electoral procedure throughout member states, then the Community could be deemed somehow to be 'deficient' in participatory terms.

What the commitment to direct elections provided from the outset, however, was an *inherent institutional dynamic* within the Assembly for the practical achievement of direct elections, and a mechanism for a *perpetual normative questioning* of the constitutional construct of the EC/EU itself. Direct elections, following the logic of Monnet, were 'the only way to get the question [of integration] away from officials and into the hands of the people at large, and to make the latter really feel that they were participating in something new' (William Hayter (who was the UK Minister in Paris in 1952) in Bullen and Pelly 1986:889). In the absence of direct elections, or in the absence of popular engagement with the 'European project', the legitimacy of that project and the institutional construct of 'Europe' would remain open to question (see Chapter 3).

In the event it took 22 years before the first direct elections were held in June 1979. The intervening period was characterized by the EP's constant assertion of the principle that a directly elected parliament at the European level would afford democratic legitimacy to the legislative outputs of the Community. Counterposing this view was the belief – most vividly expressed in 1960 by the then French Prime Minister, Michel Debré – that the EC was simply an intergovernmental association of European states. In this vision he did 'not see what direct elections by universal suffrage of a political assembly dealing with technical bodies or with higher civil servants can accomplish' (cited in Westlake 1994a:17). Such resistance took a draft convention (1960), a revised convention (1976), numerous parliamentary resolutions, reports of the EP's Political Affairs Committee (most notably the Pleven and Patjin Reports), threats to take the Council to the Court of Justice (1969) and enlargement of the Community (1973) before it was overcome and European elections were eventually held on 7–10 June 1979. Nugent observes (2006:258): 'That the first direct elections were not held until 1979 is witness to the feeling of some member governments . . . that direct elections were rather unwelcome, both because they had supranational overtones, and because they might be followed by pressure for institutional reform in the EP's favour.' As the post-1979 history of the EP reveals, member governments were justified in fearing increased pressure for institutional reform on the part of a directly elected EP. Before examining the period after 1979, however, some of the most important developments in the period 1957–79 need to be noted.

Formal structures and informal changes, 1957–79

The Treaty of Paris and the two Treaties of Rome thus provided the constitutional blueprint for the EEC, EC and EU. For some thirty years after the formation of the EEC the institutional configuration provided by the 1957 treaties was to remain unaltered in essence. Amendments and supplements to the treaties were made and added, but the institutional (im)balance – which pivoted on the initial compromises between intergovernmental and supranational organizations made in the 1950s – was never formally challenged.

If, in this sense, the treaties could be regarded as the 'tablets of stone' for the constitutional development of the EU, they also possessed some of the geological qualities of magmatic rocks – hard on the outside but malleable and fluid on the inside. Whereas formal amendments to the treaties chipped away at the surface of the constitutional stonework, an internal interinstitutional dynamic soon became activated at the heart of the constitutional edifice. For long periods, however, analysts of the EU's development, and particularly of the evolution of the EP, looked only at the formal surface of the treaties and ignored the magmatic interinstitutional changes occurring beneath the surface.

In preface to examining the formal changes that were effected in the 1957–79 period, one informal change, of major symbolic importance, needs to be noted. This was the decision, taken on 30 March 1962, for the Assembly to call itself the European Parliament. However, the formal title 'Assembly' remained unaltered in the treaties until the adoption of the Single European Act in 1986.

Merger Treaty 1965

In October 1960 the Assembly had adopted a resolution calling for the merger of the three Councils of the different Communities, and the combination of the EEC and Euratom Commissions with the ECSC's High Authority. Westlake (1994a:20) argues that Parliament's reasoning was that 'it, as well as the cause of integration, stood to gain from such a move, since a single Commission, still beholden to Parliament, could only gain in authority'. In 1965 the treaty establishing a single Council and a single Commission of the European Communities (known as the Merger Treaty) was signed and in 1967 it came into effect. The powers exercised by the merged institutions still rested on the founding treaties, though one innovation made in Article 4 was the acknowledgement of a Committee of Permanent Representatives (COREPER) to prepare for Council meetings. With the institutionalization of COREPER the intergovernmental nature of the EEC was reaffirmed.

Budgetary provisions: treaty reforms, 1970 and 1975

Parliament achieved formal recognition as part of the 'budgetary authority' after the Treaty Amending Certain Budgetary Provisions of the Treaties was signed in Luxembourg in April 1970. In adopting a system of 'own resources' financing, the Community required member states to contribute to collective resources while allowing the Council and Parliament jointly to determine the overall limits of expenditure within the revenues made available by member states. The 1970 Treaty changes were consolidated by further revision in 1975. The combined effect of these amendments was to secure for the Parliament four major powers. First, the EP acquired, within certain limits, the right to increase or reduce Community expenditure without Council approval; second, it could redistribute spending between budget sectors; third, it was granted the power of rejection of the annual budget or of supplementary budgets; and, fourth, it was given the exclusive right to approve, or not to approve, the way in which the Commission spent the money voted in the budget (for details see Corbett *et al.* 2007:248–9; see also Chapter 7). This exclusive right of discharge was hailed by the EP itself as 'in effect the first full *legislative* power under the EEC Treaty' (European Parliament 1978:21, emphasis added). Since 1975 the budgetary powers of the Parliament were not subject to formal Treaty revision until the, aborted, Constitutional Treaty in 2004 and the subsequent Lisbon Treaty. However, they had been subject to five interinstitutional agreements (in 1982, 1988, 1993, 1999, and 2006) which further enhanced the budgetary and scrutiny capacities of the EP.

Conciliation

In making the EP a joint budgetary authority the Treaty amendments of 1970 and 1975 not only gave Parliament the capacity to influence the Council's policy development, but also generated new possibilities for institutional conflict. It was partly to anticipate and avoid budgetary conflicts that a 'conciliation' procedure was introduced by a joint Declaration of the Council, Commission and Parliament in 1975.

The Council recognized that the new budgetary powers of the EP might be used to prevent the implementation of contested legislation with budgetary consequences. In these circumstances, the Council was willing to negotiate and agree a method of resolving potential conflicts. Under this procedure, if the Council wished to diverge from the opinion of the EP on 'Community acts of general application which have appreciable financial implications', then the issue was to be referred to a Conciliation Committee composed of equal numbers of

MEPs and members of the Council. At the conclusion of conciliation negotiations, the Council retained the sole right to adopt the act in question. Ultimately, therefore, Parliament did not have the capacity to force concessions out of the Council, but rather enjoyed the right to ask ministers in the Council to reconsider disputed proposals. Before direct elections in 1979 the conciliation procedure was used on only five occasions, and to little positive effect as far as Parliament was concerned. After direct elections, however, the number of conciliations and their qualitative impact upon Community legislation increased steadily (see below).

Irrespective of its policy impact, which was severely limited in the early years, the conciliation procedure was to prove of importance for four other reasons. First, it acknowledged the need for a linking mechanism between Council and Parliament which would allow the latter to consider financially significant legislative measures before they were formally adopted. In so doing, there was an implicit recognition that 'effective budgetary control calls for some say in legislation giving rise to expenditure' (Committee of Three 1979:76). Second, it provided a direct and unfiltered link between Council members and MEPs. In this sense it implanted Parliament into the direct consciousness of the Council and helped to develop closer working relations with the EP. Third, the Parliament had an incentive to extend the scope of the procedure beyond conciliation on budgetary matters to other important legislative proposals. And MEPs proved adept at extending the reach of the procedure through the creative amendment of its own Rules of Procedure (see European Parliament 1979: Rule 22(a)). Fourth, conciliation provided an institutional dynamic for the EP to press for further interinstitutional agreements in order to extend the procedure. Parliament was assisted in this respect by the Council's willingness to convene 'informal conciliations' and to adopt a flexible interpretation of the phrase 'with appreciable financial implications'. This enabled conciliations to be held on legislation which did not fall strictly within this category.

Again the specific details of the extension of the procedure need not distract us from the general point that the EP, throughout its history, has proved willing to maximize its limited formal powers by seeking creative informal agreements with other institutions and through internal procedural innovations. What the introduction of the conciliation procedure in 1975 vividly illustrates is the use of procedural precedent to lever more far-reaching institutional change at some future date. Without being too deterministic it is possible to conclude that the 1975 conciliation procedure 'acted as the precursor of the much more developed system of conciliation that exists under co-decision' (Corbett *et al.* 2007:211).

A directly elected Parliament: small steps and large strides, 1979–87

Immediately before direct elections one authoritative evaluation of the European Parliament concluded that:

> The European Parliament is *not* a parliament (or, more accurately *not much* of a parliament) because it fails to meet a series of basic political, constitutional and decision-making requirements concerning the performance of legislative, financial and control powers. (Herman and Lodge 1978:65)

Certainly, at the time of direct elections in 1979 there were many who either were sceptical of the EP's capacity to effect a fundamental redistribution of power without formal changes in the EP's advisory and supervisory powers, or who believed that increased 'democratization' of the EC's policy-making process was unlikely to result simply from the process of direct elections (see Dinan 1999:84–5; Nicoll and Salmon 2001:3 1). Both analyses were correct in identifying the basic fact that European elections in themselves neither altered treaty-based interinstitutional relations nor enhanced the participation of directly elected representatives in the EC's legislative process. But both analyses underestimated the dynamic effects of direct elections in stimulating MEPs to press for more far-reaching institutional changes.

In practice, direct elections were to have a positive impact at three different levels. The first was at an 'attitudinal' level. MEPs' own expectations were reoriented and the attitudes of the other European institutions to the EP were reappraised. The second was a structural shift in the balance between national parliaments and the EP. The third was an underlining of the traditional strategy pursued by the EP in seeking a dual enhancement of its powers: indirectly, through *petits pas* (small steps); and, directly, through promotion of treaty-based fundamental constitutional revision which was to culminate, successively, in the Single European Act (SEA), the treaties signed in Maastricht, Amsterdam and Nice, the aborted Constitutional Treaty, and the Lisbon Treaty. However, before examining these treaty revisions, we will examine the incremental advances made by the EP in the period between direct elections in 1979 and the entry into effect of the SEA in 1987.

Attitudinal change

One early, and extremely important, indication of changed attitudes on the part of other EC institutions to the directly elected EP came in the Court of Justice's 1980 *Isoglucose* ruling (for details see Kirchner and

Williams 1983). The ruling of the Court in Case 138/79 annulled a regulation which had been adopted by the Council before Parliament had formally delivered its opinion. The Court held that the Council had infringed the procedural requirement of the consultation procedure set out in Article 43(2) EEC. The significance of the consultation procedure in the view of the Court was that:

> [It] is the means which allows the Parliament to play an actual part in the legislative process of the Community. Such power represents an essential factor in the institutional balance intended by the Treaty. Although limited, it reflects at Community level the fundamental democratic principle that the peoples should take part in the exercise of power through the intermediary of a representative assembly. (quoted in Westlake 1994a:24)

In this statement the Court clearly identified Parliament as having its own source of democratic legitimacy, in which case the Council could no longer disregard Parliament's opinions without being in violation of the Treaty. Hence, just one year after the first direct elections, Parliament appeared to have become 'in the eyes of the Court . . . a vital and major institution within the Community' (Kirchner and Williams 1983:179).

Correspondingly, the attitudinal relationship between the Parliament and the Commission was affected by direct elections. After 1979 the Commission increasingly looked towards the EP for legitimation of its actions and proposals. The result was that 'although the Parliament was still practically dependent on the Commission, the Commission was becoming politically dependent on the Parliament' (Westlake 1994a:25). In the first two years of the new Parliament, MEPs rapidly moved to increase this political dependence through a series of resolutions and through amendments to the EP's Rules of Procedure on 26 March 1981 (see Lodge 1983:30–1; Kirchner and Williams 1983: 180–1).

Rule changes and procedural innovation

The 1981 Rules of Procedure doubled the number of rules from 54 to 116 (European Parliament 1981). New Rules 35 and 36 were of particular significance in introducing a mechanism of delay into the procedure for producing a parliamentary opinion. In order to maximize the advantage derived from the *Isoglucose* ruling, the new rules allowed for the referral of draft opinions back to the appropriate committee. This provided for the postponement of a vote on a Commission proposal until the Commission had expressed its position on the amendments proposed by Parliament. The threat of delay was particularly potent on those matters requiring an urgent response by Parliament. This innovation of 1981 was to serve as an important precedent, over two decades later, for further extension of the EP's legislative power – when applied to a rejection of a Commission proposal at first reading in codecision (see Chapter 8). But this is to get ahead of the story; staying in 1981 for the moment, it was clear by this date that the EP, in policy areas covered by consultation, had began to edge away from the lowest category of legislative influence, towards the modest influence/power category in line with Mezey's notion of constraints (identified in Chapter 1).

Not only was Parliament provided with a mechanism to lever concessions out of the Commission but also, through pressing for the acceptance of its amendments by the Commission, Parliament sought indirectly to influence the Council's decisions. Council could only change a revised Commission proposal by unanimity. In this manner, not only did the rule changes affect the practice of EP-Commission relations and the perception of each institution held by the other, but they also marked a psychological turning-point in the EP's relations with the Council. If, as Lodge (1983:33) argues, the internal procedural changes rested 'on the premiss that the EP has a moral and political obligation to EC voters to represent their interests by affecting . . . the content of EC legislation', then after direct elections this premiss was never explicitly challenged by the Council. Thereafter, the EP gradually became ever more focused in the collective 'mind's eye' of the Council.

Questions

The creative use of parliamentary procedures was also evident in the enhanced inquisitory role the EP accrued to itself over time. Under the EEC Treaty the Commission alone was held responsible for replying 'orally or in writing to questions put to it by the Assembly or by its members' (Article 140). The Council was to 'be heard in the Assembly in accordance with the conditions which the Council shall lay down in its rules of procedure'. Even before direct elections, however, Council accepted (in 1973) that it should answer parliamentary questions and (in 1976) extended this agreement to cover political cooperation meetings of foreign ministers. This acceptance of 'informatory accountability', in the sense of acknowledging the basic right of Parliament to be informed about the actions of Commission and Council, was further entrenched by the Solemn Declaration on European Union signed in 1983. In accordance with this Declaration Council undertook to answer all parliamentary questions addressed to it. The important point for our discussion is that this symbolic advance was made on the basis of a political convention rather than a Treaty obligation.

Legislative initiative

Informal innovations also contributed to the enhancement of the legislative role of the EP (and to the potential relocation of the EP into the modest power category in Mezey's schema and into Norton's 'policy influencing' category) even before formal treaty revisions were effected in the 1980s and 1990s. As noted above, the Commission alone under Article 155 of the Treaty of Rome was empowered to formulate recommendations for legislative action; yet, through astute use of its own rules, the EP created for itself a right of legislative initiative. Parliament adopted procedures – most notably 'own initiative reports' – that enabled it to forward draft proposals for legislation to the Commission (see Judge 1993:190–3; Judge and Earnshaw 1994:264–6). In this manner, the EP was able to insert its ideas at the formulation stage of the legislative process; either to bring a new issue onto the agenda, or to express a view on matters upon which it did not have to be formally consulted. In this sense the EP also began to edge towards Norton's 'policymaking' group of legislatures in its tentative development of a capacity to 'generate alternative policies'. Moreover, as Lodge notes (1989:66) the use of 'own initiative reports' provided a simple device which, 'when handled shrewdly by MEPs . . . was to prove extremely useful: it was the basis of the draft treaty establishing the European Union in 1984. It was also a useful vehicle for increasing formal EP-Commission contact on a future legislative agenda.'

Interinstitutional agreements

However, before examining the role of the EP in formal treaty revision, one further informal strategy is worthy of examination. As noted above, the Council, Commission and Parliament signed a joint declaration in 1975 to establish a conciliation procedure for legislation with 'appreciable financial implications'. Since direct elections in 1979, Parliament has consistently sought the extension of interinstitutional agreements to regularize its relationship with the Commission and Council. Once having established working conventions and practices with the other institutions, Parliament has been adept at transforming these informal arrangements into something more tangible, particularly during periods of formal treaty revision. A pattern has thus emerged where in the aftermath of treaty amendment, Parliament has been able to secure interinstitutional agreements to ease the implementation of new working patterns and connections between the institutions. In this manner the 1988 agreement on budgetary matters flowed from the implementation of the Single European Act, and negotiations surrounding the introduction of the Maastricht Treaty led in 1993 and 1994 to a series of interinstitutional agreements designed to facilitate the new working relationships among the three institutions. In turn the implementation of the Amsterdam Treaty brought in its wake the 1999 interinstitutional agreement on financial matters and the Framework Agreement on Relations Between the European Parliament and the Commission of July 2000 (see Chapter 7). Similarly, the Nice Treaty, the protracted post-Nice gestation of the Constitutional Treaty, and the necessity of dealing with the practicalities of decision-making in the void surrounding the Treaty's ratification, brought in their wake new interinstitutional agreements on budgetary discipline and sound financial management in 2006 (see Chapter 7), on comitology, in the form of a new Council Decision, in 2006 (see Chapter 8) and a new Framework Agreement with the Commission in 2005 (see Chapter 7).

Formal treaty reforms

Draft Treaty on European Union

The 'small steps' strategy adopted by the EP after direct elections in 1979 was accompanied by a parallel strategy of promoting a 'qualitative leap' towards further integration. Initially the majority of newly elected MEPs in 1979 were predisposed in favour of taking 'small steps' and of developing the role assigned to them by the existing treaties. Within a very short period, however, the inability of existing European institutions to deal with the problems arising from the 'eurosclerosis' of the 1970s and early 1980s led to demands for comprehensive constitutional reform from both within and outside the EP (see Capotorti *et al.* 1986:9–10). From outside, a joint initiative of the foreign ministers of West Germany and Italy – Hans-Dietrich Genscher and Emilio Colombo – led to the publication of the Genscher–Colombo Proposals in November 1981. These proposals constituted a draft European Act and sought to identify the principles and institutional reforms which would enhance European integration without a formal revision of the Treaty of Rome. At the heart of these principles was a recognition that the ideal of an EC identity should be promoted, the European Council should act as the source of political guidance within the Communities, there should be greater cooperation on foreign and security matters, and that the position of the EP within the decision-making process should be 'improved' (for details on the proposed improvements see Lodge 1982:279–83). The Genscher–Colombo Proposals made little headway and culminated only in 'a vague, insubstantial assertion of the Community's international identity' in the form of a 'Solemn Declaration on European Union' (Dinan 1999:98). Nonetheless, the Proposals heightened the profile of further political and economic cooperation on the EC's agenda. Moreover, they provided reinforcement of the position of those within the European Parliament who favoured a strategy of far-reaching constitutional reform.

In fact the EP had been kept informed of the Genscher–Colombo deliberations and had offered its strongest support for the ministerial initiative. In parallel, in July 1981, 170 MEPs signed a motion calling for fundamental reform of the EC. This motion was promoted by members of the 'Crocodile Club'. This all-party group of MEPs, which derived its name from the Strasbourg restaurant which had hosted the group's inaugural meeting in 1980, was committed to fundamental reform of the institutional procedures of the EC and a redefinition of the powers of the Community. In addition to the motion calling for Treaty revision, the EP also established in July 1981 a new Committee on Institutional Affairs. The sole task assigned to the new Committee was to draft a new constitutional framework for the EC (Lodge 1984:378).

Altiero Spinelli, one of the founders of the postwar federalist movement, was appointed general rapporteur of the Committee and, along with six co-rapporteurs, produced general guidelines for the reform of the treaties. These guidelines were accepted by Parliament in a resolution of 6 July 1982. At their centre was support for the principle of subsidiarity, and for a new institutional balance which would lead to greater equality between the Council and the EP, and which would further acknowledge the democratic legitimacy of the Parliament. These guidelines were eventually translated into the Draft Treaty on European Union which was adopted by the EP on 14 February 1984 by a vote of 237 to 31.

The first line of the preamble to the Draft Treaty indicated that its purpose was 'continuing and reviving the democratic unification of Europe'. The Draft Treaty aimed to provide a single and comprehensive constitutional text for a new political entity to replace the existing Communities. While keeping the institutional configuration of the EC – Council, Commission, Court of Justice and Parliament (with the European Council elevated to the fifth institution) – the Draft Treaty redressed the EC's intergovernmental imbalance in favour of enhanced democratic participation by a supranational Parliament. This redress was most evident in Article 36 which stated unambiguously that 'The Parliament and the Council of the Union shall jointly exercise legislative authority with the active participation of the Commission.' Correspondingly, Parliament was to constitute jointly with the Council the budgetary authority of the Union. In both cases, the Council was to lose its capacity to block progress through inaction, as approval had to be given within specified time limits (Articles 38 and 76). Moreover, within the Council, majority voting was expected to become the general rule. The Draft Treaty also specified an enhanced oversight role for Parliament in its relations with the Commission. While the Commission was to retain the right of legislative initiative, it was envisaged that an acceptable legislative programme would have to be submitted to Parliament before the Commission could take office.

Single European Act 1986

In the event, the institutional blueprint of the Draft Treaty failed to guide the intergovernmental conference convened after the Milan summit of June 1985. What the IGC produced instead was amendment of the EEC Treaty to: incorporate new policy areas (including environment, research and technological development, and regional policy); complete the internal market by the end of 1992; put European foreign policy cooperation on a legal basis; and provide formal recognition of the meetings of Heads of State and Government in the European Council. The discussions in the IGC were pervaded by a general feeling that little policy development, especially in regard to the completion of the single market, could be achieved unless the process of decision-making in the EC was reformed. A synergy was thus engendered – in large part intentionally through the creative perspicacity of Commission President Jacques Delors – between economic reform and institutional reform (see Noël 1989:3–14). The central dynamic of this synergy was a recognition that the project of the 1992 single market could be effected only if the political process of the EC was made more efficient. In turn, it was acknowledged that greater efficiency raised, as its corollary, a need for the further democratization of the decision-making process.

Greater efficiency was to be effected through two linked reforms of the Council. On the one side, unanimity had to be replaced by greater majority decision-making; on the other, the Council had to delegate some of the burden of implementing its own decisions to the Commission. With majority voting, however, came the prospect that ministers from any particular state might be outvoted, thus calling into question the ability of their own national parliaments to control the preferred outcomes of the Council negotiating process (see Westlake 1994a:27). If the lines of accountability between national ministers in the Council and national parliaments became blurred in these circumstances, there was a specific counter logic, therefore, to enhancing the legislative scrutiny and control of the EP. When combined with a more general federalist logic – which was shared by some member states, particularly Germany and Italy, and by the Commission – for an increase in the legislative powers of the European Parliament (see Dinan 1999:118), the case for constitutional reform became overwhelming.

Ultimately, the confluence of these specific and general logics resulted in the introduction of the 'cooperation procedure' in the SEA. This applied to most of the legislation needed to effect the internal market and added, in effect, a second reading to the traditional legislative procedure of consultation. The SEA also gave Parliament, through an assent procedure, equal rights with the Council for the ratification of accession treaties and association agreements. However, despite these enhancements of the EP's legislative powers, the incremental procedural changes fell far short of the general powers of codecision envisaged in Parliament's original Draft Treaty.

The response of the EP to this shortfall was predictably critical. Although disappointed with their new powers, MEPs recognized that cooperation was, nonetheless, a *new* power and that, with judicious use, it had the potential for future development. From the outset senior MEPs and officials within Parliament were acutely aware of the strategic political implications of the procedure (as indeed were officials in the Commission, but for different reasons). Both institutions were sensitive to the new interinstitutional dynamic that had been created by the procedure; and both were aware of the changes in institutional priorities and working routines needed to maximize the effect of the SEA.

Interinstitutional dialogue

While seeking to maintain its autonomy and independence, the Commission had a vested interest in ensuring that its own legislative initiatives did not stall because of interinstitutional rigidities or textual ambiguities in the Treaty itself. It adopted, therefore, a flexible attitude to Parliament, working out a number of interinstitutional agreements and informal understandings, as well as adopting a more formal 'code of conduct' (at Parliament's urging) in 1990. These changes in attitude and working practices were themselves testimony to the fact that Parliament now had to be taken seriously, not least because of the very practical advantage of securing its support at an early stage of the legislative process. What proved to be far more contentious, however, and indeed gave rise to much tension between the Commission and Parliament, was the issue of 'comitology': that is, the Commission's specification in draft legislation of the type of committee needed to assist it in the performance of executive functions (see Chapter 8).

The new rules adopted by Parliament in 1986 also envisaged a monitoring procedure (Rule 41) whereby the preparation of a common position by Council would be monitored by the rapporteur and chairman of the relevant committee. Some observers hoped, optimistically, that such monitoring would 'serve to check that the Commission is keeping its promises on amendments and effectively upholding amendments it has accepted . . . [and serve, indirectly] to prevent the Council from adopting a common position that strays too much from Parliament's position' (Fitzmaurice 1988:395). In practice, however, the reality of EP–Council relations under cooperation diverged significantly from this optimistic prognosis.

Moving beyond the SEA

With hindsight, however, the SEA conformed to the historical pattern of the EP's insatiable quest for 'the democratic unification of Europe' (Draft Treaty on European Union preamble). In this quest, dramatic 'qualitative leaps' were aspired to, but 'small steps' were achieved pragmatically and cumulatively to significant effect. Certainly the SEA did not put the EP on a co-equal footing in the legislative process, but what it did do was provide new opportunities for the EP to seek 'further refinements of the cooperation procedure, further amendments to the treaty and the revival of the draft Treaty establishing the European Union' (Lodge 1989:76). With increasing momentum after the elections of 1989, the EP issued a series of reports and resolutions highlighting the constitutional deficiencies of the SEA and calling for further 'democratization' of the EC's institutional structure.

The demands of the EP for a reconsideration of the SEA's institutional legacy were to find increased resonance in certain member states in the context of wider economic and political developments in Europe. The decision to convene an intergovernmental conference on economic and monetary union (EMU) taken by the European Council in 1989, alongside the emerging movement towards German reunification, and the political transitions in East and Central Europe, combined to prompt a general consideration of 'European Political Union' (EPU) within the integrationist debate on 'European Union' (see Wessels 1991:9–11; McAllister 1997:199–228). Predictably, the EP was proactive in seeking to widen the debate to include institutional reform. Particularly influential in this respect were the reports issued by the EP's Institutional Affairs Committee under the names of its rapporteurs David Martin and Emilio Colombo (see Corbett 1993a; Lodge 1994:75; Corbett *et al.* 2007: 346–7).

Rather than propose fully elaborated treaty revisions, Parliament's resolutions adopted on the basis of the Martin reports canvassed pragmatic, but far-reaching, procedural reform and expansion of the EC's competences (*Official Journal of the European Union*, Series C 96, 17 April 1990:114–18; OJ C 231, 17 September 1990:97–105, available through EUR-lex, at http://eur-lex.europa.eu). The key proposals envisaged in the Martin reports included the following: codecision for the EP with the Council; election of the Commission president by Parliament on a proposal from the European Council; generalized majority voting in the Council; greater cooperation between the EP and national parliaments; a limited right of legislative initiative by the EP; the creation of parliamentary committees of inquiry; reinforcement of Parliament's control over finance; and extension of the competences of the EC. The Martin reports ultimately proved crucial in defining the agenda of the IGC convened to consider political union in parallel with the IGC on EMU (Corbett *et al.* 2007:346).

While most member states agreed with the basic objectives of European Political Union – redressing the democratic deficits; expanding Community competences; strengthening subsidiarity; increasing the efficiency of decision-making – significant differences emerged in the IGC on how these were to be implemented (see Pryce 1994:36–52; Nugent 2006:84–5). Although the EP was not a direct participant in the IGCs, it made its views known, nonetheless, through its reports and debates; and pressed, successfully, for the establishment of an interinstitutional committee to serve as a forum for discussions between the three institutions. The EP also pursued a parallel strategy of involving national parliaments in deliberations upon treaty reform. Meetings with the European Affairs committees of national parliaments were convened and, more significantly, a Conference of Parliaments of the Community, or 'Assizes' to use a traditional French term, was held in Rome in November 1990 (see Westlake 1995; Judge 1995:89–90). The Assizes proved of some significance in adopting, a month before the IGCs opened, a declaration that endorsed all of the EP's main proposals for treaty revision. At the heart of the Rome Declaration was a call for a Union 'on a federal basis', a Union in which, moreover, the European Parliament would exercise a power of real codecision. In this sense the Assizes 'helped to place firmly on the agenda of the IGC virtually all the issues that had been raised by the EP . . . [and] gave ammunition to those governments favourably disposed towards the proposals and helped shape expectations with regard to the IGCs' (Corbett 1992:275).

The journey from Maastricht to Amsterdam

As the negotiations proceeded and Parliament's exorbitant demands came nowhere near being met, a torrent of speeches and resolutions condemning the IGCs flowed out of Strasbourg . . . As expected, the results of the Maastricht summit disappointed Parliament. (Dinan 1999:143)

Manifestly, while the European Parliament did not secure all it wished for, Dinan's dismissive assessment of Parliament's impact needs some qualification on at least two grounds. First, there is little doubt that many of the new treaty provisions, particularly those concerned with the extension of the powers of the EP itself, would not have been included in the Maastricht Treaty had it not been for the unremitting pressure of the EP. Second, Parliament obtained significant changes in the two areas it had identified as in need of specific change: the Community's legislative procedure and its involvement in the appointment of the Commission. Overall, therefore, a more balanced assessment is provided by Corbett (1994:223) in his statement that 'Maastricht constitute[d] an important step forward ... for the European Parliament.' This view was shared by Lodge (1994:80) who concluded that the 'TEU significantly augmented the potential scope of the European Union's popularly elected arm of the legislature'.

In terms of the enhancement of the EP's legislative influence the Treaty on European Union (TEU) was of significance in introducing a new legislative procedure – almost universally referred to as the 'codecision procedure' (under the Lisbon Treaty the new nomenclature would be the 'ordinary legislative procedure'). Although its scope was more limited and its operation more complex than initially envisaged by Parliament, nonetheless it was greeted by influential commentators as 'a remarkable step forward' (Westlake 1994a:146) and 'of fundamental importance to public perceptions of Parliament's role: it can no longer be accused of lacking teeth' (Corbett 1994:210). For the first time Parliament was now an equal partner in the legislative process, with acts adopted under the procedure jointly signed by the presidents of Council and Parliament, and with an absolute right of veto over significant areas of EU legislation. To echo Mezey's (1979:25) words, a right of veto is 'the most telling constraint that the legislature can place on the policy-making process'. After Maastricht, and under codecision, the EP – with its capacity to 'modify and reject executive proposals' – met Mezey's (1979:26) analytical requirements, noted in Chapter 1, to be located in the category of legislatures with 'strong policy-making power'.

As a consequence, informal interinstitutional linkages expanded in response to codecision. Immediately after the Maastricht Treaty came into effect 'informal conciliations and trialogues – involving the Council presidency, EP committee chairpersons and members of the Commission – emerged as crucial arenas for informal bargaining' (Peterson 1995:86). Informal negotiation also increased 'upstream' – with bargaining occurring earlier in the legislative process. At a broader institutional level, one of the early outcomes of codecision was the conclusion of horizontal agreements between Parliament and Council (and the Commission) on 'comitology' (see Chapter 8) and on 'amounts deemed necessary'. The net result of the dialogue between Parliament and Council was the confirmation of an increasingly bipartite bargaining process and this, in turn, placed the Commission in a considerably more ambiguous, and weaker, position than in the cooperation or consultation procedures. The ultimate logic of the Commission's position was that it needed now to act in a more evenhanded manner between Parliament and Council in its search for legislative agreement.

Maastricht also extended and enlarged the assent procedure to new areas and categories where international agreements required Parliament's assent. The powers over the appointment of the Commission were increased (see Corbett 1994:214; Hix and Lord 1996; Hix 1997). The TEU also saw further consolidations of the formal power of the EP in several other ways: first, it conferred a right of legislative initiative upon Parliament in so far as it allowed the EP to request the Commission to bring forward legislative proposals; second, it recognized the petitioning procedures of the EP and empowered Parliament to elect an Ombudsman to deal with matters falling within the competence of the EC; third, it required the President of the Central Bank to provide an annual report to Parliament and gave Parliament the right to be consulted on the appointment of the Bank's President and board members; and, fourth, it enabled Parliament to bring the other institutions before the European Court where its own prerogatives had been infringed.

Alongside these formal enhancements and extensions of its powers Parliament also sought to maximize, through its own internal procedures and through informal pressure, its own contribution to the EU's decision-making process. In conformity with the historical practice of combining 'small steps' with 'qualitative leaps', Parliament continued to work simultaneously for further practical procedural gains and more wide-ranging treaty reforms. In 1993 it negotiated a series of interinstitutional agreements with the Commission and the Council on the EU's finances; 'democracy, transparency and subsidiarity'; implementing the principle of subsidiarity; the proceedings of the conciliation committee; and the Ombudsman (see Corbett 1993b:31–5). A year later it concluded an interinstitutional agreement on committees of inquiry. The year 1994 also saw the adoption of new Rules of Procedure designed to maximize the impact of the formal powers conferred by the TEU. As Judge *et al.* (1994:31) noted at the time, 'internal procedural reform [was] designed to impact more widely on interinstitutional relations'. In this manner, the Commission was prompted to table amendments to its own proposals directly in EP committees, rather than having to wait until after Parliament's formal first reading (European Parliament 1994:Rule 56(3)). Under Rule 32 a two-stage procedure was introduced for the approval of the

Commission, which effectively provided for a veto on the Council's choice of Commission President (see Hix 1997:2). Similarly Rule 33 secured an undertaking from the Commission President that he would present the Commission's programme to the Parliament and that the Council would be invited to attend this presentation. In reviewing the rule changes effected in 1994, Nicoll (1994: 403–10) reached the conclusion that their cumulative effect was to enhance the EP's bargaining position relative to both the Commission and the Council. In particular he noted that 'it was only to be expected that the new rules would give the Council trouble. If they did not, the Parliament would think that it was not doing its job' (Nicoll 1994:409).

The 1996 intergovernmental conference

Similarly, the EP would have considered itself to have been failing in its self-ascribed 'job' had it not continued to press for further treaty reform after Maastricht. In fact, the Maastricht Treaty provided an inbuilt incentive for Parliament – precisely because one of its provisions (Article N) was for the convening of an IGC in 1996 to consider further revision of the Treaty. A second incentive came in the simple fact that in the three years since the TEU came into effect 'policy making in the Union ha[d] not settled down into stable and agreed routines' (Laffan 1997:295). A third incentive arose out of a heightened awareness that, without reform, the institutional capacity of the EU could be seriously weakened with the enlargement of the Union to 15 member states in 1995, and potentially 27 within ten to fifteen years (Laursen 1997:61).

The IGC was preceded by the creation of a 'Reflection Group'. Composed of 18 members – one from each member state, one representative from the Commission and two from the EP – the group's main task was to map out the parameters of the debate on the revision of the TEU. The IGC was convened subsequently at the Turin European Council in March 1996. For the first time the EP was accorded a formal role in an IGC. Despite opposition from France and the UK, it was agreed that the Parliament should be given a role similar to that of the Commission. In the event, the President of the Parliament was allowed to address and exchange views with foreign ministers at each of the IGC's monthly meetings, and two representatives from the EP held detailed monthly meetings with ministers' representatives. During the course of the IGC Parliament received copies of all working documents and position papers produced for IGC meetings.

Before the first meeting of the IGC, Parliament and the Commission submitted 'opinions' setting out their respective priorities for the ensuing discussions. The position of the EP was summarized in its resolution of 17 May 1995 on 'The Functioning of the Treaty on European Union with a View to the 1996 Intergovernmental Conference – Implementation and Development of the Union' (OJ C 151, 19 June 1995:56–67). The essence of this position was that Parliament should have equal rights with the Council in all areas of legislative and budgetary competence; have a strengthened role in the fields covered by the first and second pillars (European Communities and Common Foreign and Security Policies) and with regard to EMU; be involved in any decision on its own seat; its assent should be required for members of the various European Courts and the executive committee of the European System of Central Banks; it should have the rights to initiate legal actions and request the opinion of the Court of Justice on the compatibility of international agreements with the treaty; the Commission should be required to respond to Parliament's legislative initiatives; and, finally, that the total membership of the EP should not exceed more than 700.

The Amsterdam Treaty

The result of fifteen months of deliberations by the IGC was the Amsterdam Treaty that was agreed by Heads of State and Government on 17 June 1997 and signed later that year on 2 October. The protracted process of revision which culminated in the Amsterdam Treaty is noteworthy in itself. The 1996 IGC marked the third cycle of constitutional revision to be undertaken in just over ten years. Certainly this rolling process of constitutional change throughout this decade facilitated the EP's self-ascribed 'system development' role (see Wessels and Diedrichs 1997:6), if for no other reason than because other EU institutions, and significant member states, were receptive to the *principle* of change, even if they were not necessarily convinced by the specific proposals for reform advocated by the EP. Indeed, a putative institutionalization of the principle of constitutional review and revision within the treaties themselves seems to have emerged in this period. Thus, just as Article N of the TEU made the commitment to hold an IGC on the operation of the treaty in 1996, so, correspondingly, the Amsterdam Treaty (in the Protocol on the Institutions with the Prospect of Enlargement of the European Union, Article 2) called for the convening of an IGC 'to carry out a comprehensive review of the provisions of the Treaty on the composition and functioning of the institutions' at least one year before any future enlargement increases the number of member states to above twenty. In this manner constitutional review, and the opportunity for the EP to champion further change, became embedded in the future (see below).

Provisions relating to the European Parliament

History teaches us that the EP has never been satisfied with the piece-meal enhancements of its powers in successive treaty revisions. The response of the EP to the Treaty of Amsterdam provided no major exception to this general rule. *A Report and Initial Evaluation of the Results* (of the IGC and the New Amsterdam Treaty) (European Parliament 1997a), produced by a working party of the Parliament's General Secretariat, found the outcomes on the EP's powers and position in the legislative process to be less than impressive.

Nonetheless, specific significant advances were secured. Most importantly, the codecision procedure was extended to 23 new cases: eight of these referred to new provisions; the other 15 cases referred to existing treaty provisions to which other procedures had previously applied. After Amsterdam the codecision procedure applied to a total 38 legal bases (with a further extension to two other cases within two years of the Treaty coming into force). Codecision was now the general rule where qualified majority voting applied in Council (with the main exception being agricultural policy). At the same time Article 189B (which set out the procedure in the Maastricht Treaty) was amended to streamline the procedure (see Chapter 7). The Amsterdam Treaty virtually eliminated the cooperation procedure (with the exception of EMU matters).

The EP's role in the procedure for appointing members of the Commission was strengthened and its right of approval of the appointment of the President of the Commission was confirmed. Another 'definite success for the EP' (European Parliament 1997b) was the new paragraph 5 of Article 190 which enabled the EP to lay down the regulations and general conditions governing the performance of the duties of its members (albeit 'with the approval of the Council acting unanimously'). The preceding paragraph of Article 190 confirmed the right of the European Parliament to draw up a proposal for elections by direct universal suffrage in accordance with a uniform procedure in all member states. In turn, Article 189 limited the number of MEPs to 700 – the ceiling proposed by the EP.

On the downside, a major regret of the EP, however, was the insertion of the protocol on the location of the seats of the institutions which specified that the European Parliament was to have its seat in Strasbourg, with additional plenary sessions in Brussels. Under this protocol, committees of the EP would continue to meet in Brussels and the General Secretariat of the European Parliament and its departments would remain in Luxembourg. In other words, the EP's demand to decide on its own seat itself was rejected (see Chapter 6). Similarly, nothing came of the idea of increasing the EP's control over 'comitology' (see Chapter 8). Nor was the EP's access to the Court of Justice increased. Moreover, the Amsterdam Treaty did not grant the EP a real right of legislative initiative alongside the Commission, in part because Parliament did not make a direct request to this effect.

If the outcomes of Amsterdam are assessed in terms of 'winners' and 'losers' then Elmar Brok MEP, a Parliament representative at the IGC, was in no doubt that 'if there is one winner in the Amsterdam Treaty, then it is the European Parliament' (quoted in Dehousse 1998:603). This view was shared by many beyond the EP itself. Thus, political scientists Moravcsik and Nicolaidis (1998:22) maintained that what was 'particularly striking' about the Amsterdam Treaty was 'the increase in parliamentary power'. Similarly, constitutional lawyer Renaud Dehousse identified the Parliament as 'the institution that has most benefited from the Treaty of Amsterdam' (1998:603).

The road from Amsterdam to Nice

IGC 2000: Parliament's aspirations

The signing of the Treaty of Nice on 26 February 2001, following the IGC inaugurated a year earlier in February 2000, constituted the fourth treaty reform within a thirteen-year period. The imminent enlargement of the EU – to a likely total of 25 member states by 2004 and a further increase to 27 then expected by 2010 – added urgency to the re-examination of the institutional questions left unresolved by the Treaty of Amsterdam (the so-called Amsterdam 'leftovers').

The EP identified two 'interrelated imperatives' for the agenda of the 2000 IGC: first, democratization of the EU's institutions; and, second, improvement in their effectiveness (PE 303.546 2001:17). Under-pinning these broad 'imperatives' were three specific institutional questions which had been left unresolved by the Amsterdam Treaty: the scope of unanimous voting in Council under the codecision procedure, the weighting of votes in the Council and the composition of the Commission. The EP outlined its objectives for the IGC in a report by its Constitutional Affairs Committee (rapporteurs Giorgos Dimitrakopoulos and Jo Leinen, PE 231.873 1999) and in its resolutions adopted on 3 February 2000 (OJ C 309, 27 October 2000:85–6; PE 232.649 2000) and 13 April 2000 (OJ C 40, 7 February 2001: 409–19; PE 232.758 2000).

As the representative institution of the 'Union of the Peoples', the EP drafted a long wish-list of reforms for consideration by the IGC. This list included the incorporation of the Charter of Fundamental Rights into the new Treaty; the 'constitutionalization' of the existing texts of the treaties by joining them into a single document; consolidation of the EU's international status; and encouragement of closer cooperation when the EU was incapable of collective action.

More specifically, and of more immediate relevance to the concerns of this chapter, Parliament called for the reform of the EU's decision-making processes. The EP's belief in the concept of 'dual legitimacy' and its ultimate objective of bringing the 'rights of the countries making up the Union . . . into balance with democratic requirements' (PE 303.546 2001:19) found reflection in its calls for the reweighting of votes in the Council along with extended use of the codecision procedure.

The EP's resolution of 13 April proposed that the Commission President should be elected by the EP from among candidates put forward by the Council. The Commission President, in agreement with the member states, would then appoint the other members of the Commission subject to the conditions of the existing investiture procedure. The EP's resolution also called for the Commission President to be able to ask Parliament for a vote of confidence. If a majority of MEPs did not offer their support in such a vote then the Commission should resign. Such enhanced involvement in the appointment and dismissal procedures of the Commission would mark significant steps towards a 'parliamentary model' of governance as outlined in Chapter 1.

In terms of Parliament's own internal organization, the resolution of 13 April confirmed that the maximum number of MEPs should remain at 700 as agreed at Amsterdam. The EP also declared that the new Treaty should 'provide for the possibility' that some MEPs could be elected in a single European-wide constituency, in which case each voter would have two votes – one for a European list and one for a national list of candidates. At least one citizen from each member state should be included on the European list.

The resolution also called for the drafting (within 12 months of the Treaty coming into effect) of a statute on political parties which would specify the conditions for the recognition and funding of European political parties. In addition, there was support within the EP for the amendment of Article 289 to allow MEPs to decide by an absolute majority on the location of the EP's seat and all of its meetings.

The EP's views were conveyed at the IGC by Elmar Brok and Dimitris Tsatsos who attended the meetings of the Group of Representatives as observers from the EP. In addition Nicole Fontaine, as President of the European Parliament, participated in an exchange of views before each ministerial session and IGC meeting of Heads of State and Government (see European Council 2000a:1). These arrangements represented an incremental advance in the EP's participation in the 2000 IGC beyond that in the 1996 IGC (see Gray and Stubb 2001:7; Yataganas 2001:248).

The Treaty of Nice

The reaction of the EP to the Treaty of Nice was predictable: the changes were insufficient to meet Parliament's aspirations but at least they were a step in the right direction. Yet, as with Maastricht and Amsterdam, even before the ink was dry on the signatures to the Treaty, the EP was looking beyond the new settlement to the 'post-Nice process'. The EP recognized that the 'semi-permanent Treaty revision process' (de Witte 2002) provided it with the opportunity to sustain its traditional integrationist dynamic. MEPs believed that the hesitant steps of Nice could be lengthened and quickened in the 'deeper and wider debate about the future development of the European Union' proposed in the Declaration on the Future of the EU (European Council 2000b:Annex IV). In particular, the Declaration recognized 'the need to improve and to monitor the democratic legitimacy and transparency of the Union and its institutions, to bring them closer to the citizens of the Member States'. What was notable was that there was to be wide-ranging debate prior to the next IGC scheduled for 2004 which was to involve the EP alongside the Commission, national parliaments, and 'all interested parties' (such as political, economic and academic groups, and 'representatives of civil society'). These 'post-Nice procedures' were immediately identified as a way of levering further democratic advance for the EP within an enlarging EU (see Corbett 2001; Duff 2001).

Outcomes versus aspirations

Under the revised Article 214 the Commission President was to be nominated by a qualified majority of the Council acting at the level of Heads of State and Government. The nomination was then to be subject to approval by the EP. In essence, the adoption of qualified majority voting (QMV) would prevent a single member state exercising an effective veto over the nomination of the Commission President, as the UK had done with Jean-Luc Dehaene in 1994. Moreover, in accordance with Parliament's stated preferences, the role of the President was to be strengthened. The President was now empowered to decide on the internal organization of the Commission; to change the distribution of portfolios during the term of office; to appoint Vice-Presidents after collective approval by the college; and to enforce, with the support of the college, the resignation of a member of the Commission.

While these reforms were seen by the EP as an enhancement of the 'supranational and independent nature of the Commission' (OJ C 47E, 21 February 2002:110; PE 294.755 2002), and while Parliament's involvement in the appointment procedure was increased marginally, other important proposals – for the parliamentary election of the President and for the Commission to be subject to a vote of confidence – were quickly discarded at the IGC. In this specific regard, the advance towards a more 'parliamentary system' of governance – through effective involvement in the appointment process of the executive – was stalled at Nice.

In terms of the EP's own composition, the Treaty of Nice revised the total number of MEPs upwards from the ceiling of 700 to 732. The response of the EP itself was unambiguous. The EP berated the absence of any 'demographic logic whatsoever' (PE 294.737 2001:13) to the proposed allocation of seats per member state. Moreover, it expressed its concern that there was the possibility that the 732 ceiling 'may be exceeded by a considerable margin' if there were few accessions before 2004 but many between 2004 and 2009 (for details see PE 294.737 2001:11–13). What was clear, however, was that the decisions over the total number of MEPs and the distribution of MEPs per member state remained firmly and exclusively in the hands of the Council. What was also suspected within Parliament was that the Council had used the composition of the EP to counterbalance the decision reached over the weighting of votes in the Council (PE 303.546 2001:24). Paradoxically, while this continued external control over the EP's size and membership, and its inability to determine its own seat, inhibits the internal 'institutionalization' process, nonetheless Nice did acknowledge the external significance of the EP in the EU's institutional matrix (see Yataganas 2001:276).

Indeed, illustrations of the growing significance of the EP came, first, with the extension of the EP's legal powers to enable it to challenge acts of other EC institutions before the European Court of Justice; second, in the incorporation of the legal basis for a statute (to be adopted under the codecision procedure) for European political parties and their funding (see Chapter 5); and, third, with the prospect of the adoption of a statute for MEPs, the requirement for unanimous decision in Council on this matter was changed to qualified majority.

However, offsetting these positive outcomes, the EP found that one of the 'most unsatisfactory aspects' of the IGC was the failure to accept the principle of linking the codecision procedure to all legislative measures adopted by a qualified majority in Council (OJ C 47E, 21 February 2002:109; PE 294.755 2001). Parliament's pre-IGC position had maintained that, as a general rule, there should be qualified majority voting in the Council, accompanied by codecision with Parliament. This linkage was necessary in Parliament's opinion in order to 'reconcile efficiency in the decision-making process with the democratic legitimacy of the procedures' (PE 303.546 2001:27). Yet the actual outcome in the Nice Treaty failed to meet the EP's aspirations. Qualified majority voting was to be applied to 35 new cases (22 immediately upon the entry into force of the Treaty and the others at a later date or after a unanimous decision by the Council). At no time, however, was the issue of a general linkage between QMV and the codecision procedure involving the EP considered systematically by member states at the IGC (PE 294.737 2001:18). In the event, the codecision procedure was extended only to six areas that had previously required unanimity. Significantly, excluded from codecision were the areas of financial regulations, internal measures for the implementation of cooperation agreements, and the Structural Funds and Cohesion Fund. All of these important policy areas remained subject to the assent procedure. (The assent procedure was also extended to include Article 7 (TEU) on fundamental rights, and enhanced cooperation under the first pillar.) The exclusion from codecision of the three important areas with major budgetary implications simply perpetuated 'an indefensible mismatch between Parliament's budgetary and legislative powers' in the view of the Constitutional Affairs Committee (PE 303.546 2001:28).

After Nice the EP was formally involved in 66 per cent of all first-pillar matters and 37 per cent of all second- and third-pillar matters (combining all legislative measures subject to the consultation, cooperation, codecision or assent procedures). Moreover, some 25 per cent of the articles of the first pillar were covered by the codecision or assent procedures alone (Wessels 2001:210). In other words, Nice represented a further incremental extension of the scope of the EP acting as a co-equal legislative partner with the Council. While the formal view of Parliament was that this extension was 'manifestly insufficient' (PE 303.546 2001:28), another view was more positive in recognizing that 'it is only a small extension . . . but it is an extension, it is better than the status quo and we will come back and fight for more' (Corbett 2001).

The Constitutional Treaty

Drafting the Treaty

As noted above, a Declaration on the Future of Europe was annexed to the Nice Treaty, which called for 'a deeper and wider debate about the future development of the European Union'. The EP's Constitutional Affairs Committee maintained that this debate should be conducted through a Convention (following the precedent set in 2000 by the Convention charged with drafting the EU's Charter on Fundamental Rights) to prepare for further treaty reform (PE 303.546 2001:para. 38; see also Dinan 2004:35; Corbett *et al.* 2007:352). Parliament confirmed this proposal in its resolution on 31 May 2001 (OJ C 47 E, 21

February 2002:108). Although few governments were initially supportive of this proposal, extensive lobbying by the EP, and eventually the Belgian Council Presidency, culminated in the Laeken Declaration of December 2001 and the creation of the Convention on the Future of Europe in February 2002. In this respect the EP acted as a policy entrepreneur in formulating and promoting an institutional mode of treaty reform which was designed to break with the established IGC method, and hence alter the negotiating dynamic after the disappointments of the Nice Treaty (see Judge and Earnshaw 2008). The Convention worked over sixteen months, between February 2002 and June 2003 – through 11 working groups, 26 plenary sessions and nearly 50 meetings of its praesidium – to produce a draft Constitutional Treaty which was then presented to the European Council in June 2003 (for details see Crum 2004; Magnette and Nicolaïdis 2004; Beach 2005:179–88; Nugent 2006:116–20).

Outside observers and MEPs alike readily conceded that the EP had made a significant contribution to the drafting of the Constitutional Treaty. Thus, for example, Beach (2005:207) observed that the 'fingerprints of the EP are scattered throughout the Constitutional Treaty, and in many ways it reads like an updated and lengthened version of the EP's draft treaty establishing the European Union from 1984'. Similarly, the Constitutional Affairs Committee was willing to acknowledge that the EP had 'exerted a major influence on the draft constitutional Treaty' (PE 347.119 2004:15). Moreover, the EP's influence extended to the IGC where, for the first time, the EP's President represented the EP at meetings of Heads of Government, and two other EP representatives were formally involved in all ministerial IGC meetings.

The outcomes of the Convention's deliberations and of the IGC was the Treaty Establishing a Constitution for Europe which was eventually agreed at the Brussels' European Council in June 2004, and signed on 29 October 2004 at a ceremony in Rome – symbolically in the same building in which the 1957 EEC and Euratom Treaties had been signed. The Treaty generated a protracted and arcane debate about whether it was simply a treaty or a constitution. One of the main points of disputation was whether the incorporation and simplification of existing treaties into a single document, which provided a more comprehensible structure and a particular formal status, marked a qualitative step-change towards a federal Europe (see Church and Phinnemore 2007:54–5). Sidestepping this debate here, we may say that the significance of the Constitutional Treaty for the purposes of the present analysis is that it sought to resolve institutional issues which had been exacerbated by enlargement and which had been left unresolved in the Nice Treaty.

The Constitutional Treaty: broad overview

In broad-brush strokes, the Constitutional Treaty (OJ C 310, 16 December 2004) merged the various existing treaties into a single document and created a single entity, the European Union, with a single legal personality at international level. It abandoned the three-pillar structure in favour of a single corpus of the Union. The general provisions of the Treaty set out the values, principles and objectives of the EU, making it clear that the Union's competences were conferred by the member states and that member states and the EU operate in accordance with the principle of 'sincere cooperation' in carrying out the specified tasks of the treaties. The common values underpinning the Union were identified as 'respect for human dignity, freedom, democracy, equality, the rule of law and respect for human rights' (Article 2). The Treaty also listed in Article I-8 the symbols of the Union (including a flag, anthem, motto, and currency). Title II set out the democratic principles to be observed in the performance of the activities of the Union (see below) and Article 8c mapped out the enhanced contribution of national parliaments in ensuring that the principle of subsidiarity was respected. The Charter of Fundamental Rights was given binding legal force in its incorporation in the Treaty.

At an institutional level, the Treaty established the position of the European Council as a body autonomous from the Council of Ministers. A President of Council was to be elected by the members of the European Council for a thirty-month term, renewable for one further term. The person elected could not hold national office. The Council of Ministers was to be presided over by rotating teams, of three member states, for a period of eighteen months with each team member occupying the chair for six months. A double majority voting system in the Council of Ministers was to be adopted after 2009 to take account of both population (65 per cent of the EU population) and member states (55 per cent of states). The EP had supported the double majority principle throughout the Convention and IGC. On the other hand, the Convention's proposal, which had been strongly supported by the EP, for the Council to be constituted as a separate 'Legislative Council' when acting in a legislative capacity, was rejected. Nonetheless under the new Treaty, the various configurations of the Council were to be split into two parts to separate legislative activities from other non-legislative deliberations, and to enable public access to legislative meetings (Article I-24(6)). One new configuration to be created was a distinct Foreign Affairs Council, to be chaired by an EU Minister of Foreign Affairs – who would also be a Vice-President of the Commission.

The issue of the size of the Commission had generated heated discussion in the Convention. The Treaty settled, however, for the pragmatic solution of maintaining representation of each member state until 2014, and, thereafter, reducing the Commission's size to two-thirds of the number of member states. Member states would nominate Commissioners on a strictly equal rotational basis. The role of the Commission President was strengthened in terms of the internal organization of the Commission (Article I-27(3)), and in terms of the right to request the resignation of individual Commissioners. The responsibility of the Commission President to the EP was also enhanced (see below).

The Treaty clarified, and defined the appropriate legal status of, the competences of the Union – the Union's exclusive competences, shared competences with member states, and actions taken to complement action by member states. Falling outside these three categories were foreign and security policies and the coordination of economic and employment policies. As noted above, a new Minister for Foreign Affairs was to be created with responsibility for coordinating all aspects of the EU's external relations, and for conducting foreign and security policy. Unanimity in Council was to continue to be the rule in CFSP matters. Internally, the Treaty incorporated significant enhancements of judicial cooperation in criminal matters and police cooperation (without affecting the special arrangements applying in Denmark, Ireland and the UK). Overall, however, the Treaty did not increase the Union's competences. Moreover, the Treaty refined the enhanced cooperation provisions (Article 10), while at the same time establishing, for the first time, a procedure for 'voluntary withdrawal from the Union' (Article I-60). The clear implication was that 'involvement in the Union and in the furtherance of its policies is something that must be chosen freely on the basis of a genuine political commitment' (PE 347.119 2004:41).

Parliament: specific institutional issues

Article I-46 of the Constitutional Treaty provided a clear statement that 'the functioning of the Union shall be founded on representative democracy' and that 'citizens are directly represented at Union level in the European Parliament' (OJ C 310, 16 December 2004:34). The size of the EP was to be limited to 750 members. From this unambiguous base, the Treaty then rapidly reaffirmed the ambiguous legacy of the dual legitimation strategy, of also having the representation of member states – through the European Council and Council of Ministers – who 'themselves [are] democratically accountable either to their national parliaments, or to their citizens' (Article I-46(2)). Whereas this was simply a restatement of existing principles, the Treaty, in its commitment to 'the principle of participatory democracy' (Article I-47), formalized a further, novel, ambiguity at the heart of the 'democratic life of the Union'. In affording 'citizens and representative associations the opportunity to make known and publicly engage their views in all areas of Union activity', the Treaty not only incorporated indirect processes of consultation and dialogue but extended the right of participation to more direct modes of 'citizens' initiatives' (Article I-47(4)). The tensions between the principles of 'representative democracy' and those of 'participatory democracy' will be examined later (see Chapter 9); for now, the focus of attention will be the ambiguous relationship between the EP and the Council.

The EP's Constitutional Affairs Committee had no doubts that the 'Constitution undeniably represents a significant enhancement of the democratic dimension of the EU' (PE 347.119 2004:23). In future the Committee believed that 'the public will have a clear perception that European law is adopted by the chamber which represents them and by the chamber which represents States' (:23). In particular, the extension of codecision to most areas of EU competence was seen 'basically [as] a matter of putting into practice the fundamental idea of the twofold legitimacy of the EU as a union of States and of citizens' (:23). The Constitutional Treaty expanded codecision (now renamed as the 'ordinary legislative procedure') to 50 new legal bases covered in 69 articles. Included in these were those policy areas where the EP's legislative involvement had been limited historically – agriculture and fisheries, and the areas of freedom, security and justice, and European research. In particular the long-standing and acrimonious institutional dispute over comitology (see Chapter 8) was addressed in Article I-37 by making the rules and general principles of implementing powers exercised by the Commission subject to codecision, and, hence, to agreement with Parliament. However, there still remained exceptions to this general principle of codecision where 'special legislative procedures' enabled Council to decide by unanimity (22 areas), or where the EP was simply to be consulted (5 areas), or in one case where QMV was used but with the assent of the EP. More generally the Constitutional Treaty simplified and clarified legal instruments into six types: laws, framework laws, regulations, decisions, recommendations and opinions. A clear hierarchy of instruments was established (Article I-33); and a new category of 'delegated regulations' was introduced which created the possibility of legislative acts making provision for the Commission to adopt 'executive measures', subject to the approval of Parliament or Council. This delegation by the co-legislators would empower the Commission to adopt regulations to 'supplement or amend non-essential elements of the law or framework law' (Article I-36(1)).

In addition, the budgetary powers of the EP were extended significantly to the extent that 'finally Parliament must be recognised as an equal arm of the Budgetary authority' (PE 347.119 2004:75). The Treaty simplified the budgetary procedure. It ended the distinction between compulsory and non-compulsory expenditure, thus extending the EP's control to all EU expenditure. Moreover, the Treaty formalized the multiannual financial framework, and provided a mechanism to ensure that negotiations took place between Parliament and Council over the framework (see Chapter 7).

There was a further increment in the contribution of the EP to the appointment of the Commission President. Article I-27 confirmed that the President was to be elected by the EP, on a proposal from the European Council acting by qualified majority. This reflected the EP's earlier adoption of the word 'election' in its Rules of Procedure (European Parliament 2004, Rule 98). In addition, the European Council was specifically charged to 'tak[e] into account the elections to the European Parliament' when proposing a candidate for Commission President. Once the President had, acting in common accord with the Council, selected the other members of the Commission they would, along with the newly created Union Minister for Foreign Affairs, be 'subject as a body to a vote of consent by the European Parliament'. Upon securing this consent the Commission would then be appointed by the Council (Article I-27 (2)).

The Lisbon Treaty: a slight detour on the path set by the Constitutional Treaty

Elmar Brok, who was one of the EP's representatives at the IGC on the Constitutional Treaty, echoed earlier parliamentary responses to other treaty reforms in his assessment that 'Not everything in this constitution is perfect, but I think the decisive thing is that it is better than what we have at present' (EP Debates 11 January 2005, available at http://www.europarl.europa.eu). Nonetheless, Parliament's opinion, as expressed through its Constitutional Affairs Committee and in its overwhelming positive vote in plenary (EP Debates 12 January 2005), was 'firmly in favour' of the Constitutional Treaty. Accompanying the delight, however, was also a prescient acknowledgment that 'We must now do everything possible to ensure that this draft becomes reality rather than existing only in black and white' (Leinen, EP Debates 11 January 2005).

The chances of the Constitutional Treaty being consigned to exist only in 'black and white' increased enormously with the negative referendum votes on ratification in France and the Netherlands on 29 May and 1 June 2005. In mid-June 2005 the European Council called for a 'period of reflection' but without stipulating how this reflection was to be structured or conducted. In this vacuum the EP asserted for itself a 'leading role in the European dialogue' (PE 364.708 2005:6–7). In identifying itself as being of 'critical importance' in promoting the engagement of citizens and national representative institutions 'to clarify, deepen and democratise' the public debate about the future of European integration (PE 364.708 2005:5) the EP launched a series of deliberative forums in 2006. These included two joint parliamentary meetings of European and national parliamentarians in May and December to consider the 'Future of Europe' and a series of 'citizens forums'. The identified need for a coordinated and meaningful dialogue between leaders and led was perhaps recognition by MEPs that, in their desire to lead other EU leaders in the Constitutional Convention, they had themselves become disconnected from ordinary citizens.

Significantly, Hans-Gert Pöttering, in his inaugural programme speech as President of the European Parliament in February 2007, made clear that 'The European Union needs a new departure, a renewal . . . politicians are expected to exercise leadership' (EP Debates 13 February 2007). He also emphasized that 'This House stands by the Constitutional Treaty – about that we must not allow there to be any doubt', and that the EP must be appropriately involved in translating the Treaty into 'a legal and political reality'. But, in doing so, Pöttering also recognized that 'we must convince the public of our actions' and that 'we need a new pact between the citizens of Europe and their political institutions in the European Union'.

Ultimately, however, the European Council meeting in Brussels sought to reforge a 'new pact' beyond the specific confines of a 'constitution'; and reached an agreement on 21 to 22 June 2007 to convene an Intergovernmental Conference. The IGC was mandated to finalize the texts of a Reform Treaty and a Treaty on the Functioning of the Union (TFEU). It was unprecedented for such a detailed mandate for an IGC to be set out in advance. The conclusions of the Brussels European Council made it quite clear that the new treaties would not have a 'constitutional character' and that the 'term "Constitution" will not be used' (Council of the European Union 2007a:16). It was also made equally clear, however, that the institutional changes and innovations agreed during the 2004 IGC were to be 'inserted into the Treaty by way of specific modifications in the usual manner' (Council of the European Union 2007a:20). While Parliament's resolution on the convening of the 2007 IGC regretted 'the loss of some important elements that had been agreed at the 2004 IGC', it went on to welcome 'the fact that the mandate safeguards much of the substance of the Constitutional Treaty' (Texts adopted 11 July 2007, P6_TA(2007) 0328). Indeed, this view reflected the fact that the main proposals relating to the EP had survived unscathed and would eventually feature in what was to become the Lisbon Treaty.

Lisbon October 2007

The IGC completed its deliberations in Lisbon in October 2007. Final agreement was reached after a number of demands made, and reassurances sought, by individual member states had been satisfied. For its part, the EP also won a last-minute declaration to the Treaty relating to the appointment of the High Representative of the Union for Foreign Affairs and Security Policy. The specific issue arose because of the possibility that the High Representative would, given the determination of the Heads of State and Government to ratify the Lisbon Treaty by the end of 2008, be appointed in early 2009. This would take place before the 2009 European elections and the normal timetable for the nomination and investiture of the 2009–2014 Commission. In these circumstances the EP's representatives noted, before the final IGC session, their determination 'to defend Parliament's prerogative to "elect" the whole college of Commissioners, including the High Representative, as well as to protect the Commission President's role in approving his/her appointment' (European Parliament 2007:1). Eventually the declaration promised that 'appropriate contacts' would be made between the European Council and the EP for the first appointment process.

At the level of detail, the size of the EP was to be restricted to not more than 751 members. At the final stage of negotiations in the IGC the maximum number of MEPs was raised from 750 through the formula that Parliament's President was to be additional to the EP's membership; thus effectively adding another member. This served to satisfy Italy's demand for an additional member above the strictly 'degressively proportional' allocation of seats based on population. After 2009, Italy was thus to have 73 MEPs, the same number as the UK. It was also agreed, in accordance with proposals submitted to the IGC by Parliament, that no member state would have fewer than six representatives, or more than 96. At a more general level, the foundational principle of representative democracy was established in Title II (Article 10) of the Lisbon Treaty (TEU). Significantly the role of national parliaments was enhanced in the extension of the period to consider draft acts to eight weeks and through a revised mechanism for ensuring compatibility with the principle of subsidiarity (Protocols to the Lisbon Treaty; see also Cm 7174 2007:23–4). Article 14(1) reproduced Article I-20 of the Constitutional Treaty on the joint exercise, with the Council, of legislative and budgetary functions, and reaffirmed the power of the EP to elect the President of the Commission. Article 17(7) reproduced the European Council's responsibility to take into account the outcomes of EP elections in proposing a candidate for Commission President.

Furthermore, the term 'ordinary legislative procedure' was incorporated throughout the Lisbon Treaty. However, the Treaty retained the

longstanding terminology of regulations, directives, decisions and recommendations rather than adopting the new typology, and the hierarchy, of 'laws' and 'framework laws' of the Constitutional Treaty. In
fact, many of the clarifications of the Constitutional Treaty were
muddied in such convoluted statements as, 'Legal acts adopted by legislative procedure shall constitute legislative acts' (Article 289(3)
TFEU), or in the provision for an 'emergency brake' to be applied to
the codecision procedure leading to the suspension of the procedure
pending review by the European Council (see for example, Article 48
TFEU, for measures affecting national social security systems or,
Articles 82 and 83 TFEU, in the area of criminal justice). Clarity was
also lost in a proliferation of opt-outs, opt-ins and derogations (which
proved necessary for agreement on the mandate for the Lisbon Treaty
to be reached in the first place).

The 'ordinary legislative procedure', or codecision, was to be the
norm throughout the new treaties, with the procedure reformulated in
clearer language (see Chapter 7). Codecision was thus extended to
many areas of policy, such as agriculture and trade, from which it had
been absent in the past. Moreover, the pillar structure of the treaties
was collapsed. In general, codecision was to apply where Council
voted by qualified majority. In total, 30 existing legal bases were
modified to use codecision and 13 new legal bases were introduced
which would require codecision (see CEPS 2007:7). In specific
instances, however, 'special legislative procedures' would apply. In
such cases Council would decide, usually by unanimity, and the EP
would merely be consulted. The policy areas to be covered by these
'special legislative procedures' included the possible creation of a
European Public Prosecutor's Office, fiscal measures in the energy
sector, passports and identity cards, family law, police cooperation,
and discrimination. Equally, 'special legislative procedures' were to be
applied to those areas where Parliament adopted a measure with 'the
participation of the Council' (Article 289 TFEU). The cooperation
procedure was abolished, and the assent procedure became 'consent'
(see Chapter 7).

On the budget, the distinction between compulsory and non-compulsory expenditure was finally abolished, and Parliament won the power
of 'consent' over the multiannual financial perspective. The insertion of
conciliation into Article 314 of the new Treaty, in regard to the annual
budgetary procedure, served to formalize long-standing practice but
added specific time-lines (see Chapter 7).

The EP was also confirmed as having the right, along with any
member state or the Commission, to propose amendments to the
treaties. The default mechanism for recommending treaty amendment
by an IGC was to be a Convention convened by the European Council,
unless Parliament 'consented' not to call a Convention (see Chapter 9).

A simplified treaty amendment process was agreed for Part Three of the Treaty on the Functioning of the Union, relating to internal policies and action of the Union. Here the European Council was empowered to amend the treaty provisions, after consulting Parliament, as long as the competences of the Union are not increased. Similarly, the European Council would be able to decide by unanimity, with the consent of Parliament (in this case 'given by a majority of its component members'), to move to either qualified majority in Council, or to the 'ordinary legislative procedure' in those cases where either unanimity or a special legislative procedure is enumerated in the treaties (with the exception of the military and defence provisions of the treaties).

Conclusion

The simple point of the historical review in this chapter is that the 'location' of the EP as a 'parliament' has changed over time. Equally, the nature of the integrationist project in Europe, and the EP's location within that project, has also changed over time. 'Seen in historical perspective, the process is impressive in its continuity. In little more than [a few decades] the Parliament has moved from the status of a consultative assembly to that of a fully-fledged legislative body' (Dehousse 1998:605). It has become easier, therefore, to locate the EP in a typology of legislatures as its formal legislative powers have been enhanced through successive treaty amendments. After Maastricht, Amsterdam and Nice, and certainly after the Lisbon Treaty, the EP – with its capacity to 'modify and reject executive proposals' – can be located in Mezey's category of legislatures with 'strong policy-making power'. Equally, if Norton's criteria of the ability to 'generate alternative policies' is used, then, since Maastricht, the EP has had a formal but restricted right to initiate legislative measures. In this sense it bordered on Norton's category of a 'policy-making' legislature.

What is equally impressive is that the EP has been instrumental in 'relocating' itself within the institutional architecture of the EU. In so doing, it has invoked federal constitutional blueprints and called for 'qualitative leaps' to implement those blueprints. In addition, however, it has also secured incremental, pragmatic and ultimately vital consolidations of its powers through 'small steps' of interinstitutional agreements, informal compromises and the creative use of its own internal procedures. However, while relocating itself in this manner the EP has always been aware that it is not 'part of a finished institutional system, but rather part of one in a process of evolution and requiring change' (Corbett *et al.* 2007:343). This almost missionary belief in change was made clear in the EP's announcement, in its resolution on the convening of the 2007 IGC, of 'its firm resolve to put forward, after the 2009 elections, new proposals on a further constitutional settlement for the Union' (Texts adopted 11 July 2007, P6_TA(2007)0328; PE 393.029 2007). In this sense the evolutionary process is perpetual.

Chapter 3

Linkage, Elections and Legitimacy

> Whatever else legislatures do they connect the people to their government in special ways. (Loewenberg and Patterson 1979:167)

In the context of the EU this general statement, which Loewenberg and Patterson believe is universally applicable to all legislatures, is problematic on at least three counts: first, what constitutes 'the people' of the EU; second, what constitutes the EU's government; and, third, what are the special ways in which this connection takes place. The answer to the third question is provided in fact by Loewenberg and Patterson (1979:166) who maintain that 'the word *representation* describes that relationship'. In this chapter we aim to examine the electoral linkage at the core of the process of representation and in so doing to analyse the concepts of the 'people', European 'demos', legitimacy and democracy. However, as Chapters 1 and 2 made clear, discussion of the EP's role in the representative process of the EU cannot be discussed in isolation from conceptions of its roles as a legislature and of its location within a multi-level system of governance.

This chapter starts by examining the electoral procedures structuring the 2004 European parliamentary elections, the nature of transnational party competition, and the dominance of national political contexts before analysing the concern with low turnout at these elections. This analysis is then located within a broader-ranging discussion of legitimacy and 'linkage'.

The European Parliament and direct elections

> The obvious starting point is that the European Parliament constitutes the representative-democratic element par excellence in the structure of the Union ... the European Parliament is the only body serving the whole Union which is directly elected. (Blondel *et al.* 1998:10)

This might be the obvious starting-point but, as we will soon discover, discussion of the EP as a representative-democratic institution brings with it a host of theoretical and practical complications. Before becoming immersed in the complications let us deal first of all with the 'simplicities' of the electoral process itself. For our purposes the most straightforward, if not necessarily the easiest, way to analyse EP elections is to start with the latest election and work backwards, drawing out salient historical and analytical points where appropriate.

2004 elections

Electoral procedures

Barely one month after the enlargement of the EU to 25 member states, elections for the EP were held in June 2004. In total some 350 million voters were eligible to vote across the 25 member states and of those 58 million EU citizens had acquired the right only one month earlier. In the event, however, only 45.7 per cent of EU citizens chose to exercise the right to vote, and participation was particularly low in the new member states (see below).

Initially, as noted in Chapter 2, Article 138 of the 1957 EEC treaty had empowered the Common Assembly to draw up proposals for direct elections 'in accordance with a uniform procedure in all Member States'. After 40 years struggling to adopt a uniform system the principle of uniformity was eventually ceded in the Amsterdam Treaty to allow for European elections to be conducted 'in accordance with principles common to Member States'. And once the UK had moved away from the simple majority (first-past-the-post) system in the 1999 EP elections, agreement between the EP and Council was reached in 2002 on the principle that EP elections would be conducted on the basis of proportional representation, using the list system or the single transferable vote (PE 313.380 2002; OJ L 283, 21 October 2002:1).

Even after the 2002 agreement, however, significant diversity of electoral procedures persisted because each member state remained responsible for implementation of these common principles through national legislation. Thus, as Table 3.1 reveals, the Republic of Ireland and Northern Ireland, along with Malta, used the Single Transferable Vote; while the other 22 states used some form of list system – but with considerable variations in terms of electoral districts and preferential voting.

Electoral districts and preferential voting

In 2004 18 states based their elections upon a single national electoral district; five states used regional constituencies (Belgium, France, Ireland, Italy and the UK); and two others, Germany and Poland, had hybrid systems. In Germany, parties were able to submit either Land or federal lists. Poland had a more elaborate system with the number of seats distributed according to the number of votes received nationally per party (using the d'Hondt procedure) and then seats were allocated to each of the 13 electoral districts on the basis of turnout (using the Hare–Niemayer method).

In terms of preferential voting, the Council Decision of 2002 left open the option of preferential list voting. 17 states opted for some form of preferential voting, where the order of candidates on a list could be modified by the voter; while 8 states chose 'simple' or 'closed' lists, where voters could not re-rank predetermined lists of party candidates. Similarly, the issue of the minimum threshold required by parties to secure parliamentary representation was left to the discretion of member states (within the limits of a 5 per cent maximum). The Czech Republic, Germany, Hungary, Lithuania, Poland and Slovakia all adopted a 5 per cent national threshold, Sweden and Austria 4 per cent, Greece 3 per cent, while France utilized 5 per cent thresholds in each of its eight electoral districts.

Voting rights and eligibility

The 2004 election was the third in which citizens of the EU who resided in a member state of which they were not nationals had the right to vote and to stand as candidates on the same conditions as nationals. In practice this was not the universal right envisaged in Article 19 of the EC Treaty, as only Austria, Germany, Latvia, the Netherlands, Portugal and Spain did not impose residence or national registration restrictions upon EU citizens' right to vote. Correspondingly, only five member states did not place residence or registration limitations upon the right of non-national, EU citizens to stand as candidates (Austria, Denmark, Spain, the Netherlands, Portugal). In the event, only six non-nationals were elected in 2004 (and only 13 in total had been elected since the introduction of direct elections in 1979).

The minimum age to stand for election ranged from 18 (Denmark, Germany, Finland, Hungary, Malta, the Netherlands, Slovenia, Spain, Sweden and Portugal), 19 in Austria, 21 in Belgium, the Czech Republic, Estonia, Ireland, Latvia, Lithuania, Luxembourg, Poland, Slovakia and the UK, 23 in France, to 25 in Cyprus, Greece and Italy.

The actual date of the elections was also left to member states – with 19 states opting for Sunday 13 June, four states holding elections on one of the preceding days, and the Czech Republic and Italy staging the elections over two days. In seven states (Denmark, Finland, Germany, Greece, Hungary, Italy Lithuania and Spain) effectively only parties or formal political organizations were able to submit

Table 3.1 *2004 electoral systems and turnout*

Member state	Constituency	Electoral formula	Ballot structure	Turnout (%)
Austria	National	d'Hondt	Ordered, single vote	42.4
Belgium	Regional	d'Hondt	Ordered, multi-vote	90.8
Cyprus	National	Hare	Ordered, multi-vote	71.2
Czech Republic	National	d'Hondt	Ordered, multi-vote	28.3
Denmark	National	d'Hondt	Open, single vote	47.9
Estonia	National	d'Hondt	Open, single vote	26.8
Finland	National	d'Hondt	Open, single vote	39.4
France	Regional	d'Hondt/Hare	Closed, single vote	42.8
Germany	National/Regional*	Hare–Niemeyer	Closed, single vote	43.0
Greece	National	Hagenbach–Bischoff	Closed, single vote	63.4
Hungary	National	d'Hondt	Closed, single vote	38.5
Ireland	Regional	STV-Droop	Open, multi-vote	58.8
Italy	Regional	Hare	Open, multi-vote	73.1
Latvia	National	Sainte–Laguë	Ordered, multi-vote	41.3
Lithuania	National	Hare	Open, multi-vote	48.4
Luxembourg	National	d'Hondt	Open, multi-vote	89.0
Malta	National	STV-Droop	Open, multi-vote	82.4
Netherlands	National	d'Hondt/Hare	Ordered, single vote	39.3
Poland	National/ Regional*	d'Hondt	Closed, single vote	20.9
Portugal	National	d'Hondt	Closed, single vote	38.6
Slovakia	National	Droop	Ordered, single vote	17.0
Slovenia	National	d'Hondt	Ordered, single vote	28.3
Spain	National	d'Hondt	Closed, single vote	45.1
Sweden	National	Modified Sainte–Laguë	Ordered, single vote	37.8
UK/Britain	National	d'Hondt	Closed, single vote	38.8†
UK/N. Ireland	Regional	STV-Droop	Open, multi-vote	

*Hybrid national/regional system.
†Whole of UK.

nominations; in all other states nominations required the endorsement of a designated number of signatures or electors.

As a result of these and other dissimilarities (for example in relation to incompatibility, financing, and dual mandates) commonality across the most important procedural rules and electoral practices still remained an aspiration in 2004. In practice individual member states continued to control the precise conduct of EP elections. This led Mather to proclaim (2005:30):

> Given that the European Parliament is, as its name suggest, a *European* Parliament, it is surely only sensible for there to be a uniform *European* electoral system . . . it is likely that a single system instituted across the Community, with a set of well organised and mobilised European political parties, would better connect the citizen with the Union and further the attainment of a mature European civil society.

While the altruism in this statement should be commended, the realism of its prognosis is open to question on at least three counts: (i) the prospect of strong transnational European parties contesting elections; (ii) the development of engaged European citizens; and (iii) the attainment of a mature civil society. We will take these elements in order.

Transnational party groups/parties

While transnational party groups are a powerful force internally within the EP (see Chapter 5), externally, and paradoxically in electioneering terms, they play a subsidiary role to national parties. Thus, as Franklin points out, 'although the European Parliament contains party "groups" that sit together and co-operate in legislative matters, these groups are hardly relevant to the electoral process' (Franklin 2006:230). The selection of party candidates, the electoral campaign and, indeed, electoral success or failure itself, is determined in most member states by the profile of domestic party politics (see Hix and Lord 1997: 85–9). Where transnational party federations have been active, however, is in producing 'European' manifestos. Typically such manifestos have been 'bland, offering little more than platitudes . . . and [providing] symbolic statements of belief than statements of intent' (Smith 1999:93). This was largely the case in 2004 with few specific policy commitments – five in the case of the PSE, and 17 from the ELDR – with the EPP confining itself to a statement of general beliefs 'in favour of a union of values, a Europe for citizens, a European space of freedom, security and the rule of law'. As Stanley Crossick (*European Voice*, 10 June 2004) noted, 'all three parties favour motherhood and apple pie' and he questioned the 'policy, as opposed to presentational differences, that could be identified through reading the party manifestos'. In part, this reflected difficulties confronting the party federations in constructing a common programme on the basis of coalitions of parties with, often, diverse ideological, language and historical traditions. These difficulties had simply increased after enlargement with the inclusion of even more ideologically diverse parties in the transnational parties. Indeed many of the East and Central European parties often 'only shared names and symbols, not policies, with West European parties' (Auers 2005:748). Not surprisingly, therefore, the extent to which transnational dimensions featured in national parties' campaigns in 2004 was limited in most member states (see Chan 2005: 13; Espíndola and García 2005:233; Langdal 2005:242; Pedersen 2005:90; Raunio 2005a:105). More generally there was no attempt to coordinate campaigns across borders.

One paradox of EP elections, therefore, is that voters are mobilized around national party programmes and affiliations, yet the successful candidates elected by this process then operate in the European Parliament in transnational groupings which are largely unknown to the electorates and in some cases are not even in existence at the time of the election itself (see Chapter 5).

Second-order elections?

What the experience of the 2004 election revealed, as indeed did all EP elections since the first direct elections were held in June 1979, is that transnational and national party systems are interlinked in complex and ambiguous ways. For those politicians and scholars who believed that direct elections would lead to the creation of a new European identity on the part of voters, and hence a novel source of supranational legitimation of the EU itself, direct elections have proved to be both a practical disappointment and a conceptual quagmire.

The practical disappointment is that voters have not turned out to vote consistently in high proportions. Those voters who have voted have tended not to vote on EU issues, and transnational parties have not emerged as powerful electoral and mobilizing forces. For many commentators the reason for this is easily identified. EP elections continue to be contested not as 'European elections' but as 'second-order national contests' (Hix 2005:193).

The perspective of 'second-order national elections' was first used in the analysis of the EP elections by Reif and Schmitt (1980). Their starting premise was that in any state, elections for national representative institutions are normally the most salient for voters and parties alike. They decide 'who is in power and what policies are pursued' (Schmitt 2005:651). In this sense they constitute 'first-order elections'. Other elections, for subnational representative bodies, or in the case of the EU the supranational EP, are deemed to be less salient for voters and hence can be classified as 'second-order elections'. The major distinction between the two types of election is that 'there is less at stake' in second-order elections than in first-order ones (Reif 1985:8; Schmitt 2005:651).

Elections to the European Parliament indeed have been characterized as 'second-order' in that national political issues, national parties and the political standing of national governments at the time have dominated the campaigns. What is important to remember is that the second-order model recognizes that the same party system operates in both first- and second-order elections. In other words, the latter cannot be separated from the former in the same political system: 'Concerns which are appropriate to the first-order arena will affect behaviour, even though second-order elections are ostensibly about something quite different' (Marsh 1998:592). Nonetheless, there also tends to be a 'head' and 'heart' distinction in so far as voters may choose to follow their 'heart' in second-order elections – which are deemed to be less important and hence hold fewer policy consequences – than first-order elections (Marsh 2006:3).

Reif and Schmitt (1980) offered three broad characteristics that differentiated aggregate behaviour in European elections from national elections. They believed that in EP elections, turnout would be lower, national government parties would suffer losses, and small parties would do better than in national elections. These descriptive propositions have been tested at both individual and aggregate levels using the experience of various elections since 1979.

Before examining the data pertaining to the 2004 election, the issue needs to be raised of whether the assumption of automatic 'second-orderness' of EP elections remained the same in 2004 as it was in 1979. Significant changes had occurred in the intervening period. First, more than twice as many states elected representatives to the EP in 2004 than was the case just 15 years earlier. Second, the 2004 elections were contested on a more truly 'European' basis – transcending the Cold War East–West divide for the first time. Third, the policy salience of the EP was far greater in 2004 given the significant increase in its formal powers and the increased scope of EU policy competence generally. Fourth, the 'European issue' in itself may have helped to structure voters' preferences at EP elections and so help to explain vote change between national and European elections (see Marsh 2005:145).

Marsh (1998) provided one of the most comprehensive analyses of 'second orderness' using aggregate data derived from elections between 1979 and 1994. He re-examined Reif and Schmitt's propositions about which parties win and lose by examining the performances of governments and of individual parties in EP elections (1998:595). What he found was that 'there are election cycle effects on government support manifested at European Parliament elections' (1998:606). At a general level, EP elections served as pointers to subsequent general elections. At a more specific level, government losses were greatest when EP elections were held at their mid-term and levelled off thereafter. What was particularly striking was that Marsh discovered that these losses increased with each set of EP elections, and that these losses could not be explained in terms of increasing government losses in general elections.

In 2004, 23 of the 25 governments lost support from the preceding national elections. The exceptions were Slovakia, where the government made a 10 per cent gain, and Spain, where the newly elected socialist government made a 1 per cent gain on its national election result of one month earlier. Hix and Marsh (2005:19) provided the qualification, however, that, although governing parties continued to lose in 2004, large governing parties tended to lose most, while small parties in government did not lose as much. Nonetheless, Marsh (2005:149) concluded that the 2004 results in the EU-15 countries (plus Cyprus and Malta) provided the 'best fit' to date of the predictive model based on the timing of EP elections within the national electoral cycle. In the post-communist states, however, the model did not fit (Marsh 2005:150; Schmitt 2005:659). Voters in the new member states did not appear to use the EP elections to register a protest against incumbent national governments (see Koepke and Ringe 2006:322). There appeared to be 'no sign at all of any electoral cycle' (Hix and Marsh 2005:26).

The second proposition, that small parties gain at the expense of large parties in European elections, also found support in Marsh's 1998 analysis and in subsequent analyses of the 2004 election. In 1998 Marsh found that while there was no consistent pattern of increasing support for certain types of small parties at all elections, nonetheless, there was sufficient evidence that there had been a shift of votes from bigger to small parties, with very small parties and very large parties being the most obvious 'winners' and 'losers' (1998:606). In 2004 gains continued to be made mostly by small parties at the expense of larger parties (Hix and Marsh 2005:19; Marsh 2005:150). Notably, however, some small parties did better than others, with anti-EU or Eurosceptic parties (especially in the UK and Sweden) and Green parties performing relatively well in EU-15 states. In contrast, in the new member states, small parties did not perform consistently better in EP elections than in national elections.

While not arguing that the EU was entirely irrelevant for the results of European elections, Marsh was led in 1998 to conclude that the essential insight of the second-order model was upheld. Models based on second-order propositions did help to explain the performance of parties and governments and thus to confirm that 'European

Parliament elections take place within a wider political context and that their results can be understood in such terms' (1998:606). After the 2004 elections Marsh recorded pretty much the same verdict: 'there is little in our analysis to suggest that results in 2004 were not brought about by the forces responsible for results in 1979' (2005:159). Equally one of the initial proponents of the second-order model, Hermann Schmitt, concluded that, in the EU-15 states at least, EP elections in 2004 were 'still very much second-order elections' (2005:668).

Turnout

A major element of the second-order model was the prediction that electoral participation would be lower in EP elections than in national general elections. In terms of EP elections taken in their own right, there had been a trend of declining participation since the first elections in 1979 (see Table 3.1); and a new low of 45.7 per cent was reached in 2004. While the average turnout was largely unchanged in the EU-15 (49.8 per cent in 1999 and 49.4 per cent in 2004), several of the new member states recorded notably low participation rates. Hence, although Finland, Ireland, Italy, Luxembourg, the Netherlands and the UK all returned higher turnouts than in 1999 these gains were offset by the low turnout in the new member states. The overall average for the 10 new member states was 26.9 per cent, with Poland (21 per cent) and Slovakia (17 per cent) markedly deflating the average turnout figures in the post-communist states.

When turnout for first-order national parliamentary elections is compared with subsequent EP elections the difference in electoral participation – the so-called 'Euro-gap' – continued to increase in 2004. In 24 of the 25 states turnout was lower than at the preceding national parliamentary election (Rose 2004:3). The exception was Luxembourg, where compulsory voting and a concurrent general election sustained participation rates. The 'Euro-gap' averaged 25 per cent across the EU-25, and ranged from 3 per cent in Ireland to 53 per cent in Slovakia, and was greater in new member states than in the EU-15 – 29 percentage points and 22 percentage points respectively. However, large gaps were apparent in both EU-15 and new member states alike: 42 per cent in Sweden, 41 per cent in the Netherlands, 38 per cent in Austria; to 44 per cent in Slovenia, 35 per cent in Hungary, and 31 per cent in Latvia (Rose 2004:3).

Although turnout has been falling at each successive election, and by 2004 was down by more than 17 percentage points from the level in 1979 (see Table 3.1), this does not mean that there has been a single, linear process of decline in that period. As noted above, six member states recorded higher turnouts in 2004 than in 1999. In the UK the 2004 turnout was 6.6 percentage points above the average turnout recorded for the preceding five direct elections, in Ireland the corresponding increase was 4.9 points, and in Luxembourg it was 2.1 points (Rose 2004:7). Yet, in contrast, in France and Germany turnout in 2004 was considerably lower than the average for the five preceding EP elections. The downward trend in aggregate turnout observable in Table 3.1 thus masks notable variations across countries across time.

Why the concern with turnout?

> Direct elections ... will give this assembly a new political authority. At the same time [they] will reinforce the democratic legitimacy of the whole European institutional apparatus. (Tindemans 1976:Section V, A)

This belief that direct elections would necessarily enhance the legitimacy of the entire EU institutional framework has been at the heart of the debate about the democratic deficit in the EU. There was an assumption of an automatic correlation between an increase in democracy (through the act of voting) and an increase in legitimacy (by developing support through the participation of all the electorates of member states). Not surprisingly, given this assumption, there has been an intense concern with the level of turnout throughout the history of direct elections. This was largely because members of supranational institutions (the EP and the Commission) feared that 'a low turnout would undermine the legitimacy of the EP [or] that it might be interpreted as an expression of no confidence in the EC' (Smith 1999:110). Thus the reverse of Tindemans's logic is that if direct elections failed to provide 'a new political authority', then far from reinforcing democratic legitimacy they would simply serve to undermine that legitimacy. Yet, as we will see, the connection between turnout, democracy and legitimacy is neither that simple nor direct.

Explanations of low turnout

As noted above, one explanation is that EP elections are second-order elections. Turnout figures in Table 3.1 are used by some commentators, such as Hix (1998b:35), for example, to argue that the EU is an 'upside-down political system' where the focus of attention is on national politics. Other explanations, however, focus upon the attitudes of voters to the campaigns and activities of parties and candidates at European elections, or upon the 'institutional' variables, such as the nature of electoral systems and the requirements of voting.

Attitudinal explanations

At an individual level, part of the explanation rests in the attitudes of voters towards the EP and to the EU itself. Blondel *et al.*'s survey, based on nearly 13,000 completed questionnaires in nine languages in the wake of the 1994 EP elections, found that the most striking characteristic of voters' general attitudes to the EU was a sense of a lack of involvement rather than opposition. 'Indifference, apathy, and ignorance' characterized attitudes to the EU (Blondel *et al.* 1998:240). Correspondingly, voters' attitudes to the EP itself were not generally grounded in political knowledge or direct experience of the Parliament; but Blondel *et al.* (1998:112) found that the majority of respondents did not share the view of the relative powerlessness of the EP which is at the base of the second-order model. There were, however, notable differences among member states, but the basic problem for the EP was that a substantial proportion of its electorate had no image of the Parliament – whether good or bad. In total some 39 per cent of respondents had no affective image of the EP (1998:120).

Blondel *et al.* proceeded to raise the question of how far the probability of voting or non-voting was affected by attitudes to the campaign, the parties and the candidates, as well as more broadly to the EP and the EU. Their answer pointed to two sets of explanations. First, there were circumstantial explanations, with some 40 per cent of respondents citing pressures of time or of work, illness, or absence from home, for example, as reasons for not voting. In 2004 some 23 per cent of Eurobarometer respondents also claimed that they were too busy, had no time, had work pressures, or were away from home (2004:17). Second, there were voluntary explanations. Lack of interest was the most common reason in this category, with political distrust, inadequate information and dissatisfaction with the EP electoral system also featuring in the comments of voluntary abstainers (Blondel *et al.* 1998:243). Similarly, dissatisfaction or distrust of politics in general (22 per cent) or a lack of interest in politics *per se* (14 per cent) were among the main reasons cited for abstention in 2004. As the Eurobarometer report noted, 'the weight of the general criticisms of politics is much more significant than rejection or ignorance of European affairs in explaining the abstention in European elections' (2004:20).

Using a series of bivariate analyses, Blondel *et al.* discovered that variations in turnout were associated with European party and candidate differentials, in other words, attitudes to the EU did make a difference. At an individual level, Eurobarometer respondents in 2004 revealed that positive attitudes to the EU appeared to enhance the propensity to vote (Eurobarometer 2004:47), though these effects were relatively small in aggregate (see Hix and Marsh 2005:7). If anything the 2004 election illustrated a 'creeping Europeanization' of EP contests – with voters considering more European issues when making their choice (Manow 2005:22). With increased 'Europeanization', however, came the attendant and negative possibility that the decision to vote might be influenced by dissatisfaction with the EU (in the form of anti-Europeanization and Euroscepticism). Either way, the significance for the second-order model was that the view – that there was 'less at stake' in European rather than in national elections – appeared to have declining resonance with voters.

Institutional explanations

Institutional factors have also been used to explain differences in turnout: compulsory voting, the simultaneity of national and European elections, and the nature of the electoral system have all attracted the attention of researchers. The starting-point of such analyses is to note the differences observable in Table 3.1. Certainly voting was higher in those countries where voting is nominally compulsory – in Greece, Belgium, Luxembourg and Cyprus – and in Italy where voting is still defined by the constitution as being a 'civic duty'. But even in these high-turnout countries there was a gap between Belgium and Luxembourg and Cyprus, Italy and Greece. This pattern had been observable in previous elections in Italy and Greece and underlined the fact that even when voting was nominally prescribed, voters chose not to vote in the European elections more than in national elections. In the case of Cyprus the fact that more than a quarter of the electorate did not vote was deemed 'unusual' by Cypriot standards (Melakopides 2005:74). In reverse, Malta secured 82 per cent participation without compulsory voting. Nonetheless, compulsory voting remained the strongest predictor of higher than average turnout in 2004 (Schmitt 2005:657).

A second institutional variable was the simultaneous timing of national and European elections. Again concurrent national and European elections tended to affect, significantly and positively, turnout in 2004 (Rose 2004:5; Schmitt 2005:657) just as it had done in the 1999 EP elections (Smith 1999:120; Guyomarch 2000:169; Frognier 2002:50). Certainly in the UK the combination of local elections and EP elections had a marked effect on turnout; but the effect was variable, as holding concurrent elections had a greater effect in some areas rather than others (see Electoral Commission 2004:111–13; Curtice *et al.* 2005:193). Moreover, the introduction of all-postal voting in four regions increased turnout in these areas and added to the variability of turnout in the UK in 2004 (Electoral Commission 2004:109).

Distance in time between national and European elections has also been identified as a contextual variable influencing turnout. Thus, for example, Franklin (2006:236) maintained that the period of time between national and EP elections was an important variable in explaining the variance in turnout from country to country. The basic proposition is that voters and parties are less interested in the EP elections if national elections have occurred recently. Franklin estimated this time effect at 2.8 per cent per year: the longer the gap since the last national election the greater the potential engagement of voters in the European election. Voters in new member states in 2004 also appeared to behave just like those in established member states, in so far as there was 'an apparently identical effect of time until the next election' (Franklin 2006:5). However, Franklin's model has not gone unchallenged. Blondel *et al.* maintained, for example, that this contextual variable did not appear to have a significant effect on turnout before 1999. Using both the time elapsed since the last national election and time until the next election Blondel *et al.* (1998:227–8) found that the timing variable had little impact on turnout. Similarly, for the 2004 elections, Schmitt (2005:658) concluded that the timing of EP elections in relation to the 'first-order electoral cycle' had little significance in explaining levels of turnout.

Elections, democracy and legitimacy

What is distinctive about legitimation in liberal democratic political systems is that democratic participation is largely conceived of in terms of authorization of representatives through the electoral process (see Beetham and Lord 1998:8). In a representative democracy both election (participation) and representation (indirect decision-making) are defining characteristics of the political system. Repeated elections serve as a key incentive in encouraging representatives to take account of the views of the represented (see Manin 1997; Judge 1999).

So far we have consciously referred to 'representative democracy' and the relationship between the people and their representatives, rather than to 'representative government' and the relationship between the people and elected decision-makers in government. This is because, as we will examine below, what constitutes 'the people', and what is meant by 'government' in the EU, are the source of heated contestation. For the moment, however, we will simply focus upon the question of why low turnout and voter participation in EU-wide elections is considered to be a problem of 'legitimacy' within the Union itself.

Even at this starting-point the issues of legitimacy and of a 'democratic deficit' in the EU become immediately entangled. Again we will postpone a discussion of both the nature and of the number of 'deficits' until later, concentrating here simply upon the limited notion that direct elections provide neither sufficient authorization from, nor a clear expression of, 'European' opinion or public identity to confer legitimacy upon the actions and outputs of their representatives in the European Parliament.

From the outset direct elections were seen as a means of enhancing the 'direct legitimacy' of the representatives in the EP. European elections were identified as the process through which the actions of MEPs would be authorized and through which they would be directly accountable to the people who elected them (see Herman and Lodge 1978:74). What was particularly important in this argument was the fact that MEPs alone would be authorized on a 'European' basis, and so be able to speak on behalf of the 'European electorate'. This was a claim which neither the Commission nor the Council of Ministers could substantiate in terms of the bases of their collective tenure of office. In the words of former President of the Commission Walter Hallstein (1972:74):

> What is lacking . . . is an election campaign about European issues. Such a campaign . . . would give the candidates who emerged victorious . . . a truly European mandate from their electors; and it would encourage the emergence of truly European parties.

Such a rationale for direct elections is based on the claim that elections would elicit popular support for the process of European integration. Moreover, as Smith notes (1999:17–18), 'at no time did those who favoured direct elections question that public support could be rallied or that elections were the way to rally it'.

Given the subsequent failure of 'truly European parties' to emerge, for election campaigns to be predominantly nationally based rather than focused on European issues, and the propensity of substantial numbers of voters not to vote, then the counter logic is that MEPs do not have a convincing 'truly European mandate'. Indeed, this is the essence of the persistent streak of Euro-scepticism in some EU member states.

If the consensus before direct elections was that they would increase the EP's and EC's legitimacy, the actual experience of European-wide elections has 'lent credence to the view that [they] might exacerbate rather than mitigate legitimacy problems' (Lodge 1993:22). This is why turnout and the nature of campaigns become so important. Thus, after the 1999 elections Wilfred Martens, then leader of the European People's Party, recognized that 'in some member states, the legitimacy of the European Parliament has been put into question' (*European Voice* 17–23 June 1999).

Demos or demoi?

The discussion of legitimacy in the EU presupposes a model of representative democracy derived from the practices of modern liberal democratic nation states, where a territorially defined 'people' – commonly identified as a 'national electorate' with some identity rooted in 'nationhood' – elect their representatives in a national assembly or parliament. While a legally prescribed common EU citizenship was introduced under Article 8 of the TEU, there is a notable absence of a shared collective European identity on the part of these legally defined 'citizens'. This lack of a developed sense of European identity and loyalty has been considered 'the most serious of the obstacles to the development of political legitimacy at the European level' (Beetham and Lord 1998:33).

Yet the relationship between identity and the legitimacy of the EU's political system is not unidirectional. An essential element of the case for direct elections was the assumption that a European identity could be *created* through political participation. Similarly, other integrationist projects – through, for example, the development of institutions (European Courts, European Central Bank), symbols (flags, anthems) and substantive policy programmes (student exchanges, regional and social funds) – reflect a logic that political resources can be used to develop a sense of 'Europeanness'. By this logic the fact that European identity is relatively weak and that citizens are basically agnostic on the issue of integration does not preclude the possibility that the sense of identity can be strengthened and the agnosticism mitigated over time.

At this point in the discussion the work of Joseph Weiler is of relevance. Weiler recognizes that citizenship is as much about social reality and identity of the polity as it is about the politics of public authority (1999:337). For Weiler, citizens constitute the 'demos' (the people) of a political system:

> *Demos* provides another way of expressing the link between citizenship and democracy. Democracy does not exist in a vacuum. It is premised on the existence of a polity with members – the *demos* – by whom and for whom democratic discourse with many variants takes place . . . Simply put, if there is no *demos,* there can be no democracy. (Weiler 1999: 337)

A parliament is a democratic institution in this view because it derives its authority from the demos (through the representative process) and hence legitimizes the outputs of that process (Weiler 1997:257). When the EU is examined then it is apparent that there is no nation, no state and hence no demos. By the logic of Weiler's statement, without a demos there can be no democracy: 'If the EP is not the representative of *a* people, if the territorial boundaries of the EU do not correspond to its political boundaries, then the writ of such a parliament has only slightly more legitimacy than the writ of an emperor' (Weiler 1997: 258).

One proposal therefore is to create a demos. Thus for example, Lord concludes his book *Democracy in the European Union* with the plea for the development of transnational deliberative politics which could conceivably be built upon the construction of 'a *demos* around shared civic values' (1998:132). The linkage between institutional form and collective identity is apparent in this prescription, but in both theory and practice this is an exceedingly complex linkage to envisage.

Multiple demoi

Rather than conceive of a single demos, Weiler suggests that citizens of the EU are best conceived as belonging simultaneously to multiple 'demoi', based upon different subjective identities. One identity is ethno-culturally based and rooted in nationality and the nation state. By this view citizens are located simultaneously in a set of 'concentric circles' of identity, sharing a sense of belonging to, say, Scotland, the UK and Europe, or Catalonia, Spain and Europe. The other is understood in civic terms and a commitment to shared values which transcend ethno-cultural identification. In the case of the EU, the latter sense of belonging would stem from 'European transnational affinities to shared values' (Weiler 1999:344–5); for example, through commitments to human rights and to shared social responsibilities encapsulated in the ethos of the welfare state.

Similarly, Kalypso Nicolaïdis (2003; 2004) has argued that it is necessary to depart from the notion that a single demos is essential for a genuine identity-based political community to develop. For Nicolaïdis the EU has already developed into a 'new kind of political community: one that is defined not by a uniform identity – a *demos* – but by the persistent plurality of its peoples – its *demoi*' (2004:101). Normatively the EU should be conceived as a 'demoicracy' in the making (Nicolaïdis 2003:143). But this requires three conceptual transitions to be made: 'seeking the mutual recognition of all of the members' identities rather than a common identity; promoting a community of projects, not a community of identity; and sharing governance horizontally, among states, rather than only vertically, between states and nations' (Nicolaïdis 2004:102). Moreover, this view also requires a conceptualization of the EU as 'transnational', rather than national or supranational (2004:104), and for a 'post-national' perspective to be adopted (Nicolaïdis 2003:144). In other words, this entails a conceptualization of a future community that is not predicated on a common identity.

Demos, demoi and EU governance

In assessing the legitimacy of the EU's 'decisional procedures', two possible models emerge. One model draws directly upon existing liberal democratic, state-based notions of what such procedures entail; while the other sketches a future, as yet unrealized, post-national mode of governance.

Model 1: state-based

In the first model, the EU cannot 'escape the need for representative institutions if it is to deliver the core attribute of democratic governance, which we take to be public control with political equality' (Lord and Beetham 2001:458). Hence, parliaments are central to legitimate governance. Dehousse (1998:609) makes this point in his statement: '[A]s parliaments are regarded as the main providers of legitimacy, executive authority must derive from, and be responsible to the legislature'. Correspondingly, one persistent strand of argument in the enhancement of the EU's legitimacy has revolved around increasing the European Parliament's contribution to democratic authorization, accountability and representation (Beetham and Lord 1998:6–9; Lord 1998:15; Rittberger 2005:199).

Proposals for the democratization of the EU have been many and varied. Almost all of them, however, are concerned with the enhancement of representative *government* rather than with representative democracy as such. Attention thus becomes focused upon the capacity of elected representatives to authorize and hold decision-makers to account, as well as to influence decisions and public policies made by 'government'. This concern is reflected in Weiler's belief that 'the basic condition of representative democracy is, indeed, that at election time the citizens "can throw the scoundrels out", that is replace the government' (1999:350). A prior condition, many would argue, is that parliaments should authorize government in the first place. On either count – whether authorization or holding government to account – the fundamental problem is that there is no 'government' to authorize or to throw out.

The EU has a dual executive in which the Council and Commission share, asymmetrically, executive responsibilities for the formulation, initiation and oversight of the implementation of policies. Traditionally the democratic authorization of the Council–Commission executive was located in the indirect legitimation afforded collectively to the Council through the process of individual national elections of its members. The EU's dual executive was thus authorized indirectly by the electorates of each member state voting in national elections. If this claim to democratic authorization was tenuous for the Council it was even more so for the Commission. Before the Maastricht Treaty the President of the Commission was nominated by the 'common accord' of the member states' governments, and each Commissioner was chosen individually by national governments. While the consultative and confirmation rights of the EP were enhanced successively under the Maastricht, Amsterdam and Nice Treaties, and the Lisbon Treaty if it comes into effect (see Chapters 2 and 8), electorates in the member states still have no direct say in the selection of Commission members as they neither vote for individual Commissioners nor directly affect the choice of Commission President.

A key element of the 'democratic deficit' identified at the heart of the EC in the 1990s was 'the weaknesses and deficiencies in inter-institutional relations and specifically to the idea of inadequate parliamentary influence over the Commission and Council . . . [in particular] the impact of Euro-elections on the composition of decision-making institutions [was] seen to be flawed' (Lodge 1993:22). Throughout the past two decades the connection between authorization of an executive and the relevance of parliamentary elections was explicit in most proposals to address the 'deficit' (see, for example, Martin 1990:26; Smith 1999:68). The linkage between the 'election' of the Commission President and EP elections was clearly seen by some commentators as having the potential to 'make European elections more interesting, mitigate concerns about the accountability of the European Commission and enhance its legitimacy' (Smith 2004:33). Significantly, the electoral dimension featured prominently in the Commission appointment procedure outlined in Article 1–27 of the Constitutional Treaty and in Article 17(7) of the Lisbon Treaty (TEU) – both in the implied linkage between the outcomes of EP elections and in the 'election' of the President (the word 'election' was already used in the EP's Rules of Procedure (European Parliament 2004: Rule 98)). In Føllesdal and Hix's (2006:554) opinion this linkage could be made even more explicit, 'with candidates declaring themselves before the European elections, issuing manifestos for their term in office, and the transnational parties and the governments then declaring their support for one or other of the candidates'. More radically, others, including MEPs Nick Clegg and Michel van Hulten (2003:26), have argued that the Commission President should be directly elected by the EP, or that the whole College of Commissioners be chosen by parliamentary election (Smith 2004:46). Part of the logic of such direct election would be 'to inject new life and vigour into the electoral process' (Clegg and van Hulten 2003:26; see also Smith 2004:32).

Another basic characteristic of representative government is the ability of elected representatives to influence the policy choices of executives in accordance with the wishes expressed by voters through competitive elections. In practice in most liberal democracies this distils into a process of competitive party government. At best the EU is an embryonic system of party government (see Hix 2005:206–7), and some analysts have even begun, misguidedly perhaps, to apply the terms 'government and opposition' to legislative activity within the EP (see Hoyland 2005). At worst, some argue that such a system is neither possible nor necessary in the political culture of the EU (see Blondel *et al.* 1998:253).

Without entering into the details of the debate about the development of competitive party government, at this stage at least (see Chapter 5), the relevant part of this debate for present purposes is its emphasis upon giving the EP greater powers in the EU's legislative process and in envisaging institutional mechanisms 'to promote genuine competitive party democracy in the EU' (Hix 2005:177). In practice, paradoxically, the EP does play a more influential policy role than many of its national counterparts (see Scully 2000a; Bergman and Raunio 2001). Yet the potential to exploit this at election time is mitigated by voter ignorance and the inability of transnational parties to claim credit for what are essentially interinstitutional, intergovernmental policy outputs rather than clearly identifiable outputs of party government as such. As noted earlier in this chapter, there appears to be only a tenuous connection between perceptions of the power of the EP and electoral turnout. Despite the EP's enhanced powers, and despite recognition of this fact by knowledgeable voters, most voters still have little knowledge of the role or impact of the EP. The fact that the EP is not dismissed as a 'write-off in itself or relative to national parliaments' does not automatically lead to the stimulation of involvement or participation in European elections (Blondel *et al.* 1998:241).

Dual legitimation, dual deficit: the European Parliament and national parliaments

[T]he European Union is based on a system of dual legitimacy: the first legitimacy is based on the democratic institutions of member states ... Gradually a second source of legitimacy has been building up, mainly based on the direct elections to the European Parliament. (Neunreither 1994:312)

So far we have focused almost exclusively in this discussion of elections and legitimacy upon the 'European level' and the role of the European Parliament. However, throughout, the connections between the processes of representation at a national level and at a supranational level have intruded either implicitly or explicitly into the discussion. Moreover, conceptions of what sort of political system the EU is – whether 'type 1 governance' or 'type 2 multilevel governance' (see Chapter 2) – have provided a subconscious structuring of the debate. Thus, for example, analysis of a 'European people/demos' and 'European legitimacy' resonates with federalist notions of EU-wide democratic representation and legitimation derived from the EP (see Chapter 1). Correspondingly, an intergovernmental perspective threads through the analysis of 'second-order elections' and the assumption of limited legitimation derived from the EP. What matters are national electoral contests and national policy outputs.

The idea of a dual legitimacy, noted above by Neunreither, is intuitively attractive but upon further consideration generates a series of paradoxes and conceptual tensions. These complications are outlined at length by Beetham and Lord (1998:84–93), but the essence of their analysis is that the EU has 'created mutually complicating relationships between democratic legitimation at the national and European levels' (1998:84). Attempts to link the two levels of legitimation is not a simple problem of aggregation – of adding EU representative democracy on to existing national processes of representation. In the first instance, there are 27 national political systems displaying different characteristics (for example, majoritarian versus consensus decision rules; structures of legislative–executive relations; experiences and phasing of democratization; and the weighting of territorial and functional representation). In the second instance, the development of European representative processes, without an underpinning elite or public commitment to EU-wide electoral competition, may question the legitimacy of outputs of that process despite their actual responsiveness to public needs. Despite these difficulties the EU has consciously sought to develop dual legitimation in practice, not least through an increasing recognition that both national parliaments and the EP have roles to play in providing authorization, representation and accountability in the Union (see Chapter 9).

Model 2: *multiple demoi and multiple legitimation*

Wessels and Diedrichs believe, however, that the notion of 'dual legitimacy' does not go far enough (1997:8). They claim instead that the EP is but one element of 'multiple legitimation' within the EU; it is simply 'only one of several loci of legitimacy in the fused polity' (1999:148). The 'fused polity' is one in which it is difficult to trace accountabilities and where responsibility for any specific policy is diffuse (Wessels 1997:274). The fusion thesis assumes that national, subnational and supranational actors interact at several levels of governance in a complex and highly differentiated political system (see Chapter 1). Not surprisingly, given the emphasis upon multilevel complexity, Wessels and Diedrichs find that the orthodoxies of federalist (supranational) and realist (intergovernmental) perspectives provide inadequate conceptualizations of legitimacy in the EU. Instead, as noted in Chapter 1 , they argue that the EU is becoming a new kind of parliamentary system (1999:139). In this new system 'national and subnational institutions keep their legitimacy while at the same time the EP might acquire a share of basic acceptance and identification by the citizens. Complementary and mutually reinforcing processes of legitimacy-building are possible' (1999:148). In this 'new polity' legitimacy derives from a 'pluralistic citizenship' (Wessels and Diedrichs 1999:148). Such a 'pluralistic citizenship' resonates with Weiler's and Nicolaïdis's notions of mutiple *demoi*, but this is a citizenship and a polity of the future.

A merging of different sources of legitimacy is claimed to be apparent with the EP making an important contribution as 'a direct representative element . . . as part of a European legitimacy complementary to the national and functional one' (Wessels and Diedrichs 1997:9). Ultimately, however, it is predicted that, while the EP is unlikely to become a central representative institution comparable to national parliaments, its direct representative capacity will play an important role in bolstering 'a European legitimacy'. The important point is that the model underlines the institutional complexity and multilevel nature of the EU and highlights the elemental point that legitimacy is not a zero-sum construct where either national parliaments or the EP are the single source of 'European legitimacy'. There are other foci of legitimation and other forms of representation (see Chapter 9).

Conclusion

The simple formulation of Loewenberg and Patterson noted at the start of this chapter, about the linkage role of legislatures, captures only part of the complex linkages between 'the people' and 'government' in the EU. Equally, a simple linear model of parliamentary legitimation proves inappropriate in the EU. Empirically, the sources of legitimation within the EU are multilevel and, some would claim, are as much concerned with 'output legitimacy' – in terms of technocratic and efficient decision-making – as with 'input' notions of legitimacy derived from the processes of electoral linkage. Normatively, however, the EP 'seems to be predestined to be the main bearer of legitimacy in the Union' (Höreth 1999:250; see also Lord 2004:13–6). In part, this is because of the sheer normative strength of existing conceptions of legitimation derived from established representative democratic praxis in member states and the subsequent transposition of these ideas to the EU level. The simple fact remains that most of the political debate (in contrast to the academic debate) 'about the legitimate political order in Europe remains primarily focused on the European Parliament' (Höreth 1999:250). As Rittberger (2005:204) observes, 'Parliamentary/representative democracy [is still] the key reference point for policy-makers when they think about and debate mechanisms to legitimise EU governance' (see also Kohler-Koch 2000:528). This reference point reflects the common experiences of member states and provides institutional frames for future development. These are frames, moreover, which do not rely upon the normative aspirations surrounding notions of 'pluralistic citizenship' or 'demoicracy', and which do not entail a radical rethinking and reshaping of forms of governance.

Thus, while much academic attention has been focused upon the prescription of a future European polity which will be different and new, and which draws upon multiple (and often conflicting) sources of legitimacy, politicians have preferred to follow a simpler logic. In this logic, in Kohler-Koch's (2000:521) words, the question of EU development 'is reduced to looking for a frame to match surface indicators: representation is linked to parliament, political control to increasing parliamentary powers, and political efficiency to increasing governmental control'. In other words, politicians prefer constitutional choices rooted in their existing experiences. Not surprisingly, the best solution to problems of legitimacy in the EU, identified by many parliamentarians at least, is for further parliamentarization of the EU's political process (see Rittberger 2005:18–9). Exactly what further parliamentarization involves, and what impact it will have upon legitimation within the EU, will be examined in later chapters. More immediately, however, Chapter 4 examines the practice of representation and 'what' MEPs represent when they act on behalf of their electorates.

Chapter 4

Linkage, Representation and MEPs

Chapter 3 examined the linkage provided by direct elections between Members of the European Parliament and citizens of the European Union. In this chapter we develop the analysis of linkage by looking at how the EP acts as a representative body, and how it links citizens and decision-makers in the periods between elections. However, this immediately raises the question of what is 'representation'? It also immediately leads us to sidestep a detailed discussion of the various meanings of representation (see Pitkin 1967; Judge 1999) in favour of addressing the specific ways in which citizens are *re*-presented in the European Parliament by their elected members. In particular, we will concentrate upon the foci of representation – upon 'what' is to be represented when elected politicians act for the represented.

Four main foci are usually identified in the literature on representation. These are political parties, functional groups, territorial constituencies and broader social groupings (see Wahlke *et al.* 1962; Loewenberg and Patterson 1979:170–8; Judge 1999). The focus of representation identified by any particular legislator is not, however, simply a matter of individual choice; it is also, as Loewenberg and Patterson (1979:192) observe, 'determined for them by the electoral system through which they are chosen and by the political culture of the nation in which they live'. On both counts – given the nature of European elections and the difficulties of conceiving of a European nation or demos as discussed in Chapter 3 – the identification of foci of representation may prove to be more problematic for MEPs than for members of national parliaments. We will return to this issue later in the chapter, but for now we need to examine the extent to which MEPs do in fact identify and act on behalf of each of the four main foci noted above. Taking these in reverse order we will look in turn at: microcosmic, constituency, functional and party notions of representation.

Microcosmic representation

As we noted in Chapter 3 the concept of representation is inextricably linked with the concepts of legitimacy and legitimation. In that chapter

it was argued that direct elections are an integral part of the legitimation process and provide, simultaneously, the representatives themselves; authorization for the actions of representatives; and, in
mediated form, information upon popular preferences. In addition, the
periodic nature of elections also provides incentives for representatives
to remain informed about popular preferences in between times.

If we assume that representation is essentially about political action –
about how and why representatives can act for others, and so 'make
present' those who are not actually present at the point of decision –
then we have to start by considering 'how' the people are made present
in the first instance. One answer, at the institutional level of the representative assembly, is that the composition of the institution itself
'reflects' the composition of the wider electorate – in so far as there is
some correspondence between the social characteristics of the population at large and the membership of the legislature. Representation, in
this sense, is concerned initially less about what the legislature does
than about how it is composed. Ultimately, however, composition is
deemed of importance precisely because it affects the outputs of representative institutions. Thus, as Pitkin (1967:63) recognizes, 'proportionalists . . . are interested in what the legislature does; they care
about its composition precisely because they expect the composition to
determine the activities'.

The linkage between the 'composition' and 'action' of representative
assemblies, between inputs in terms of representativeness and outputs
in terms of legislation and policies, is most apparent in microcosmic
notions of representation (see Judge 1999:20–46). Exactly just such a
linkage is explicit in Pippa Norris's research into the backgrounds of
candidates at European elections when she notes that 'Theories suggest
that the process of recruitment, determining who becomes an MEP, is
likely to shape the decision-making and legitimation functions of the
European Parliament' (1999:88). Norris proceeds to note that the
extent to which the composition of the legislature reflects that of the
electorate from which it is drawn is of importance for at least two
reasons. First, 'legislative bodies which fail to reflect society may be
perceived as symbolically less legitimate'. Second, 'the social background of members has the power to influence the policy priorities,
role perceptions and attitudes of legislators' (Norris and Franklin
1997:185–6). Ultimately Norris concludes that:

> [A] central function of parliament is to act as a linkage mechanism,
> connecting citizens and the state, and legitimating decisions made
> by governments. In this regard social representation may be crit-
> ical. How far does the European Parliament look like a microcosm
> of European Society? (Norris 1999:96)

A microcosm of European society?

A stereotypical representative in any European national parliament is now predominantly middle-aged, male, and a 'professional politician with a middle class background, medium to high levels of education, significant political experience, and the likelihood of extended parliamentary service' (Cotta and Best 2000:505). Not surprisingly, therefore, research on the socio-economic background of MEPs shows that they too are predominantly middle-aged, with a mean age of 51.3 in 2004 (Verzichelli and Edinger 2005: 265). MEPs from the new accession states were marginally younger (mean 49.9) than members from EU-15 (mean 51.8). Even new entrants to the EP in 2004 were overwhelmingly middle-aged with 45 per cent aged between 40 and 54, and 32 per cent between 55 and 69 (Bale and Taggart 2006a:9).

MEPs have traditionally been drawn from professional occupations, with public sector employees, especially teachers and university lecturers, being proportionately overrepresented. In 2004 new recruits reinforced this pattern with some 32 per cent of first-time MEPs having been employed in education, a further 12 per cent having experience of public administration, and 7 per cent coming from a legal background (Bale and Taggart 2006b:17). Manual workers remained underrepresented in the EP in 2004, as did agricultural workers with only 2 per cent of new MEPs, thus confirming the profile of the 1994 and 1999 Parliaments which had respectively 2 per cent and 3 per cent of members with prior employment in agriculture.

In 2004 37 per cent of MEPs had also served as elected representatives to their own national parliaments at some stage in their political career. This was the highest figure since direct elections were introduced in 1979 and marked an increase from 28 per cent in 1999. The increase was accounted for largely by the 90 former national parliamentarians elected from the 10 new member states. Indeed, 56 per cent of all MEPs from the accession states had served in their own national parliament at some stage before joining the EP; whereas less than one-third, 31 per cent, of MEPs in the EU-15 states had former national parliamentary experience. Nonetheless, in five national delegations – Finland, Ireland, Luxembourg, Portugal and Sweden – former or current national parliamentarians were in the majority. In 1999, 40 MEPs had been simultaneously members of their own national parliaments and the EP; by 2004, however, the abolition of the dual mandate meant that only eight MEPs continued to be in this position (with limited, temporary derogations for two UK members from the House of Lords and six Irish representatives).

The 2004 EP also included 117 members who had some ministerial experience in national governments. This figure had increased from 64 in 1999, largely through the influx of former ministers from the accession states (*n* = 48, 28 per cent of Central and East European MEPs). The number of former prime ministers increased to eight, alongside one former acting prime minister and one former president. Indeed, the Lithuanian delegation had the distinction of including not only a former president (Landsbergis) but also a former PM (Eugenijus Gentvilas). In the EU-15 states, Belgium (6 of 24 MEPs), Finland (4 of 14), Ireland (6 of 13), Luxembourg (4 of 6) and Portugal (9 of 24) continued to return sizeable numbers of former ministers. In contrast, however, no former ministers were included in the national delegations from Germany, the Netherlands and Sweden.

An interesting aside at this point is that not only does the EP's membership contain a number of leading ex-national politicians, but, given experience to date, there is the distinct possibility that a number of future leading national politicians are also included in its membership. Indeed, it has become relatively common for MEPs to be appointed to national governments following national elections. In recent years therefore many national governments have included at least one ex-MEP. In 2007, for example, ex-MEPs were included *inter alia* in the French, German, Greek, Italian, Netherlands, Polish, Romanian, Swedish and UK governments: Roselyne Bachelot and Brice Hortefeux (ministers of health and immigration respectively in the French government), Heidi Wieczorek-Zeul and Joachim Wuermeling (development minister and state secretary for European affairs respectively in the German government), Konstantinos Hatzidakis (minister for transport and communications in the Greek government), Emma Bonino and Massimo D'Alema (trade minister and foreign minister respectively in the Italian government), Camiel Eurlings (transport minister in the Netherlands), Bogdan Klich and Barbara Kudrycka (defence minister and minister of science and higher education respectively in the Polish government), Cecilia Malmström (European affairs minister in Sweden), Adrian Cioroianu and Ovidiu Ioan Silaghi (foreign affairs minister and minister for small and medium-sized enterprises respectively in the Romanian government) and Geoff Hoon (chief whip in the UK government and formerly defence minister). In September 2006 Toomas Ilves was elected President of Estonia while a sitting MEP. Finally, unlike the 1999–2004 Commission which included three former MEPs (Busquin, Reding and Vitorino), the 2004–2009 Commission included only one former MEP (Reding) until the appointment of Antonio Tajani as Transport Commissioner in June 2008.

Former regional and local politicians are also well represented in the EP. In 1999 35 per cent of MEPs had been elected to local or regional government (Mather 2001:191). This number increased in 2004 with some 42 per cent (*n* = 171) of the new entrants having served in local government and 13 per cent (*n* = 52) having experience of regional government (Bale and Taggart 2006a:11). Several national delegations also included high-ranking local or regional politicians, with, for example, MEPs from Italy including a former regional president (Amalia Sartori of Veneto), 12 former regional ministers, and two serving mayors (Paolo Costa of Venice and Gabriele Albertini of Milan). Similarly, Spanish MEPs included Fernandez Martin, former regional president of the Canaries, and five former regional ministers.

While prior national political experience is thus a notable, but minority, feature of the career trajectories of MEPs, so too is prior membership of the EP itself. Thus in 1999 only 286 of the 626 MEPs (45.7 per cent) had served previously as MEPs, and only 14 had served continuously since 1979. In 2004 the number of re-elected MEPs fell to 42 per cent, primarily as result of the influx of new members from the 10 accession states. Even if the MEPs from the new states, who had served as observers in the session before enlargement in May 2004, are included in the numbers of 'returning MEPs', still less than half of MEPs (n = 350, 48 per cent) after June 2004 had former experience in the EP. Moreover, the 382 new members were spread across all of the political groups and constituted a majority in each group (ranging from 52 per cent in the EPP and the Greens to 71 per cent in the GUE/NGL and 74 per cent in the ID). While in the strictest sense none of the MEPs from the new states were incumbents, among the EU-15 states Greece, Ireland and Sweden returned few serving MEPs (respectively, 8 per cent, 23 per cent and 32 per cent). At the other end of the scale, over 70 per cent of MEPs from Austria and the UK, and some 68 of the 99 German MEPs (68.7 per cent), were incumbents.

Representation of women

If MEPs are as unrepresentative as national MPs in socio-economic terms, they are also disproportionately male – again in parallel with the gender profiles in nearly all of the 27 national parliaments. At the 2004 EP election 222 women (30.3 per cent) were returned as MEPs. However, as Table 4.1 reveals, there is substantial variation of female representation from one member state to another. In 18 member states the proportion of women representatives returned at the 2004 EP elections was greater than that in the closest national elections. Women constituted 58 per cent of Swedish MEPs, and over 40 per cent of the delegations from Luxembourg, the Netherlands, France and Slovenia; yet less than 20 per cent of Italian and Polish MEPs were women, and Cyprus and Malta returned no female representatives at all. Notable differences between female representation in party groups was also apparent after 2004. In descending order the proportion of female representation in each group was: Greens/EFA 43 per cent; PSE 40 per cent; ALDE 30 per cent; GUE/NGL 29 per cent; EPP-ED 25 per cent; UEN 19 per cent; and ID 8 per cent. Yet these average percentages hide significant differences within party groups. Taking the major party groups, EPP-ED and PSE, as examples, there was considerable variation across both national and party delegations. Female members constituted 82 per cent of France's representation in the EPP-ED, and 45 per cent of French PSE members. Among the UK members, women were represented at lower levels and more unevenly across party lines: 8 per cent of British EPP-ED MEPs, and 39 per cent of British PSE members, were female. In Italy the contrast was greater still with only one female member out of 24 EPP-ED MEPs (4 per cent), and five females out of 16 PSE MEPs (31 per cent).

While there has been an upward trajectory of female representation in the EP, with a marginal increase in 2004 from 30 per cent in 1999, and up from 27 per cent in 1994, the rate of increase is such that it would be well into the twenty-first century before women were likely to obtain 50 per cent representation in the EP. Such predictions are complicated, however, by the fact that the increase in female representation in EU-15 member states in 2004 was up to 32.5 per cent ($n = 185$); but the overall increase was moderated by the lower percentage of female representatives from the new member states (37 out of 162, 22.8 per cent).

The concern with female (under)-representation does however raise significant questions for the study of legislatures generally and for the study of the EP specifically. One fundamental question is: why are there so few women in the European Parliament? Yet a related question is: why, in nearly three-quarters of member states, are there more female representatives in the EP than in national parliaments? Is there a European effect?

The first question can be answered in terms of the standard variables accounting for the underrepresentation of women in most Western legislatures: opportunity structures of the wider political and party systems; discriminatory tendencies in the 'supply and demand' of candidacies; gender stereotyping; access to resources and support networks; political motivation; and institutional receptiveness (in terms of facilities and working conditions within legislatures) (see Norris and Lovenduski 1995; Norris and Franklin 1997, Childs *et al.* 2005; Lovenduski 2005). But equally, the question can be inverted to ask why there is a better representation of women in the EP than in most national parliaments.

One traditional answer has been that males have been reluctant to pursue a political career in the EP given the perception of its relative weakness in comparison with national parliaments. As Krook (2005:17) observes, the most prominent argument used to explain the selection of greater numbers of women candidates for EP elections remains that 'the European Parliament is relatively powerless compared with national parliaments and, thus, that each type of election attracts a distinct pool of potential candidates'. Freedman's survey of

Table 4.1 *Female representatives: European Parliament (2004) and national parliaments*

	European Parliament				National parliaments			
Country	*Date of election*	*Seats*	*Women*	*% women*	*Date of election*	*Seats*	*Women*	*% women*
Sweden	June 2004	19	11	57.9	Sept. 2006	349	165	47.3
Luxembourg	June 2004	6	3	50.0	June 2004	60	14	23.3
Netherlands	June 2004	27	12	44.4	Nov. 2006	150	55	36.7
France	June 2004	78	34	43.5	June 2007	577	107	18.5
Slovenia	June 2004	7	3	42.8	Oct. 2004	90	11	12.2
Austria	June 2004	18	7	38.8	Oct. 2006	183	59	32.2
Lithuania	June 2004	13	5	38.4	Oct. 2004	141	31	22.0
Ireland	June 2004	13	5	38.4	May 2007	166	22	13.3
Denmark	June 2004	14	5	35.7	Feb. 2005	179	66	36.9
Finland	June 2004	14	5	35.7	March 2007	200	84	42.0
Slovakia	June 2004	14	5	35.7	June 2006	150	29	20.0
Estonia	June 2004	6	2	33.3	March 2007	101	22	21.8
Hungary	June 2004	24	8	33.3	April 2006	386	40	10.4
Spain	June 2004	54	18	33.3	March 2004	350	126	36.0
Germany	June 2004	99	31	31.3	Sep. 2005	614	194	31.6
Greece	June 2004	24	7	29.2	Sep. 2007	300	48	16.0
Belgium	June 2004	24	7	29.1	June 2006	150	52	34.7
Portugal	June 2004	24	6	25.0	Feb. 2005	230	49	21.3
UK	June 2004	78	19	24.3	May 2005	646	127	19.7
Latvia	June 2004	9	2	22.2	Oct. 2006	100	19	19.0
Czech Republic	June 2004	24	5	20.8	June 2006	200	31	15.5
Italy	June 2004	78	15	19.2	April 2006	630	109	17.3
Poland	June 2004	54	7	13.0	Oct. 2007	460	94	20.4
Cyprus	June 2004	6	0	0.0	May 2006	56	8	14.3
Malta	June 2004	5	0	0.0	April 2003	65	6	9.2
Total		732	222	30.3				

Source: http://www.ipu.org/wmn-e/classif.htm

women MEPs in the 1999–2004 Parliament appeared to confirm that national parties were 'more willing to make an effort to present women candidates for European rather than for national elections, largely because of a continuing belief by many national politicians that the European institution is not a site of effective power, so that there is less competition for places' (Freedman 2002:181). But if this argument can be summarized in the phrase, 'where there is power there are no women; and where there is no power there are women' (Freedman 2002:179), the problem then arises of explaining why female representation continues to rise alongside each successive increment in the formal powers of the European Parliament (Krook 2005:17–18; see Chapter 7).

Similarly, difficulties arise in using the type of electoral system as an explanatory variable. Whereas, as a general proposition, proportional systems tend to enhance the prospects of female representation rather more than majoritarian systems (see Childs *et al.* 2005:80–3; Schwindt-Bayer and Mishler 2005:420), the problem in the EU is that there is no simple correlation between types of electoral systems and female representation in the EP. While the case of France, with a majoritarian system at national level and a proportional list system at EU level, appears to uphold the general proposition, the position in the UK is far less clear-cut (see Table 4.1). Equally, cross-national variation in female representation in the EP in states with proportional systems at both levels undermines the general proposition still further.

Other explanations have therefore had to be examined. One explanation has emphasized the uniqueness of the EU's polity and the opportunities for new forms of political participation and engagement associated with the concepts of integration, consensus, and identity. Freedman (2002) found, for example, that many women MEPs perceived membership of the EP less as a 'career' and more as a means to 'contribute actively to the construction of the European Union' (Evelyn Gebhardt, PSE, Germany, quoted in Freedman 2002:185). A further argument has been that women might be more likely to stand as candidates for the EP 'because they are attracted to the less confrontational political style of European politics', and that this more consensual style may result in a 'political atmosphere [that is] less misogynistic than in national parliaments' (see Krook 2005:19). More importantly, however, Krook identifies party selection processes as a 'crucial lens' for understanding the changes in female representation. In particular, she maintains that increased Europeanization, in conjunction with increased demands of women's groups and the promotion of EU gender equality policies, has impacted differentially on the calculations made by national party elites in candidate selection decisions. Ultimately, 'party selection practices for EP elections tend to replace, follow, or accompany changes in party selection practices for national elections' (Krook 2005:21).

Territorial representation

In the study of legislatures there is common agreement that 'parliamentary representation involves a territory' (Hibbing and Patterson 1986:992), or that, as Loewenberg and Patterson (1979:170) maintain, the representation of geographic areas has been 'the primary focus of representation for legislators in many countries'.

One immediate problem confronting any analysis of territorial representation in the EU is, of course, the problem of defining a 'constituency'. As noted in Chapter 3, 18 states used single national constituencies for EP elections; five states used regional constituencies (Belgium, France, Ireland, Italy and the UK); and two others, Germany and Poland, had hybrid systems. As Table 4.2 reveals, on average, each MEP represented some 627,012 people, with significant variations around this figure – most notably in Germany (with 833,653) and Luxembourg (with 75,266). When compared with national parliaments the ratio of representative to population in the EP is significantly higher. In the UK, each Westminster MP in 2006 represented on average 93,487 people, while their UK counterparts in the EP represented an average of 765,382 constituents. In Germany the respective ratios are 1:134,262 and 1:833,653, in France 1:109,557 and 1:794,667, and in Luxembourg 1:7,658 and 1:75,266. The simple fact, therefore, is that MEPs on average have to 'represent' far more individual constituents than do national politicians. However, the problem confronting MEPs is that not only do they have to represent more people, they tend to be less informed about the preferences of their electors and vice versa are less 'visible' to the people they represent than their counterparts in national parliaments (see Blondel *et al.* 1998:93; Mather 2007:64–6).

Trying to establish exactly how representatives 'act on behalf' of their electors in territorial constituencies has been a preoccupation of legislative scholars for decades (see Judge 1999:149–57). In essence, however, two main concerns have dominated the literature: one is with 'policy responsiveness' or 'policy advocacy' (see Jewell 1983:320; Norton and Wood 1993:25–8); and the other is with 'service responsiveness'.

On the one hand, a concern with 'policy responsiveness' focuses attention upon the congruence between the opinions of constituents and the views and voting behaviour of their representatives in parliament. As the main focus of the EP is, by definition, 'European policy' –

Table 4.2   *Ratio of MEPs to population (2004 election)*

Country	Number of MEPs	Population per MEP
Germany	99	833,653
France	78	794,667
UK	78	765,382
Italy	78	742,156
Spain	54	784,172
Poland	54	706,922
Netherlands	27	602,148
Greece	24	460,029
Portugal	24	436,445
Belgium	24	433,183
Czech Republic	24	425,479
Hungary	24	421,529
Sweden	19	525,037
Austria	18	452,228
Denmark	14	385,543
Slovakia	14	384,292
Finland	14	372,836
Ireland	13	309,823
Lithuania	13	265,069
Latvia	9	257,689
Slovenia	7	285,200
Estonia	6	225,183
Cyprus	6	121,733
Luxembourg	6	75,266
Malta	5	79,980
Total EU 2004	732	627,012
Romania	35	616,146*
Bulgaria	18	426,627*
Total EU 2007	785	630,736*

*2007 figures.

Note: Population statistics available at www.epp.eurostat.ec.europa.eu

that is, policy instruments to deal with European-wide problems (Marsh and Wessels 1997:229) – then one reasonable measure of establishing the congruence of opinions between MEPs and their electorates is to examine attitudes on major European-wide issues such as unification, the single currency and border controls. Indeed, in evaluating the extent of difference between the attitudes of MEPs and their electorates, Marsh and Wessels (1997:23 1) concluded that 'MEPs as a whole are more favourable to unification, more supportive of a European Currency, and more inclined to weaken border controls than are voters'. In this respect there is limited policy congruence between the opinions of the represented and their representatives in so far as 'MEPs are unlike publics in their views on European integration' (Marsh and Wessels 1997:239). This led Marsh and Wessels (1997:231) to conclude that in comparison with national parliaments 'congruence is considerably lower at the European level' and that 'distortions in representation result in elites who are unduly favourable to European integration'.

On the other hand, a concern with 'service responsiveness' draws attention to what is commonly referred to as the 'welfare officer role', with representatives carrying out 'casework' on behalf of aggrieved constituents. A further dimension of 'constituency service' is the 'promotion' of collective constituency projects, such as local industrial and economic development, environmental improvement or some other social project. Included within this conception of 'service' is what Eulau and Karps (1977:242) term 'allocation responsiveness' whereby representatives seek 'legislative allocations of public projects that involve advantages and benefits . . . accruing to a representative's district as a whole'.

The first vital link in the chain of service responsiveness is the simple ability of constituents to contact their representative in order to articulate their concerns and grievances. Research by Mark Shephard and Roger Scully (2002) revealed that in the 1999–2004 Parliament, while information was readily available via the EP website about how to contact MEPs in Brussels or Strasbourg, specific constituency contact information was less readily available and varied among national delegations. Their analysis of the web pages of national EP Information Offices, and of the EP itself, found that while 90 per cent of MEPs provided a postal address in their own countries, only 59 per cent provided a national phone number, 55 per cent a national fax number, and only 36 per cent a national email address (Shephard and Scully 2002:161).

In the event, actual requests by electors for information from, or action by, MEPs appears to be remarkably limited. Most respondents (53 per cent) to a survey of MEPs in 2000 (for details see Scully and Farrell 2001) reported that they received no more than 10 such requests per week. Only in Ireland (50 per cent) and the UK (36 per cent) were 50 or more requests received per week (Shephard and Scully 2002:163). These findings confirmed earlier survey results which revealed that contacts between MEPs and electors were 'extremely low' (Bowler and Farrell 1993:55).

In view of these figures, perhaps not surprisingly, the majority of MEPs in the 2000 survey did not rank the representation of the individual interests of individual constituents highly among their representative roles. Similarly, in a replication survey in 2006, the 'representation of individual interests of individual citizens' was the lowest-ranked aspect of MEPs' work (Farrell and Scully 2007:106). Such representation attained an average score of only 3.15 (out of 5). Nonetheless, the vast majority of respondents in 2006, 94 per cent, maintained a permanently staffed 'constituency office'; and 60 per cent held personal consultation sessions for individual voters (Farrell and Scully 2007:124). A limited 'electoral system' effect was apparent to the extent that MEPs elected under STV or open-list systems were more likely to emphasize the importance of representing individual constituents. Overall, Farrell and Scully (2007:137) concluded that there was 'a clear empirical link between the systems under which MEPs are elected and their orientation towards constituency representation'.

Earlier studies had also found a notable 'constituency size effect' in so far as MEPs from 'countries with either regional constituencies or regional listings attract more citizen contact than those from countries with national constituencies and national listings' (Shephard and Scully 2002:171; for similar findings pre-1999 see Bowler and Farrell 1993). Similarly, regionally elected MEPs were found to assign greater importance to the representation of the interests of individual constituents than MEPs elected from national lists. However, the linkage between constituency size and conception of representative role is not necessarily as direct as suggested by these findings, as a 'cultural' variable may also be discerned. Thus, for example, Farrell and Scully observed a 'British effect' with regard to constituency representation. They found a general consensus among British MEPs who believed that they had more contact with their constituents than other MEPs in other member states (Farrell and Scully 2007:178). Even among British MEPs, however, there was a clear sense that there had been a decline in constituency representation after the introduction of the closed regional list system in Britain. Certainly constituency workloads appear to have reduced after 1999. The amount of postal correspondence for British MEPs was estimated in the early 2000s at less than 100 letters per month, with probably less than one-third of letters pertaining directly to the constituency representative role (Farrell and Scully 2007:175–6).

Functional/interest representation

The third 'focus' of representation – the representation of interests – has become of increasing concern for legislatures in an age of mass democracies. Historically, most Western parliaments were able to accommodate the representation of 'functional' or 'sectional' interests pragmatically alongside territorial, individualistic or party notions of representation. Yet the tensions between the promotion of sectional interests and the defence of wider 'general' or 'public' interests by elected representatives continued to dog both the theory and the practice of representation in most liberal democracies (see Judge 1999:97–120). Equally the challenges posed by group representation to established conceptions of parliamentary representation – most notably in the formulation of 'post-parliamentary governance' – have raised fundamental normative questions about the impact of policy networks upon established liberal democratic decision-making processes in the EU and its member states. These broader issues are raised elsewhere in this book, but in this chapter we are concerned more specifically with the role of the EP and its representatives in linking organized interests and 'decision-makers' in the EU. This concern leads to an examination of the micro-dimensions of interest representation focused upon individual MEPs and their linkages with outside interests, and the macro-dimensions of interest representation at an institutional level.

Lobbying the EP

Exactly what constitutes 'interest representation' is the cause of heated academic debate but need not detain us here. All that needs to be noted is that the range of interests represented in Brussels is vast. It has been estimated that in 2007 there were some 15,000 lobbyists in Brussels (Kallas 2007:4). In terms of the number of active groups and organized interests, Greenwood (2007a:11) notes that there were some 2,376 organizations listed in the *European Public Affairs Directory* for 2006. Of these, the largest number (843) were EU trade and professional associations, followed by 429 'citizen interest associations', 295 firms with their own public affairs units, 198 regional associations and 153 public affairs consultancies. The remainder was divided fairly evenly among national trade, professional and employers federations (122), international organizations (118), law firms (115), and think tanks and training organizations (103). Within a period of five years from 2000 to 2005 the proportion of citizen interest associations increased from 20 to 30 per cent of listed organizations; whereas business interest associations accounted for 50 per cent of all EU associations in 2005 – down from 66 per cent in 2000 (Greenwood 2007a:13). Brussels has the second-highest concentration of lobbyists and civil society organizations after Washington, DC. As in the US capital, the most effective collectively organized interests and lobbyists know that 'Brussels is very much an insider's town' (Greenwood 1997a:5). They are aware that knowing who to speak to, and when, are vital resources in the informal interpersonal and interinstitutional networks operating in the Belgian capital.

Certainly there are frequent interactions between MEPs and organized interests. Indeed, the indispensability of interest representation was pointed out by Kohler-Koch who noted that because of MEPs' information deficiencies and time constraints 'they have to be open to lobbying' (1997:6). The sheer scale of interaction was revealed in one survey of MEPs in 1996 which discovered that some 67,000 contacts occurred between MEPs and interest groups each year (Wessels 1999:109). Undoubtedly this figure has increased markedly over the past decade. A more recent survey of MEPs, in 2006, recorded that 52 per cent of respondents had weekly contact with organized groups; and 40 per cent had weekly interactions with lobbyists (Farrell and Scully 2007: 124).

The three Ts: transmission, translation and timing

'Interest representation' and 'lobbying' in parliaments are normally justified in terms of information transmission, translation and timing. The transmission of information from interest organizations to MEPs is deemed essential as it provides predigested information for elected representatives who are often non-experts in the particular policy area under consideration. This 'briefing' function also allows specific groups and organizations to translate often complex and technical information into accessible data for busy elected representatives. Indeed, as Alexander Stubb (EPP-ED, Finland) noted:

> lobbying is all about interest and information . . . [MEPs] survive with few assistants and civil servants. No matter how talented they might be, an MEP is also dependent on the information provided by lobbyists. Good lobbyists can be a vital source of information. (*European Voice* 30 August–5 September 2007)

As important as transmission and translation of information, however, is the timing of its dissemination. The timing of the provision of information at the appropriate point in the EU's legislative cycle is a key resource of groups and lobbyists. Kohler-Koch (1997:9) is in no doubt that 'Timing is considered to be most essential for successful performance' and that in turn the 'timing of interest representation is dominated by the procedural rules of EU decision making'. Certainly, with the extension of the codecision procedure, and with an increased propensity to agree legislation at the early stages of that procedure (see Chapters 7 and 8), lobbyists have become increasingly aware of the need to 'act more quickly to get their views across to MEPs'.

In the case of the EP, timing is particularly acute when amendments to Commission proposals are tabled in committee (see Chapter 8). Committees that have heavy legislative loads are especially colonized by representatives of organized groups and consultants. The sessions of the EP's Environment or Industry committees, for example, regularly attract several hundred interest representatives. But the provision of information is not simply 'supply-led' but is also 'demand-led'. Committee rapporteurs, committee chairmen, vice-chairmen and shadow rapporteurs are particularly prominent 'targets' for the supply of information and, in reverse, are significant 'consumers' of information from outside organizations. Rapporteurs in drafting their reports routinely seek information not only from other EU institutions but also from interest associations and lobbyists (see Chapter 8). In addition, committee members often request draft amendments from interested organizations when the groups concerned have not already suggested their own favoured amendments. As a consequence, the process of amendment in committee is often characterized by intensive negotiation, dialogue and compromise not only among committee members but, crucially, between MEPs and affected interests across Europe.

In these interchanges the preferences of MEPs and lobbyists alike are for issue-specific briefings and the provision of detailed amendments at appropriate times. Of most use for both sides in the MEP–interest relationship is contact on 'issues of particular interest' and 'propositions for amendments to the directives under discussion' (Kohler-Koch 1997:Figure 5). The clear preference in the EP is for direct, personal, well-timed and pertinent contact, with lobbyists providing targeted information on specific legislative amendments. This contrasts markedly with the lobbying styles focused on the Commission – where continuous, longstanding and permanent relationships based around technical content are most valued by lobbyists and Commission officials (see Mazey and Richardson 2006:250).

MEPs and interest representatives not only trade substantive information on policies but also exchange 'interinstitutional' information. The reciprocal trading of information on the thinking and scheduling of legislation within the Commission or Council is a vital commodity in the MEP–lobbyist relationship. Of particular currency in this exchange is information on the work patterns of, and rate of legislative progress in, the various committees engaged in processing specific directives. Representatives of interest associations and lobbyists often provide informal monitoring for MEPs of the asymmetries of committee activity on a particular directive. They track the different deadlines imposed by the various committees for the tabling of amendments; variations in the speed of processing proposals across committees; and possible divergences of policy emphases in the different committees dealing with the same issue. In this way, interest groups with a mastery of the EP's procedural complexities and a developed surveillance capacity provide not only substantive policy briefing but also inter- and intra-institutional intelligence for MEPs.

Lobbying: 'problem' and regulation

The reciprocal transmission of information from organized interests to MEPs, and the subsequent enhancement of the informational resources within the EP, has many benefits. Nonetheless, there remains a deep-seated concern that:

> politicians risk being absorbed by the lobbyists . . . In other words, politicians who are dependent on the lobbyists for their information risk favouring those interests. There is also a risk of asymmetry, in that, obviously, groups with the biggest financial resources or brainpower can far better defend their cause than those who are spread out or badly organised. And then there is a risk for the image of democracy in the European Union. (Magnette 2006).

Historically, interest representation has been regarded as a particular 'problem' for parliaments. Elected assemblies have institutionalized the norms of the equal status and voting weight of individual representatives, and the transparency of deliberation. In practice, however, the interactions between organized interests and elected representatives often reflect inequalities of access to, and provision of, information, and translucent rather than transparent bargaining. In these circumstances fears about the representation of 'sinister interests', to use John Stuart Mill's phrase ([1861] 1910:254), are articulated and demands for regulation emerge.

Exactly such fears and demands emerged after direct elections and have increased with each successive increment in the EP's legislative powers. In an environment in which MEPs 'retain close links with particular sectors or interest groups which will help to condition their choice of priorities' (Corbett *et al.* 2007:59), what concerns MEPs and outsiders alike is just how close these links are, and what kind of resources and incentives are used to 'condition the choice of priorities'. Since 1996 the EP has operated a self-regulatory scheme by establishing a public register of lobbyists. From that date, lobbyists were effectively defined as individuals who sought an annual access pass to the EP's buildings. Instead of providing a detailed definition of 'lobbyist', this approach invoked a self-selecting, and pragmatic, logic. This logic found reflection in new Rule 9(2) (now Rule 9(4)) which provided for the issuing of distinctive photo-ID passes to 'persons who wish to enter Parliament's premises frequently with a view to supplying information to Members within the framework of their parliamentary mandate in their own interests or those of third parties' (European Parliament 2007a). Holders of such passes are entitled only to attend public meetings of the EP and have no special access other than that 'applicable to all other Union citizens' (European Parliament 2007a:Annex 9(1.3)). In return lobbyists are required to respect a code of conduct and sign a register which is available on Parliament's website.

Although a self-regulatory scheme for lobbyists had been operating in the EP for over a decade, the issue of further regulation was accelerated up the EU's agenda in 2006 with the publication of the Commission's Green Paper (COM(2006)194) in preface to the adoption of a 'European Transparency Initiative'. Ironically perhaps, the promotion of this initiative by Commissioner Siim Kallas was itself a classic example of lobbying – by some 140 'public interest' organizations coordinated under the frame of the Alliance for Lobbying Transparency and Ethics Regulation (Alter-EU) (see Greenwood 2007a:47–8). In calling for a new and more structured framework for the regulation of lobbying activities within the EU, the Commission proposed a voluntary registration system, a common code of conduct, and a system of monitoring registration of lobbyists. The aspiration was to adopt an 'inter-institutional approach to lobbying' with a 'one-stop-shop' registration process covering the Commission, European Parliament, the Committee of the Regions and the Economic and Social Committee, and to launch a new voluntary register in spring 2008 (COM(2007)127).

While the existing code of conduct for lobbyists regulates the 'external' dimension of the linkage between outside interests and MEPs, the 'internal' dimension of the 'interests' of MEPs themselves has also been made more transparent since the 1996 rule changes. Under Rule 9(1) each MEP was expected to make a detailed personal declaration of professional activities and any other remunerated functions or activities, and of 'any support, whether financial or in terms of staff or material, additional to that provided by Parliament and granted to the Member in connection with his political activities by third parties, whose identity shall be disclosed' (European Parliament 2007a:Annex 1(1)). Under the terms of Annex 9(2.1) registered assistants to MEPs are also required to make a written declaration of their professional activities and any other remunerated functions and activities. In addition, when speaking in Parliament, an MEP with a direct financial interest in the subject under debate is required to disclose that interest to the meeting orally. MEPs are also required to have completed the annual financial declaration of interests before they accepted nomination as an office-holder of Parliament or one of its bodies, or participated in an official delegation.

Initially the Register of Financial Interests could only be accessed in Luxembourg, and Strasbourg and Brussels when Parliament was meeting there. However, many MEPs, most notably Glyn Ford (PSE, UK), campaigned forcefully to have the document made publicly available. A decision to this effect was taken in principle in late 1999 and details from the Register were finally published on the official parliamentary website in July 2001. Annex 1 of the Rules of Procedure simply states, however, that 'The register may be open to the public for inspection electronically'. While most MEPs append a declaration of their financial interests to their individual web pages, some omissions remain with, for example, five (of 50) Polish MEPs in 2007 not making their declaration of financial interests available electronically.

The 'institutional lobbyists'

In addition to 'mainstream' lobbying by interest representatives, the 1990s also witnessed a dramatic increase in the lobbying of the EP by the Commission and national governments. In recognition of the EP's enhanced legislative capabilities in that decade the Commission and national governments acknowledged the necessity of maintaining a dialogue with appropriate MEPs.

The characterization of national and Commission officials as 'lobbyists' in the context of EU decision-making is certainly not new. In 1993 David Spence, for example, identified the national official as 'clearly a lobbyist of European institutions and other Member States' officials' (1993:47). Within the EP Ken Collins, then Chair of the Environment Committee, in his address to the hearing organized by the Rules Committee into lobbying in 1992, noted the difficulties in defining lobbyists. He argued that, as far as the EP was concerned, a definition should include not only 'delegations of the Council' but also 'Commission officials defending their proposals vis-à-vis Members and parliamentary committees . . . representatives of local and regional authorities [and] representatives of third countries' (PE 155.236 1992:Annex, i). Thus, while the depiction of national officials as lobbyists is not new, the greater attention paid by them to the EP is relatively new. Whereas over a decade ago Spence devoted just one short paragraph to the role of the UK permanent representation in Brussels in following EP affairs, such a cursory treatment would be unlikely in the 2000s.

EU governments willingly provide policy briefings to their own national delegations in the EP. Thus Caroline Jackson, another former chair of the Environment Committee, informed the authors in interview in September 2005 that 'the British government seeks to influence us . . . [and] provides all British MEPs with briefs on all the issues coming to the Committee. Now that is something which is very very important – it means that British MEPs are burdened with the knowledge that other people don't have of the background to legislation and indeed of the consequences in their home country.' Jackson also noted that this attention was not confined to British MEPs; 'I *know* that the

British Government does lobby other nationalities and they've made a particular effort to lobby members and governments from Eastern Europe' (Interview, Brussels, 20 September 2005).

Traditionally, much national briefing was essentially formal, taking the form of written memoranda outlining the view of national administrations on Commission proposals, or on parliamentary reports once tabled for the EP's plenary (see Humphreys 1997). What has changed since the 1990s, however, is that national officials and politicians (sometimes in alliance with their allies in Council) have started to seek to influence EP proceedings more intensively, at an earlier stage, in tandem with their evolving position in the Council of Ministers. There is also a recognition that national governments should provide tailored briefings for committee rapporteurs, other key committee actors, constituency MEPs, committee members and, ultimately, all MEPs in the run-up to plenary, together even with a voting list 'so that those who agree with your position overall know how to vote for it in detail' (Humphreys 1997:200).

Moreover, it is not unusual for individual permanent representation officials to suggest legislative amendments to their respective national MEPs in committee. Invariably these amendments parallel current national negotiating positions in the relevant working group of the Council. In this sense, national officials have started to intertwine themselves firmly into the pattern of interest representation within the EP. In addition, officials of the permanent representations sometimes also operate *collectively* in seeking to influence the EP. To this end, permanent representation parliamentary attachés, who are responsible for relations with the EP, meet before each plenary session to coordinate their positions and identify targets for direct lobbying. Obviously, at this stage, national officials will reflect primarily the position arrived at in Council. Such lobbying may be intensive. In the run-up to the EP's vote on the Members' Statute in May 1999 (a vote which ultimately went against the view of Council), one of the permanent representation parliamentary attachés commented to one of the authors that he had 'done nothing for a month but lobby the Parliament on the members' statute'.

Party representation

> Political representation is hardly thinkable without political parties. (Thomassen and Schmitt 2004:386)

In most parliamentary systems political parties form the primary mechanism of linkage between the electors and their 'government', and so conjoin the two distinct concepts of 'party' and 'government' into the notion of *party government*.

'Party government' offers, in effect, an idealized view of responsible government: one where the actions of parliamentary elites are legitimized by the electoral choice of voters mediated through the programmes of parties. The idea of 'party government', or more accurately 'competitive party government' (Schumpeter [1943] 1976), is deceptively simple and follows a logical sequence: first, each party presents to the electorate a policy programme in the form of a manifesto; second, voters make an informed choice between the competing parties on the basis of this programme; third, the successful party (or coalition) seeks to translate this programme into practice once in government; and, fourth, the governing party (or coalition) is then judged by the electorate on its success in implementing its promises at the next election.

The implications of this model for individual representatives is that they will contest elections on the basis of an agreed aggregate policy programme, and once elected will support policies in conformity with that programme and the party leadership charged with implementing that programme. The internal cohesiveness of parties within the representative parliament is thus a crucial condition of party government. What underpins the notion of party representation is a defence of party discipline and cohesive behaviour of party representatives in parliament (see Judge 1999:70–1).

When the model is applied to the EU, however, there are manifest divergences between the model and the political reality of the EU. There is no competitive party system at the European level which is analogous to competition in national state elections and which forms the basis for the selection of a government (see Chapter 3). Nor is there an EU government as such. Nor do parliamentary parties operate in a simple, bifurcated context where decisions are based on either support for, or opposition to, the policy programme of the majority party (or parties) in the EP.

That being said, however, there are elements of the model which illuminate the present workings of the EU as well as pointing to the potential development of the party system at the EU level. To identify these convergences it is necessary to examine the two different party organizational structures at this level. The first are the transnational party federations. The second, and of more direct relevance to the present discussion, are the party groups within the EP.

In a formal sense a European party system exists with 'party families' of socialists, Christian democrats, liberals, regionalists and green parties organized into transnational party federations. In a practical sense the importance of these transnational federations in delimiting representative roles for their members is remarkably limited. As noted in Chapter 3, although the transnational federations coordinate EU-wide manifestos, these bland statements hold little resonance for most voters. If the notion of 'party representation' is based upon political parties supplying different policy platforms for voters to choose from, then, in Thomassen and Schmitt's (2004:389) opinion, 'a competitive European party system ... does not exist' (see also Franklin 2006:228–9; Raunio 2006:308). Similarly, the transnational federations do not form the basis of electors' choices.

The paradox of the party system in the EU is that while European party federations outside the EP are of restricted significance, the party groups within the EP are of vital importance to the daily operations of the Parliament. Party groups determine the composition of leadership positions within the Parliament, such as the President and Vice-President, and committee chairs. They also determine the agenda of the EP, the allocation of speaking time in debates, and the appointment of committee rapporteurs in the processing of legislation (Hix 2005:91; Corbett *et al.* 2007:70). In this sense, internally within the EP, a 'truly European party system clearly exists' (Thomassen and Schmitt 1999:134).

While the internal organization of party groups and their wider structural implications for the EP itself will be considered in Chapter 5, the primary concern here is with how and why MEPs act as party representatives within the EP. Katz's (1999) research into the role orientations of MEPs found that they were more likely to give priority in decision-making in the EP to their party than to voters. Admittedly, party influence was ranked well below the use of 'own judgement' by MEPs (Katz 1999:64), but, nonetheless, the influence of party voters was greater than among respondents from national MPs in Katz's sample. Moreover, MEPs placed greater emphasis upon the influence of their party as an *organization* than upon the views of party voters. However, the findings of two more recent surveys, conducted in 2000 and 2006, admittedly using different questions to establish how MEPs conceive of their representative roles, found a different emphasis among MEPs in the 1999–2004 and 2004–2009 Parliaments. In both 2000 and 2006, greater importance was afforded to the views of party supporters among the electorate than to the views of the national party or to an MEP's EP party group. But in aggregate the differences were modest (see Scully and Farrell 2003:271–2; Farrell and Scully 2007:105). While there is a clear 'partisan' dimension in the role orientations of MEPs it remains unclear how far these orientations point towards the development of a bifurcation of roles in the EP commonly associated with 'party government' (see Chapter 5).

The 'how' of representation: representative style

Thus far we have examined the main foci of representation – of 'what' is represented, whether social groups, territorial constituencies, functional interests or political parties. But the other dimension of representation – the 'style' of representation – of 'how' representatives act on behalf of the represented also needs some consideration. Typically the actions of representatives have been located on a continuum from the position of 'independent trustee' through 'politico' to 'mandated delegate' (Wahlke *et al.* 1962). At the respective ends of this continuum the representative is held either to act independently of voters' opinions or interests; or, alternatively, to take instructions from his or her electors (see Judge 1981, 1999). In between, a representative may act as a 'politico' and adopt either a trustee or a delegate style at different times on different policy issues.

When MEPs in the 1994–1999 Parliament were asked to rank the factors most likely to influence their decisions – own judgement, the views of own party voters, or the view of national party or EP group – some 74.7 per cent ranked their own judgement in first place (Katz 1999:64). One initial plausible explanation of the pronounced preference for 'trustee' role orientations in the EP might very well be the absence of 'party government' and the corresponding absence of notions of party representation. One difficulty with this explanation, however, as noted above, is that (if trustee orientations are ignored) then party is clearly identified by MEPs as of importance for the performance of their representational roles. Another difficulty is the simple fact that MPs in national parliaments, with systems of party government, also rank highly a trustee orientation (71.8 per cent). This leads Katz to conclude that representatives might simply identify a socially approved answer, or, more persuasively, that they are able to accommodate notions of independence within a broader frame of 'party representation' (1999:64). In other words, the practice of representation is not unidimensional and representatives may draw upon a range of ideas about representation and adopt a series of orientations (see Judge 1999:58–60; Scully and Farrell 2003:271; Farrell *et al.* 2006:8). In this regard MEPs are certainly not unique.

Conclusion

One objective of this book is to assess the extent to which the EP can be located within the academic analysis of legislatures. Certainly, the EP provides the only direct linkage between EU decision-makers and the 27 electorates of the EU. In this sense, as the only directly elected supranational representative institution in the EU, it is unique. Despite this unique position it displays, nonetheless, characteristics of representation commonly associated with national parliaments in Western liberal democracies. Whether this is a 'good thing' is open to question. For example, those 'proportionalists' who believe that the EP should be a microcosm of European society are disappointed to discover that MEPs are, in aggregate, just as middle-aged, middle-class and Caucasian as their counterparts in national parliaments. Equally, those concerned with the potential of 'interest representation' to subvert the 'democratic' wishes of the electorate are just as wary as their national counterparts of the representation of 'sinister interests' and the need to regulate the relationships between representatives and the lobbyists, the political consultants, and the public affairs executives who inhabit the corridors of the EP. If anything, the enhanced legislative impact of the EP in the past two decades has simply intensified these concerns in Brussels and Strasbourg.

Even the belief that the EP at least was distinguishable from national parliaments in the weakness of notions of 'party representation' and the underdevelopment of a parliamentary party system has been undermined in the light of recent research (see Hix *et al.* 2007). If the role orientations of MEPs display characteristics of 'party representation' then so too are their daily activities in the EP structured by their party group affiliation. Given the influence of party groups in structuring the conceptions of roles and the actual voting behaviour of MEPs, then one analyst at least believes that 'the post-1999 EP operates very much like any domestic parliament in Europe' (Hix 2001b:685). While this may be an overstatement, as there remain marked differences between the EP's party system and national parliamentary systems based upon party *government*, nonetheless it highlights the importance of party in the representative process of the EP. And it is to one particular aspect of party representation – party groups – that we now turn in Chapter 5.

Party Groups in the European Parliament

Chapter 4 raised some of the issues surrounding the representative/ linkage role of political parties and the extent to which notions of transnational party competition are appropriate for the study of the EU. In this chapter we examine the role played by party groups in the internal workings of the EP. Not only do parties link the people to decision-makers but they also link, structure and regularize interactions between decision-makers themselves. In this respect the EP is no different from most other parliaments and legislatures in that parties provide the organizational lubricant for the smooth operation of the institution. A clear link can be discerned between the effective organization of the EP and the structure of party groups within that institution. Indeed, the best way to analyse party groups, for our purposes at least, is as aggregations of individual representatives as an institutional response to the complexities of decision-making in an environment characterized by information overload, linguistic proliferation, territorial diversity, ideological heterogeneity and technological complexity.

The very structure of decision-making itself in the EU – both in the nature of its legislative procedures and in its multilevel dimensionality – affects the organizational imperatives of party groups within the EP. The nature of the EU legislative process is such that it requires fluid parliamentary majorities across policy areas and across legislative procedures. This is in contrast to the fixed and consistent majorities required in many national parliaments in support of, or in opposition to, a party government. Moreover, the nature of interinstitutional bargaining in the EU is such that the EP has to engage simultaneously with intergovernmental and supranational (and sometimes national) institutions and so has to be able to accommodate and articulate national and transnational demands in tandem. Hence, party groups within the EP cannot be understood in isolation from the institutional context in which they have developed and within which they function.

Development of transnational party groups

Transnational party groups have been such a long-standing feature within the EP that it is worthwhile remembering that there were alternative organizational forms that could have been adopted. One possibility was, of course, for MEPs to organize as national blocs (Henig and Pinder 1969:476–7). Another was simply for representatives to sit as individuals – as independent trustees. Indeed, the original 78 nominees to the ECSC Common Assembly sat in alphabetical order and carried symbols of neither national nor party allegiance. But neither organizational precept – individualism or nationality – offered an effective solution to the institutional requirements of a body charged with the monitoring and supervision of a supranational executive. From the outset, therefore, there was an institutional predisposition in favour of transnational cooperation within the Assembly. Indeed, as noted in Chapter 2, within the first six months of the Common Assembly's creation, party groups had formed, and by June 1953 they had been officially recognized in the Assembly's standing orders. Even before the official formation of groups there had been agreement among delegates that the committees of the Assembly should 'reflect political tendencies as well as the balance between nationalities' (Raunio 1996a:65).

The three major West European, postwar party constellations of Christian Democrats, Socialists and Liberals provided the initial groupings in the Assembly. These three groups have been in continuous existence ever since, and have remained the largest groups in the EP. Moreover, the absence of other groups in the formative years of the Assembly from 1953 to 1965 helped to inculcate 'a tradition of political group oligopoly' (Westlake 1994a:185). Since then, a number of other groups have emerged and maintained a continuous existence across several parliaments (Group of the European United Left and Greens), and a number of others have come and gone (for details see Hix and Lord 1997:77–9; Corbett *et al.* 2007:71–5). Still others emerged during the course of the 2004–2009 Parliament (see below). Nonetheless, throughout, the oligopoly of the major groups has remained largely intact.

Certainly, the limited number of party groups has provided organizational benefits in the form of the routinization of working practices and has brought 'stability, consistency, and functional efficiency to the Parliament' (Raunio 1996a:67). In return, the party groups have been conferred with specific institutional rights and privileges in terms of financial assistance, staffing and accommodation (see below). In this manner, there have been incentives for Parliament as an institution, for party groups and for members themselves to consolidate transnational cooperation internally within the groups.

Over time the exact number of transnational groups in the EP and their longevity and composition has been influenced by several key variables. First, group formation was influenced by successive enlargements in 1973, 1981, 1986, 1995, 2004 and 2007 which brought more MEPs, more parties and more ideological diversity into the EP.

Second, the changed political priorities in member states – with advances of parties of the centre right in the 1980s, of the social democratic left in the late 1990s, and with the growing importance in the early 2000s of environmental, nationalist and regionalist parties, alongside a return of more centre-right parties to governing coalitions – also impacted on the group profile within the EP. Third, the end of the cold war not only affected the structures of national party systems but also 'led to a reconfiguration of forces and relationships within the EP' (Ladrech 1996:301).

Rules on size and formation

In response to the changing constellation of parties finding representation in the EP there has been a succession of rule changes to regulate the size and formation of groups. Before 1999, a group could be established exclusively from MEPs drawn from a single member state. In the major overhaul of the Rules of Procedure in 1999 the minimum number of MEPs required to form a group was linked for the first time to a distribution of group members across more than one member state (European Parliament 1999 Rule 29(2)). In 1994 the then ruling party in Italy, Forza Italia, had formed from its own representatives the EP group Forza Europa. At that time the minimum threshold for group formation was 26 members from one member state. After enlargement in 1995 the minimum threshold was increased to 29 where MEPs came from one state. In 1999 the minimum threshold was reduced to 23 with MEPs drawn from at least two member states. The threshold was reduced still further to 18 if members came from three member states, and to 14 if drawn from four or more member states. In 2007 the threshold was 20 members from at least a fifth of member states (that is six of them). After the creation of the far-right Identity, Tradition and Sovereignty Group (ITS) in January 2007 Socialist MEPs argued that, in an EU of 27 member states, the threshold was too low and should be raised to 40 MEPs from eight states (*European Voice* 18 January 2007).

Under Rule 29(1), there is the convoluted interpretation that:

> Parliament need not normally evaluate the political affinity of members of a group. In forming a group together under this Rule, Members concerned accept by definition that they have political affinity. Only when this is denied by the Members concerned is it necessary for Parliament to evaluate whether the group has been constituted in conformity with the Rules. (European Parliament 2007a)

The basic requirement that members share broad 'political affinities' had existed in the rules since the earliest days of the Common Assembly, and its significance was that it prevented heterogeneous collections of MEPs nominally joining together to accrue the organizational and financial benefits of group membership. The addition of the interpretative statement to Rule 29(1) concerning the denial of political affinity followed the attempts in July 1999 – of five MEPs from the French Front National along with seven Radicals from Italy (Lista Emma Bonino) and other unattached representatives – to establish a Technical Group of Independent Members (TDI). Significantly, not only was the group ideologically diverse but its members also proclaimed openly that they did not share 'political affinities'. It was further proposed that the parties of the right and far right might join with the Italian Radicals of the Lista Emma Bonino.

The formation of the TDI Group was rejected in Parliament's plenary on the grounds that its membership did not display the necessary requirements of 'political affinity'. A subsequent attempt by Italian non-attached members to allow for the formation of a 'Mixed Group' – to allow 26 non-attached MEPs from nine parties in six member states to benefit from the procedural and financial advantages of a political group – also failed to secure the necessary parliamentary support.

However, members of the putative Technical Group challenged Parliament's rejection in the Court of First Instance. On 25 November 1999 the President of the Court ruled that the Technical Group could remain in existence until the Court's judgment was delivered (Case T-222/99). The Technical Group was formally terminated in October 2001 after the Court rejected the appeal against the EP's decision not to recognize the existence of the TDI Group (Joined Cases T-222/99, T-327/99 and T-329/99). In the intervening period between September 1999 and October 2001, Parliament's Committee on Constitutional Affairs examined the whole issue of technical and mixed groups and adopted a report in June 2000 (which was subsequently modified in September of that year (PE 232.762 2000)). The Committee's proposal for the rewording of Rule 29(l), and the amendment of other rules, was eventually adopted in plenary in June 2002, so removing the most apparent areas of discrimination regarding the rights of independent members (notably those relating to the threshold for tabling resolutions to wind up debate and representation on conciliation delegations).

Parliamentary-specific activities

Party groups within the EP are best regarded as 'parliamentary specific' (Ladrech 1996:294) in that their intra-parliamentary activities are largely divorced from the standard campaigning and electioneering functions associated with political parties in nation states. As we saw in Chapter 3, European elections are still basically contested on national political terrains with national political parties jealously guarding the right to select candidates for the EP and to structure subsequent campaigns. Where transnational party federations have been active is in the formulation of transnational manifestos and, to a limited extent, in the coordination of campaigns. Nonetheless, the actual detailed organization and running of the campaigns in each member state has been left to national parties. A division of labour has thus emerged between national parties, transnational party federations and political groups in the EP. A Court of Justice ruling in 1986 – that EP groups could not use funds derived from the EP budget (under item 3708) to fund election campaigns – simply reinforced this division of labour. The Court ruled that it was *ultra vires* for Parliament, via its political groups, to support any kind of election campaign in the absence of a uniform electoral system (see Case C-294/83, the *Green Group* v. *European Parliament,* judgment of 23 April 1986). Since that ruling EP funds have been used in principle only for the dissemination of group information and have been suspended even for such activity thirty days before a European election. A report by the Court of Auditors in 2000 went a step further and declared illegal the system whereby party federations tended to rely on their respective political groups in the EP as their main source of finance, even beyond campaign funding (see below; see also Lightfoot 2006:305).

One of the consequences of this division of labour has been a fracturing of the normal liberal democratic linkage between the activity of representatives in Parliament and their electoral accountability. In the EU, what MEPs do, or what their party groups do in the EP, is not the primary determinant of reelection (Hix *et al.* 2007:28), or, for MEPs, of reselection. Yet, paradoxically, party groups are the primary organizational determinant of what happens in the EP. Precisely because political groups are the backbone of the EP's internal organization significant rights and financial resources have been conferred on them by the institution itself. Thus, in addition to the funds previously provided under budget item 3708 for informational purposes, the groups also received financial assistance under item 3707 for administrative and secretariat support. In 2001 all funding for the political groups was placed on a single budget line, item 3701. This was a result of criticisms made by the Court of Auditors about the legality and regularity of transactions made by the political groups. The Court proposed, in its Special Report (13/2000), that all appropriations for the groups be placed under a single budget heading 'to end the highly theoretical distinction between political and information activities' (Court of Auditors 2000:11 in OJ C 181, 28 June 2000). In 2007, nearly €50.6

million was provided under this budget line, and when expenditure on technical facilities, office accommodation, meeting rooms and other organizational support is added, the total support for political groups amounts to approximately 15 per cent of the EP's €1.42 billion budget.

Towards a European party statute

The problems discovered by the Court of Auditors in respect of the legality and regularity of the financial transactions of political parties, and the recommendation that 'consideration should be given to drawing up transparent rules to be applied to the financing of these parties' (OJ C 181, 28 June 2000:para. 64), served to highlight the need for a regulation on the statute and financing of European political parties. However, such a need had been acknowledged earlier, in December 1996, with the adoption of a resolution on the constitutional status of European political parties (OJ C 20, 20 January 1997:29).

Article 191 of the Maastricht Treaty had acknowledged that: 'Political parties at European level are important as a factor for integration within the Union. They contribute to forming a European awareness and to expressing the political will of the citizens of the Union.' But there was no accompanying operational clause that would allow for the implementation of this article. Hence, the Commission proposed, during the 2000 IGC, that Article 191 be amplified further, and transformed into a legal base suitable for the adoption of a statute relating to the formation and funding of European political parties. This mirrored the proposal made by Parliament in its November 1999 resolution on the IGC (OJ C 189, 7 July 2000:224). As a result, the Nice Treaty negotiators added a second paragraph to Article 191, providing for a statute for European parties to be adopted, via codecision. The IGC also agreed a declaration which sought to guard against the EU acquiring competency in party funding rules nationally, and which reiterated that EU finances 'may not be used to fund, either directly or indirectly, political parties at national level'.

After a protracted process of negotiation (see Judge and Earnshaw 2003:124–6; Schönlau 2006:144–6), Regulation (EC) 2004/2003 on the 'regulations governing political parties at European level and the rules regarding their funding' was agreed in November 2003 (OJ L 297, 15 November 2003:1). During these negotiations it became clear that, given the extent of disagreement among member states and among party groups themselves, if legislation were to be agreed before the elections of 2004 then attention would need to focus on issues of financing rather than upon the more vexed question of the legal status of parties. It also became clear, however, that issues of finance could not be considered in complete isolation from considerations of the legal personality of parties. While the EP still favoured a comprehensive statute – covering the definition, legal status, and operating procedures as well as the financing of political parties – it welcomed, nonetheless, the proposed regulation as 'an important first step' towards a European party statute (PE 323.576 2003:26; see also Lightfoot 2006).

The regulation sought, in Article 2, to define a political party as 'an association of citizens which pursues political objectives, and which is either recognised by, or established in accordance with, the legal order of at least one Member State'. To be recognized at the European level a political party had to fulfil four basic conditions. First, it needed to have a legal personality in the member state in which it was located. Second, it had to be represented in at least one quarter of member states in the EP or in national parliaments or regional parliaments and assemblies, or alternatively had to have received at least 3 per cent of votes at the most recent EP elections. Third, it needed to observe in its programmes and activities the principles on which the EU was founded. And fourth, it had to have participated in elections to the EP or to have expressed the intention to do so (OJ L 297, 15 November 2003:2 Article 3).

The regulation set out procedures for an annual application process for funding; verification of political parties; declaration of the sources of funding for donations above €500; prohibition of certain donations – those made anonymously, or from the budgets of political groups in the EP, or those exceeding €12,000 per year and per donor, or funds from the general budget of the EU. The appropriations were to be distributed annually, with 15 per cent distributed in equal shares among registered parties, and the remaining 85 per cent distributed in proportion to the number of MEPs in each party. Significantly, no more than 75 per cent of a European party's budget could be charged to the EU. As Bardi (2006:19) observes this 'makes national parties, above all the stronger and richer ones, decisive in constituting and maintaining Europarties'. The EP was made responsible for the implementation and administration of the funding process, and was required to review the application of the regulation by no later than 15 February 2006.

When the regulation came into effect in 2004 eight parties had established independent structures outside of the EP and so were able to receive funding at the start of the 2004–2009 Parliament. These were the European People's Party, Party of European Socialists, European Liberal, Democrat and Reform Party, European Green Party, Party of the European Left, European Democratic Party, Alliance for a Europe of the Nations, and the European Free Alliance. Two other parties were later established just before the November 2005 registration deadline – the Alliance of Independent Democrats in Europe and the

EU Democrats. In 2007 €10.4m was made available for the funding of European political parties.

From the outset, the regulation encountered significant criticism and was subjected to three legal challenges, one by the Front National, one by Emma Bonino and the other MEPs of the Lista Emma Bonino, and one by 'SOS Democracy' – a grouping of Eurosceptic MEPs primarily from the (1999–2004) EDD Group but including also well-known British Conservative Eurosceptics such as Roger Helmer and Daniel Hannan (Cases T-13/04, T-17/04 and T-40/04 respectively). All three actions sought the annulment of the regulation on the grounds that, among other things, it was discriminatory against smaller parties, it granted implementing and decision-making powers to the EP, and it did not provide adequate guarantees that funds would not be used for activities by national parties. The Court of First Instance ruled the three actions inadmissable in July 2005. The Front National appealed against this decision, though its appeal was dismissed in July 2006 (Case C-338/05, OJ C 224, 16 September 2006:18).

The Constitutional Affairs Committee, in accordance with the provisions of the regulation, duly produced a report in February 2006 on the operation of the regulation and made nine recommendations for change (PE 367.786 2006:6–7). The main proposals related to the phasing of payments; the development of longer-term funding plans; a relaxation of the restrictions upon the capacity of parties to build reserves; and an increase in the levels of financial support provided to parties. Moreover, the Committee's rapporteur, Jo Leinen, called upon the Commission to produce proposals on how political foundations could be used to support the informational and educational roles of European parties. Indeed, during Parliament's processing of the 2007 EU budget, a proposal was agreed for the financing of a pilot project for the establishment, development and functioning of European political foundations (a call for proposals for support was published in July 2007; see OJ C 159, 12 July 2007:15). Eventually, in June 2007, the Commission duly adopted a proposal to amend the regulations governing political parties to allow for the establishment of European political foundations, the carrying over of 25 per cent of income from one year to the first quarter of the next, and the possibility of accruing savings of up to 100 per cent of a party's annual average income (COM(2007)364). The Commission's proposal made clear that:

> appropriations received from the EU budget may also be used for the financing of campaigns conducted by the political parties at European level in the context of European Parliament elections, provided that this does not constitute a direct or indirect financing of national political parties or their candidates.

The Commission's proposal was eventually agreed with Council at first reading in November 2007, with MEPs voting 538 votes in favour, 74 against and 10 abstentions. An associated amendment to the Financial Regulation (Regulation 1605/2002) was also deemed necessary by Council and was supported by Parliament's Budgets Committee. While broadly in line with the Commission's proposal, Parliament's agreement with Council also proscribed the use of EU funds to finance referendum campaigns, and the receipt of donations from third-country governments or undertakings under the 'dominant influence' of a third-country government (Regulation 1524/2007, OJ L 343, 27 December 2007:5). It also enlarged upon the transparency requirements for party funding. Austrian Green MEP Johannes Voggenhuber commented that: 'These new rules will create a true European political landscape in Europe, which is less determined by conflicting national interests. This is a decisive step towards a genuine European democracy and towards a European public' (quoted in *EurActiv.com* 30 November 2007).

Structures and staffing

The structure and staffing of each party group is linked, obviously, to its size. Generally, the larger groups tend to have larger bureaux (executive committees) and more staff. The structure of group bureaux is not specified in the EP's rules, and each group's organization is different. In general, the bureau in each group is composed of a chair, president or leader (and co-chairs in the case of the Greens, the UEN, and Independence and Democracy), vice-chairs and treasurer along with other members. Procedures for selecting and/or electing group bureaux differ across the groups but in all cases the basic principle is one of reconciling intra-group national and political interests. In the larger groups the influence of national party leaders is inevitably at work during the negotiations, usually after European elections, to determine the choice of a group leader. Agreements reached are often part of a larger package which may include the group's candidate for EP President, in addition to the parliamentary group's leader, the group's treasurer, group secretary-general, and the leader of the extra-parliamentary party confederation. Negotiations about future parliamentary and party group office holders have increasingly started well before the elections. The outcome of such negotiations *de facto* reflects national and political balance in the group, along the lines of an 'imperfect d'Hondt' system. Thus, in 2004, EU socialist party leaders decided upon Josep Borell Fontelles as Socialist candidate for the EP presidency, Martin Schulz (Germany) as group leader, Linda McAvan (UK) for treasurer, and David Harley (UK) became secretary-general of the group (and was replaced by Anna Colombo (Italy) in 2006). In April 2004 Poul Nyrup Rasmussen (Denmark) had narrowly defeated Giuliano Amato as leader of the Party of European Socialists. Group bureaux also frequently include parliamentary officers such as EP Vice-Presidents, quaestors or committee chairs. Leaders of national delegations within groups are also frequently members of their group bureau. Over the years the role of national delegation leaders within EP party groups has increased. On some occasions, on the most politically sensitive issues, intra-group decision-making is conducted initially among leaders of national delegations (manifestly at the expense of formal group procedures).

In the larger groups there is also a mechanism for ensuring a pro-rata reflection of the size of each national delegation in the number of members in the bureau. For example, in the EPP-ED there is one coopted bureau member for every ten members per national delegation. The PSE Group also has a policy of gender equality. Its internal rules provide that there should be at least four men and four women on the group bureau; but in 2007 this minimum was only just met with four women representatives on the ten-member PSE Bureau.

Group chairs are normally elected from the larger national delegations. After the 2004 election only the PSE and UEN chose new leaders. This was in contrast to 1999 when each group, with the exception of the Liberals, elected new EP leaders. The respective chairs in 2007 were: for the EPP-ED, Joseph Daul, a French member of the Union pour un Mouvement Populaire who was elected after Hans-Gert Pöttering became President of the Parliament in January 2007; for the PSE, Martin Schulz, a German SPD member; for the Alliance of Liberals and Democrats for Europe (ALDE), Graham Watson, a UK Liberal Democrat; and for the Union of Nations (UEN) Brian Crowley, an Irish Fianna Fáil representative, and Cristiana Muscardini, an Italian Alleanza Nazionale member. Daniel Cohn-Bendit of the German Greens and Monica Frassoni of the Italian Federazione dei Verdi co-chaired the Greens/European Free Alliance. Francis Wurtz, a French Communist, was the chair of the Confederal Group of the European Left/Nordic Green Left (GUE/NGL). In turn, the Independence and Democracy Group was co-chaired by Jens-Peter Bonde (JuniBevaegelsen) from Denmark; and Nigel Farage from the UK Independence Party. Bruno Gollnisch, a French Front National representative, chaired the Identity, Tradition and Sovereignty Group (ITS) until its disintegration in November 2007.

The position of group chair is of considerable importance within the EP. In addition to providing internal political leadership, chairs also represent the group in its external dealings with other groups, most notably in the EP's Conference of Presidents. Many necessary deals are struck, and alliances forged, in informal meetings of group chairs.

Nonetheless, the scope for independent action by group chairs is limited in practice by the need to maintain consensual and collective decision-making within the group.

Group meetings

The important role of group chairs and of the bureaux in securing intra-group agreement on policy and institutional decisions is evident in 'group weeks'. These are scheduled into the EP's annual cycle and are held in Brussels in the week before plenary sessions in Strasbourg. In addition, each group meets on several occasions, normally four, throughout the Strasbourg plenary week and prior to plenary sessions in Brussels. Elaborate arrangements are in place within each group to allow time to formulate and articulate common perspectives on the issues before Parliament and to mobilize support. In this process the group chair, bureau members and, especially, national delegation leaders play a key role in aligning the policy preferences of national delegations and of the transnational group itself. Indeed, the traditional working pattern, within the EPP-ED and PSE at least, is for group chairs to structure group debates on important issues around statements from leaders or spokespersons of national delegations.

Group meetings also allow for the coordination of EP committee decisions with group positions. Hence, 'group weeks' also include collective meetings of the committee coordinators for each group (effectively the group 'spokespeople' on each of the EP's committees), with committee chairs from the group usually in attendance. The committee coordinators' meeting is normally scheduled early in 'group week', and the outcomes of these deliberations guide subsequent discussion in the group as a whole. In this manner, party group preferences (which reflect broader party and national stances) are reconciled, or at least accommodated, with EP committee positions. In the course of intra-party deliberations committee coordinators and committee chairs attune their respective group positions to the policy preferences formulated within their committees.

The regularity of group meetings, their format and the attempt therein to reconcile various political preferences – party, nationality, committee – provide vivid evidence of the necessity of ensuring a style of 'qualified supranationalism' and collective internal decision-making (see Hix and Lord 1997:128). This style seeks to maximize transnational agreement while allowing for reasoned national and other political divergences from the group position when necessary. Continual consultation within the bureaux and within the wider group is thus a defining feature of group leadership in the EP.

The need for protracted consultation and the frequency of group meetings serve in turn to restrict independent action by group leaders. What is apparent also is that on those occasions when the processes of consultation and collective deliberation unravel, the position of the group leader becomes precarious. This was well illustrated by Pauline Green's fate as Leader of the PSE after the 1999 Commission crisis and the European elections of that year. Her interventions in the Commission crisis and her apparent responsiveness at that time to instructions from her national party leadership in London led to open criticism of her leadership. More particularly, after the significant reduction in the numbers of UK Socialist MEPs after the 1999 election Pauline Green was forced to stand down as leader of the Socialist Group (see *European Voice* 17–23 June 1999).

Each group is entitled to a number of administrative and support staff. The precise number varies in accordance with the size of the group, as well as with the number of working languages used by each group (see Corbett *et al.* 2007:82). In 2007 a total of 883 party group posts were budgeted for. The largest group, the EPP-ED, employed over 178 officials, while the smallest, the Identity, Tradition and Sovereignty Group (ITS), employed only 12 before its disbandment in November 2007. Naturally, political affiliation and nationality are important criteria in securing a post in a group, but objective selection criteria of written and oral tests and language tests are now the norm in the larger groups. Most group officials are employed on temporary contracts but enjoy some *de facto* job security. (However, the entire staff of the European Democratic Alliance group was made redundant in 1999 when its largest contingent of French Gaullist MEPs transferred *en masse* to the EPP group). Notably, several group officials have used their group position to launch their own careers as MEPs. Three MEPs in the 2004–2009 Parliament, Richard Corbett of the PSE, Caroline Jackson of the EPP-ED, and Monica Frassoni of the Greens, had followed this career route.

Composition of groups

Table 5.1 indicates the number of MEPs from each member state in each political group.

European People's Party (Christian Democrats) and European Democrats (EPP-ED)

In February 2008 the EPP-ED was the largest group – with 288 MEPs drawn from 49 parties from across all 27 member states. In 1999 the

Table 5.1 Political groups by member state (at 24 February 2008)

	EPP-ED	PSE	ALDE	UEN	Greens/EFA	GUE/NGL	Ind/Dem	Nonattached	Total
Austria	6	7	1		2			2	18
Belgium	6	7	6		2			3	24
Bulgaria	5	5	5					3	18
Cyprus	3		1			2			6
Czech Republic	14	2				6	1	1	24
Denmark	1	5	4	1	1	1	1		14
Estonia	1	3	2						6
Finland	4	3	5		1	1			14
France	18	31	10		6	3	3	7	78
Germany	49	23	7		13	7			99
Greece	11	8				4	1		24
Hungary	13	9	2						24
Ireland	5	1	1	4		1	1		13
Italy	24	15	14	13	2	7		3	78
Latvia	3		1	4	1				9
Lithuania	2	2	7	2					13
Luxembourg	3	1	1		1				6
Malta	2	3							5
Netherlands	7	7	5		4	2	2		27
Poland	15	9	5	20			3	2	54
Portugal	9	12				3			24
Romania	18	10	6					1	35
Slovakia	8	3						3	14
Slovenia	4	1	2						7
Spain	24	24	2		3	1			54
Sweden	6	5	3		1	2	2		19
UK	27	19	11		5	1	10	5	78
Total	288	215	101	44	42	41	24	30	785

Source: www.europarl.europa.eu/members/expert.do?language=EN

EPP-ED, with 233 MEPs, had overtaken the PSE to become the largest group for the first time since the introduction of direct elections. This newly found preeminence was to have significant repercussions for the legislative orientation and the working patterns of the EP. Equally, the growth in size had its own internal repercussions for the EPP-ED as its ideological coherence became ever more dissipated. Indeed, even before the 2004 and 2007 enlargements, leading French MEP Jean-Louis Bourlanges observed that the EPP-ED was starting to be 'characterised by organised indiscipline' (quoted in *Agence Europe*, 12 April 2000).

At its inception the EPP was a fairly cohesive grouping of Christian Democratic parties from the six founding member states (for details see Fitzmaurice 1975:69–85; Pridham and Pridham 1981). Uniformly, the national Christian Democratic parties were predominantly centre-right and pro-federalist in orientation. Successive enlargements, however, incorporated within the EPP a number of other centre-right parties which neither subscribed to Christian Democratic values nor shared a federalist vision for Europe.

The extent of ideological diversity of the group found reflection in its change of name after the 1999 election to the Group of the European People's Party and European Democrats. The name change was prompted in large part by UK Conservative MEPs who were keen to signal the changed ideological balance inside the group. While the largest contingent in the EPP remained the traditional backbone of the German CDU, the second-largest national party delegation after 1999 was the UK Conservatives. This was a UK delegation characterized by internal divisions over European integration and which contained an increased number of overtly Eurosceptic members. The third-largest national party delegation was the Italian Forza Italia, a populist rightist party with several of its MEPs openly 'Gaullist' in defence of national sovereignty. Indeed, seven other Italian right-wing parties found representation in the EPP-ED. The rightward drift was most starkly revealed, however, with the decision of the Austrian ÖVP in 2000 to join in a domestic governing alliance with the far-right Freedom Party (with the ÖVP's MEPs still retaining membership of the EPP-ED). The then group leader, Hans Gert Pöttering, openly acknowledged the diversity within the group but did not see such ideological variety to be a significant problem. However, some traditional Christian Democrats within the group were less sanguine about the diffusion of the original principles of the EPP and shortly after the 1999 election established a loose grouping, the Schuman Group, to combat the rightward drift and 'to regroup those who strongly believe in European integration and centre politics' (Gil-Robles, cited in GPC 2000:17).

The ideological diversity of the EPP-ED was extended still further with the addition of 22 parties and 79 MEPs from the 12 new member states after the enlargements in 2004 and 2007. Overall the membership of the EPP-ED grew by 16 per cent, and after the elections in Bulgaria and Romania in 2007, some 30 per cent of its members came from the new member states.

The diversity of group members finds reflection in the Group's Rules of Procedure (EPP-ED 2006) which allow for three categories of membership. The first consists of those parties which are full members of the EPP and have automatic inclusion. The second is those parties which subscribe to the political programme of the EPP and which are committed to pursue 'the process of federal unification and integration in Europe'. The third category is allied members who subscribe to the basic principles of the group but who maintain the right to 'promote and develop their distinct views on constitutional issues in relation to the future of Europe' (EPP-ED 2006: Rule 5).

The distance between the Eurosceptic ED members – the UK Conservative party and the Ulster Unionists, along with the Czech ODS, two Portuguese Partido Popular MEPs and one Italian Partito Pensionati MEP – and Christian Democrats in the EPP was particularly pronounced. The official commitment by David Cameron, upon his election to the leadership of the UK Conservative Party in 2006, to withdraw Conservative MEPs from the alliance with the EPP to form a new anti-federalist EP group after the 2009 elections, did little to lessen the ideological tensions within the EPP-ED. The UK Conservative Group for Europe, a pro-European group affiliated to the UK Conservative Party, acknowledged these tensions on its website: 'There are certainly some parties in the EPP we would describe as wet, federalist or not "One of Us"' (www.cge.org.uk/18.html). One British Conservative MEP was even more critical in his observation that:

> even in economic and fiscal policy, where there is supposed to be the greatest commonality of interest, we don't influence the EPP but, instead, are compromised by its agenda ... We ... look forward to ending the practical disadvantages in our EPP affiliation that have rendered us invisible and toothless. (Van Orden, 2006:11)

If the British Conservatives were to leave the EPP-ED, then one of their most likely partners would be the Czech Civic Democratic Party (ODS). Significantly, within the EPP-ED, the ODS was still regarded with suspicion by some German EPP MEPs who had initially opposed its inclusion in the EPP-ED on the grounds that they believed the Czech party to be 'anti-European and anti democratic' (*European Voice* 4 March 2004).

Group of the Party of European Socialists (PSE)

Until 1999 the PSE had been the largest group in the EP since the first direct elections in 1979. However, with only 180 MEPs returned in June 1999, some 53 fewer members than the EPP-ED, it was forced to relinquish its pole position. Most of the decline in PSE numbers from 221 immediately before the 1999 elections was accounted for by the loss of 33 UK Labour Party MEPs. The PSE remained in second place after the 2004 elections. With the addition of 18 members from Bulgaria and Romania the numbers of PSE MEPs rose to 218 after May 2007, but dropped gain to 215 after the Romanian elections in November 2007. However, after the 2004 elections, only 33 MEPs came from EU-10 countries and the reduced contingents from the UK Labour Party and the German Social Democrats meant that the French and Spanish Socialists were the largest national parties.

Unlike the EPP-ED, after 2004, the PSE drew its members from only 25 of the 27 member states, with no representatives from Cyprus and Latvia. Nonetheless, the PSE remained far more ideologically coherent than the EPP-ED – despite a marked ideological difference between the more traditional socialism of the Spanish and French PS and the 'modernizers' among the UK Labour members. This division within the ranks of the PSE, combined with the increased representation of French and Spanish members after the 2004 election and, crucially, the UK Labour government's participation in the invasion of Iraq, led to the group favouring incoming Spanish Socialist MEP Josep Borrell as its candidate for the President of Parliament for the first half of the 2004–2009 mandate. Borrell was preferred to the long-standing British Labour member Terry Wynn, who had served as chair of Parliament's Budget Committee in the 1999–2004 Parliament.

Alliance of Liberals and Democrats for Europe (ALDE)

The ALDE group combines members of two separate transnational European political parties – the European Liberal, Democrat and Reform Party (ELDR) and the European Democratic Party (EDP). The latter was formed in the wake of the 2004 election by the French UDF's François Bayrou and Francesco Rutelli of the Italian Democrazia è Libertà – La Margherita. According to Bayrou, the EDP was a response to increasing Euroscepticism and was committed to the 'validity of the federal model' while 'reconcil[ing] initiative and solidarity' (*Agence Europe* 10 December 2004). While the ELDR represents the traditional liberal, mainly centre-left, core of the ALDE group, EDP membership of ALDE brought French UDF members from the EPP-ED (where they had resided since the early 1990s) back to the ALDE group, along with eight Italian members from the Margherita list and two other Italian radicals from the Lista Bonino.

In February 2008 ALDE's 101 members were drawn from 22 member states and 32 national parties, with the EDP constituting 25 MEPs from five parties. The group also included independents from Ireland (Marian Harkin) and Cyprus (Marios Matsakis). The UK Liberal Democrats were represented by 11 MEPs and provided the group leader, Graham Watson. The UDF from France had ten members. The ALDE also benefited from the return of seven FDP members from Germany, the first time the FDP had secured representation in the EP since 1989.

The ALDE group occupies the ideological centre ground in the EP and as such sees itself as the 'voice of reason and rationale, of principle and purpose' (ALDE 2006:7). Undoubtedly, ALDE has played a pivotal role in many decisions and provided the swing vote in the investiture of the Barroso Commission (see Chapter 7).

Internally, however, there are tensions as the British, Finnish, Hungarian, Italian and several other member parties of ALDE see themselves as natural allies of the centre-left, while other members of the group (including the Bayrouistes, Danish Venstre, the German FDP and the Dutch VVD) are more inclined towards the centre-right. In addition to these left–right tensions, another potential division within the group is between the integrationist/federalist majority and the more Eurosceptic centre parties from the Nordic countries (Raunio 2006:298).

Union for Europe of Nations (UEN)

The Union for Europe of Nations adopted its name in 1999, and was the successor to the Europe of Nations group that had been formed in 1994 by anti-Maastricht French MEPs and Danish Eurosceptics. In 1994 some 90 per cent of the 30 members of the UEN came from just three countries: France, Italy and Ireland. In contrast, Portugal and Denmark provided just three members between them. In 2002 the UEN's membership was substantially reduced after the departure of nine members of the French RPFIE to join the non-attached members.

As Fieschi (2000:524) noted for the 1994–1999 Parliament, 'The Europe of Nations group is a motley gathering.' This observation was even more accurate during the course of the 2004–2009 Parliament. Indeed, it was not readily apparent that the UEN would survive immediately after the 2004 elections, given that Fianna Fáil initially held discussions with ALDE. Once the UEN was reconstituted, the original Italian, Irish and Danish parties rejoined (but this time there were no representatives from France) to form a group with a total of 27 members. They were joined later by four members of the Italian Lega Nord who had migrated from the ID group through the non-attached members before joining the UEN. These parties from the old member states were subsequently joined by representatives from the Polish Law and Justice Party, the Latvian Fatherland and Freedom Party, and two parties from Lithuania – the Liberal Democrats and the Peasants and New Democratic party. In 2005, 13 Polish MEPs joined to bring the total of Polish UEN MEPs to 20. By 2007 the Polish contingent included representatives from five different party lists, including five from the League of Polish Families (who had initially joined the ID group) and three former EPP-ED members who had been elected on the list of the Polish People's Party. With the addition of these new members the UEN had nearly doubled in size from 27 in 2004 to 44 in 2007, and had become the fourth-largest group in the EP. With the increase in size came increased ideological diversity. One UK Socialist MEP characterized the UEN as 'a mix of hard right (Alleanza Nazionale and Dansk Folkeparti) . . . more moderate right wingers (Fianna Fáil) . . . the far right Italian Lega Nord and the deeply homophobic League of Polish Families' (Claude Moraes, *Tribune* 19 January 2007).

Group of the Greens/European Free Alliance (Greens/EFA)

Of all the groups in the EP the Greens/EFA benefited least from the post-2004 enlargement. Indeed, the Greens was the only party group in 2007 not to have any representatives from the 12 new member states, and the EFA had only a single Latvian member representing 'For Human Rights in United Latvia'. In the 1999–2004 Parliament the Greens/EFA, with 48 members, had been for a time the fourth-largest group – before three German defections reduced its size to below that of the GUE group. In 2004, although the overall share of Green/EFA MEPs fell from 7.2 per cent before enlargement to 5.7 per cent post-enlargement, the group regained its fourth position – until the expansion of the UEN group, noted above, returned the Greens/EFA to fifth place.

The Greens are dominated by the German Die Grünen (with 13 MEPs) with the French Les Verts providing a further six representatives. The dominance of the German Greens, and their generally less hostile attitude to the EU (see Bomberg and Carter 2007:S101), impacted upon the policy positions of the group in the EP and reinforced the campaign message that Greens 'want Europe to become a real power for environmental protection, peace and social justice' (Greens/EFA 2004).

The European Free Alliance was initially formed in 1981 as an enabling framework for cooperation among regionalist parties seeking greater independence for their nations and regions. The Nationalist parties from Scotland (SNP) and Wales (PC) and a separatist party in Catalonia (ERC) continue this tradition and have now been joined by a Danish Socialist People's Party representative, who chose to join the

EFA rather than the Nordic Green Left, and a Latvian MEP whose party supports stronger ties with Russia. Two other Dutch MEPs are associated with the Greens/EFA, one of whom is the former Commission official, Paul van Buitenen, who exposed financial irregularities within the Commission in the late 1990s.

Confederal Group of the European Left/Nordic Green Left (GUE/NGL)

The origins of the GUE/NGL are to be found in the communist, euro-communist or left-socialist parties of the 1970s. With successive enlargements the group expanded its territorial scope to include, by the time of the 1999–2004 Parliament, representatives from Denmark, Finland, France, Germany, Greece, Italy, Netherlands, Portugal, Spain, and Sweden. Indeed, the extension of the group's title to include 'Nordic Green Left' was the result of the admission of Swedish and Finnish members after enlargement in 1995. In the 1999 parliament the GUE/NGL eventually emerged as the fourth-largest parliamentary group, with 50 members after 2002, after a number of defections from other groups.

After the 2004 elections the GUE/NGL's representation dropped from 7.8 per cent before enlargement to 5.6 per cent in 2004 and 5.2 per cent in 2007. By 2007 it was the sixth-largest group in the EP. In Finland, France, Spain, and Sweden the communists and former communist parties lost ground in 2004, whereas the German PDS gained an extra seat to make it the largest delegation with seven seats. Two MEPs from Sinn Féin, representing respectively the Republic of Ireland and Northern Ireland, joined the group for the first time in 2004. In the new EU-10 states representatives were only returned in the Czech republic (six seats) and in Cyprus where the AKEL won two seats. No GUE/NGL representatives were returned for Bulgaria or Romania in 2007.

The Constituent Declaration of the Group states: 'The Confederal Group of the European United Left is a forum for cooperation between its different political components, each of which retains its own independent identity and commitment to its own positions' (GUE/NGL 1994). The desire of individual parties to maintain their independent identities and own positions has created problems for group cohesion in the EP (see below; see Lazar 2002:91–2).

Independence and Democracy Group (ID)

The Independence and Democracy Group was the immediate successor to the Group for a Europe of Democracies and Diversities (EDD) which had been formed after the 1999 election and was 'open to members who were critical of further European integration and centralization' (www.europarl.eu.int/edd). The EDD's 16 MEPs represented five parties from four member states. The largest contingent of six representatives was from the French list Chasse, Pêche, Nature, Traditions. Representing hunters, fishermen and rural voters, this list was specifically opposed to EU legislation infringing the privileges of blood sportsmen. These French rural Eurosceptics were joined in the 1999–2004 Parliament by three Eurosceptic Danish members from the former Europe of Nations Group (one of whom subsequently left the group), and by two of the three UK Independence Party MEPs elected in 1999 who favoured UK withdrawal from the EU. In addition, the EDD also included MEPs from three separate fundamentalist Calvinist parties.

After 2004 the renamed group comprised 38 members from 10 member states. By 2007 the defections of eight members of the League of Polish Families and four members of the Lega Nord, all to the UEN, along with the loss of two members of the UK Independence Party and one member of the Swedish June List, reduced the total number of ID MEPs to 24. Nearly half of the remaining members belonged to UKIP, and Nigel Farage of UKIP acted as co-chair of the group alongside Jens-Peter Bonde of the Danish June Movement.

The enlarged group was both ideologically more heterogeneous and more right-wing than its predecessor. The UKIP was committed to the UK's withdrawal from the EU while most other members retained a critical but reformist position on the EU. The divisions in the group were heightened by the diversity of fundamentalist religious groups represented by the Catholic League of Polish Families, the Dutch Calvinist Christian Union and the Greek Orthodox traditionalist party (LAOS).

Identity, Tradition and Sovereignty Group (ITS): January–November 2007

The accession of Bulgaria and Romania in January 2007, and the inclusion of 14 representatives of far-right nationalist parties among their national delegations, enabled other far-right parties, most notably the French Front National, to achieve their long-held ambitions to form a group in the EP for the first time since 1994. The ITS passed the threshold for group formation, of 20 members from at least six member states, with seven MEPs from the French Front National, five from the Greater Romania Party, three from Belgium's Vlaams Belang, two Italians (including the granddaughter of Benito Mussolini), one Austrian from the Freedom Party, one Bulgarian, and one defector from UKIP. The former UKIP MEP, Ashley Mote, was removed from the UKIP whip shortly after the 2004 election after it emerged that he was to be prosecuted for a series of housing benefit frauds. In September 2007 Mote was sentenced to nine months in prison after being found guilty of falsely claiming benefits.

In publishing a statement of its founding principles, the group also complied with the requirement that political group members accept that 'by definition that they have political affinity' (European Parliament 2007a Rule 29(1)). These principles included 'recognition of national interests, sovereignties, identities and differences', as well as commitments to 'Christian values, heritage, culture and the traditions of European civilisation', 'the traditional family as the natural unit within society', 'the freedoms and rights inherited by all and the rule of law'. The ITS also made clear its opposition to 'a unitary, bureaucratic, European superstate' (www.its-pe.eu).

Despite denying that the group was essentially racist and antisemitic (see *European Voice* 11 January 2007) the leader of the ITS, Bruno Gollnisch from the French Front National, was fined €5,000 and given a six-month suspended sentence for denying the Holocaust by a French court in January 2007. Certainly the other major political groups in the EP made clear their disapproval of the new group by preventing the appointment of two ITS members to committee vice-chairs, to which the ITS was entitled under the d'Hondt system. The leader of the PSE, Martin Schulz, stated at the time that members of his group would 'never vote for a fascist' (quoted in *European Voice* 1 February 2007).

In the European elections in Romania on 25 November 2007 the Greater Romania Party failed to reach the 5 per cent electoral threshold and so lost the five seats it had occupied in the EP since accession. This loss would have signalled the disbandment of the ITS, had the group not already imploded on 14 November – only days before the election – when the Greater Romanian Party's MEPs withdrew from the ITS in protest at 'racist' comments directed against Romanians by a fellow ITS member, Alessandra Mussolini.

Non-attached members

Before the Romanian election in November 2007 some 13 MEPs remained unattached to any political group, because either of ideological incompatibility or of personality conflicts with members of existing groups, or simply because members preferred the scope for individual action beyond the constraints of group structures. Initially, immediately after the 2004 elections, there were 28 non-attached members, many on the far right of the political spectrum and many of whom migrated to the ITS upon its formation in January 2007. Italy, Slovakia and the UK each had three non-attached members, Poland had two, while Austria and the Czech Republic provided the remaining two MEPs. After the disintegration of the ITS and the Romanian election there were 30 unattached MEPs by February 2008. From 2005 the non-attached members from the UK included Roger Helmer, a staunchly Eurosceptic British Conservative and former member of the

EPP-ED. He had been excluded from the EPP-ED in June 2005 for insulting its then leader Hans-Gert Pöttering. Reflecting upon the uneasy position of British Conservatives within the EPP-ED (see above), Helmer felt 'relieved' to leave the EPP-ED and queried why other British Conservatives were still 'sleeping with the enemy' (quoted in *Agence Europe* 14 June 2005). Helmer was joined by another Eurosceptic British Conservative, Daniel Hannan, in February 2008. Hannan became a non-attached member after expulsion from the EPP-ED for claiming that Hans-Gert Pöttering's interpretation of the EP's Rule 19 had conferred upon the President 'arbitrary power' and so could be compared with the Enabling Act passed by Hitler in 1933 (EP Debates 31 January 2008).

There was little in common among the representatives from the League of Polish Families, the French Front National, the Northern Ireland Democratic Unionist Party, the former UKIP member, the Austrian populist, or the Italian left-of-centre Socialist Unity for Europe list members. But, under Parliament's Rule 31, the non-attached members were able to share a secretariat, to employ staff and use rooms which have been set aside for them on an occasional basis.

National party delegations

As noted above, the transnational party group system within the EP has been underpinned by institutional incentives: both direct material incentives of financial and administrative assistance and the benefits derived from the maximization of institutional power and associated policy influence. Nonetheless, the fundamental bedrock of the party group system in the EP has remained individual national parties.

'Size matters' in the EP party groups. The larger national delegations are in a very strong bargaining position within the groups (see Raunio 1996a:72). Leadership positions (for the EP's bureaux and for nominations to parliamentary posts) are normally distributed in accordance with broad principles of proportionality within groups among national delegations (using the d'Hondt method). In turn, leaders of national delegations are elected by their respective national party colleagues and represent their parties in intra-group negotiations and often take decisions on their behalf in the bureaux. Elaborate mechanisms are in place to tie national delegations into party group agreements. Indeed, decisions at group level are routinely preceded by discussions within national party delegations. As noted above, meetings of national delegations are consistently held in 'group weeks' and during plenaries, with preliminary negotiations among national delegations normally taking place before important group decisions are taken.

Correspondingly, parallel meetings and contacts between leaders of national delegations and their own domestic parties are an essential part of the decision-making process within party groups. Indeed, as the EP's legislative role expanded and became more institutionalized in the 1990s, contacts between MEPs and their national parties increased and became more routinized (Raunio 2000:220–1). Another stimulus came with the upheavals in national politics associated with the ratification process of the Maastricht Treaty. Given the unpreparedness of national parties and the 'intellectual vacuum' surrounding the debate about EU integration at the time, party groups were presented with the opportunity to assert their status in relation to their national counterparts (Ladrech 1996:299). As the issue of integration came to prominence in domestic politics, so EP party groups found their policy positions to be both more pertinent to national deliberations and also the subject of increased attention by national party officers.

In the larger delegations contacts with national parties are formalized through EP leaders serving on the executive bodies of the national parties (Raunio 2000:213). Thus, for example, the leader of the UK's European Parliamentary Labour Party (EPLP) sits on the party's National Executive. However, informal modes of communication are equally important, with national party leaders and their officers maintaining regular phone contact with their counterparts in the EP's larger delegations. Government parties are especially sensitive to maintaining regular contacts with their respective EP party leaderships. Sometimes national party influence may even be exerted indirectly via other governments. Thus for example, during the processing of the working time directive in 2005, which brought British Labour members into conflict with the British Labour government over limits on working hours, it was reported that Tony Blair sought to dilute Parliament's stance through having British concerns relayed by his Spanish counterpart José Luis Rodríguez Zapatero, one of whose Spanish Socialist MEPs, Alejandro Cercas, was Parliament's rapporteur on the legislative proposal (*Financial Times* 23 March 2005).

Not only do national delegations feed national party perspectives into transnational group deliberations; they also serve as informational conduits in the reverse direction – between the EP and domestic political parties. In fact, as Scully (2000b) points out, 'One of the major contributions that MEPs make is to help their national parties and governments *understand* the issues operating at the European level.'

Party cohesion: national vs European party group?

If '[d]epartures from party loyalty are observable in all legislative parties in democratic countries' (Loewenberg and Patterson 1979:229), then one expectation would be that such 'departures' would be greater in transnational parties than national ones (see Attina 1990:576–8; Hix 2001a:57–8). One specific set of problems undermining cohesion in transnational party groups in the EP is that 'their subcomponents are not merely factions or tendencies, but fully formed political parties in their own right, with proud histories as self-governing organizations in the national arena' (Hix and Lord 1997:141). Moreover, the incentives for national parties to exert influence over their MEPs' voting decisions have increased in parallel with the enhancement of the legislative powers of the EP. In these circumstances a secular trend towards increased intervention by national parties to control the activities of their European representatives might well be anticipated.

Offsetting such a trend, however, is the reality that the very protractedness of intra-group bargaining in the EP enhances the independence of national party delegations from direction by their party leaderships 'back home'. The constant process of negotiation and deliberation between national delegations normally results in compromises most group members are willing to support and if necessary vote for in plenary. This is why so much time is devoted in the larger groups to building consensus by incorporating and reconciling the views of national delegations to agreed group positions. Indeed, the very complexity of the EP's political environment – with some 175 parties from 27 member states operating in seven transnational political groups for most of the 2004–2009 Parliament – makes it usually both extremely difficult and organizationally inefficient for national parties to bind their MEPs to strictly defined and predetermined policy preferences. Only where issues are closely delimited, clearly defined and with limited possible outcomes are national party mandates likely to produce anticipated results. One such recurring issue has been the choice of the Commission President. Empirical analysis of the EP's vote on the confirmation of Jacques Santer as Commission President in 1994 and of Romano Prodi in 1999 found that although there was a clear ideological divide on this issue, MEPs were strongly influenced by the preferences of their national parties (Hix and Lord 1996; Gabel and Hix 2002). While the choice of José Manuel Barroso in 2004 reflected greater party polarization in the EP than previous nominations, nonetheless, British Labour MEPs and Spanish Socialists still voted against the PSE position in accordance with their national parties' preferences (see Magnette 2005:79).

In the context of bargaining within the EP it is more problematic and less efficient for national delegations to be tied to predetermined national bargaining positions. In these circumstances domestic parties generally have little to gain from mandating their representatives in the EP. To do so would 'simply condemn them to being outvoted, and [to deny] them the flexibility to negotiate their way into winning coalitions' (Hix and Lord 1997:129). In which case, as Scully argues, a lack of bargaining flexibility in such multi-actor, multidimensional bargaining can be harmful (Scully 2000b:18). A plausible option for most parties is thus 'to see their MEPs enjoying a limited, or conditional independence' (Scully 2000b:19).

Hix *et al.* (2007:133–6) approach this bargaining relationship from a principal-agent perspective, and conceive of MEPs as the agents of two principals: their national parties and their European political groups. Each principal has a range of incentives (both positive and negative) with which to seek to influence MEPs' support for the respective party line. European party groups have positive incentives in the form of control of the policy agenda and the allocation of leadership positions both within the party and within Parliament, such as committee chairs and rapporteurships. The European party groups, however, have few negative sanctions (see below) but do actively monitor the behaviour of their members in terms of voting, through 'whips', and in committees through group coordinators (see Chapter 6). Given that the larger groups have greater influence over both the EP's agenda and the allocation of official positions, one hypothesis is that the voting behaviour of individual MEPs would be structured according to European party group alignment and that this would be particularly the case in the larger groups.

A second, and counterposed, proposition is that while party group leaders may seek to exercise internal control in the EP, national party elites actually exert powerful external control through candidate selection and wider party patronage. National parties control the selection of party candidates in European elections, the development of national party policy programmes, direct access to national party positions and indirect access to national government positions. In fact, given the relative weakness of internal 'whipping' systems in the EP, there are few sanctions available to party group leaders to curb dissent by national delegations on policy issues with a high salience in domestic party arenas.

The intriguing question that has occupied scholars is what happens when an MEP's two principals are in conflict. Existing studies pointed to the fact that, where there were conflicts between party group and national party preferences, MEPs were more likely to vote in accordance with the latter rather than the former (Brzinski *et al.* 1998; Kreppel 2002:208; Raunio 2006:300–1). Perhaps not surprisingly, therefore, Hix *et al.* confirmed that MEPs rarely voted against their national parties between 1979 and 2004 (2007:143). Specifically, MEPs were nearly twice as likely to vote against their party group as they were their national party (2007:145), and, generally, national parties were, on average, twice as influential in determining which ways MEPs voted as European parties were (2007:144–5).

A linked question is, why are MEPs more prone to follow national party direction than European party group preferences? The first part of an answer is that MEPs are rarely forced to make a choice between national party and European party group. In nearly 90 per cent of recorded voting decisions in the 1999–2004 Parliament there was no difference between national party and European party preferences. This reflected a longer continuity, where in the overwhelming majority of roll-call votes since 1979, national and European parties voted the same way (Hix *et al.* 2007:137). What is apparent, therefore, is that national party delegations have acted strategically since direct elections to find consensus within their European party group in order to maximize the chances of policy success when competing with other European party groups in Parliament.

Intra-group cohesion

In a monumental study of voting behaviour in each of the five parliaments between 1979 and 2004, Hix *et al.* recorded five distinctive trends in terms of party cohesion (Hix *et al.* 2007 which drew on earlier research reported in Hix 2001b; Hix 2002a; Hix *et al.* 2005; Hix and Noury 2006). The votes examined are roll-call votes. The authors acknowledge that such votes account for only a third of all votes in the EP, and that there are problems of 'selection bias', but claim, nonetheless, that 'roll-call votes are used for the more important decisions in the European Parliament' (2007:29–30). For the moment, we will accept this claim at face value and simply review trends identified by Hix *et al.* First, party groups were generally more cohesive than national groups in the EP. Second, as party group cohesion has increased, voting cohesion in national groups has declined. In essence, therefore, 'voting in the European Parliament is primarily along party lines rather than national lines, and increasingly so' (Hix *et al.* 2007:88). Third, cohesion within party groups has increased as the main party groups have increased in size; and the two largest groups – EPP-ED and PSE – have tended to be more cohesive than the smaller groups. Fourth, intra-group cohesion has increased as the powers of Parliament have increased (2007:104). Fifth, more MEPs from parties in government, and increased pressure from parties in national governments upon those MEPs, is associated with more cohesion rather than less in European political parties (Hix *et al.* 2007:102).

Party cohesion is measured by Hix *et al.* by means of an 'Agreement Index', where a score of 1 indicates that all members of a party vote together, and a score of 0 means that members of a party split their votes evenly between yes votes, no votes and votes to abstain (Hix *et al.* 2007:91–2). The votes recorded in the data set are all roll-call votes cast from July 1979 to May 2004 – nearly 15,000 votes by over 2000 MEPs. From this impressive data set the researchers claim that they are able to 'analyse exactly how politics inside the European Parliament has evolved' (2007:31). The 'exactness' of the analysis, and the nature of the data used, will be examined shortly; but for now the main find-ings of Hix *et al.* will simply be noted.

The conclusion that party groups were generally more cohesive than national groups in the EP is substantiated in the average Agreement Index score of 0.809 for the six main political groups across the 25-year period. This is in contrast with the significantly lower average score of 0.603 for national groups across this period. The increase in the average relative cohesion score of the main party groups rose from 0.814 in the first Parliament to 0.889 in the 1999–2004 Parliament, whereas the average score for each national group declined from 0.667 to 0.589. Hix *et al.* (2007:95) also found that the combined average relative cohesion score for the EPP and PSE increased from 0.821 to 0.914. The observation that intra-party cohesion has increased as the powers of Parliament have increased is confirmed in the finding that there was an 11 per cent increase in the cohesion scores of party groups after the Amsterdam Treaty (2007:102). The further general conclusion, that the percentage of MEPs from parties in government is positively associated with greater party group cohesion, is borne out in the significant effects revealed in Hix *et al.*'s econometric models (2007:100).

When Hix and Noury (2006) examined voting behaviour in the first eighteen months of the 2004–2009 Parliament, immediately after enlargement in 2004, they discovered continuing stable levels of party cohesion. Despite a considerably more heterogeneous composition, in terms of political, economic and ideological profiles of new members, they found that party group cohesion had remained remarkably stable since enlargement and, if anything, absolute party cohesion had risen slightly. Cohesion along national lines remained considerably lower than cohesion along party group lines, though it had increased margin-ally in relative terms, by 0.053 when comparing the 25 member states with the 15 states in the 1999–2004 Parliament. There was, however, some evidence of more cohesive national voting in some of the new smaller member states – such as Estonia, Latvia and Slovenia – but this might have been as much a function of national group size as one of cohesion. Equally Hix and Noury found that size remained of impor-tance for the two main groups EPP-ED and PSE – with relative cohe-sion scores of 0.858 and 0.900 respectively for the period after 2004, compared with 0.866 and 0.901 in the 1999–2004 Parliament. ALDE suffered the greatest decline in relative cohesion from a score of 0.882 to 0.870. Given the political and ideological diversity of the new ALDE group, noted above, this finding was perhaps predictable. Ultimately Hix and Noury (2006:20) concluded that in the immediate aftermath of the 2004 enlargement 'cohesion of the political groups in the European Parliament remains high and has neither increased nor declined significantly'.

Inter-group coalitions and competition

Intra-party cohesion is of major significance in parliamentary systems where 'government' and 'opposition' are defined in relation to competing and disciplined parties; and where the successful processing of policy is dependent upon governments securing and sustaining parliamentary voting majorities. In this competition government and opposition are differentiated in terms of structured voting blocs. Manifestly, the interinstitutional location of the EP and its own internal organizational logic has not required the creation of a competitive pattern of party politics. Historically, in the absence of a simple split between government and opposition parties in the EP, and notwithstanding the claim by some Socialist MEPs that they would take up the role of 'official opposition' to the incoming Barroso Commission (see *Parliament Magazine* 28 February 2005), variable legislative coalitions have formed around specific policy positions. This does not mean necessarily, however, that voting patterns are unpredictable. In fact, the reverse is the case. Traditionally, there has been an underlying consistency and predictability to voting in the EP. For long periods, a system of 'political group oligopoly' operated where the PSE and Christian Democrats constituted a winning coalition to meet the requirements, both political and procedural, for the exercise of legislative influence.

Substantiation of this 'tradition of oligopoly', or more accurately perhaps of 'duopoly', had been provided in studies of voting patterns in the 1989–1994 and 1994–1999 Parliaments. Analyses of voting in these parliaments had found that the PSE and EPP had, depending on the type of procedure, joined together on 60 to 75 per cent of votes (Hix and Lord 1997:139; Kreppel 2000a:344–5; 2002:142–51). Plus, more often than not, PSE and EPP MEPs were joined by a majority of ELDR group members (PSE-ELDR 81 per cent; EPP-ELDR 75 per cent).

What needs to be explained therefore is why the PSE-EPP duopoly emerged with such regularity. One explanation is that the majority of members within the two party groups held similar policy preferences on many basic issues within the broader commitment to a social-market, regulated economy and to the promotion of further European integration. Another simple explanation is that much of the legislative work of the EP is highly technical and does not necessarily involve recourse to ideology and partisanship to reach voting decisions. A further, common explanation of the formation of the PSE–EPP duopoly and 'grand coalitions' is as a response to the absolute majority requirements of certain legislative and budgetary procedures. As Corbett *et al.* (2007:109) point out, 'Usually, the Socialists and EPP must negotiate compromises if Parliament is to amend Council's position. They are the only two groups that alone can combine to obtain an overall majority and have been since before direct elections'. In practice, historically, there has been a reinforcing dynamic between procedural rules and the political configuration of the PSE–EPP coalition which was 'centripetal and stabilising' (Hix and Lord 1997:162).

Clearly, voting rules have a marked impact on coalition formation – but they are not the exclusive or the primary explanation of coalition formation. Kreppel (2000a:346, original emphasis), for example, argues that 'it is the *institutional system* of checks and balances which require ideological moderation for effective legislative influence'. Her contention is that the level of cooperation between the major party groups of the PSE and EPP is best explained by the simple fact that the EP has to work with the Commission and Council to process legislative outputs. Both of these other bodies institutionalize consensual and non-confrontational decision-making processes, and within this wider institutional context it is rational for groups within the EP to conform to a non-adversarial style of decision-making. Thus, in 'a political system where numerous, ideologically diverse actors have "veto power" . . . over the legislative process we should expect gradual and moderate change to be the norm' (Kreppel 2000a:346). In other words, the process of interinstitutional bargaining impacts upon the internal bargaining between party groups in the EP (see also Hix and Lord 1997:148).

Development of left–right politics?

In examining the extent to which groups collude or compete Hix *et al.* (2007:148) reach the conclusion that 'party competition and coalition formation in the European Parliament occur along the classical left–right dimension, and that the two main political groups vote together less than they used to'. The overall finding is that the closer two party groups are on a left–right spectrum the greater the propensity to vote together. This pattern was found to be consistent across the 1994–1999, 1999–2004 and 2004–2009 Parliaments (Hix and Lord 1997:158–66; Raunio 1997: 101–6; Hix and Noury 2006: 1; Hix *et al.* 2007:150–51). In a sense, given the amorphous nature of party groups and their 'big tent' approach to group membership, statistical confirmation of a propensity to vote with proximate groups which, as noted above, have ideologically indistinct and overlapping borders, is perhaps of little surprise. Thus, in the first eighteen months after the 2004 election, the EPP-ED voted 83 per cent of the time with the UEN, and 78 per cent of the time with ALDE (this was an increase on the respective figures for the 1999–2004 Parliament of 71 and 68 per cent respectively), while the PSE voted 72 per cent of the time with the Greens/EFA and 75 per cent with ALDE (Hix and Noury 2006:30).

Hix *et al.* also noted that as the EPP-ED and PSE became more ideologically differentiated after 1999, and as the distance of the policy positions between them increased, so the proportion of times they voted together decreased. In this sense the researchers reiterate their claim, made on numerous previous occasions, that the main party groups are becoming more competitive (2007:158). The percentage difference in terms of voting agreement between EPP-ED and PSE did indeed decline from the high levels of 71 per cent and 69 per cent in the 1989–1994 and the 1994–1999 Parliaments, to 65 per cent in the 1999–2004 Parliament, and 67 per cent in the 2004–2009 Parliament. While Hix *et al.* use these figures to indicate increased group competitiveness, the simple fact remains that the overwhelming majority of roll-call votes, some two-thirds or more, have consistently witnessed cooperation rather than competition between the two largest groups. Even Hix and Noury (2006:11) eventually acknowledge that the figures they present 'can be thought of in two ways: either the two main parties are equally as competitive as they were in the previous parliaments or they are equally as cooperative'. While Hix *et al.* choose to emphasize the former, many observers more closely associated with the EP choose to emphasize the latter (see Shackleton 2006:112; Corbett *et al.* 2007:109–10; Westlake 2007:342–4).

In placing the emphasis upon competition Hix *et al.* argue that the policy positions of party groups and the ideological distance between them are strong predictors of how often groups will vote together. They estimate that a 1 per cent decrease in ideological distance between two parties on the left–right dimension will result in a 6 per cent increase in the probability that the two parties will vote together (2005:228). This helped to explain why the ELDR showed an increased propensity to vote with the PSE in the 1999–2004 Parliament – because the ideological distance between the two had decreased; whereas the enlarged ALDE group in the 2004–2009 Parliament was ideologically closer to the EPP-ED and hence more willing to vote with the EPP-ED in roll-call votes (see Hix and Noury 2006:12; Hix *et al.* 2007:157–9). The changing ideological position of party groups is thus identified as the main factor explaining intergroup competition and, as such, the EP is 'very much like most other democratic parliaments, in that it is dominated by political parties and left-right politics' (Hix and Noury 2006:20). This is seen by Hix and his co-authors as a 'very positive message' and accompanies a belief that increased competition between parliamentary groups and between European political parties is the route towards future 'healthy democratic outcomes' in the EU (Hix *et al.* 2007:218). Exactly what implications these findings hold for the future development of parliamentarism in the EU will be examined in Chapter 9; for the moment, however, we need to examine the validity of the findings themselves.

Roll-call votes in the EP: finding what you want to find?

Hix and various co-authors have consistently and vehemently insisted that roll-call votes are an appropriate data source with which to test hypotheses about voting cohesion in the EP. They have acknowledged problems in the use of roll-call data but have largely sidestepped these problems and sought sanctuary in the assertion that 'it is reasonable to assume that roll-call votes are used for the more important decisions' (Hix *et al.* 2007:30). As such, it appears, therefore, that roll-call votes have some intrinsic importance in themselves as the public record of MEPs' voting behaviour.

The first problem, readily accepted by Hix, is that 'roll call votes do not tell the complete story of voting behaviour in the EP' (Hix 2001b:667–8). A more complete story would have to include votes in committees and the many votes in plenary which are conducted by a show of hands, or through electronic voting, but in which the votes of individual MEPs are not recorded. The 'story' of voting at present, therefore, is at best partial and reveals simply that roll-calls are held on a small minority of votes. Indeed, there is no agreement as to the extent of roll-call voting. Kreppel and Tsebelis (1999:941) estimated that only 15 per cent of votes involved a roll-call: Gabel and Carrubba (2004:3) and Thiem (2006:2) claim roll-calls account for 25 per cent of total votes; while Hix and co-authors settle for 'roughly a third' (2007:29). More damagingly, Westlake (2007:346–7) argues that there is no accurate, or readily available, means by which the exact proportion of roll-call votes can be estimated. At best, therefore, estimates of the proportion of roll-call votes in the EP resemble unsubstantiated guestimates.

While the small proportion of roll-call votes is not in itself pathological to the testing of hypotheses about voting behaviour, it does mean that the 'quality of our inferences' about such behaviour 'depend[s] crucially on the sampling properties of RCVs' (Carrubba *et al.* 2006:692). Stated at its simplest, for generalizations to be made about the universe of votes it has to be assumed that the sample constituted by roll-calls is a random selection of votes (Thiem 2006:2; Carrubba *et al.* 2006:692). The issue then becomes as follows:

> What if the selection of votes for roll call is based on exactly those characteristics of voting behaviour and legislative competition that we wish to study? Specifically, what if party groups, which are the most common source of roll call vote requests, select votes for roll call based on their expectations of the level of group cohesion and of the type of political conflict associated with the vote? If so, then the votes that are hidden from view – i.e. those not decided by roll call – may be very different from roll call votes in terms of party group cohesion and the character of political conflict.

Consequently, roll call votes may not provide a reliable source of information about legislative behaviour and the impact of ideology and nationality on EP politics. (Gabel and Carrubba 2004:3)

Unfortunately for Hix *et al.*, successive studies (Carrubba and Gabel 1999; Gabel and Carrubba 2004, Carrubba *et al.* 2006; Hug 2006; Thiem 2006) have demonstrated that roll-call votes are not a random sample. They are used strategically by party group leaders to signal their group's position variously to voters, interest groups, other party groups and other EU institutions (see Kreppel 2002:128–9; Thiem 2006:8) or alternatively to reveal the position of another group. In both cases the requesting group (normally roll-call votes are requested by party group leaders in the name of their group, but may also be called by at least 40 MEPs) ask for roll-call votes if they anticipate cohesive voting behaviour in their own group. Empirical studies have found that the decision to request a roll-call vote is endogenous to the expected level of cohesion (Gabel and Carrubba 2004:4), and hence a roll-call vote sample 'reveals rather high levels of party group cohesion while hiding votes with lower cohesion' (Thiem 2006:18). In other words, the decision to call a roll-call vote is 'hardly random' (Hug 2006:7). Moreover, if roll-call votes are used for 'signalling' group positions the sample of roll-call votes also proves to be endogenous to the policy space or issue area of votes. Thus, for example, Carrubba *et al.*'s findings reveal bias in the issue areas covered by roll-call votes. Some issue areas (using 'responsible committee' as a proxy for such areas) are significantly overrepresented in roll-call votes while others are not represented at all. This leads Carrubba *et al.* (2006:702) to argue that privileging the importance of the left–right cleavage in the EP may prove to be dubious. The danger is that other dimensions of policy conflict may be missed precisely because roll-call votes are not a representative sample of issue areas. Thus, for example, Carrubba and co-authors have found that, in the period they studied, the 'libertarian-traditional' dimension tended to be hidden from view in roll-call voting. A major reason for this was the fact that none of 50 votes on issues handled by the Women's Rights Committee were roll-call votes. As a result, one of the key aspects of the 'libertarian-traditional' dimension – women's rights, especially the right to decide on abortion – was obscured in a data set derived from roll-call votes (Gabel and Carrubba 2004:7; Carrubba *et al.* 2006:702).

While Hix *et al.* (2007:30) acknowledge some of the 'potential problems of "selection bias"' they claim, as noted earlier, that 'it is reasonable to assume that roll-call votes are used for the more important decisions in the European Parliament'. Their critics, however, are united in pointing out that this assumption 'is not necessarily true' (Westlake 2007:346) and that the evidence 'strongly suggests that [party group] leaders are making sure that the most important votes are specifically not decided by roll call' (Gabel and Carrubba 2004:5). This conclusion is reached on the basis of an analysis of the types of motions voted upon in roll-call votes. Carrubba *et al.* (2006:699) found, for example, that roll-call votes are called disproportionately on non-legislative resolutions and that, even with legislative votes, the 'most legislatively consequential votes . . . [are] massively under-sampled'. This is confirmed in Westlake's observation, based upon his long experience of the EP, that 'almost certainly, most . . . "important decisions" are not taken by RCV' (2007:346).

Overall, therefore, Gabel and Carrubba (2004:7) conclude that roll-call votes are 'not used for the most important decisions, they are not called on the full range of issues, and they are not called proportionately by party group'. In which case serious doubt is cast upon existing findings in the EP voting behaviour literature. The broad doubts about the nature and extent of left–right party competition have wider ramifications for the debate about the future parliamentarization of the EU, and these issues will be examined in Chapter 9. At a more specific level, doubts – about the potential to generalize behavioural patterns of voting and party cohesion from the restricted sample of roll-call votes – have led some analysts to advocate the abandonment of roll-call analysis and to seek different ways of examining voting behaviour (see Septembri 2006). Most other critics are less radical, however, and instead counsel caution in the interpretation of roll-call data and point to the need to recognize why and under what circumstances roll-call votes are called. If roll-call votes are used strategically to encourage intra-party cohesion and to signal inter-party differences then statistical analysis of roll-call votes will find exactly that!

Conclusion

One obvious conclusion of this chapter is that politics in the EP is dominated by party groups. Moreover, these pan-European groups remain overwhelmingly cohesive in their voting behaviour in roll-call votes despite their increasing internal heterogeneity. As noted earlier, there are no fewer than 175 national parties represented in the EP, with the largest group, the EPP-ED, encompassing 49 national parties. In addition to this heterogeneity, the fact that national parties still control nomination procedures for MEP candidacies removes a traditional incentive for greater party cohesion which is available to most party leaders within national legislatures. On top of these disincentives the absence of 'party government', and an institutional divide between 'government' and 'opposition' in the EU, also is a force moderating political group cohesion in the EP.

For these reasons EP groups remain less cohesive than party groups in member states' legislatures (see Raunio 2006:301). Nonetheless, empirical evidence reveals that MEPs vote predominantly along partisan rather than national lines. In so doing, MEPs frequently structure their voting behaviour along a policy dimension which corresponds to a traditional 'left-right' ideological conflict in most national party systems. In aggregate, while different party coalitions form on different policy issues, a willingness to seek consensus between the two largest groups is still the dominant feature of voting behaviour in the EP. The willingness of the major party groups to cooperate with each other is, in part, a reflection of the realities of interinstitutional bargaining in the EU policy process. Simply stated, an ideologically polarized EP would be unable to generate the necessary majorities at the later stages of the legislative process to impact upon EU policies. In these circumstances 'the party groups are forced to produce moderate proposals if they are to have any influence at all' (Kreppel 2002:216).

Party groups work within an institutional context that has changed dramatically with successive treaty reforms and enhancements of the legislative role of the EP. In part, the securing of formal legislative power has underpinned the informal commitment of party groups to seek consensus in order to maximize the policy impact of the EP. In part also, the extension of formal power has increased the importance of exerting institutional controls over the activities of party groups and their members. In this sense, as Kreppel postulates, there is a dynamic relationship between the organization of the EP as an institution, the party system and the party groups:

> [E]xogenous increases in the legislative authority of a parliament directly affect the development of the internal organizational structures, the party system (coalitions + number of parties) and the internal development of the parties themselves (albeit weakly). Each of these in turn then indirectly affects the evolution of the others. (Kreppel 2002:218–19)

It is to the internal organizational structures that we now turn in Chapter 6. Before doing so, it is worth committing to memory (for Chapter 9) the conclusion provided by Hix *et al.* (2007:180) that, in party terms:

> Politics in the European Parliament is surprisingly like in other democratic parliaments. The main dimension of voting behaviour both within and between the European political parties is the classic left-right dimension of democratic politics [and is] dominated by left-right positions and driven by the traditional party families of domestic European politics.

Chapter 6

Internal Organization

How legislators choose to organize themselves is one of the most fundamental issues confronting parliamentarians and students of legislatures alike. Different forms of legislative organization impact differently upon the internal relations between individual representatives, and upon the external relations of parliaments with other political institutions within the wider political system. Moreover, the choice of rules and procedures affects both the process of legislative decision-making and the nature of legislative outputs themselves. Not surprisingly, therefore, long before 'new institutionalism' (and its rediscovery of the importance of political institutions) became fashionable in academic circles, questions of legislative organization and institutional design had been of historic concern to parliamentarians and legislative scholars alike.

The central organizational question confronting legislatures is: how do elected representatives effectively and efficiently organize themselves in order to make collective decisions on the multiplicity of complex issues demanding their attention? In other words, what are the strategies available to legislators to cope with informational overload and environmental uncertainties? As already seen in Chapter 5, one powerful institutional device for dealing with the problems of collective decision-making has been the organization of political parties. In this chapter, however, attention will be focused upon the organizational form of Parliament itself: upon its rules and procedures, upon formal institutional leadership positions, and upon the all-important internal division of labour in the form of its committees. The importance of legislative organization should not be underestimated, for not only have issues of institutional design and organization remained a preoccupation of historic parliaments and new assemblies alike but, as Krehbiel (1991:2) points out, they have continued to shape:

> the collective expression of policy objectives, the level of expertise that is embodied in legislation that seeks to meet legislative objectives, the effectiveness with which legislation is implemented, and, ultimately, the importance of the legislature in the governmental process.

Legislative organization seeks to manage complexity. Most legislatures start, at least, from a fairly simple institutional configuration: whether

147

bicameral or unicameral. A 'legislature' remains, nonetheless, a singular institution; most parliaments take for granted their location in a single city, and, in most national assemblies, representatives communicate with each other in a single language, or a highly restricted range of official languages. In the case of the European Parliament, however, none of these assumptions holds. It is a co-legislator in partnership with an external intergovernmental institution – the Council – which in turn, arguably, is part also of a dual executive. It has three geographical locations. It is unique in being the only transnational directly elected representative institution in the world. It is one of the largest elected chambers in the world. And it has 23 official working languages which produce 506 possible language combinations for representatives to communicate effectively with each other. Hence, even before confronting the standard interinstitutional and policy complexities facing all legislatures, the EP has to deal with its own specific organizational complexities arising from a peripatetic existence and a multilingual and multinational composition.

Seat

It has long been lamented by MEPs themselves that they have no direct control over where the Parliament sits. The right to determine where the European Parliament meets is conferred by the treaties upon national governments (Article 289; Article 341 of the Lisbon Treaty (TFEU)). The Amsterdam Treaty reaffirmed and detailed this right:

> The European Parliament shall have its seat in Strasbourg where the 12 periods of monthly plenary sessions, including the budget session, shall be held. The periods of additional plenary sessions shall be held in Brussels. The committees of the European Parliament shall meet in Brussels. The General Secretariat of the European Parliament and its departments shall remain in Luxembourg. (Protocol on the location of the seats of the institutions, Amsterdam Treaty)

Yet apparently most MEPs, if given the choice, would prefer a single seat for the European Parliament, and many would prefer Brussels to Strasbourg. Thus, for example, an online poll of MEPs conducted by the Campaign for Parliamentary Reform in the 2004–2009 Parliament found that 89 per cent of 306 respondents were in favour of a single seat, and 81 per cent would like to see that seat in Brussels (*Parliament Magazine* 18 June 2007, Issue 248:4).

However, when MEPs have been given the opportunity they have been reticent to effect such a move. Thus, for example, in July 2007

Parliament voted against seeking to extend the mandate of the IGC to include consideration of the removal of the EP's seat from Strasbourg (by 370 votes to 280 with 33 abstentions). Undoubtedly, some MEPs who were in favour of this proposition were reluctant to support it while also urging member states to stay within the mandate agreed for the IGC. Similarly, a proposal to hold additional 'micro-plenaries' in Brussels during 2008 (see Chapter 7) was lost by 331 votes to 320, with 24 abstentions. Such 'micro-plenaries' were perceived by many MEPs to constitute a further step away from Strasbourg.

So the questions remain: why do MEPs still lead a peripatetic existence and why has a 'single seat' still not been agreed? The simple answer, long acknowledged by the Council itself, is that 'the decision on a seat is essentially of a political nature' (Council letter, 20 December 1974, quoted in Earnshaw 1985:79). If the question of a single seat for Parliament remains unresolved, at least the issues have been clarified and the number of options has been reduced over the years. One option, effectively removed as early as 1981, was a triangular rotation of meetings between Strasbourg, Brussels and Luxembourg. Since that date Parliament has refused to schedule its plenary sessions in Luxembourg (with few exceptions, the last being in 1986 when the Strasbourg chamber was being enlarged).

The original triple location emerged at the inception of the ECSC when the dual executive of the Council and the High Authority was located in Luxembourg. It made some sense, therefore, to locate the secretariat of the Common Assembly in close proximity to the staff of the Council and the High Authority. Yet representatives to the Common Assembly convened initially in the only fully equipped multi-lingual parliamentary building available at the time – the Parliamentary Assembly of the Council of Europe in Strasbourg. As most members of the Common Assembly also sat in the Council of Europe's Assembly there was a reinforcing pragmatic reason for meeting in Strasbourg. Plus, Strasbourg had a historic claim to host representatives of supra-national European institutions as it was imbued with 'the spirit and memory of Europe' (President of the EP, EP Debates 15 December 1999) – which continues to be evoked today – and served as a powerful spatial symbol of Franco-German postwar reconciliation. Moreover, as long as the Assembly was seen primarily as a deliberative body, there was no immediate necessity for its members to interact directly with, or be physically located close to, the executive institutions and the bureaucracies of the EC. Significantly, however, when Assembly members performed their consultative functions in the legislative process – with the emphasis upon scrutiny of executive actions through the committee system – they preferred to work close to where the executive action was. And, after the Treaty of Rome in 1957, the centre of the EC's legislative 'action' increasingly became Brussels.

The routine of holding committee meetings in Brussels, and of scheduling plenary sessions in Strasbourg, with occasional plenaries in Luxembourg, became the established working pattern in the decade after the Treaty of Rome. However, in the subsequent decade – from 1968 until direct elections in 1979 – Parliament began to hold more plenary sessions in Luxembourg, not least because of the convenience of holding its meetings where its secretariat was based (Corbett *et al.* 2007:33).

Gradually, however, after the first direct elections in 1979, Luxembourg lost out to Strasbourg despite considerable investment in a new parliamentary building (including a hemicycle) to accommodate the enlarged parliament on the Plateau du Kirchberg. In fact, within six months of the formation of the new directly elected EP, its members questioned the intergovernmentalist restrictions placed upon Parliament's location. MEPs asked the Political Affairs Committee and its rapporteur, Mario Zagari, to examine this issue. Eventually, in July 1981, on the basis of Zagari's report, MEPs adopted a resolution in favour of a single seat. As an interim measure, they agreed to restrict plenary sessions to Strasbourg and committee meetings primarily to Brussels.

Not surprisingly, the Luxembourg government, given its substantial financial investment in a new hemicycle, contested Parliament's decision in the Court of Justice. In February 1983 (Case C-230/81) the Court ruled that the EP had no obligation under the *status quo* to meet in Luxembourg, and in the same month the EP voted to convene an additional part-session in Brussels rather than in Luxembourg. A subsequent attempt by Parliament, in July 1983, to move its secretariat away from Luxembourg foundered, however, on a successful challenge made by the Luxembourg government in the Court of Justice (Case C-108/83).

Thereafter, various attempts to rationalize the location of the EP, through parliamentary resolutions in October 1985 and January 1989, resulted in further court cases initiated by the Strasbourg and Luxembourg authorities. Both feared that Parliament's support of building projects in Brussels, and the increased scheduling of sittings in the Belgian capital, would residualize the EP's presence in their respective cities (C-258/85 and joined cases C-213/88 and C-39/89).

These fears were only heightened when, in January 1992, the EP's President signed the lease for a new parliament building in Brussels. (Later, in 2000, an agreement was reached between the EP and the Luxembourg government which guaranteed that at least 50 per cent, and a minimum of 2060, of the EP's Secretariat would continue to be based in the Grand Duchy.) The ultimate intention of Parliament was to reduce the number of meetings in Strasbourg and schedule additional meetings in Brussels. The response of the French government was swift and decisive. At the European Council summit in Edinburgh in December 1992 the French government secured an agreement that Strasbourg should be considered the normal venue for the EP's monthly part-sessions. What was unusual about the Edinburgh declaration was the exact specification of the number of meetings to be held in Strasbourg. The Parliament immediately questioned the legality of the European Council's decision (in its resolution of 16 December 1992 OJ C 21 1993:107) and demonstrated its opposition to any detailed intervention in the scheduling of its internal affairs by ignoring the decision and scheduling only 11 and 10 sessions in Strasbourg in 1993 and 1994. When the EP scheduled only 11 Strasbourg sessions in 1996 the French government sought the overturn of this decision in the Court of Justice. In October 1997 the Court ruled that only after 12 sessions (or 11 sessions in election years) had been scheduled in Strasbourg could additional sessions then be held in Brussels (Case C-345/95).

This minimum number of Strasbourg meetings was incorporated in the protocol of the Amsterdam Treaty noted above, but controversies still continued to erupt over the number of days required to constitute a plenary session, and the possible compression of two plenaries into a single week. Indeed, on 14 June 2000 MEPs voted by 277 to 232 with 28 abstentions to discontinue Friday sittings of the Strasbourg plenary. No such sittings have been held subsequently. In March 2000 Parliament's Committee on Constitutional Affairs proposed that Article 289 of the EC Treaty should be amended to allow the EP to decide 'by an absolute majority of its members, on the location of its seat and all its meetings' (PE 232.758 2000:6). The Committee's proposal was incorporated into the EP's resolution of 13 April 2000 (OJ C 40, 7 February 2001:41) on proposals for the IGC and supported in plenary by 401 in favour, 77 against and 9 abstentions. However, it was not accepted by member states (see Chapter 2).

Not surprisingly, with the impetus provided by new cohorts of MEPs, the issue of Parliament's seat was revisited in the 2004–2009 Parliament. On the one side, many members from the EU-10 states experienced particular transportation difficulties in reaching Strasbourg given the absence of direct flights to any of the new member states, while on the other, some new MEPs regarded the traditional symbolism of Strasbourg as 'the spirit and memory of Europe' as 'an anachronism' (Alexander Alvaro, German MEP, quoted in *The Guardian* 1 November 2006). In May 2006, a group of MEPs, constituted as 'The Campaign for Parliament Reform', launched a citizens' initiative. The purpose of the initiative was to collect a million signatures calling for the EP to be located in one seat in Brussels. The significance of the figure of a million signatures was that, if the European Constitution had been in force, under Article 1-47 such an initiative could have been used to invite the Commission to consider introducing legislation on such a matter. Indeed, the initiator of the petition, Cecilia Malmström (ALDE, Sweden), symbolically presented the petition with a million signatures to the Commission on 21 September 2006, and in the following week presented the petition to the Finnish Presidency.

The issue of the seat was further propelled up Parliament's agenda with the disclosure, in April 2006, that Parliament had been overcharged by €1m a year on the rent of two of its buildings in Strasbourg. This disclosure led to an investigation by a working group of the Budgetary Control Committee and to an extended audit by the Court of Auditors. Indeed, the Budgetary Control Committee, for the first time in its history, decided to delay approving the Parliament's accounts (for 2004) while the investigation was under way. Eventually, the Committee found no evidence of illegality in the excessive rental payments and voted in favour of discharge. One month later, on 23 October 2006, the Bureau took the unanimous decision to purchase the Winston Churchill and Salvador de Madariaga buildings in Strasbourg.

In parallel, the then President, Josep Borrell, had been mandated by Parliament to raise the one-seat issue at the European Council's June 2006 summit. However, the Austrian presidency made it clear that it would not allow a debate on Strasbourg's future to proceed. Nonetheless, the issue reemerged in January 2007 during the election campaign for the new EP President. Two of the candidates, Jens-Peter Bonde and Monica Frassoni, argued strongly in their campaigns that the next President should promote the cause of a single seat. While the new President, Hans-Gert Pöttering, made no such commitments, his successor as leader of the EPP-ED, Joseph Daul, was prepared to argue that 'the seats of all the institutions need to be talked about'; and to raise the possibility that if 'Strasbourg has the right to a European institution' and 'if it's not going to be the Parliament then something else should go there' (*European Voice* 11 January 2007).

Ultimately, however, the decision on the EP's seat rests with Council and still requires unanimity. One proposal to entice the French government to contemplate change was to hold European Council meetings in Strasbourg as a *quid pro quo* for Parliament sitting exclusively in Brussels. A written declaration tabled in early 2006 by leading members of the Campaign for Parliamentary Reform noted that, whereas the EP interacted daily with the Brussels-based Commission and Council, the European Council did not do so and hence its quarterly meetings need not be held in Brussels. The declaration proceeded to call 'for the sessions of the European Parliament to be held in Brussels and the meetings of the European Council in Strasbourg' (Written Declaration 0033/2006, PE 373.818 2006). On 12 November 2007 the Campaign for Parliamentary Reform sent a letter to the new

French President, Nicolas Sarkozy, asking him to consider such alternative uses for Strasbourg. His response, made at a meeting of the EP's political groups in Strasbourg on 13 November, was emphatic: 'I am a flexible politician but on this question there can be no possibility' (*European Voice* 22 November 2007).

Costs of a multiple seat

The costs of maintaining a triple seat are substantial. In 2006 some €142m was spent on the EP buildings, including €40.56m for rent and lease payments and €73.38m on associated costs such as cleaning and maintenance, energy, security, and insurance (EU Budget 2007: budget item 200). This marked a saving of over €132m from 2005, primarily as a result of the continued policy of Parliament purchasing its own buildings (the Konrad Adenauer building in Luxembourg in 2003, the D4 and D5 buildings in Brussels in 2004 and 2005, and the Louise Weiss, Winston Churchill, Salvador da Madariaga and IPE3 buildings in Strasbourg). In 2005 over €97.87m was expended on property purchases and, in 2006, three buildings in Strasbourg were bought for €143.125m.

In addition to the financial costs of investment in, and maintenance of, two hemicycles, associated office accommodation (with 3971 offices in Brussels and 2360 in Strasbourg), leisure and recreational facilities, and logistical expenses, there are also the time-costs attendant upon communicating and commuting between split sites. The cost of transporting members, staff and documentation between Strasbourg and Brussels for 12 four-day sessions has been estimated at over €200m per year (*Financial Times* 15 May 2006; Eco-Logica 2007:13), while the variable costs of an ordinary four-day session in Strasbourg are about 33 per cent higher than in Brussels. An estimated 13,209 working days are lost by officials and interpreters in travelling between the EP's split sites (*Sunday Times* 22 May 2005). Commuting between Strasbourg and Brussels accounts for 16 per cent of the EP's annual budget. Moreover, with growing environmental concern about carbon emissions, opponents of the EP's split site began to emphasize the additional emissions associated with parliamentary sessions in Strasbourg. A report commissioned by the Greens/European Free Alliance in 2007 quantified the total CO_2 inventory associated with Strasbourg at 18,901 tonnes per annum. This calculation was based on energy consumption in buildings, travel and freight movements, and 'purchasing behaviour and expenditure' related to the 'Strasbourg operation' (Eco-Logica 2007:55).

Not surprisingly, many MEPs fear that the ultimate cost of the split site is a debilitating negative public image of a 'travelling circus' or of 'shuttle democracy'. As Cecilia Malmström (2007) noted:

Everybody, everywhere, no matter how little they know about the European Union and its institutions, they know about the commuting. They have all seen the photographs of the dozens of lorries filled with boxes of paper driving between the two cities. It is a question that has disgraced the European Parliament for a long time, it gives hard working politicians a ridiculous image and it brings huge expenses to the taxpayers. We are the only parliament in the world that has no say over where it sits as this is decided by the member states and written in the Treaties.

Speaking in tongues

On 1 January 2007, with the accession of Bulgaria and Romania, and the recognition of Irish as an official language of the EU, the number of official languages used in Parliament increased to 23. From an initial four languages in 1957 (Dutch, French, German and Italian), each successive enlargement brought more official languages, so that by 1995 the number stood at 11, and, with eastern enlargement in 2004, nine new languages brought the total to 20. Whereas in 1957 there had been 12 possible language combinations, by 2007 there were 506. Moreover, Bulgaria's accession added the Cyrillic alphabet to the Latin and Greek alphabets already in use.

In a continent where language has played such an historic role in helping to define and bolster conceptions of nationhood, it is hardly surprising to find the vigorous maintenance of linguistic identities in an institution constituted of representatives from the many diverse and disparate cultural and linguistic traditions of Europe. Equally unsurprising is the defence of linguistic equality in the EP's rules of procedure and various resolutions adopted by Parliament.

The principles of linguistic sovereignty have held particular resonance in the EP at times of enlargement. In May 1994, for instance, in the face of new elections and the 1995 enlargement, a resolution was adopted which upheld the 'right to use one's own language' in the EP (Resolution 6 May 1994 OJ C 205 1994:529). At the same time the 'strict equality' in the use of all the EU's official languages was reaffirmed; as was the undesirability of implementing language restrictions in an 'institution composed of elected representatives'. The issue of the number of official languages resurfaced later in two reports for Parliament's Bureau. The first was on multilingualism in the EP, and was drafted by Jean-Pierre Cot in 1999. The second, on preparing the EP for enlargement, was submitted to the Bureau in early 2001 by EP Vice-President Guido Podesta. While the Cot report countenanced radical change and the limiting of interpretation to only a single or a restricted range of languages, the Podesta report reaffirmed 'multilinguacy, and especially the principal of equality between languages' in the EP. Podesta's report added that, with enlargement, it would be necessary 'to continue to guarantee that MEPs may speak and hear their own language in all the meetings and that all the documents are translated into these official languages' (quoted in *Agence Europe* 25 January 2001).

The importance of linguistic equality is institutionalized in the EP's 2007 Rules of Procedure. Rule 138.1 holds that 'all documents of the Parliament shall be drawn up in the official languages', and rule 138.2 confirms that 'all Members shall have the right to speak in Parliament in the official language of their choice'. Simultaneous interpretation of speeches in plenary from one official language into all other official languages is also guaranteed in Rule 138.2. Rule 150.6 makes it clear that: 'Amendments shall be put to the vote only after they have been printed and distributed in all the official languages, unless Parliament decides otherwise. Parliament may not decide otherwise if at least forty Members object.' Furthermore, Rule 57.1 requires that before the Parliament's President announces the receipt of the documents containing Council common positions they are translated into the official languages. The need for precision in understanding detailed, technical and complex legislative documents is one powerful reason for maintaining this requirement. In the case of legislation processed under the codecision procedure, for example, a small group of parliamentary lawyer-linguists liaise with their counterparts in the Council to ensure equivalence in the various language versions of legislative texts. Lawyer-linguists are also now included, along with other officials, in Parliament's Tabling Office. This office is charged with 'formal and linguistic verification of all texts tabled to plenary' – in essence to 'quality assure' the texts produced by MEPs and staff, as well as to identify issues of admissibility.

While the principle of linguistic equality remains sacrosanct, the proliferation of official languages has occasioned significant pragmatic accommodations to be made in the daily routines of translation and interpretation. In April 2004 Parliament's Bureau revised its Code of Conduct on Multilingualism, which had been introduced in February 1999. The new Code came into effect on 1 May 2004, the day of EU-10 enlargement, and sought to manage Parliament's language resources in accordance with the principles of 'controlled full multiculturalism' (PE 338.978/BUR 2004:Article 1.1). In essence this entailed more planning and prioritization in the use of resources, but, more radically, the updated code required 'language profiles' to be drawn up for meetings beyond plenary to take account of the 'languages requested and actually used' (PE 338.978/BUR 2004:Article 4.1). New rule 138.2 reflected this change in its statement that 'interpretation shall be provided in committee and delegation meetings from and into the official languages used and requested by members and substitutes of that committee or delegation'. Similarly, an accommodation was made in 2007 for documents dealt with in plenary to be automatically translated into 21 languages, but with only some documents automatically translated into Irish and Maltese.

Difficulties in recruiting interpreters for the nine new languages in 2004, and the three new languages in 2007, led to an extension of the 'exceptional' derogations from Rule 138 which had initially been introduced as a transitional measure following eastern enlargement. In December 2006 Rule 139.1 was amended to allow the transitional period to be extended until the end of the 2004–2009 Parliamentary term. During this period 'derogations from the provisions of Rule 138 shall be permissible if and to the extent that, despite adequate precautions, interpreters or translators for an official language are not available in sufficient numbers'. Ironically, just such derogation was needed in June 2006 when the Culture and Education Committee's meeting to discuss a report on multilingualism had to proceed without a full complement of interpreters (*European Voice* 29 June 2006). Although, by the end of 2006, Parliament had appointed hundreds of linguists, including 252 translators, for the new languages, MEPs from the new member states still had cause for concern about the language difficulties encountered in their daily parliamentary activities. Indeed, the report of the Constitutional Affairs Committee, in making the recommendation for the amendment of Rule 139, noted the 'serious difficulties' in recruiting Latvian, Lithuanian, Slovakian and Slovene interpreters, and coverage of Maltese and Irish was deemed to be 'extremely problematic' (PE 380.576 2006:7).

In these circumstances pragmatic linguistic shortcuts have been devised to ensure efficient translation and interpretation processes. Six 'pivot' or 'relay' languages are used for translation purposes, where the source language (say Hungarian) is translated either into English, or French, German, Italian, Polish or Spanish, and then retranslated from the these languages into another (say Maltese).

Other pragmatic responses to the proliferation of languages in the EP have been the use of external, freelance translators – with 36 per cent of work outsourced in 2005 (with 43 per cent of EU-10 translation outsourced); limitation of the size of documents to be translated; and timetabling restrictions for the submission of texts for consideration in committees and delegations. A text has to be available for translation ten days in advance of any formal parliamentary meeting in which it is to be considered in all languages. Legislative and initiative reports in single or first reading have to tabled 15 working days or three calendar weeks before the plenary at which they are to be considered. Nevertheless, there are still frequent complaints from MEPs of documents only being available in the more widely used languages, or being available only at the very last minute. In a resolution of 7 June 2007 MEPs noted that they were 'highly concerned' by the fact that translations of documents were frequently unavailable in all languages for debates in committees. This often led to debates in committee being postponed because one or more language version of committee papers was not available and MEPs regretted 'a situation which has a negative impact on the committees' proceedings and leads to an inefficient use of available resources' (Texts adopted 7 June 2007, P6_TA(2007)237).

Away from the formal proceedings in the chamber and committee rooms the translation and interpretation conventions within political groups are less rigid. The PSE, for example, with members from 25 states, uses only four languages (English, French, German and Spanish) for most internal documents. Similarly, within the EP's own secretariat, there is a convention of using just French and English. And there is a growing tendency for original texts sent to the Parliament's translation services to be produced in either of these two languages. In fact, French and English now account for two-thirds of original texts sent for translation, with English alone accounting for nearly 50 per cent of texts sent by committees for translation. In contrast, the combined EU-10 languages accounted for less than 20 per cent of pages translated.

Costs

Over a third of parliamentary staff is employed to provide linguistic services. Indeed, the EP is the biggest user of interpreter services of all the EU institutions and, in fact, of all international organizations in the world (European Parliament 2005a:84). In 2005 some 85,340 interpretation days and 1,078,000 pages of translation were undertaken by 350 staff interpreters and 543 staff translators assisted by numerous auxiliary interpreters and translators (over 50 per cent of interpretation and 36 per cent of translation was outsourced). Over €41.7m was spent on interpreters and conference technicians in 2005 (European Parliament 2005a:12, budget item 1870) and an estimated €99m was spent on translation (2003 figures calculated by Court of Auditors 2006:23 (OJ C 284 2006:01); the EP has not traditionally calculated the total cost of translation services).

In addition to the financial costs there are also efficiency costs associated with working in so many different languages. Although Parliament's translation Directorate-General has specific quality control procedures, MEPs remain concerned about the quality of translation of technical and specialist texts. Misunderstandings between members and the tabling of unnecessary amendments are two common results of imprecise translations (see Corbett *et al.* 2007:41). There is an additional problem of translators trying to identify the precise linguistic meaning of often technical amendments across the full range of the EU's legislative competences. Equally, incomprehension and a lack of spontaneity are frequently observed in debates in plenary and committees as a consequence of cultural nuances and inflexions being lost in the literal interpretation of words. The cut and thrust of deliberation, and the value of rhetoric, is certainly lost in simultaneous interpretation of multilingual debate.

Moreover, the whole process of decision-making is affected by the time constraints imposed by the need for interpretation. Fixed working hours for plenary and for committees are agreed between interpreters and Parliament. Any extension of these hours has to be authorized in advance, and occurs only in exceptional circumstances. This impacts upon the scheduling of committee meetings as the capacity to run parallel meetings is influenced by the number of interpreters available at any one time. In practice this limits parallel sessions to a maximum of 12 at any one time. Moreover, given the lower priority afforded to other meetings, such as working groups or committee coordinators' meetings, interpretation is often difficult to arrange, with a resultant impact upon levels of mutual understanding. The restrictions imposed by the practicalities of translation, noted above, have impacted adversely upon the length of committee working documents and explanatory statements attached to committee reports. Significant time lags have become a feature of the work of the EP with considerable time lapses between the transmission of a text and its emergence as a translated document in all languages. In turn, consideration of such texts in committee and plenary is delayed; further delay may be occasioned by the requirement to translate amendments into all languages; and the final version of a committee report has to be tabled at least ten working days before the beginning of the session week at which it is to be considered.

While many of these problems are of long standing they have been exacerbated by the logistical contortions required to accomodate 506 language combinations. Indeed, such problems are destined to increase with further enlargement and with the possible recognition of regional languages (such as Catalan and Basque). If the 'right to use one's own language' is one of the basic principles underpinning Parliament's organization, and serves to guarantee that Parliament remains 'open to the citizens of Europe' (PE 369.878 2006:3), then the associated financial and logistical costs are still, at least in the opinion of Alex Stubb (EPP-ED, Finland), 'a small price to pay for democracy' (*E!sharp* January–February 2007:57).

Formal parliamentary leadership

The organization of legislatures is very different from the organization of bureaucracies. Legislatures organize themselves; they are not organized by outside authorities. Legislatures are organizations of members who are nominally equal to each other, who do not, therefore, stand in the relationship of authority and subordination to each other as do members of hierarchical organizations. (Loewenberg and Patterson 1979:164)

Nevertheless, universally, legislatures have designated leadership roles and, hence, hierarchical organizational structures. What distinguishes legislatures from many other organizations, however, is the fact that elected representatives select their own leaders. The EP is no exception to this general rule. Similarly, the EP is no exception to the rule that parties and parliamentary committees provide the main, invariably parallel, and sometimes competing, foundations of legislative leadership structures. The concentration of power in the reinforcing structures of party groups and of formal committees correspondingly finds reflection in the official leadership positions in the EP.

These positions have at their pinnacle the individual office of President and the collective offices of the 14 Vice-Presidents. Operating in tandem with the Presidency are the collective bodies of the Conference of Presidents, the Bureau, the College of Quaestors, the Conference of Committee Chairmen, and the Conference of Delegation Chairmen. The Conference of Presidents and the Bureau provide direction and supervision of the broad managerial, administrative and financial dimensions of the EP's operations. The Conference of Committee Chairmen and the Conference of Delegation Chairmen have more specific concerns with the organizational dimensions of the EP relating to the processing of substantive legislative and policy outputs.

The Presidency

In a comparative study of presiding officers in democratic assemblies Stanley Bach (1999:210–13) identified five activities in which all such officers are expected to engage. First, there was the ultimate responsibility for the management of the assembly; second, responsibility for the allocation of the assembly's resources among members and party groups; third, organizing the agenda and working schedule; fourth, chairing plenary sessions and interpreting Rules of Procedure; and fifth, controlling debates. Bach also identified a sixth role exercised by many presiding officers and that was to act in a partisan capacity. (It should be noted, however, that in many legislatures the presiding officer is expected to detach himself or herself from overt party activity.) However, in legislatures where the partisan character of the position of presiding officer is openly recognized, then it 'is deemed both natural and proper for the majority party to choose its leader (or one of its leading members) to occupy the primary position of authority in the body it controls' (Bach 1999:212–13).

Choice of President

In the case of the EP, the choice of the President is clearly influenced by party political considerations. Since direct elections in 1979, a convention has emerged whereby the President, along with other parliamentary officers, is chosen every two and half years. Elections for these posts are held in the month after the June EU ballot, and then in the January session two and a half years later. Moreover, since 1989 there had been a tacit agreement between the two largest groups, the PSE and EPP, to alternate the two presidential terms, with the largest group holding the office in the first term and the smaller group holding it in the second. Thus, in 1989, the EPP supported the Socialist Enrique Barón Crespo and in return the PSE did not contest the 1992 mid-term election against the EPP's candidate Egon Klepsch. In the 1994–99 Parliament the split presidency continued with Klaus Hänsch of the PSE serving in the first half and José Maria Gil-Robles serving in the second half of the term. The agreement between the two largest political groups foundered, however, in the wake of the 1999 EP election. The PSE decided to contest the elections for the first time in a decade on the stated grounds that the EPP's rightward ideological trajectory and its internal instability had undermined the tacit understanding between the two groups (*European Voice* 15–21 July 1999). In the event, the EPP-ED worked out a 'constitutive agreement' with the ELDR, part of which was a deal to divide the presidency – with Nicole Fontaine of the EPP occupying the post for the first half of the term and the ELDR leader Pat Cox serving as President in the second half. In 2004 the EPP-ED and the PSE renegotiated their earlier agreement to split the Presidency. As a result Josep Borrell Fontelles (PSE, Spain) served in the first half of the 2004–2009 Parliament, and Hans-Gert Pöttering (EPP-ED, Germany) became President in 2007. However, the renewal of the deal on a split presidency prompted opposition to this arrangement among other political groups. A multi-party 'Fair Chair' campaign was subsequently launched in November 2006 to contest the election of the President. As a result, Pöttering was challenged by Jens-Peter Bonde (co-leader of the ID group) who received 46 votes, Monica Frassoni (Greens/EFA group leader) who secured 145 votes, and Francis Wurtz (GUE/NGL group leader) who obtained 48 votes in January 2007.

  Box 6.1 lists the functions performed by the EP's President. Most of the five activities identified by Bach are evident in this list: management of the assembly; allocation of its resources; organization of the agenda and working schedule; chairing plenary sessions and interpreta-

Box 6.1 *Functions of the President of the EP*

- Responsible for the application of the Rules of Procedure of Parliament, and, to this end, plays a steering role in all the activities of Parliament and its bodies.

- Signs the EU budget into being following Parliament's vote on it at second reading. During the procedure, chairs the EP/Council conciliation delegations.

- May, under the EP/Council codecision procedure, chair the EP/Council conciliation committee. Jointly with the President-in-Office of the Council, signs all legislative acts adopted by codecision.

- Addresses the European Council prior to each of its meetings, stating Parliament's viewpoint on the subjects on the agenda in the framework of a debate with the heads of state and government.

- When an intergovernmental conference is held for the reform of the treaties, takes part in the meetings of the government representatives where these are organized at ministerial level.

- Represents Parliament in its international relations, and, in this connection, undertakes official visits within and outside the EU.

Source: www.europarl.eu.int/president/function/en/default.htm

tion of the Rules of Procedure; and control of debates. Similarly Bach's expectations that presiding officers generally represent the assembly in its formal relations with other government institutions and external bodies finds confirmation in Box 6.1. A cursory glance at the President's list of engagements in any one month would reveal a punishing schedule of symbolic and ceremonial meetings with heads of state and visiting dignitaries; meetings with heads of government and ministers of member states; publicity and promotional opportunities; and visits to states both within and beyond the borders of the EU. One example of the high profile role now played by Parliament's President was the invitation extended to Pöttering to take part in the celebrations to mark the French national day in July 2007, and to attend the reception at the Elysée Palace. Other invitees included the President-in-Office of the Council, Portuguese prime minister Jose Socrates, the Commission President, José Manuel Barroso, and the High Representative for CFSP, Javier Solana. Pöttering was also the first 'foreign' visitor received by Nicolas Sarkozy following his election as French President.

In addition, the EP President plays a significant role in representing the EP in its interinstitutional relations with the Council and Commission as well as in its wider interactions with international agencies, institutions and governments. A fair degree of discretion is often afforded to the President in performing this interinstitutional role.

The Vice-Presidents

The President is assisted by 14 Vice-Presidents who act formally as substitutes for the President in his or her absence. In this capacity they chair plenary sessions, and act as surrogate representatives for the President in the conduct of the EP's external relations. They also participate in the work of the Bureau in their own right (see below). To stand any chance of election, nominees for Vice-President invariably have to have the official backing of the political groups. The rank ordering of the allocation of responsibilities among the Vice-Presidents is also primarily determined by the political groups. In 2007 four of the five highest-ranked portfolios were held by members of the EPP-ED – Rodi Kratsa-Tsagaropoulou (Greece), Alejo Vidal-Quadras (Spain), Edward McMillan-Scott (UK), and Mario Mauro (Italy) – but with Gérard Onesta (Greens/EFA, France) holding the second ranked position. Miguel Angel Martínez Martínez (PSE, Spain), the sixth-highest-ranked Vice-President, held the highest of four PSE positions.

Each Vice-President concentrates upon specific duties. In addition, three Vice-Presidents are appointed to serve as permanent members of the Conciliation Committee with the Council (see below), and two serve as leaders of the EP's representatives on the Conference of European Affairs Committees (COSAC) (see Chapter 9).

Quaestors

After the election of the Vice-Presidents, MEPs are balloted upon the election of six 'Quaestors'. The number of Quaestors was increased from five to six in 2007, and as with the Vice-Presidents, nomination for election as Quaestor is usually made by the political groups; though MEPs have occasionally overturned the preferences of party group leaders by electing 'non-official candidates', such as Richard Balfe in the 1999–2004 Parliament and Astrid Lulling (EPP-ED) in the 2004–2009 Parliament. Lulling displaced the 'official' Liberal candidate in 2004 and retained her position again in 2007 to serve alongside James Nicholson (EPP-ED), Mia De Vits (PSE), Ingo Friedrich (EPP-ED), Szabolcs Fazakas (PSE), and Jan Mulder (ALDE).

The Quaestors are responsible for administrative and financial matters of direct concern to the performance of the role of the individual MEP and act in accordance with guidelines laid down by the Bureau (European Parliament 2007a:Rule 25). The responsibilities of Quaestors cover the allocation of offices, provision of equipment, employment conditions of MEPs' assistants, security arrangements, official cars and financial questions on expenses and fees. Such matters often excite strong passions among MEPs, and, as a consequence,

---

Box 6.2   *Main duties of the Bureau (Rule 22)*

- Takes financial, organizational and administrative decisions on matters concerning members and the internal organization of Parliament, its Secretariat and its bodies.
- Takes decisions on matters relating to the conduct of sittings.
- Decides the establishment plan of the Secretariat and lays down regulations relating to the administrative and financial situation of officials and other servants.
- Adopts provisions concerning non-attached members
- Draws up Parliament's preliminary draft estimates.
- Adopts the guidelines for the Quaestors.
- Is the authority responsible for authorizing meetings of committees away from the usual places of work, hearings and study and fact-finding journeys by rapporteurs.
- Lays down the implementing rules and implements the procedures as specified in the 2004 party statute.
- Appoints the Secretary-General.

Source: European Parliament (2007a).

---

meetings of the Quaestors 'are robust affairs' (Corbett *et al.* 2007:124). In addition, Quaestors serve in a consultative capacity in the Parliament's Bureau.

The Bureau

The Bureau is the regulatory body that is responsible for Parliament's budget and for administrative, organizational and staff matters. Its membership consists of the President and Vice-Presidents along with the Quaestors (who sit in on its meetings in a non-voting capacity). Members are elected for a term of two and a half years. The main duties of the Bureau are listed in Box 6.2, but it also considers organizationally sensitive issues on an ad-hoc basis as in, for example, establishing a working group in 2006 to consider a 'Charter of Members Assistants'. In practice, however, the Bureau operates in the 'political shadow' of the Conference of Presidents (Westlake 1994a:195).

Conference of Presidents

The Conference of Presidents is one of the organizational powerhouses in the EP with responsibility for the broad political direction of

Box 6.3   *Main duties of the Conference of Presidents (Rule 24)*

- Takes decisions on the organization of Parliament's work and matters relating to legislative planning.
- Is responsible for matters relating to relations with the other institutions and bodies of the European Union and with the national parliaments of member states.
- Is responsible for matters relating to relations with non-member countries and with non-Union institutions and organizations.
- Draws up the draft agenda of Parliament's part-sessions.
- Is responsible for the composition and competence of committees, committees of inquiry and joint parliamentary committees, standing delegations and ad-hoc delegations.
- Decides how seats in the Chamber are to be allocated.
- Is responsible for authorizing the drawing up of own-initiative reports.
- Submits proposals to the Bureau concerning administrative and budgetary matters relating to the political groups.

Source: European Parliament (2007a).

Parliament (see Box 6.3). It meets regularly, at least twice a month, and consists of the President of Parliament and the chairs of the political groups (including, after November 2007, one delegate from the non-attached Members who does not have the right to vote). The Chair of the Conference of Committee Chairs also attends on a non-voting basis (see below).

Conference meetings are held behind closed doors in order to facilitate consensual agreements (Rule 23(3)). When a consensus cannot be reached, however, votes are taken and weighted in accordance with the number of members in each political group.

The prime purpose of the Conference is to 'cut deals between the Groups regarding Parliament's business' (Corbett *et al.* 2007:124). Given the preeminence of the EPP-ED and the PSE, the duopoly of power noted in Chapter 5 finds institutional expression in the meetings of the Conference of Presidents. Smaller groups can easily be outvoted and so have an incentive to find consensual outcomes. The political and partisan sensitivity of agreements worked out in Conference is reflected in the fact that minutes of its meetings are carefully checked and approved by its members before dissemination to all MEPs. This both reinforces the perception of consensual outcomes and also minimizes the political fall-out likely to result from divergent interpretations of conference deliberations.

Conference of Committee Chairs and Conference of Delegation Chairs

A monthly meeting brings the chairs of parliamentary committees together to discuss organizational matters common to all committees and to help formulate draft plenary agendas (Rule 26). Because the committee chairs are significant politicians in their own right, drawing their authority from their formal parliamentary status but also buttressed by their position within a political group, they are a powerful force within the EP. With 'their collective finger on the Parliament's legislative pulse' (Westlake 1994a:194) the chairs play a considerable role in ensuring the stability of the EP's legislative biorhythms by settling demarcation disputes between committees, resolving common difficulties and monitoring progress of legislation through the committee cycle. The Conference elects its own chair, who, in turn, attends the Conference of Committee Presidents as the committee chairs' representative.

The EP has an extensive system of delegations which link Parliament with other parliamentary institutions and countries outside the EU. In 2007 there were 35 delegations. These were grouped into interparliamentary delegations, joint parliamentary committees, and parliamentary cooperation committees. Interparliamentary delegations are created to facilitate contacts with the parliaments in non-EU countries. Joint parliamentary committees (JPCs) bring together representatives of the EP with members of parliaments in accession countries or in states that have association agreements with the EU. In 2007 there were three 'Europe' JPCs (one each for Croatia, Macedonia and Turkey) and two 'non-Europe' JPCs (with Chile and Mexico arising out of specific EU agreements). Six Parliamentary Cooperation Committees also operated in 2007 as part of partnership and cooperation agreements signed between the EU and states of the former Soviet Union.

In addition the EP is represented in three other joint parliamentary assemblies. The Parliamentary Assembly of the African, Caribbean and Pacific regions and the EU (ACP-EU) brings together 77 MEPs and 77 representatives of parliaments from African, Caribbean and Pacific countries. The 'Euromed' Parliamentary Assembly had its initial meeting in March 2004 and brings together representatives from the EP (45 MEPs), national parliaments of EU member states (75 MPs) and 120 representatives from non-EU Mediterranean parliaments. In November 2006 the EP-Latin American Parliamentary Assembly was inaugurated.

Although delegations tend to operate relatively informally, their proliferation has led to a tightening of the rules under which they operate in the EP. Each delegation has its own chair and two vice-chairs who are elected by the plenary along with committee chairs (see below) on the basis of nominations made by the political groups to the Conference of Presidents. Their activities are coordinated in the Conference of Delegation Chairs, which meets once a month to discuss common organizational and scheduling issues. This Conference, in consultation with the Foreign Affairs and Development Committees, drafts a calendar of future interparliamentary meetings and draws up implementing provisions for the operation of delegations.

Secretariat

Parliament's work is organized by a Secretariat, headed by a Secretary-General, with a staff of just over 5000 in 2007 grouped in eight Directorates-General. Of these officials, as noted above, up to a third are employed in the linguistic services. A further 800 or so are temporary staff employed, and recruited directly, by the political groups (see Chapter 5). The permanent officials of the EP are thus relatively few in number and are recruited directly by external open competitions. Upon appointment they become European civil servants who are subject to the Staff Regulations of Officials of the European Communities, and a vital part of their employment conditions is their independence.

While the Staff Regulations do not allow for posts to be reserved for nationals of any specific member state, there is an attempt, especially at the highest grades, to ensure a spread among nationalities. Party affiliation, however, is not precluded and leading officials may have clear party pedigrees. Indeed, at the most senior levels this is now almost a prerequiste. In 2007, a Danish national, Harald Rømer, became Secretary-General upon Julian Priestley's retirement. Rømer was only the sixth incumbent since 1958. Rømer had at one stage or another been the Secretary General of the old ED group, Deputy Secretary General of the EPP, and *chef de cabinet* of EP President Nicole Fontaine in 1999. Rømer's predecessor, Julian Priestley, before becoming Secretary-General in 1997, had at one stage in his career run the Secretariat of the PSE group and then been *chef de cabinet* to Parliament's President, Klaus Hänsch. David Harley, a former Secretary General of the PSE group, became Deputy Secretary-General in 2007. Similarly, Klaus Welle, *chef de cabinet* to President Hans-Gert Pöttering, was a former Secretary General of the EPP-ED group, and is a potential candidate to replace Rømer in due course as Parliament's Secretary General.

Despite 'carrying out their duties in a politically neutral way' (Corbett *et al.* 2007:193), the permanent officials of the EP historically have been proactive in the creative exploitation of Parliament's formal powers and informal procedures. In the past, such 'activist' officials sought appointments particularly in the legal service and to the secretariats of the most prestigious and influential parliamentary committees (see below). Yet, with the expansion of Parliament's powers, successive increases in its size, and widening geographical and ideological diversity of its members, the integrationist zeal of officials has been moderated in recent years, and there is every prospect that the secretariat will be obliged to 'assume a more technical role than it has done in the past' (Corbett *et al.* 2007:201).

Formal organization: committees

Committee structure

From the outset the EP operated primarily through a committee system. Despite its advisory remit and its remarkably limited legislative functions, nonetheless the Common Assembly of the ECSC established seven standing committees in its first year of existence. The number of parliamentary committees increased to 13 after the establishment of the EEC and Euratom in 1958, and increased again to 16 after direct elections in 1979. Thereafter, the number increased gradually to 20 before a review of the committee structure in 1999 reduced the number to 17. The number was reinstated at 20 after a further review in 2004.

At the start of the twenty-first century, the EP's specialized committees are at the heart of its legislative, and non-legislative, work. Chapters 7 and 8 examine in detail both how the committees operate and their contribution to the decision-making processes; here, however, we will concentrate upon the organization of the committees themselves.

2004 review of committees

In increasing the number of committees to 20 in 2004 several of the changes effected in the preceding review of 1999 were reversed. The review in 1999, immediately before the June election, had heralded the first systematic reorganization of the committee structure since direct elections in 1979. (An earlier, far less systematic and unsuccessful attempt to rationalize the committee structure had been proposed in the 1989–94 Parliament by the then PSE Group leader Jean-Pierre Cot.) The 1999 review was prompted, in part, by the incremental increase in the numbers of committees over the years (from 16 in 1979 to 20 in 1999); in part also by the changed legislative priorities of the EP resulting from the Amsterdam Treaty; and, in part too, to redress some of the imbalances in workload that had arisen from the initial functional allocation of committee responsibilities. Although radical proposals were made to reduce the number of committees to between

12 and 14, in the event, the rationalization of the committee structure was only partly fulfilled in the 1999–2004 Parliament. Even so, deep tensions emerged over the existence of certain committees and the respective remits of each committee. Thus, for example, one of the most controversial aspects of the 1999 review was the transfer of responsibility for the legal protection of consumers to the Legal Affairs Committee from the Environment Committee (though the latter retained responsibility for the broader aspects of consumer policy).

The 2004 review reflected, in turn, changed priorities, both organizationally within the EP and more broadly within the hierarchy of EU policies. Ultimately, however, the major precipitant of reform was the increased number of MEPs after enlargement who had to be accommodated within the committee structure. If anything, it was easier to reallocate responsibilities in 2004 – within the context of increased numbers of committees – than it had been in 1999 when the number of committees was reduced. Nonetheless, there were still significant 'turf wars'. Thus, for example, the Environment Committee, which had retained responsibility for most aspects of consumer protection in 1999, lost this responsibility to a new Internal Market and Consumer Affairs Committee in 2004. Correspondingly, the Legal Affairs Committee lost its responsibilities for general internal market measures to the new Internal Market Committee. Other changes included the creation of a new International Trade Committee, which assumed the former external trade responsibilities of the Industry Committee; and the division of the Regional and Transport Committee into two separate committees – Transport and Tourism, and Regional Development. Significantly, the Fisheries and Women's Rights Committees were both retained despite persistent questioning of their respective roles. The Fisheries Committee had resisted merger with the Agriculture Committee in 1999 and the Women's Rights Committee, while promoting the mainstreaming of women's issues in the work of other committees, opposed the formal organizational integration of its own membership into other committees.

The extent of variation in committee workload can be seen in Table 6.2. Despite the 2004 reorganization, there remains a marked imbalance in the workloads of the various committees with six of the 20 accounting for half of all adopted reports. Table 6.2 lists the number of reports produced by each committee between July 2004 and July 2007. There are two main broad categories of reports: legislative and non-legislative.

The legislative category can be broken down further in accordance with the legislative procedure in operation – consultation, cooperation, codecision or assent (see Chapter 7 for details). Within these legislative categories the number of codecision reports was heavily skewed towards three committees, with the Environment, Transport, and Legal

Table 6.1 *Parliamentary committees and chairs, 2007*

Committee	Chair	Full members
Agriculture and Rural Affairs	Neil Parish (EPP-ED, United Kingdom)	47
Budgetary Control	Herbert Bösch (PSE, Austria)	38
Budgets	Reimer Böge (EPP-ED, Germany)	50
Civil Liberties, Justice and Home Affairs	Jean-Marie Cavada (ALDE, France)	60
Constitutional Affairs	Jo Leinen (PSE, Germany)	29
Culture and Education	Nikolaos Sifunakis (PSE, Greece)	38
Development	Josep Borrell Fontelles (PSE, Spain)	35
Economic and Monetary Affairs	Pervenche Berès (PSE, France)	51
Employment and Social Affairs	Jan Andersson (PSE, Sweden)	52
Environment, Public Health and Food Safety	Miroslav Ouzký (EPP-ED, Czech Republic)	68
Fisheries	Philippe Morillon (ALDE, France)	38
Foreign Affairs	Jacek Saryusz-Wolski (EPP-ED, Poland)	84
Industry, Research and Energy	Angelika Niebler (EPP-ED, Germany)	54
Internal Market and Consumer Protection	Arlene McCarthy (PSE, United Kingdom)	43
International Trade	Helmuth Markov (GUE/NGL, Germany)	33
Legal Affairs	Giuseppe Gargani (EPP-ED, Italy)	28
Petitions	Marcin Libicki (UEN, Poland)	38
Regional Development	Gerardo Galeote (EPP-ED, Spain)	57
Transport and Tourism	Paolo Costa (ALDE, Italy)	51
Women's Rights and Gender Equality	Anna Záborská (EPP-ED, Slovakia)	40

Table 6.2 European Parliament committee reports, July 2004 to July 2007

Committee	Consultation	Codecision (reports in 1st reading)	Codecision (recommendations in 2nd or 3rd reading)	Assent	Budgetary procedure	Discharge procedure	Own-initiative+	Rules of Procedure	Immunity	Inter-institutional agreement	TOTAL
Agriculture	53	1					10				64
Budgetary Control	14	2		1		56	8				81
Budgets	11	2	1		44		3			9	70
Civil Liberties, Justice and Home Affairs	77	24	3	1			25				130
Constitutional Affairs	4						7	9		4	24
Culture and Education	4	13	9				14				40
Development	1	5	1	2			25				34
Economic and Monetary Affairs	29	20	1				35				87*
Employment and Social Affairs	6	13	4				21				44
Environment, Public Health and Food Safety	11	47	23				19				100
Fisheries	53	1	1	1			11				67
Foreign Affairs	14	3		14			44				75
Industry, Research and Energy	21	12	5	1			21				60
Internal Market and Consumer Protection		13	9				9				31
International Trade	11	1		12			14				38
Legal Affairs	32	46	3	1			13	2	26		123
Petitions							10				10
Regional Development	2	5	1	6			14				28
Transport and Tourism	23	31	18				14				86
Women's Rights and Gender Equality		4	3				19				24
TOTAL	366	243	82	39	44	56	336	11	26	13	1216

Source: Calculated from http://www.europarl.eu.int/committees/home_en.htm

* 2 cooperation procedures
+ Including Green Papers, Strategy Documents, and Commission reports.

Affairs committees accounting for around 52 per cent of all codecision reports. The addition of the legislative activities of the Economic, Industry, Internal Market, and Civil Liberties committees leads to a total of 79 per cent of codecision reports being produced by just seven committees. The second 'non-legislative' category includes 'own-initiative' reports, reports on Commission communications, green papers and strategy documents, as well as those relating to budgetary procedures and interinstitutional agreements. As can be seen from Table 6.2, there is a rough correlation between a high legislative workload and the production of relatively few own-initiative reports – and vice versa.

Membership

The 2004 review of the committee structure was implemented in the July session of the new Parliament. This conformed to established practice where the number of committees, the size of their memberships and the allocation of responsibilities are decided at the first July session of a newly elected parliament. Individual committee assignments are then allocated in accordance with Rule 177 (European Parliament 2007a):

> Members of committees and committees of inquiry shall be elected after nominations have been submitted by the political groups and the Non-attached Members. The Conference of Presidents shall submit proposals to Parliament. The composition of the committees shall, as far as possible, reflect the composition of Parliament.

As is the case in other legislatures, there is intense competition to serve on some committees and less competition to serve on others (see Neuhold 2001:4; McElroy 2002:10). In the first three parliaments, the Foreign Affairs Committee (despite limited formal powers) and the Budgets Committee (with more extensive formal powers) were particularly regarded as high-status committees, and competition for seats on these committees was intense. More recently, in the 1999–2004 and 2004–2009 Parliaments, membership of the most proactive legislative committees, such as Environment and Economic and Monetary Affairs (ECON), has been heavily contested.

Most MEPs serve as a full member of one committee and as a substitute on another. Substitute members normally have full speaking and voting rights (if acting as a replacement for an absent full member). They may also serve as rapporteurs and draftsmen (especially if they have acknowledged expertise in the policy area under consideration). Some committees are deemed to be 'neutralized committees' which, because of their procedural focus, for example Petitions, or specialist concern, for example Budgetary Control, would be unlikely to attract sufficient members to serve on them if MEPs were limited to full service on only one committee. The pay-off for membership of a 'neutralized committee' is that it does not prejudice an MEP's chances of becoming a full member of another committee.

Ultimately, as with most other legislatures, the choice of committee is not an unrestricted preference of the individual representative. Instead, committee assignments are determined by political groups in rough proportion to their respective numerical strengths in plenary. Groups also endeavour to maintain a proportionate national balance within their representation on committees. As a result, there is a close correspondence between the membership of committees and the overall party group composition of the chamber. There is no doubt, therefore, that there is 'a strong tendency to consider both partisan and national proportionality issues when committee seats are assigned' (McElroy 2006:12). In addition, an informal, if weak, seniority principle operates in the larger groups where longer-serving MEPs may press prior claims over newly elected MEPs to appointment on the most prestigious and oversubscribed committees. Certainly, previous tenure on a committee is significantly correlated with chances of reselection for that committee (McElroy 2006:17).

Within the broad parameters set by party groups, individual representatives seek appointment to specific committees. The mix of individual career preferences and personal goals plays a decisive part in the choice of committee assignments (Corbett *et al.* 2007:128–9). The most powerful incentives prompting service on particular committees have been found to derive from personal interest in a policy area and/or prior occupational experience. Successive studies have revealed clear evidence of the importance in the assignment process of the occupational and interest group attachments of committee members (see Bowler and Farrell 1995:231–4; Mamadouh and Raunio 2000:8; McElroy 2006:17–18). In combination the criteria deployed by party groups and individual group members in the allocation of committee assignments allow for the development of 'a process of coordinated – even controlled – specialization' (Bowler and Farrell 1995:241; see also McElroy 2006:17). This echoes the earlier contention of Judge (1981:38–40, 46–8) that the practices of 'party representation' and shared party values may facilitate a division of labour among members of the same party group in a legislature.

Committee bureau

Once committee members have been selected, each committee then elects its own officeholders of a chair and four vice-chairs, known collectively as the committee's 'bureau'. The bureau and especially the chair play a powerful role both internally within the committee, and in the committee's external relations in the EP itself and in its dealings with other EU institutions and national governments and interests beyond the EP. As is the case with other formal officeholders in the EP, committee chairs hold office for half-parliamentary terms and are thus subject to reelection midway through a parliament. In practice, this has resulted in a considerable turnover of committee chairs for most committees. During the lifetime of the 2004–2009 Parliament, for example, 11 of the 20 committees changed their chair.

Although formally 'elected', in practice committee chairs and vice-chairs are chosen on the basis of negotiation among political groups. Groups choose which committees to chair in accordance with the proportional d'Hondt system – whereby the order of allocation is determined by alternation between the political groups according to size. Thus, after the 2004 election, the EPP-ED, as the largest group, could claim the first, third, fifth, seventh, ninth, 12th, 17th, 19th and 21st choices. The PSE, as the second-largest group, gained the second, fourth, eighth, tenth, 16th, 20th and 23rd choices. The ALDE had the sixth, 13th and 22nd choices, the Greens had the 11th, and the GUE/NGL had the 15th choice. Independence and Democracy had the 18th choice and UEN had the 24th choice.

In making its choices for chairs in 2004 the EPP-ED ranked the Foreign Affairs Committee as its first choice. Although having no legislative powers, this Committee had a high political profile. In 1999 the Foreign Affairs Committee had been ranked as the EPP-ED's second choice, and Elmar Brok had become chair. By 2004 Brok, as one of Parliament's leading German Christian Democrats, was the obvious candidate within the EPP-ED to retain his chairmanship. Indeed, he was one of only two committee chairs to retain his position after the 2004 election; the other was Giuseppe Gargani (EPP-ED, Italy) on the Legal Affairs Committee.

Within the EPP-ED, given the decreased numbers of UK Conservative MEPs after the 2004 elections, the German contingent had a claim to two of the group's key chairs, rather than the one occupied by Brok in 1999. Offsetting its first choice of the Foreign Affairs Committee (as an important but essentially non-legislative committee) the EPP-ED selected as its second choice the Committee on Environment, Public Health and Food Safety (as a highly influential and highly active legislative committee) and nominated Karl-Heinz Florenz (EPP-ED, Germany) as its chair. The EPP-ED also secured the committee chairs of Budgets (Janus Lewandowski, Poland), Industry (Giles Chichester, UK), and Agriculture (Joseph Daul, France). Lewandowski was one of only three MEPs from new member states to gain a committee chair. The chairs of the Regional Affairs, Legal Affairs and Women's Rights Committees were also occupied by EPP-ED members after 2004.

The PSE, in making its seven choices in 2004, opted for a rank-order of Economic and Monetary Affairs (chaired by Pervenche Berès, France), International Trade (Enrique Barón Crespo, Spain), Employment (Ottaviano Del Turco, PSE, Italy), Internal Market (Philip Whitehead, PSE, UK), Culture (Nikolaos Sifunakis, Greece), Constitutional Affairs (Jo Leinen, Germany), and Budgetary Control (Szabolcs Fazakas (Hungary). The ALDE chose the chair of the Civil Liberties Committee (Jean-Louis Bourlanges, France), the Greens gained the chair of the sub-committee on human rights (Hélène Flautre, France), and the GUE/NGL chose the chair of the Development Committee (Luisa Morgantini, Italy).

At mid-term, in January 2007, eight committees elected new chairs including leading committees such as Foreign Affairs, Budgets, Environment, Industry, Agriculture, and Development and International Trade. A key factor in the mid-term reshuffle was the claim of MEPs from the new member states that they should occupy significant parliamentary positions. As early as July 2004 some newly elected members had expressed their disappointment at the limited number of committee chairs and other parliamentary positions on offer to MEPs from the EU-10 states. The former prime minister of Slovenia, Alojs Peterle, had noted at the time that 'better representation in these posts from the new member states . . . would have sent out a signal to citizens in these countries that the Parliament takes enlargement of the Union seriously' (quoted in *European Voice* 22 July 2004). In January 2007 the vociferous demands for chairmanships for members from new member states, and the lack of agreement between – and within – the political groups, led to a delay of several weeks before agreement was reached on the allocation of committee chairs.

Most controversy occurred within the EPP-ED group and especially between its German and Polish members. The elevation of Hans-Gert Pöttering to the Presidency of Parliament incurred contingent costs under the d'Hondt system for the German group in the EPP-ED. This enabled the Polish EPP-ED members to displace German Elmar Brok as chair of the Foreign Affairs Committee and secure the former Polish foreign affairs minister, Jacek Saryusz-Wolski, as his replacement. (At one stage the German Chancellor, Angela Merkel, became involved in mediating between Brussels and Warsaw over this issue.) Karl-Heinz Florenz, similarly, lost the chair of the Environment Committee to Czech Miroslav Ouzký. The knock-on effect was that German EPP-ED member Angelika Niebler displaced Giles Chichester as the chair of the Industry Committee, while Neil Parish (Conservative, UK) gained the lower-priority chair of the Agriculture Committee.

On the socialist side, confusion rather than controversy reigned in January 2007. In particular, Spanish PSE members generated considerable uncertainty. Initially, it was unclear whether they preferred the Development Committee, for former Parliament President Josep

Borrell, or the Trade Committee, which had been chaired until 2007 by the Spanish Socialist Barón Crespo. Eventually, Borrell became chair of the Development Committee; and GUE member Helmut Markov took over as chair of the International Trade Committee.

Once the chairs have been selected a similar process of proportionate interparty distribution of vice-chairs then takes place. Thus, for instance, in the case of the EPP-ED's first-choice committee in 2004, Foreign Affairs, Toomas Ilves of the PSE gained the first vice-chair, Geoffrey van Orden of the EPP-ED was appointed second vice-chair, and the Baroness Nicolson of Winterbourne of ALDE became the third vice-chair. At mid-term in 2007, these three were replaced by four new vice-chairs (Libor Rouček, PSE, Czech Republic;: Michael Gahler, EPP-ED, Germany; Janusz Onyszkiewicz, ALDE, Poland; and Ioan Pascu, PSE, Romania).

Final decisions on committee office-holders are taken at the first plenary session following the European election and any revisions, contingent upon the wider choice of presidency and bureau, are made by the political groups at that time. The grip of political group control is just as apparent at the mid-term review of committee leadership positions. Political groups have been prone to reallocating committee bureau positions at mid-term to reflect the internal political balance among their own members. One consequence of this propensity of political groups to rotate committee leadership positions is the under-mining of specialization, reputation for expertise and a 'collective memory' of procedural and institutional affairs at the top of the committee structure. The one clear exception remains Ken Collins (PSE, UK) who served as chair of the Environment Committee for 15 out of the 20 years he served as an MEP. Only Willy de Clercq, as the chair of the External Economic Relations Committee from 1989 to 1997, and Diemut Theato, as chair of the Budgetary Control Committee from 1994 to 2004, came anywhere close to Collins for accumulated service as chair of a single committee. In contrast, other important committees have changed their committee chairs with remarkable regularity. The Legal Affairs Committee had 12 chairs in the period 1979–2007, while the Employment and Social Affairs Committee had 13 and Foreign Affairs had 11 chairs in the same period.

Only very rarely is a nomination made by one group challenged by another group. On such occasions it is usually backbench members of the relevant committee who are responsible for the challenge. One example was provided, however, in July 2004 when Socialist members of the Women's Rights Committee opposed the nomination of Anna Záborská (EPP-ED, Slovakia) as chair. Záborská was an open opponent of abortion and gay rights and had not supported anti-discrimination legislation in Slovakia. Given this track record, British Socialist member Mary Honeyball referred to Záborská's nomination as a 'very

provocative choice by the EPP which put [Socialist members] in a difficult position' (quoted in *European Voice* 29 July 2004). Predictably,
therefore, Záborská's election met with opposition from non-EPP-ED
members during the constituent meeting of the Women's Rights
Committee in July 2004. Equally predictably perhaps, this led EPP-ED
members to challenge the election of Pervenche Berès (PSE, France) to
the chair of the Economic and Monetary Affairs Committee – an election scheduled for the following day after the vote of the Women's
Rights Committee. Eventually, Záborská was elected after Socialist
members did not take part in the ballot for the chair of the Women's
Committee, thus allowing Záborská to be elected with 15 votes in
favour, four against and three abstentions. In turn this allowed Berès
to take up the chair of ECON – as originally agreed as part of the deal
made by party group leaders.

Group coordinators

Political group coordinators play an important role in coordinating the
activities of group MEPs in and across committees. Together with the
committee's bureau, group coordinators arrange a committee's agenda,
and facilitate the working of the committee by discussing forthcoming
votes, the tabling of amendments and broader political problems before
they surface in the full meeting of the committee. In particular, coordinators negotiate the distribution of rapporteurships among the groups
represented on the committee. In turn, it is then the responsibility of the
group coordinator to allocate a specific report within his or her own
group. The group coordinator also decides which substitute member
may vote in the absence of a full committee member from the group.
Generally the coordinator is responsible for orchestrating the activities
of group members on a committee and for performing many of the
functions associated with 'party whips' in other legislatures: convening
pre-meetings to formulate the group's position on forthcoming votes in
the full committee, working out a schedule of speakers, ensuring attendance at key votes, and communicating information on the progress and
outcomes of committee deliberations to the wider group. The performance of all of these tasks, however, is complicated by the internal segmentation of groups along national as well as ideological lines.

Allocations of rapporteurships are based loosely on the principle of
proportionality. Within each committee the allocation between groups
is based usually on an informal 'points' system. Each group receives a
quota of points in proportion to its numerical strength in the committee. (In the Budgets Committee, however, the points quota is determined in accordance with the number of group MEPs in Parliament as
a whole.) Corbett *et al.* (2007:140) provide a concise summary of the
normal procedure:

Reports and opinions to be distributed are ... discussed by the committee coordinators who decide the number of points each subject is worth, and then make bids on behalf of the Group, the strength of their claim being based in theory (but not always in practice) on the relationship between the number of points already used by the Group and their original quota. A controversial issue may be the subject of competing bids.

But the precise bidding system varies among committees, not least because the process is entirely informal. In the Environment Committee, for example, the point value of a report depends on the number of groups willing to bid. If four groups express an interest then the point value is four, and if two groups make a bid the value is two points. Less contentious reports normally have a value of two or three points, with opinions having a value of one point. The 'neutralized committees' mentioned above rarely use a points system, while others, such as the Research, Technological Development and Energy Committee in the 1994–99 Parliament, operated a strict hierarchical points system for different types of report, with the committee secretariat deciding the value (for details see Mamadouh and Raunio 2000:14–15). Some reports, which no group particularly wants, may have a zero points value. Yet another model is provided by the Legal Affairs Committee, where codecision proposals 'cost' two points, reports on Commission Green and White Papers one point, and opinions for other committees half a point. The Legal Affairs Committee before 2004 also adapted the system further – with a group 'paying again' to retain the report at second reading. In theory, therefore, the rapporteurship could thus change between readings. Normally, however, rapporteurships remain with the same group (if not necessarily with the same person) at second reading (according to Rule 59).

Overall, the allocation system works effectively with very few formal votes taken in committees to decide rapporteurships. As Ken Collins, former chairman of the Environment Committee, noted in interview, the selection of rapporteurs is 'a combination of a kind of auction and a kind of elaborate game of poker' (Wurzel 1999:12). In this game coordinators play side-games whereby a particular political group's bid for a particular report may secure support (or acquiescence) from other coordinators because of their implicit approval of the bidding group's potential nominee as rapporteur. Equally, there is the counter proposition, that a coordinator may allow a particular report (sought by a less able member of the same group) to be allocated to another group to ensure that the committee ultimately receives a well-drafted report. When the chips are down in this game of poker, however, the biggest groups hold the biggest stakes and operate an effective duopoly in the allocation of the most politically controversial and prestigious reports.

Once a group secures a particular report it is then allocated to a specific member of the group. At this point considerations of nationality and expertise, sometimes as conflicting principles, come into play. A detailed study of the distribution of reports and rapporteurships in committees found that, on the one side, 'the size of national delegation predicts rather well its share of reports' (Mamadouh and Raunio 2000:25). Equally, on the other side, it was also confirmed that 'within committees certain MEPs are recognised as experts on specific issues, and that these representatives are assigned as rapporteurs on these topics' (Mamadouh and Raunio 2000:30). Particularly among group coordinators and members who have served on the same committee for many years, nationality is often discounted and is ranked well below other selection factors such as specialization within the committee, negotiation skills, and respect among other political groups. Obviously, overall, some balance will be maintained among group members of different nationalities – but this is seldom explicit. Similarly, where a particular issue has a specific national dimension it can work against – as well as in favour of – members of that nationality becoming rapporteurs.

Because of the growing importance of the EP in the EU's legislative process, and the significance of committees within the EP itself, increased academic attention has come to be focused upon the selection of rapporteurs (see for example Mamadouh and Raunio 2003; Kaeding 2004, 2005; Benedetto 2005; Hausemer 2006; Hoyland 2006). Despite the deployment of sophisticated quantitative techniques the findings tend to underline the basic observations noted above: there is a rough proportionally in the allocation of rapporteurships among political groups; within this overall proportionality groups contest the allocation of reports through consensual bidding processes; but there is disproportionality *within* political groups which reflects the different emphases placed upon expertise and nationality in the choice of individual reports (see Mamadouh and Raunio 2003:343–8; Benedetto 2005:85–6; see also Kaeding 2004:367, 2005:97–99 who emphasizes the disproportional distribution of rapporteurships within party groups and national delegations). Exactly how rapporteurs once appointed fulfil their roles, and how reports are dealt with, will be examined in detail in Chapter 8.

Temporary committees/Committees of Inquiry

Under Rule 175, 'Parliament may at any time set up temporary committees, whose powers, composition and term of office shall be defined at the same time as the decision to set them up is taken; their term of office may not exceed twelve months, except where Parliament extends that term on its expiry' (European Parliament 2007a). There are two basic types of temporary committee. First, there are committees formed in accordance with Rule 175 and whose powers and mode of operation are determined exclusively by Parliament. Between 1979 and 2004 15 such committees were established. These dealt with such matters as: European economic recovery (1983), budgetary resources (1984), 'making a success of the Single Act' (1987), Community legislation necessary to permit German unification (1990), the 'Delors II' package (1992), employment (1994/5), monitoring action taken subsequent to the report of the BSE Committee of Inquiry (1997), assessment of the implications of a communications interception system known as ECHELON (2000), examination of developments in the field of human genetics and other new medicine technologies (2001), and the management of, and the impact of, the foot-and-mouth crisis (2002). In 2004 a temporary committee, of 50 MEPs chaired by the then President Josep Borrell, was established to consider the policy challenges and budgetary means of the enlarged Union 2007–2013. Its remit was 'to define the European Parliament's political priorities for the future financial perspective both in legislative and budgetary terms' and its report was adopted in June 2005 (OJ C 124E, 25 May 2006:373). The following year saw the creation of a temporary committee to investigate the alleged use of European countries by the CIA for the transportation and illegal detention of prisoners. The committee's report was accepted at the February 2007 plenary in the full glare of international media attention (OJ C 124E, 29 November 2007:309). Similarly, the decision in April 2007 to establish a temporary committee on climate change attracted widespread press interest. Karl-Heinz Florenz, the recently deposed chair of the Environment Committee, was appointed rapporteur. In presenting the committee's work programme he made it clear that the committee would not confine itself to a single report given the cross-cutting nature of climate change. It was intended to progress the committee's enquiries through a series of public hearings and conferences beginning in the autumn of 2007, as well as by convening an 'agora' (a parliamentary meeting with civil society organizations) on energy and climate change.

The second type of temporary committee is the Committee of Inquiry. Soon after direct elections in 1979 the EP started to use such committees to draw attention to specific policy issues and to assert its rights of scrutiny over the actions of other Community institutions. Nine Committees of Inquiry were established between 1979 and the adoption of the Maastricht Treaty. These ranged from the handling of nuclear materials, through transfrontier crimes linked to drug trafficking, and the use of hormones in meat, to racism and fascism. However, these investigatory committees had no formal standing or legal recourse beyond the EP itself. In other words, the committees were dependent upon the voluntary cooperation of other EU institutions and national authorities in the pursuit of their inquiries.

This changed with the addition of a new article in the Treaty of Maastricht which provided a legal base for the EP's Committees of Inquiry and specified that provisions relating to the right of inquiry should be worked out by common accord by the Council, Commission and Parliament (see Shackleton 1998:116–17). Eventually, after detailed negotiations extending over fifteen months, an interinstitutional agreement was reached between the three institutions and, shortly thereafter, Parliament revised its internal rules to accommodate the new provisions. At the beginning of 1996 the first Committee of Inquiry – into the Community's transit regime – was established under the chairmanship of John Tomlinson (PSE, UK). The committee had 17 full members and 17 substitutes, and met 37 times over a period of thirteen months. While the transit committee was conducting its extensive inquiry, a second Committee of Inquiry into the BSE crisis was established in July 1996. The BSE committee was chaired by German Christian Democrat Reimer Böge. It held 31 meetings and produced its report (in February 1997 with Manuel Medina Ortega as rapporteur) within six months of its inception.

In his detailed assessment of the impact of the transit and BSE committees Shackleton (1998:123–7) draws a contrast between their limited formal powers and their impact on both public and policy debates as well as upon actual policy outcomes. In comparison with Committees of Inquiry in most member states' parliaments, the EP's committees' powers to call witnesses, enforce their attendance and elicit evidence were severely circumscribed. Nevertheless, both committees secured significant press and media coverage and made an impact upon specific policy programmes and upon the EU's policy process itself (for details see Shackleton 1998:125–7). However, little use was made of such committees thereafter. Nearly a decade passed before a further Committee of Inquiry was established in January 2006 to examine the alleged mismanagement of the UK insurance company, Equitable Life. On 19 June 2007 Parliament's plenary accepted the recommendations of the Committee of Inquiry that the UK government should compensate victims of the company's mismanagement and that wide-ranging changes should be made in the drafting and implementation of EU financial services legislation (P6_TA-PROV(2007)0264; PE 386.573 2007).

Conciliation Committee

As will be seen in Chapter 7, codecision is the most significant legislative procedure in the EU (and the details of this procedure will be examined in the next chapter). At this point in the discussion of the internal organization of the EP, however, it is advisable to examine the structure and workings of the Conciliation Committee. This committee effectively constitutes the final stage of the codecision procedure itself (for full details see European Parliament 2004a).

The Conciliation Committee is an interinstitutional body and, unlike the other committees considered in this chapter, is not, therefore, an exclusively parliamentary organization. Representatives of both the EP and Council meet in the Conciliation Committee with the express purpose of reaching agreement on a joint text on the legislative proposal under consideration (see Chapter 7). Representatives of the Commission are also present at the meetings of the committee, which are held mostly in Brussels.

The Conciliation Committee has a total membership of 54, with 27 members of the Council or their representatives and an equal number of MEPs. Parliament's Conference of Presidents determines the political composition of the EP's delegation at the beginning of each legislature, but not the precise membership (which varies with each committee). From January 2007 there were 11 EPP-ED representatives, nine from the PSE, four ALDE, and one each from the Greens/EFA, EUL/NGL and UEN. Each political group also appoints substitute members who may take part in the proceedings of the delegation. Although nominally having a membership of 54 members, by the time political advisers, technical experts, legal experts and other support staff are represented over 100 people may actually be in attendance at the Conciliation Committee.

The membership of the EP's delegation is appointed for each separate conciliation, with the exception of the three Vice-Presidents of the Parliament who serve as permanent members of the Conciliation Committee. (The permanent members constitute part of the quota of the respective political groups.) In the second half of the 2004–2009 Parliament the three Vice-Presidents who served on the Conciliation Committee were Alejo Vidal-Quadras and Rodi Kratsa-Tsagaropoulou, both of whom were from the EPP-ED, and Mechtild Rothe from the PSE. The rapporteur and the chair of the committee responsible are also members, and most other members are selected by the party groups from the 'committee responsible' or from committees that have provided an opinion on the legislative proposal under consideration (under Rule 64). Moreover, the delegation normally includes the group spokespersons on a specific proposal, and party group coordinators in the main committee responsible are often appointed.

Representatives from the Commission also are normally invited to the meetings of the EP delegation (and of the Council delegation).

Several meetings of the EP's delegation may be necessary prior to formal Conciliation Committee meetings. These 'prior meetings' provide opportunities to discuss future strategy or the outcomes of negotiations (on trialogue or other informal meetings: see Chapter 8). These delegation meetings are usually held in Strasbourg.

The delegations are supported by a Conciliations Secretariat. The main tasks of the Secretariat are to prepare and organize the meetings of the delegations, prepare background notes for delegation members, assist in the running of the conciliation procedure, draft compromise texts, and prepare reports for plenary on the outcomes of conciliation. Perhaps more importantly, the Secretariat maintains and develops contacts with all of the leading participants in the conciliation process – especially with relevant officials in the Council and Commission, and with the secretariats of relevant EP committees, with Parliament's legal service, and with the Jurist Linguists to ensure the legal verification of texts throughout the codecision process. The Conciliations Secretariat also plays an important role in informing MEPs and interested publics of the process of conciliation itself and of the progression and processing of legislation under the codecision procedure. The importance of Parliament's conciliation unit in oiling the wheels of the conciliation process was noted by Garman and Hilditch (1998:280–1) who highlighted the significance of the exploratory meetings convened between the conciliation units of Parliament and the Council which ultimately facilitate compromises in the Conciliation Committee itself.

As for the full Conciliation Committee, any number of meetings may be convened within the six- or eight-week deadline stipulated in the codecision procedure. The maximum number to date has been four meetings – on the Fifth Research Framework Programme in 1998. In the 2004–2009 Parliament, however, the trend has been towards reaching agreement within a single meeting of the Conciliation Committee – though such agreement is often the product of three or more prior trialogue meetings. In the period July 2004 to December 2006, 11 legislative proposals were subject to conciliation and in all but two cases the conciliation procedure was formally opened and concluded at the same meeting of the Conciliation Committee. In the other two cases agreement was reached at a second meeting of the Conciliation Committee.

Rules of procedure

Parliaments . . . are divided internally into various subgroups, such as chambers, parties, and leadership bodies. Legislative output depends on the powers vested in these subunits of parliamentarians. Legislative organization is not simply a matter of what substructures exist: what ultimately matters are the rights or authorities given to these units. Moreover, the rights are tied up with sometimes arcane and complex rules by which the legislature does its work. (Strøm 1995:69)

As Chapter 2 revealed, Article 25 of the ECSC Treaty conferred upon the Common Assembly the right to adopt its own rules of procedure. That right was to prove vital to the evolution of the Assembly and, later, to the European Parliament. Indeed, throughout the history of the Parliament MEPs have proved adept at extending the reach of their powers and influence through the creative amendment of the EP's own Rules of Procedure. Moreover, Chapter 2 also underscored the point made by Evans (1999:632) that 'Seemingly minor decisions about rules made early in a legislature's existence . . . can have profound consequences for institutional development'.

Indeed, a 'philosophy' has been discerned behind the rules which has sought the strengthening of the EP's position in the legislative process 'from the beginning to the final decision' (Rømer 1993:2–3), as well as making its internal organization more efficient and, more widely, maximizing its interinstitutional impact (see Judge *et al.* 1994:31). This 'philosophy' was clearly expressed by Richard Corbett, in his report as rapporteur on the rule changes to be effected upon the introduction of the Amsterdam Treaty:

> Parliament has traditionally taken the Treaties and tried to stretch them like a piece of elastic, in order to enhance the efficiency and democratic accountability of the Union. Of course Parliament cannot contravene the Treaties in its Rules of procedure but the Treaties inevitably leave scope for interpretation and room for imagination. (PE 229.204 1999:87)

Between 1979 and 2002, well over 1000 rule changes were proposed by the Rules/Constitutional Affairs Committee (Kreppel 2002:107–20; PE 229.204 1999; PE 304.283 2001). Admittedly, some two-thirds of these amendments were minor, technical or clarificatory, and a substantial proportion were never adopted. Many more were inspired by significant treaty revisions – the SEA, Maastricht, Amsterdam and, eventually, Nice. Nonetheless, in quantitative terms alone they reflect the internal dynamism of the institution and the perpetual quest for the enhancement of the EP's standing within the EU's interinstitutional structures. Moreover, in qualitative terms, the incessant rule changes have reflected at least four major organizational requirements of the EP, which have varied over time and in their relative emphasis (see

Kreppel 2002:104–5): first, to increase the efficiency of its internal organization (in terms of leadership structures, committee division of labour and so on); second, to regulate and institutionalize party group activities (in terms of the prerogatives of large groups, protection of the rights of small groups and the organizational requirements of technical groups and non-affiliated members); third, to address increments in the EP's powers and competencies arising from treaty revisions; and, fourth, to sustain an integrationist dynamic (in terms of setting the agenda of future interinstitutional relations by innovative procedural changes as illustrated, for example, by the development of the appointment process of the Commission).

Intergroups

'Intergroups' are unofficial groupings of MEPs who share a common interest in a particular cause or interest. In 2007 there were some 25 formally registered intergroups. Despite the 'unofficial' nature of these groups, it is estimated that between 40 and 80 were in existence at any one time in the 2004–2009 Parliament (Corbett *et al.* 2007:165; European Parliament 2007c; Greenwood 2007a:38). There is such diversity among intergroups in terms of size, membership, frequency of meetings, and links with political groups and outside interests that it is difficult to make generalized statements about their activities.

Nonetheless, Corbett *et al.* (2007:185) list the benefits of intergroups for the EP as enabling MEPs to focus on a 'particular set of issues of specific national, constituency or personal concern', to specialize, to make contacts with outside interest groups on an informal basis, and to facilitate political contacts outside their own political groups. In the area of cancer research and treatment, for example, there are a number of formal and informal intergroups which aim to impact upon parliamentary activity; these include the registered Health and Consumer Intergroup as well as the informal European Parliamentary Group on Breast Cancer (EPGBC), 'MEPs against Cancer' (MAC) and the Cervical Cancer Interest Group (CCIG). The EPGBC was an active advocate of the Resolution on Breast Cancer in the Enlarged EU adopted by Parliament in October 2006 (OJ C 313E, 20 December 2006:273). MAC actively promoted a parliamentary resolution on cancer, which was adopted in late 2007 in advance of the Slovenian EU presidency (in the first half of 2008) which had announced its intention to focus on cancer as part of its health policy priorities.

There are, however, also certain disbenefits associated with intergroup activity. Indeed, concern with the operations of a few intergroups and their close connections with outside lobbies led the Conference of Presidents in 1995 to ratify an agreement to reaffirm and underline the unofficial status of such groups. Intergroups were expected to make clear that they were not organs of the EP, they did not speak on behalf of Parliament, and they were not entitled to use the EP's logo or its official title in any communications or printed materials. Specific rules were also drafted in the same year to bring intergroups into line with the rules concerning lobbyists and the declaration of financial interest of MEPs and their assistants (see Chapter 3). In 1999 further restrictions were placed on the creation of intergroups when they were required to have the support of at least three party groups before they could be constituted.

In addition to the concerns that some groups merely served as a 'front' for certain organized interests (see Corporate Europe Observatory 2006:4–5), there was also concern that the sheer scale and activism of intergroup networks constituted 'a rival centre of attention to official parliamentary activities, and in certain circumstances may undercut the latter' (Corbett *et al.* 2007:185). Thus, on occasion, the clash of timing of intergroup meetings with official parliamentary committee meetings and plenary debates has adversely affected attendance at the latter. Similarly, outside speakers occasionally quibble at attending committee meetings after appearing at intergroup sessions.

Plenary

As noted earlier, the EP was required by the protocol to the Amsterdam Treaty (and in the Lisbon Treaty) to schedule 12 plenary sessions a year (formally titled 'part-sessions') in Strasbourg, with additional plenary sessions held in Brussels. Effectively, with the ending of Friday sittings in 2000, each Strasbourg plenary part-session lasts just three and a half days. Not surprisingly, this episodic and curtailed working schedule heightens the premium placed upon formalism in the EP's plenaries.

Moreover, in formal terms, the treaties only recognize Parliament as a collectivity in plenary under its President. (In the Lisbon Treaty, however, Articles 121 and 284 TFEU make reference to the Parliament's competent committees. The former has its antecedents in Maastricht, and the latter grants the EP the possibility of calling the President of the ECB and other members of the Executive Board to appear before its committees.) Thus, although the working methods and organization of the EP revolve around the committees and political groups, only decisions reached in plenary have the imprimatur of Parliament. In other words, while committees are indisputably the practical locus of decision-making, the outcomes of their deliberations still have to receive the formal approval of the EP as a whole. Final votes on legislative proposals can only take place in plenary.

The formal pre-eminence of plenary is reflected in the fact that the proceedings on the floor of the chamber are published verbatim in the *Official Journal* and are available the following day on the EP's website. In contrast, debates within committee are simply minuted and the minutes made available on the EP's website, though often only some months later. (However, one of the innovations in Parliament's rule changes in June 2002 was to ensure, exceptionally, the production of a verbatim report of the presentations of the President of the European Central Bank made to Parliament's Economic and Monetary Affairs Committee.) The formal recording of plenary proceedings also partly explains the often stunted and formalistic contributions to debate – as speakers are strictly apportioned across political groups, time limits are rigidly enforced, and, correspondingly, individual speeches tend to be regimented and frequently scripted (see Chapter 7). Moreover, given the time constraints and the need to record accurate decisions, voting is usually separated from debate, confined to specific voting times, and ordered in accordance with standard procedures for the taking of votes (see Corbett *et al.* 2007:174–6).

Conclusion

This chapter has examined how the EP has responded to the complexities of making collective decisions in a peculiarly heterogeneous environment. The EP's peripatetic existence and its use of 23 working languages has served only to exacerbate the generic problems encountered by all elected representative bodies in processing highly complex and often technical issues in an informed manner.

The absence of a 'government' removes one authority hierarchy from within the EP, which in most other Western parliaments provides an identifiable decision-making cue for individual members – simply whether to support or oppose the position adopted by the 'government'. Other hierarchies of party and parliamentary leadership roles have thus developed, and conjoined, to mitigate the centrifugal organizational forces at work in the EP. Most importantly of all an internal division of labour, structured around committees, has developed to offset these forces. The committees provide the main institutional mechanism for the processing of legislative proposals. Notably, they enjoy considerable autonomy under the rules of the EP, and as nodal points of influence they have organizational consequences for party groups. So much so, that party groups seek both to control the memberships of the committees and to coordinate their own internal activities around the work of committees.

One of the themes of this chapter, and more generally of the book, has been that institutional design and organizational adaptation has been a persistent feature of the EP. At a formal level, the specification of decision-making procedures in the treaties has had internal organizational ramifications, and successive treaty reforms have stimulated attendant organizational changes within the EP. Equally, however, at a more informal level, the creative amendment of the EP's own Rules of Procedure has mirrored an institutional dynamism and an almost perpetual quest for the enhancement of the EP's standing within the EU's interinstitutional structures.

Chapter 7

Formal Powers

> Although we must expect the real influence of legislators will be at variance with their constitutional powers, we nevertheless need to know what scope constitutions give to legislatures before we can consider some of the more complex problems of legislative influence. (Blondel 1970:30)

Heeding Blondel's words, this chapter examines the formal powers conferred upon the EP before the complexities of legislative influence are analysed in Chapter 8. Almost by definition, such an examination is comparative in nature as it requires an assessment of the powers of the EP in relation to other institutions involved in the EU's legislative process, and also invites some assessment of the powers of the EP in comparison with those of national parliaments. In particular, in line with Mezey's ideas outlined in Chapter 1, this chapter will examine the capacity of the EP to constrain the legislative activities of the 'dual executive' of the Commission and Council. However, this does not mean that constraints are to be analysed solely in negative terms – of preventing action – but should also be seen as positive incentives to promote cooperative interinstitutional collaboration. Moreover, as Chapter 2 revealed, the formal powers of the European Parliament have to be viewed in tandem with informal modes of influence. How these formal and informal dimensions interact will be examined in Chapter 8; in the meantime the powers of the EP will be outlined in relation to the processing of legislation, budgetary control, appointment and dismissal of EU institutions, and scrutiny and control of EU institutions.

Legislative powers

Starting in the twenty-first century: codecision

Codecision2

Most studies of the legislative role of the EP start with a historical review of the incremental advances made since the inception of the EC. Equally most studies note the limited formal legislative powers of the EP before the SEA, Maastricht and Amsterdam Treaties. In fact, some

188

studies still seek to argue that, even after Nice, 'at the European level we find a weak European Parliament' which 'lacks (legislative) powers and cannot hold the executive fully accountable' (Krouwel 2004:12; 4). But what this chapter argues is that an analysis of the EP in the early twenty-first century should start with the formal powers currently possessed by the EP, and a recognition that the EP is presently and undisputedly a co-legislator in most important policy areas with the Council of Ministers. The 'weak image' is no longer linked to legislative reality. The present reality is that the EP is a major player in the legislative process. For this reason we start the examination of formal legislative powers with the codecision procedure.

With the implementation of the Amsterdam Treaty after 1 May 1999, codecision became what the EP itself described as the 'normal legislative procedure' or 'the standard procedure'. Indeed, the term 'ordinary legislative procedure' is used in the Lisbon Treaty, and this is the term that would also have featured in the Constitutional Treaty. The post-Amsterdam procedure is the second version of codecision, the first being introduced after the Maastricht Treaty, and hence is sometimes referred to as 'codecision2'. Despite the fact that the second version is widely regarded as remaining a highly complex procedure (see Figure 7.1), it represents a considerable simplification of the initial codecision procedure. The Lisbon Treaty simplified the terminology of codecison further. In particular, it removed reference to Council adopting a 'common position' (Council now simply adopts a 'position' as does the EP when adopting amendments). In this terminological change the equality of Council and Parliament in the operation of the procedure was further underlined.

In 2007, 43 areas of Community action, extending over 35 treaty articles, were covered by the procedure. This meant that well over 50 per cent of Commission proposals tabled under the first pillar were processed under codecision. Under the Lisbon Treaty codecision would apply to all areas where EU legislation is adopted by QMV in Council (unless an explicit provision is made to the contrary). As noted in Chapter 2, the Lisbon Treaty extends codecision substantially – to the extent that it would apply to 95 per cent of EU primary legislation. In so doing, the areas historically excluded from co-legislative authority – most notably agriculture and trade policy – would be subject to codecision.

The simplest way of conceiving of the procedure is in terms of three stages, or readings, with eight termination or 'exit' points for legislative outcomes.

Under codecision the whole process starts with the Commission proposing legislation to the European Parliament and the Council. Until the implementation of the Lisbon Treaty the Commission retains the sole right of legislative initiative in the case of the codecision. Prior to the Amsterdam Treaty cooperation among the member states on justice and

Figure 7.1 *Codecision2 procedure*

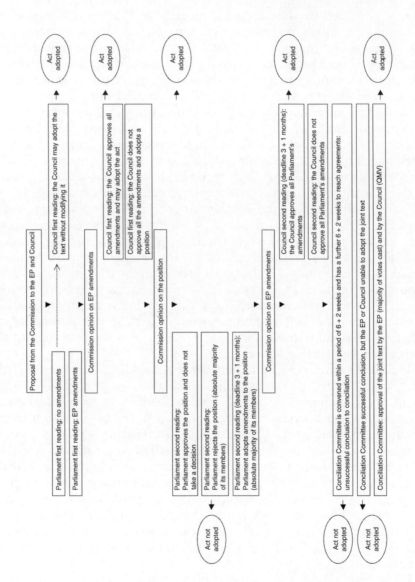

Proposal from the Commission to the EP and Council

Parliament first reading: no amendments

Council first reading: the Council may adopt the text without modifying it

Act adopted

Parliament first reading: EP amendments

Commission opinion on EP amendments

Council first reading: the Council approves all amendments and may adopt the act

Act adopted

Council first reading: the Council does not approve all the amendments and adopts a position

Commission opinion on the position

Act adopted

Parliament second reading:
Parliament approves the position and does not take a decision

Act not adopted

Parliament second reading:
Parliament rejects the position (absolute majority of its members)

Parliament second reading (deadline 3 + 1 months):
Parliament adopts amendments to the position (absolute majority of its members)

Commission opinion on EP amendments

Council second reading (deadline 3 + 1 months): the Council approves all Parliament's amendments

Act adopted

Council second reading: the Council does not approve all Parliament's amendments

Conciliation Committee is convened within a period of 6 + 2 weeks and has a further 6 + 2 weeks to reach agreements:

Conciliation Committee unsuccessful conclusion: conclusion to conciliation

Act not adopted

Conciliation Committee successful conclusion, but the EP or Council unable to adopt the joint text

Act not adopted

Conciliation Committee: approval of the joint text by the EP (majority of votes cast) and by the Council (QMV)

Act adopted

home affairs (under the 'third pillar') remained intergovernmental, while under the Amsterdam Treaty some third-pillar competences were brought within the first pillar. The Lisbon Treaty collapsed the pillar structure and, in so doing, would bring decision-making within the entire 'area of freedom, security and justice' into the scope of supranational legislation. Even so, an exceptional provision for a quarter of member states to have the right of initiative, along with the Commission, in the areas of judicial and police cooperation (Article 76 (TFEU)) remained in the Lisbon Treaty. With the implementation of the Lisbon Treaty the 'ordinary legislative procedure' would also apply to recommendations made by the European Central Bank to amend the Statute of the European System of Central Banks (Article 129 (TFEU)), requests by the Court of Justice to establish specialized courts (Article 257 (TFEU)) and the amendment of the Court's statute (Article 281 (TFEU)).

Once submitted to Parliament and Council, the draft regulation, directive or decision is examined in Parliament, primarily by the relevant parliamentary committee (see Chapters 6 and 8), and, where appropriate, amendments to the Commission's text are tabled before the plenary adopts an 'opinion'. Council simultaneously considers the Commission's proposal and subsequently decides whether to accept or reject the EP's amendments (in the wording of the Lisbon Treaty, the EP's 'position'). If no amendments are proposed or, alternatively, if all the amendments contained in the EP's opinion are acceptable to Council, then Council may, by qualified majority, adopt at this early stage an act 'in the wording which corresponds to the position of the European Parliament'. These represent the first and second, successful, exit-points.

Once Council's position is forwarded to Parliament, a three-month time limit is activated, within which Parliament can, variously: unconditionally approve it or fail to take a decision; reject it by an absolute majority of its members; or amend Council's position, again by an absolute majority of its members. At this second-reading stage, if the EP approves the Council's position, or alternatively does not take a decision, then an act is adopted in accordance with the Council's position. This is the third, successful, exit point. If the Council's position is rejected the legislation falls. This is the fourth exit-point, and the first at which there is an unsuccessful legislative outcome. Where amendments are proposed, the amended text is returned to the Council and to the Commission. The Commission has to decide whether to accept or reject Parliament's amendments.

If the Commission favours the amendments, and if Council decides to accept all of Parliament's amendments, a qualified majority in Council will secure the adoption of the text. Alternatively, unanimity is required in Council to adopt the EP's amendments for which the Commission does not offer its support. In either case, this is the fifth exit point. Where the Council rejects one or more of the EP's amendments the proposal is automatically referred to the Conciliation Committee. Negotiations on a compromise text have to be conducted within a period of six weeks. The role and composition of the Committee is set out in Article 251 (Article 294 of the Lisbon Treaty (TFEU)) and reads as follows:

> The Conciliation Committee, which shall be composed of the members of the Council or their representatives and an equal number of members representing the European Parliament, shall have the task of reaching agreement on a joint text, by a qualified majority of the members of the Council or their representatives and by a majority of the members representing the European Parliament within six weeks of its being convened, on the basis of the positions of the European Parliament and the Council at second reading.

If conciliation fails to produce an agreed joint text the sixth exit-point is reached and the act falls; otherwise bargaining between Council and Parliament produces a joint text which incorporates agreement on individual EP amendments (according to the Lisbon Treaty this would be 'on the basis of the positions of the European Parliament and Council'). This text is agreed independently of the opinion of the Commission, though it may 'take all necessary initiatives with a view to reconciling the positions of the European Parliament and the Council' (Article 294). At this point, the European Parliament, acting by an absolute majority of the votes cast, and Council, acting by a qualified majority, each have a period of six weeks in which to adopt the joint text. This constitutes the seventh and final positive exit point. An eighth and negative termination point is reached where one of the co-legislative institutions votes against the joint text and the act fails.

The importance of codecision2 is that it provides the EP with a veto which it lacked under preceding legislative procedures. Failure to reach agreement between Council and the EP results in the failure of legislative proposals. The prospect of producing a negative outcome serves to focus the collective minds of Council and Parliament to reach positive compromises. As Corbett *et al.* (2007:216) note, 'This right to say "no", whether at second reading or during conciliation, gave Parliament a bargaining position which it hitherto lacked regarding Community legislation.' However, a small caveat is needed here, as an 'emergency brake' system was built into the Lisbon Treaty for legislative proposals which a member state believed affected 'important aspects of its social security system' (Article 48, TFEU), or 'fundamental aspects' of its criminal justice system (Articles 81 and 82, TFEU). Under this 'braking system' a member state would be able to refer a proposal under the 'ordinary legislative procedure' to the European Council and thereby suspend the operation of codecision2 for four months. In the case of Article 48 this may ultimately render an act 'deemed not to have been adopted'. In the case of Article 82, where consensus does not materialize in the European Council within four months, the Lisbon Treaty would provide for a simplified transition to enhanced cooperation (for those member states wishing to follow such a route).

Consultation

As noted in Chapter 2, the consultation procedure was the initial legislative procedure from which the cooperation and codecision procedures ultimately derived. What Chapter 2 also revealed was that the capacity of the EP to affect legislation under this procedure was entirely conditional upon both the Commission and the Council incorporating parliamentary amendments into a proposal. Even after Amsterdam, the consultation procedure featured in no less than 66 treaty provisions (Maurer 1999a:9) and continued to be applied to significant areas of EU policy such as: agriculture, the harmonization of indirect taxation, private sector competition, the harmonization of national provisions affecting the internal market and specific measures relating to industrial policy, nuclear energy and radiation, as well as to fiscal aspects of environmental policy (for a full list see Corbett *et al.* 2007:211–2). The Amsterdam Treaty also introduced a new form of consultation under the third pillar (Article 34(2)(b,c,d)) for the purpose of approximation of laws and regulations relating to police and judicial cooperation. Under the new procedure Council could set a deadline of not less than three months within which Parliament had to submit its opinion. If an opinion was not provided within the deadline then Council could proceed to adopt the measure unilaterally. This form of consultation was abolished by the Lisbon Treaty.

Under the Lisbon Treaty the consultation procedure, which would become a 'special legislative procedure', is retained *inter alia* for the establishment of the European External Action service (Article 27, TEU), treaty amendment – where the EP is consulted by the European Council (Article 48 TEU), the adoption of directives to ensure coordination and cooperation between member states for diplomatic and consular protection (Article 23 TFEU), provisions concerning passports, identity cards and residence permits (Article 77 TFEU), family law (Article 81(3) TFEU) and operational cooperation between police forces (Article 87 TFEU). In most cases the use of the consultation procedure under Lisbon would be associated with the requirement for unanimity in Council.

Assent procedure

The assent procedure was introduced by Articles 8 and 9 of the Single European Act and subsequently extended in the Treaties of Maastricht, Amsterdam, Nice and Lisbon. In the event of the Lisbon Treaty being implemented, the assent procedure would also be renamed (in line with the Constitutional Treaty) as 'consent'. Consent is simply 'an "authorisation" without which a legislative act cannot be definitely adopted by the Council' (Maurer 1999b:46). In the first instance, under the SEA, Parliament's assent was required before Council could enact association agreements with third countries and the accession of new member states. Maastricht and Amsterdam added further areas to the scope of the assent procedure: sanctions for the breach of fundamental human rights; special tasks entrusted to the European Central Bank; amendments to the protocol on the European System of Central Banks; specific aspects of the organization of the Structural Funds and the creation of the Cohesion Fund; uniform procedures for European elections; and international agreements under Article 300(3) covering specific institutional frameworks, budgetary implications, or entailing amendment of legislation adopted under codecision. In turn, the Nice Treaty required the assent of the EP under Article 7 (TEU) before the Council could decide that there was a clear risk of a serious breach of fundamental rights. Assent was also extended to enhanced cooperation under the first pillar. In two cases, relating to the duties of the Ombudsman and the general conditions governing the duties of MEPs, the assent of the Council (its 'approval') was required for Parliament to act. In these specific cases, the assent procedure was reversed. The assent procedure thus covers aspects of both external relations and internal EU legislative competences.

In the Lisbon Treaty the consent procedure would be extended further to such matters as the (non) establishment of a Convention for the revision of the Treaty (Article 48 TEU; see also Chapter 9), agreements for withdrawal from the EU (Article 49 TEU), and the adoption by Council of a regulation laying down the multiannual financial framework (Article 312 TFEU).

Corbett *et al.* (2007:231) describe the assent procedure as 'a cruder form of codecision in that there is no scope for Parliament to put forward amendments to the measure in question'. Indeed, one weakness of the procedure is that it does not provide a mechanism whereby the EP and the Council can settle their differences. In fact, some commentators argue that the power is a 'nuclear' one and hence MEPs are reluctant to use it (Smith 1999:76). Nonetheless, it is a significant power and comparable with the ratification procedures possessed by most national parliaments in relation to international agreements. Moreover, it is not simply negative. As Dietmar Nickel (1999:5) argues:

we are confronted with a misunderstanding . . . power is often construed as being the negative use, a decision not to do something. This is just wrong. You use your assent power for instance for an enlargement as much when you vote in favour as when you say no.

Ultimately the most pressing constraint upon the EP's negative use of the consent procedure is simply that in most instances withholding consent is a blunt weapon if Parliament is anxious to see association agreements, enlargement or other favoured internal legislation come into effect.

Initiation of legislation

The EP has, through 'own-initiative reports' under Rule 45 and members' 'motions for resolution' tabled under Rule 113, been able to participate indirectly in the initiation of legislation (see Chapter 2; Judge 1993:191–3; Judge and Earnshaw 1994:263–6). Own-initiative reports are drafted by the responsible committee and adopted by a majority of MEPs present at plenary as with other reports and resolutions. Since 1982 the Commission has agreed in principle to pursue any parliamentary initiative to which it did not have major objections. On the occasions when it has objected the Commission has explained its position to Parliament. More generally it has also reported regularly to the relevant committee on progress made on parliamentary initiatives. The classic example of the EP's legislative initiative remains the ban on the import of baby seal skins (as early as 1982), though more recent examples include the 1998 proposal to ban tobacco advertising which had its origins in a parliamentary initiative in 1990.

The Maastricht Treaty granted the EP a comparable right to that of the Council to initiate legislative proposals. Under Article 192 the EP, acting by an absolute majority of its members, was empowered to request the Commission 'to submit any appropriate proposal on matters on which it considers that a Community act is required for the purpose of implementing this Treaty'. Parliament's experience with the procedure has been mixed. One of the earliest examples of the use of the provision was Parliament's request in May 1994 that a liability regime for environmental damage should be established in EU law. Parliament's proposal followed an earlier Commission proposal on civil liability for damage caused by waste, which had sat before Council for some years before eventually being withdrawn, and a Commission Green Paper on environmental liability published in 1993. Parliament also held a joint hearing with the Commission on environmental liability during the same year. However, only in January 2002 – nearly eight years after the original parliamentary initiative –

did the Commission submit a legislative proposal providing for environmental liability. Even then, the Commission was only prompted into action by Parliament's threat to derail another of the Commission's proposals – on the deliberate release of genetically modified organisms – if the proposal on liability was not submitted.

A somewhat more expeditious application of Article 192 (then 138b) occurred with legislation on the settlement of claims arising from traffic accidents outside the claimant's country of origin. Adopted in October 1995, Parliament's resolution under Article 138b sought a Commission proposal to harmonize national provisions relating to liability in car insurance, and thereby to protect consumers and the victims of traffic accidents. Some half a million tourists were involved in accidents in a member state other than their own each year, and an obvious legal vacuum existed in EU law in settling accident claims. In October 1997 the Commission brought forward a proposal (COM(97)510 final), in line with Parliament's request, and this was approved in Parliament's first reading in July 1998. In December of that year Council reached a political agreement on the proposal, and reached a formal common position in May 1999. Parliament's second reading took place in December 1999, and the measure was agreed in conciliation in March 2000, with formal adoption in May 2000.

In early 2000 the boundaries of Article 192 were pushed still further. On this occasion, the European Ombudsman (see below) creatively proposed, in a special report submitted to the EP President, that Parliament should use the procedure to request the Commission to submit a proposal for a regulation on a code of good administrative conduct in the EU institutions (*Agence Europe* 20 April 2000). Some years after that, a new Framework Agreement of May 2005 (signed in the wake of the investiture of the Barroso Commission – see below), obliged the Commission 'to take account of any requests made, pursuant to Article 192 of the Treaty establishing the European Community, by Parliament to the Commission to submit legislative proposals, and [to] provide a prompt and sufficiently detailed reply thereto' (see European Parliament 2007a, annex XIII, para. 14). The Lisbon Treaty proposes to extend Parliament's right of initiative by granting the EP the right to initiate treaty revision (Article 48 TEU).

Written declarations

Parliament's Rules of Procedure have provided, since they were first revised following direct elections (see European Parliament, 1981), for written declarations to be submitted by MEPs. If signed by a majority of members, these declarations are then announced in plenary, published in Parliament's minutes and forwarded to the institutions named therein (as with other parliamentary resolutions). The procedure remained relatively unused until the 1999–2004 Parliament. However, in the 2004–2009 Parliament there was increasing use of the procedure, especially to focus attention on issues for which committee and plenary time would be difficult to attain (for example in Chapter 6 it was noted that a written declaration was used to raise the issue of the EP's seat).

Most written declarations call for Commission action; and they are taken seriously by Commission officials as an indicator of parliamentary concern. Written declarations may also serve to chart preliminary ideas for future committee own-initiative reports, other committee initiatives, or legislative proposals. Thus, for example, written declaration 52/2007, on the need for a comprehensive strategy to control cancer, was tabled by leading members of the Environment Committee in 2007 and secured a majority of MEPs' signatures in September 2007. In turn, this led to an 'oral question with debate' tabled by the same Committee (with a resolution to wind up debate) in plenary in April 2008. Similarly, written declaration 40/2007, which called for a ban on the use of non-human primates in experiments, secured a majority of signatures in September 2007 and preceded the long-awaited submission of a Commission proposal to amend Directive 86/609 on animal experimentation.

While many written declarations are tabled, relatively few are adopted. Between January 2004 and December 2006 only 14 written declarations were adopted, while 220 lapsed without having gained sufficient signatures. The vast majority of lapsed declarations received fewer than 100 signatures. Most written declarations result from wider campaigns outside Parliament. One example was a declaration adopted in 2006 which called on the Commission and Council to develop an EU diabetes strategy by means of a Council Recommendation on diabetes prevention, diagnosis and control. This declaration had its origins in a campaign to improve the treatment of diabetes across the EU conducted by the International Diabetes Federation – Europe Region, and the Federation of European Nurses in Diabetes. Indeed, written declarations are unlikely to garner sufficient signatures to be adopted unless there is extensive lobbying of MEPs by campaign groups in support of the declaration. The simple logistics – in requiring MEPs to be physically present to sign the proposed declaration either just outside the plenary during part-sessions or in a specific room in Parliament's building when part-sessions are not in progress – requires sustained organizational endeavour to secure the required number of signatures.

Budgetary powers

Chapter 2 chronicled the acquisition of significant budgetary powers by Parliament after the creation of the EC's 'own resources' in 1970 and further treaty revision in 1975. While these formal powers remained little altered until the drafting of the Lisbon Treaty, Parliament's influence upon the EU's finances was extended with the signing of successive interinstitutional agreements. The first was signed in 1988 and by 2007 four had been signed in total (see Chapter 2).

Julie Smith (1999:74) notes that 'The EP's role in budgetary affairs is highly significant, since it has a much larger say than most national parliaments.' If anything, however, the EP's budgetary powers are the reverse of those traditionally exercised by parliaments. Whereas national parliaments have historically focused upon exercising control over the raising of revenues – under the rallying cry of 'no taxation without representation' – and thereby subsequently and indirectly influencing expenditure decisions, the EP has exercised control over expenditure but has had little say over the raising of revenue. This 'peculiarity' in the exercise of the EP's budgetary powers is a reflection of the EU's own unique financial arrangements. The EU has three revenue sources aggregated in its 'own resources': 'traditional own resources' such as duties charged on imports from non-EU countries (about 15 per cent of revenue in 2007); a VAT resource – a uniform percentage rate of the VAT revenue in member states (15 per cent); and a contribution from member states, calculated from a base rate of their respective gross national income, and reflecting their ability to pay (69 per cent) (European Commission 2007a).

Whereas Parliament has had no power to vary revenues, since the treaty revision of 1975 it has accumulated significant powers over expenditure. Even so, Parliament's control over expenditure had been limited (until the Lisbon Treaty, see below) by the technical, and largely artificial, distinction made in the EU between 'compulsory' and 'non-compulsory' expenditure. Expenditure which resulted directly from the application of treaty obligations was deemed 'compulsory'. In contrast, 'non-compulsory' spending was defined as 'avoidable expenditure where the Union enjoys broad discretion as to the level of expenditure that it incurs' (Corbett *et al.* 2007:259). Exactly what this distinction meant in practice was the cause of a 25-year struggle between the EP and Council. At the same time as MEPs battled to increase the proportion of non-compulsory expenditure they simultaneously sought to increase the maximum level of expenditure permissible under the treaties. According to the pre-Lisbon Article 272, Parliament, with the agreement of the Council, could propose an increase in the annual maximum rate of increase in non-compulsory expenditure calculated by the Commission prior to the submission of its preliminary draft budget for the following year. In making its calculation the Commission was required to take into account macro-economic indicators in member states such as levels of economic growth, government spending and the rates of inflation. For 2007 the maximum rate of increase was calculated at 4.2 per cent.

Given the relatively low voting hurdles that had to be jumped (at least in comparison with increasing own resources), there were few disincentives for MEPs not to seek to increase the maximum rate of increase. 'The result was that the Parliament spent much of the 1980s up to 1988 trying to convince the Council to agree to an increase in the maximum rate' (Westlake 1994a:125). In reverse, the Council spent much of the 1980s trying to curb spiralling EU expenditure, largely fuelled by agricultural transfers, in the face of severe macroeconomic problems in member states. On three occasions, in December 1979, 1982 and 1984, Parliament expressed its dissatisfaction with the draft budget by finding the necessary two-thirds majority for rejection and, as a result, Council was required to submit a new draft. In view of the persistent annual disputes over the maximum rate of increase, as well as those over the classification of expenditure, it was generally acknowledged that some reform was required of the budget process. Reform eventually came in the context of the reexamination of the EU finances in the 'Delors-1 Package' (see Laffan and Lindner 2005:199–200) when an Interinstitutional Agreement on 'budgetary discipline and the improvement of the budgetary procedure' was signed between the Council, the Commission and the EP. This Agreement entered into force in July 1988 and largely resolved two of the main points of friction between the institutions. First, it adopted a five-year financial perspective in which it was agreed to respect the expenditure levels proposed in six categories of expenditure. Within this five-year horizon a detailed financial framework for each year could then be agreed. Importantly, this arrangement severed the linkage between increases in compulsory expenditure and reductions in the amounts available for non-compulsory expenditure. Effectively the Council conceded a substantial increase in non-compulsory expenditure, with a specific commitment to the doubling of expenditure on the Structural Funds, by the end of the first five-year period. Such a commitment could only be fulfilled, however, if the normal calculation of the maximum rate of increase was exceeded. Moreover, the Interinstitutional Agreement included the provision that the institutions could agree to exceed the permissible maximum rate in advance of any specific annual agreement. In so doing, the 1988 Agreement 'transformed the argument about the maximum rate of increase' (Corbett *et al.* 2007:261). In the event, however, it did not remove all disputation from the budget process.

In particular, Parliament's attempts to maximize the rate of increase continued to meet with opposition from the Council. Ever willing to advance a creative interpretation of procedures, the EP argued that it could increase spending to the maximum permitted level in each category and then assume that the overall total was acceptable to the Council. Council on the other hand proved unwilling to accept this assumption and threatened to challenge it in the Court of Justice in 1992. This threat was dropped when the matter was resolved during the 1992 Edinburgh European Council when agreement was reached on a new financial perspective for the period 1993 to 1999 (Nugent 2006:432). The main elements of this financial perspective were incorporated in a new Interinstitutional Agreement signed in 1993.

In 1999 a further Interinstitutional Agreement (for details see OJ C 172, 18 June 1999) marked not only the resolution of the differences over technicalities – of classification of expenditure and maximum rate of increase – but also confirmed the changed priorities of the EP in the use of its budgetary powers. In turn these changed priorities reflected wider changes in the interinstitutional relationship between Council and Parliament. The EP's initial strategy of maximizing its policy influence through the budgetary process (at a time of limited legislative powers), and the ensuing endemic competition with the Council, gave way to cooperation with the Council on management issues. As Laffan and Lindner (2005:202) note, this change meant that the budgetary process 'lost its place in the interinstitutional spotlight and became the domain of budgetary experts, [who] cooperated closely and developed a routine of adopting annual budgets in time and without major tensions'.

In accordance with the Interinstitutional Agreement of 1999 the Commission presented proposals, in February 2004, for a new financial perspective for the period 2007–2013. Parliament established a Temporary Committee (see Chapter 6) and eight months of deliberations culminated in its report (PE 353.270 2005) which, in turn, formed the basis of Parliament's resolution of 8 June 2005. Against the backdrop of the Lisbon Strategy, periods of low-growth rates in many eurozone states, and the inclusion of ten new member states – all with expectations of budgetary transfers in their favour – the negotiations on the new Financial Perspective proved to be particularly protracted. The Budgets Committee's rapporteur, Reimer Böge, noted at one late stage that, without agreement between Council and the EP, 'the possibility of an absence of FP/IIA [Financial Perspective/Interinstitutional Agreement] should be envisaged and the consequences, mainly for legislation, anticipated' (PE372.062 2006:51). This followed an earlier threat by the Budgets Committee to suspend the IIA and move to annual budget setting unless Council responded positively to the EP's negotiating position (*European Voice* 9 March 2006). Eventually, after a series of monthly trialogues in early 2006, an agreement was reached. Although Parliament remained disappointed at the additional increase in the budget, nonetheless, Reimer Böge, concluded that: 'Parliament was not just obsessed with figures – we wanted reform of policy, new instruments, the cutting of red tape and guarantees for Parliament's role on foreign policy instruments – and a proper role in the 2008–9 review. We have managed to get these qualitative aspects on board in a satisfactory way' (European Parliament 2006). These qualitative aspects, along with a new Financial Framework (a renaming of the Financial Perspective), were incorporated in the new IIA signed on 17 May 2006 (OJ C 139, 14 June 2006).

The Lisbon Treaty proposed both to simplify and transform the EU's budgetary procedure. As noted above, this transformation reflected three decades of deliberation, and often disagreement, between the EP and Council. The new Treaty would resolve four of the main issues of contention between the two institutions. First was the provision for the adoption of a multiannual financial framework (covering at least a period of five years) by Council acting unanimously with the consent of Parliament. Second, the distinction between compulsory and non-compulsory expenditure was abolished, thus giving Parliament a 'decisive voice on the whole of budget' (PE 347.119 2004:32). Third, the Commission was required formally to submit a draft budget to Council and Parliament rather than a preliminary draft budget, which Council then, in turn, would submit to Parliament. Fourth, specific conciliation processes in relation to the budget were specified, whereby Parliament effectively gained parity with Council over the adoption of the budget. The 'maximum rate of *increase*' was also removed from the Treaty.

Under Article 314 (TFEU) the EP would be a twin arm, alongside the Council, of the 'budgetary authority'. What this would mean in practice, post-Lisbon, is that Parliament would be able to propose amendments to any expenditure, as long as it stayed within the ceilings defined by the multiannual financial framework. Generally, the EP would remain dependent upon Council's acceptance of its proposals but it would be able to over-ride Council (by an absolute majority and three-fifths of votes cast) where Council rejected an agreement on the budget reached in conciliation. Finally, where conciliation failed to agree a joint text, a new draft budget would have to be submitted by the Commission.

Discharge

As noted above, Parliament has increasingly become concerned to ensure sound financial management in the implementation of the EU's budget. In this task the EP is assisted by the Court of Auditors which conducts detailed audits of the accounts of all EU bodies. The Court of Auditors examines the accounts of all revenue and expenditure and verifies their 'legality, regularity . . . and examines whether financial management has been sound' (PE 167.189 1997:2). The Court then produces an annual report which includes separate sections detailing the activities of each of the institutions in that financial year. In addition, since the Maastricht Treaty, the Court of Auditors has been required to issue a 'statement of assurance on the reliability of the accounts and the legality and regularity of the underlying transactions for each financial year'. The annual report and the statement of assurance are subsequently forwarded to the EP, which, since 1975, has had the exclusive right to approve (grant a discharge) or disapprove (not grant a discharge) the Commission's implementation of the budget. The actual processing and assessment of the Auditors' reports is entrusted to the EP's Committee on Budgetary Control, which recommends whether or not Parliament should discharge the Commission's handling of the budget.

'The power to grant or not to grant discharge therefore represents the strongest expression of Parliament's political control over the Commission as regards its responsibility in implementing the budget' (PE 229.285 1998:5). In fact, so great was the negative power implicit in a refusal to grant discharge that neither the treaties nor the Communities' Financial Regulation formally contemplated the consequences of such a refusal (Corbett *et al.* 2007:291). On the only occasion before 1999 that Parliament refused to grant discharge, in November 1984, the Commission was within weeks of its planned termination of office and hence the procedural logic – that a motion of censure or the Commission's resignation would follow – was not fulfilled.

Corbett *et al.* (2007:290) make clear that discharge 'is much more than an annual ritual: it is as much a *power* as a procedure'. It is a formal statement that the EP accepts the manner in which the Commission has implemented the budget. In making its judgement Parliament has asserted its right to require the Commission to provide all necessary information (this would be given treaty status in Article 319(2) TFEU) and to ensure that the 'Commission should take all appropriate steps to act on observations by the European Parliament relating to the execution of expenditure' (Article 319(3) TFEU). In recent years the EP, acting through its Committee on Budgetary Control, has used the process of discharge to investigate allegations of financial mismanagement, fraud and irregularities. In so doing, it has encountered problems in eliciting information from the Commission and in securing an adequate response to its observations and recommendations (see PE 226.077 1998). In these circumstances the EP devised a strategy of postponing a decision on discharge, and thereby giving notice to the Commission that it expected missing information to be provided or remedial action to be taken, or both, by a given deadline. Implicit in the postponement of discharge was a threat. This threat was made explicit in the Budgetary Control Committee's report on the postponement of discharge for the 1996 financial year (PE 226.077 1998:20):

> [I]n proposing that the discharge be postponed, it is by no means your rapporteur's intention to start a witch hunt against the Commission leading eventually to its inevitable resignation. On the contrary, this is constructive criticism, and your rapporteur . . . just wants to set the ball rolling. The Commission must be aware, however, that if it fails to heed the barking of the watchdogs, no-one will protect it from the bloodhounds.

This warning proved to be prophetic in view of the ensuing events over the discharge of the 1996 budget and the subsequent resignation of the Santer Commission in 1999 (for details see Judge and Earnshaw 2002:349–52).

In 2002 Parliament revised the discharge procedure to allow Parliament, by simple majority vote, to grant or postpone discharge in April of each year. If postponement is recommended then Parliament revisits the issue in October (European Parliament 2007a:AnnexV). The six-month delay is designed as a means of exerting pressure on the Commission to respond to parliamentary concerns before the final vote.

Appointment and dismissal

The Commission

It was noted in Chapter 1 that characteristic features of a parliamentary system include the authorization of political executives by the legislature and the fusion of executive and legislative roles. Moreover, '[i]n a parliamentary system, the chief executive . . . and his or her cabinet are responsible to the legislature in the sense that they are dependent on the legislature's confidence and that they can be dismissed from office by a legislative vote of no confidence or censure' (Lijphart 1984:68). The logic of this system, therefore, is that the executive should retain the confidence of the legislature because it derives both its legitimacy and its authority from the representative parliament. An important corollary of this logic is the general belief that 'Parliaments are supposed to control the operation of the executive'

(Dehousse 1998:598). The exact degree of control is determined, in turn, by the formal and informal constraints that the legislature is able to place upon the executive and vice versa (see Blondel 1973:45–54). This returns us to Mezey's (1979:25) notion of constraint identified at the beginning of this chapter and in Chapter 1. The constraints of concern here are those that the EP can exercise over the formation and dismissal of the Commission. There are both negative and positive dimensions to these powers, and variations in the degree of constraint attendant upon the exercise of these powers.

Appointment of the Commission

Historically the EU's process for the appointment of the Commission was intergovernmental, consensual and driven by domestic political considerations (Jacobs 1999:3). Initially the EP had no say in the appointment process, but then through gradual increments attained the dual right to be consulted upon the choice of the Commission President, and also to assent to the choice of the College of Commissioners as a whole. The main change effected in the Amsterdam Treaty was that the appointment of the President of the Commission was no longer simply contingent upon consultation with Parliament but was now dependent upon the formal approval of the EP. In turn the influence of the President over the choice of the College of Commissioners was enhanced. This was taken a step further in the Nice Treaty, with the European Council nominating and approving the President and College by qualified majority (Article 214(2)).

In practice, however, the changes effected in the Amsterdam and Nice Treaties marked an incremental advance on already existing procedures adopted by the EP after the Maastricht Treaty. After Maastricht the EP as a whole, rather than just its enlarged Bureau, was involved in the consultation process in the choice of Commission President. Moreover there was a formal vote to record Parliament's verdict. In drafting its new rules, to take account of the Maastricht changes, the EP decided that it would 'approve or reject the proposed nomination [of Commission President] by a majority of the votes cast' and, further, 'vote its approval of the Commission by a majority of the votes cast' (European Parliament 1993, Rules 32 and 33 respectively). Implicitly the EP maintained that if a negative vote was recorded then the nominee would be withdrawn (Hix 2000b:98). This interpretation found confirmation in 1994 when Jacques Santer, at the time that his nomination for Commission President was initially canvassed, made it clear that he would withdraw if Parliament voted against him. Further confirmation came from the then Council Presidency (Germany) that a new candidate would have to be found in the event of a negative vote by the EP (Hix 2000b:98).

In addition, the Maastricht Treaty synchronized the Commission's term of office with that of Parliament. The intention was that the broadly coterminous mandates of the EP and the Commission would facilitate 'parliamentary scrutiny and control as well as the feeling of Commissioners that they are accountable to Parliament' (Corbett *et al.* 2007:269). To maximize parliamentary control the EP sought to establish the principle of 'prior authorization' whereby individual Commissioners-designate would appear before its committees to identify the Commission's policy priorities (see Judge and Earnshaw 2008).

In amending its Rules of Procedure after Maastricht, new Rule 33 (now Rule 99, European Parliament 2007a) requested 'nominees proposed for the various posts of Commissioners to appear before the appropriate committees according to their prospective fields of responsibility'. These hearings were to be held in public, and, significantly, were scheduled before the confirmation vote was to be taken. Each Commissioner-designate was requested to make a statement to the relevant committee and answer questions. The main objectives of the hearings, as described by the EP itself, are:

- [To] provide an opportunity for the parliamentary committees to get insight into the personalities of the various Commissioners designate and to hold an extensive exchange of views on the priorities of the various Commissioners designate with regard to their respective areas of responsibility.
- In case of approval of the Commission, the hearings serve in this way to establish a working relationship between parliamentary committees and their Commissioners at the earliest possible moment.
- Finally they also serve as an initial benchmark for examining the subsequent performance of the Commissioner concerned. (European Parliament 2004b)

January 1995 saw the first use of 'confirmation hearings' for Commissioners, when the newly enlarged Parliament scrutinized nominees for the Santer Commission. No formal votes were held at the end of each committee hearing, simply because the EP had no power to reject individual nominees. Instead, each committee chair wrote to the President of the Parliament expressing the committee's evaluation of each Commissioner-designate. In turn, the President of the Parliament convened a press conference to discuss the published conclusions of the committees. Although negative comments on individual Commissioners were voiced (particularly on Ritt Bjerregaard and Padraig Flynn), they had little tangible effect on the outcome of the vote on the Commission as a whole, other than the reallocation of one aspect of Commissioner Flynn's portfolio (see Corbett 1995:40–1). Nonetheless, at the time, Fitzmaurice (1994:183) identified the new Maastricht confirmation provisions as possibly 'one of the most significant of the institutional reforms' in that they 'could imply a more parliamentary Commission in the long term'.

The second confirmation hearings were held in September 1999 when the new Parliament considered nominees for Romano Prodi's Commission. The basic format of the 1995 hearings was retained. One significant innovation in the 1999 hearings, however, was a common written questionnaire which all nominees were required to return two weeks in advance of the scheduled committee meetings. What also characterized the interview process in 1999 was the increased levels of preparation on both sides from those apparent in 1995. A further characteristic was the increased partisanship of proceedings, with EPP MEPs openly critical of the overall left-of-centre bias of the incoming Commission and of specific Socialist Commissioners-designate. In particular, Philippe Busquin, former Belgian Walloon socialist leader, encountered sustained hostile questioning from EPP members of the Industry Committee on his alleged proximity to a number of domestic political scandals. In return, Socialist MEPs responded in kind with fierce criticisms of Spanish Christian Democrat Loyola de Palacio, and succeeded in delaying for a short period the decision on her nomination.

Appointment of the Barroso Commission

The appointment of the Barroso Commission in 2004 confirmed just how influential the EP had become in the selection of the Commission. It also confirmed the developing partisanship underpinning the selection process. Indeed, one observer concluded that the episode pointed demonstrably to 'the emergence of disciplined political parties within the European Parliament' (Murray, 2005:1).

Immediately after the elections in June 2004, the European Council nominated the Portuguese prime minister, José Manuel Durão Barroso, after an initial acrimonious exchange in Council over the respective claims of the preferred nominee of Germany and France, the Belgian prime minister Guy Verhofstadt, and his strongest competitor Chris Patten, the British Commissioner for External Relations. In the background to this dispute, the EPP-ED group in Parliament insisted that the nominee for Commission President should reflect the party outcome of the EP elections itself. In this respect the EPP-ED articulated informally what the Lisbon Treaty proposes formally – that the Council should take into account the elections to the EP in choosing a candidate for Commission President (Article 17(7)).

Once nominated as President-designate, Barroso then met with Parliament's Conference of Presidents and attended party group meetings. After two days of plenary debate, Barroso was 'elected' (the term used in the EP's Rules of Procedure), on 22 July, with 413 MEPs voting in favour, 251 voting against, and 44 abstaining. For the first time, following the rule changes of 2002, the vote was by secret ballot (thereby tending to nullify lobbying by national capitals in support of the European Council's nominee). For the first time also, the vote was more clearly differentiated along party lines; with the EPP-ED group voting in favour and the bulk of the PSE, Green and GUE groups voting against (Corbett *et al.* 2007:269).

A list of Commissioners-designate was then compiled from the list of nominees proposed by member states. The final list was adopted on the basis of the Council acting 'by common accord' with Barroso. Although Barroso was restricted in this manner in the choice of Commissioners, he was able to exert some influence in raising the numbers and profile of female Commissioners and in allocating specific Commission portfolios. In late September and early October 2004 all 24 Commissioners-designate attended 'confirmation hearings' of the relevant parliamentary committee (or committees).

Before attending the hearings each Commissioner-designate was asked to complete a written questionnaire. Each questionnaire was divided into two sections: the first included nine questions covering personal and professional experience relevant to the prospective role as Commissioner; independence in carrying out duties; views on the future development of the European Union; conceptions of the Commission's democratic accountability to the European Parliament; and commitment to gender mainstreaming. The second section dealt with specific matters relating to the policy portfolio of each Commissioner. Replies to the second section averaged just over 14 pages and varied in length from three pages (Dalia Grybauskaité, Commissioner-designate for Financial Programming and Budget) to 36 pages (Rocco Buttiglione, Commissioner-designate for Justice, Freedom and Security). Because Commission officials were deeply engaged in the drafting of responses, the direct involvement of Commissioners-designate was not always immediately apparent. In part, this reflected a propensity by committees to ask questions which 'often delved into a level of minute detail that was inappropriate at the outset of the mandate of the Commission and before the college had been able to formulate substantively its future work programme' (PE 355.359 2005:9). Moreover, answers to the first section were closely coordinated by Commission officials. This was readily apparent in answers to the question, how do you envisage the nature of your responsibility to the European Parliament? All replies offered a variation of Margot Wallström's answer:

> It is of prime political importance that the European Parliament, as the only directly elected European institution, should hold commissioners and the entire college to account ... As Commissioner

> I will work to ensure that I and my colleagues fully respect and implement the commitments between our two institutions signed in July 2000. . . . Mr Barroso has already assured Parliament that he would not hesitate to ask a Commissioner to resign if he or she clearly underperformed or failed in his or her duties under the Treaty.

All hearings were held in public and lasted up to three hours, with nominated Commissioners making brief oral statements followed by question-and-answer sessions in the respective committees. Proceedings were also broadcast live – on Europe by Satellite (EbS). There was unprecedented media coverage, stimulated initially by concerns about possible conflicts of interest and the financial probity of some Commissioners (Kroes, Dimas, Boel, Udre) and the lacklustre performance of another (Kovács). However media coverage increased exponentially when the Italian Commissioner-designate for Justice, Freedom and Security, Rocco Buttiglione, made controversial statements about homosexuality and the rights of women during his hearing (see Beukers 2006:27).

After each hearing, each committee convened a meeting of group coordinators to enable a preliminary assessment of the performance of each Commissioner-designate to be reached, and for a letter of evaluation to be drafted. The Chair of the committee responsible, or the co-Chairs where there had been a joint hearing, then had the responsibility of signing the letter and forwarding it to the President of the EP. In turn, an extraordinary meeting of the Conference of Presidents was called to consider the evaluation letters, on 13 October 2004, before the letters were forwarded, without comment, to Mr Barroso. The letters were posted simultaneously on the Parliament's website.

Although marked 'confidential' the contents of each letter were widely known before the Conference of Presidents met. In particular, the fact that the Civil Liberties Committee had voted 27 to 26 against the endorsement of Buttiglione's nomination, and 25 for to 28 against his appointment but to a different remit, attracted massive press and parliamentary speculation. Similarly, the negative assessment of Kovács by the Industry, Research and Energy Committee – with 'most Members of the Committee . . . not convinced by his professional competence in the energy field nor his aptitude to assume the high office he has been proposed for' (PE 349.302/BUR/12 2004) – prompted heated discussion within, and beyond, the EP.

The fact that the Conference of Presidents forwarded the letter to Barroso without comment was itself a reflection of the deep intra- and inter-party divisions over the negative assessments of Buttiglione and Kovács. Initially it was believed by the leaders of the EPP-ED, PSE and ALDE that some reassignment of the remits or changes of portfolios within the Commission would overcome the immediate possibility of rejection of the entire College of Commissioners (see Beukers 2006:30–2). These beliefs were made known to Barroso in the course of consultations with the major political groups. However, by the time Barroso met with the Conference of Presidents on 21 October, and announced that he would not accept the rejection of either Buttiglione or Kovács, opinion within the PSE and ALDE groups was beginning to harden against the two Commissioners-designate. Socialists and many Liberals 'remained united in their opposition to Buttiglione, despite heavy pressure from London and Berlin to back the original Commission line-up', and this unity eventually enabled them to outmanoeuvre the EPP-ED, which continued to back Barroso's original line-up (Murray 2005:1).

Thereafter, Barroso's intransigence, in contemplating neither the removal nor a change of portfolios for Buttiglione or Kovács, reinforced opposition within the PSE and ALDE (with the Greens/EFA and GUE/NGL already committed to the replacement of Buttiglione and the reassignment of the portfolios of Kovács, Boel, Dimas, Kroes and Udre). The extent of this opposition was clear on 26 October, the eve of the planned vote on investiture, from the absence of a parliamentary majority in favour of Barroso's team. The following morning Barroso announced the postponement of the presentation of his proposed Commission to Parliament.

After consultations with national governments, a process facilitated by the meeting of the European Council for the signing of the Constitutional Treaty on 29 October, a successor for Buttiglione was found (Franco Frattini). Further changes became necessary after the withdrawal of Udre's nomination by the Latvian government on 30 October and the reassignment of Kovács to the Taxation and Customs portfolio. With these changes in place the EPP-ED, PSE and ALDE announced that they would vote in favour of the revised College. A second round of hearings for Frattini, Kovács and Andris Pielbags (the new Latvian Commissioner-designate for Energy) was held on 15–16 November; and on 18 November Parliament voted to approve the new Commission (449 votes in favour, 149 against, with 82 abstentions). Barroso's team was then formally appointed by the Council on 19 November.

Censure and dismissal of the Commission

Under Article 201 (Article 234 TFEU) the EP has the capacity to force the Commission to resign as a body if a motion of censure is carried by a two-thirds majority of the votes cast, representing a majority of the members of the European Parliament. Yet the EP has never successfully used this formal power, notwithstanding the resignation of the Santer Commission in 1999. However, the fact that no censure motion has been successful has not prevented the EP from tabling such motions. Twelve motions were tabled between 1972 and mid-2007. All failed to come close to meeting the double majority requirement of the procedure. The closest censure vote before the 'Commission crisis' of 1999 was on the handling of the 'BSE crisis' in 1997 when 73 per cent of MEPs voted but only a quarter (118) of those who voted supported the motion (see Lord 1998:89; Maurer 1999a:54–5). In June 2005, in the first few months of the Barroso Commission, a motion alleging unethical behaviour by the Commission President was tabled by the ID Group but was supported by only 35 MEPs out of the 659 who voted.

In part, the procedural inhibitions on the exercise of this power, whereby a double majority is required in Parliament, limit the chances of successfully removing the Commission. In larger part, however, the failure to adopt a motion of censure is because the power of dismissal is a 'nuclear weapon' in Parliament's procedural armoury. As noted repeatedly throughout this book, Parliament and Commission histori-cally have shared a common institutional perspective which has been reinforced by close working arrangements and interinstitutional agree-ments between the two institutions. In Hix's words (2005:60), 'the EP is aware that the Commission, as a fellow supranational institution, is more often an ally against the Council than an enemy'. As a result, Parliament has proved reluctant to deploy the negative weapon of censure. Moreover, the fact that the weapon is targeted at the Commission collectively, and aimed at the College of Commissioners as a whole, means that it is an indiscriminate weapon.

Nonetheless, the mere existence of a censure procedure contains 'the ever-present threat of potential sanction' (Westlake 1994a:115) and as such serves to ensure that both the Parliament and Commission has a vested interest in securing interinstitutional cooperation rather than conflict (see Judge and Earnshaw 1999:7). Indeed, the Commission from the outset was extremely sensitive to any suggestion that the power might be used. In this sense, the negative power of censure and dismissal helped to forge a positive and constructive relationship between Parliament and the Commission. As such it has played a central role in the political and constitutional development of the European Union.

Yet the dismissal of individual Commissioners was not countenanced formally as part of this constitutional development. Indeed, the censure procedure is the obverse of the appointments procedure, for just as the EP consents to the formation of the College of Commissioners as a col-lectivity, and not to the appointment of individual Commissioners (other than the President), so MEPs censure the Commission as a whole and not as individual Commissioners. Despite several attempts before 1999 to extend the right of dismissal to individual

Commissioners, successive IGCs and treaty revisions failed to incorporate such a provision.

The events surrounding the resignation of the Santer Commission and the appointment of the Prodi Commission in 1999 did, however, highlight the issue of the responsibilities and accountabilities of individual Commissioners. This issue was addressed formally for the first time in the *Framework Agreement on Relations Between the European Parliament and the Commission* (European Parliament 2000). Points 9 and 10 of the agreement explicitly addressed the responsibility of individual Commissioners, while still maintaining that collective control rested with the Commission President.

The Framework Agreement was updated immediately after the appointment of the Barroso Commission. The 'major innovations' in relation to the political responsibilities of Commissioners (PE 355.690 2005:8) included in the 2005 Framework Agreement largely reflected the demands outlined in a joint resolution, tabled by the EPP-ED, PSE, ALDE and UEN, and which was adopted on 18 November – immediately before the vote of approval for the new Commission. Beukers (2006:42) is in no doubt that this 'clearly indicated that some agreement on these issues [of responsibility] was to be seen as a condition for approval'.

The final text of the Framework Agreement was agreed on 26 May 2005 and signed by the Presidents of the Parliament and the Commission. Under the heading 'Political Responsibility' the following statements were found:

2. Each Member of the Commission shall take political responsibility for action in the field of which he or she is in charge, without prejudice to the principle of Commission collegiality . . .
3. If Parliament decides to express lack of confidence in a Member of the Commission, the President of the Commission, having given serious consideration to that decision, shall either request that Member to resign, or explain his or her decisions to Parliament. (PE 355.690 2005:11; European Parliament 2007a: Annex XIII)

While emphasizing the individual responsibility of each Commissioner, the Framework Agreement was careful to ensure that the ultimate decision on the fate of an individual Commissioner continued to reside in the hands of the Commission President. It was the President who had to calculate whether a vote of confidence would ultimately be sufficient to trigger a vote of censure if a dismissal, or an adequate explanation of the decision not to seek the resignation, was not forthcoming. Parallels with the appointment process, and especially with the Buttiglione saga, can thus be made. In essence, in this case in relation to responsibility, Parliament has interjected a 'smart bomb' into its armoury, whereby through action directed against individual Commissioners it can signal the possible use of the 'nuclear option' against the entire Commission if it does not like the Commission President's response on the individual case.

Appointments to other EU bodies

In addition to its formal powers over the appointment of the Commission the EP is also involved in the nomination processes for the Court of Auditors, the European Ombudsman, the European Central Bank, and the executive boards of some EU agencies (such as the European Medicines Agency and the European Environment Agency). As Westlake (1998:432) notes, 'all [of these powers] are interrelated and, in procedural terms, have borrowed from each other'. But Westlake's assessment needs to be qualified in two ways. First, a distinction needs to be made between appointments, on the one hand, to quasi-parliamentary institutions such as the Court of Auditors and the European Ombudsman and, on the other, to quasi-executive bodies such as the European Central Bank. Second, there was little procedural borrowing in the appointment procedure of the European Ombudsman.

The European Ombudsman

The post of European Ombudsman was introduced by the Maastricht Treaty. The Ombudsman is empowered to investigate complaints of maladministration by EU institutions or (non-judicial) bodies. Any EU citizen or 'any natural or legal person' residing in a member state may contact the Ombudsman directly or alternatively route their complaint through an MEP. The duties of the Ombudsman are regulated by Parliament and are annexed to the EP's Rules of Procedure. (The Commission expressed its opinion on the rules governing the performance of these duties and they were also approved by the Council.) The Ombudsman is 'parliamentary' in the literal sense of being appointed by Parliament. Indeed, Westlake (1998:437) refers to the office as the 'parliamentary ombudsman'. The EP exercises exclusive control of the nomination process, with member governments, unusually in EU appointments, having no input. At least 40 MEPs from at least two Member States are required to make a nomination. Moreover, the Ombudsman's term of office is synchronized with that of the EP itself and nominations are made by MEPs immediately after each parliamentary election.

In making its decision on the appointment of the Ombudsman the Petitions Committee holds public hearings which take the form of interviews with all of the nominated candidates. A list of interviewed candidates is then presented, in alphabetical order, for decision by the full Parliament. In this regard the parliamentary appointment process of the Ombudsman is distinctly different to the EP's other appointment procedures. The vote is decided by simple majority, though at least half of all MEPs have to be present. In the event of a tie the rules provide for the eldest candidate to be appointed (European Parliament 2007a: Rule 194).

Jacob Söderman was elected as the first Ombudsman and he was reelected, narrowly, for a second term in October 1999. Upon his retirement he was succeeded by Nikiforos Diamandourous in April 2003. Mr Diamandouros was reelected by the new Parliament in January 2005. Diamandouros works closely with the Petitions Committee to which he presents an annual report as well as reporting to plenary. The Ombudsman's office is located in the EP buildings in Strasbourg. His budget is annexed to the EP's budget.

In the event that the Ombudsman no longer fulfils 'the conditions required for the performance of his duties or is guilty of serious misconduct' then, at the request of the European Parliament, he may be dismissed by the Court of Justice (http://www.euro-ombudsman.eu.int/home/en/default.htm).

Court of Auditors

The Court of Auditors was established in 1975 with the merger of the two separate audit bodies of the EEC and Euratom and the ECSC. Under Article 248(4) (Article 287(4) TFEU) the Court of Auditors exists to help the twin arms of the budgetary authority (Parliament and Council) 'in exercising their powers of control over the implementation of the budget'. The EP had pressed hard for the creation of a single audit body and as a result 'has always had a proprietorial, and almost paternal, attitude towards the Court' (Westlake 1994a:47). From the outset, the EP was given the right to be consulted in the appointment of its members (Article 247; Article 286 TFEU). This was the first time the Parliament had been involved in the EU's appointment process, and, in line with its wider expansionist procedural creativity (see Chapter 2), it sought to maximize its influence beyond the formal power of consultation. This it did by establishing the practice after direct elections of using its Budgetary Control Committee to hold hearings, loosely based on the American tradition, in which nominees were questioned on their experience and views. Recommendations were then made by the committee to the EP as a whole for its decision on whether or not to approve the nominees.

What should be remembered at this point is that there was no treaty provision for such hearings, and there was no formal obligation upon nominees to appear before the committee. What the EP was able to count on, however, was the political calculation that any candidate who refused to attend a hearing would be highly unlikely to receive positive parliamentary support. More of a gamble was what would happen if Parliament expressed a negative opinion upon a nominee. This occurred for the first time in 1989 when the nominees of the French and Greek governments failed to receive a favourable opinion. The outcome was inconclusive as the French replaced their initial candidate while the Greek government ignored Parliament's opinion. Some within the EP identified the French response as setting an 'important precedent' (Westlake 1998:433) and as a reinforcement of Parliament's position (Jacobs 1999:5), but such assessments were strongly qualified by events in 1993. On this second occasion, the EP's opposition to a nominee from Portugal and to the reappointment of the Italian government's nominee was completely ignored by the Council, thus revealing 'the inherent weakness of the European Parliament's position' (Corbett 1999:5) when its informal procedures collided with formal treaty prescriptions. In 2004 Parliament's Budgetary Control Committee, when scrutinizing nominees made by the ten new member states, recommended support for the appointment of eight candidates but expressed a negative opinion on the Slovakian and Cypriot candidates. The Cypriot government then withdrew the nomination of Constantinos Karmios before the vote in plenary; but the Slovakian government maintained the candidacy of Julius Molnar who was duly appointed by Council despite a negative vote in the EP.

In November 2007, when recommending approval of seven replacement members of the Court, the Budgetary Control Committee called once more for the review of the appointment procedure. The Committee's rapporteur, Inés Ayala Sender, recommended that: 'a much closer cooperation between Parliament and Council (ECOFIN) on the nomination procedure be established. Parliament should receive information on the candidates proposed by each Member State in due time. In a medium term perspective, Council and Parliament should agree on a more coherent and efficient nomination procedure' (PE 396.489 2007:5).

European Central Bank

With the implementation of the Maastricht Treaty in 1993 the formal consultation of the EP was extended to include the nomination of the nominees for President, Vice-President and members of the executive board of the European Central Bank (ECB). Formally the EP had equal consultative rights with the Council in assessing the merits of the nominee for the President of the European Central Bank. In practice, however, the European Council acted on the basis of a proposal from the ECOFIN Council (Westlake 1998:433). Despite his appointment being a foregone conclusion, the nominee, Baron Alexandre Lamfalussy, was asked to respond to a written questionnaire and was subjected to three hours of questioning in the Committee on Economic and Monetary Affairs. Similarly, Lamfalussy's successor, Wim Duisenberg, was subjected to the same rigorous process of scrutiny in 1997. Again what is of significance is that both candidates were under no formal obligation to appear at the parliamentary hearings, but both responded quickly and positively to the invitation to do so. Certainly, in the case of Lamfalussy's appearance before the Economic and Monetary Affairs Committee, a key precedent had been established.

The precedent set by hearings held for the President of the European Monetary Institute (the precursor of the ECB) proved to be of direct relevance to the appointment process of the ECB. In adopting the process of 'confirmation hearings' the EP sent the message to Council that it would seek to maximize its powers beyond the mere consultation afforded to it under the Treaty. In particular, given Parliament's dissatisfaction with the limited political control of the ECB conferred in the Maastricht Treaty, it was predictable that the EP would seek to define the terms of any future dialogue with members of the ECB – and to do so through the medium of the confirmation hearings. In this respect the written questionnaire sent to all nominees was of vital importance (1998 was the only occasion when all candidates were appointed at the same time). The questionnaire covered the topics of the personal and professional background of the candidates, issues of monetary and economic policy, decision-making processes of the ECB, and, more pointedly, the issue of the democratic accountability of the ECB. Indeed, one of the positive results of the process was the commitment of the President-designate Wim Duisenberg to maintain a regular dialogue with the EP and to appear before its Economic and Monetary Affairs Committee on at least a quarterly basis. Moreoever, Duisenberg announced that he would withdraw his candidature if the EP failed to approve his nomination. These concessions have rightly been seen as strategic advances in securing enhanced accountability of non-elected EU bodies to the EU's only directly elected institution (see Corbett 1999:12). Westlake (1998:437) was even more upbeat in his assessment of how these advances were secured: 'Once again, Parliament brilliantly exploited the potential of its own internal rulemaking autonomy in order to create effective [confirmation] procedures.'

While not believing that the existing system constituted a confirmation procedure as such, Jean-Claude Trichet – during the process of his appointment as successor to Duisenberg in September 2003 – did tell the Economic and Monetary Committee:

I am convinced that the existing procedure of hearings by the European Parliament, and the consequent giving of its opinion, are of great importance. I believe, as a citizen, that an official confirmation procedure would be indispensable in a totally federal political structure. Should political Europe evolve in this direction official confirmation would, in my eyes, become necessary. (PE 333.044 2003:22)

In the meantime, Trichet was keen to stress the significance of the dialogue between the ECB and the EP:

I have meetings with the European parliament at least five times a year – de facto even more frequently because I can participate once or twice a year in colloquiums … So that makes, perhaps, five, six, meetings a year including – which does not happen in the US – a hearing with the plenary session of the European parliament. (*Financial Times* 17 May 2007)

Certainly, in the absence of any legal requirement for the ECB to report to Parliament (other than for the President of the ECB to provide an annual report) or to explain its policy actions to it, the EP had nonetheless been able to secure informal practical undertakings to this effect (see de Haan and Eijffinger 2000:402). In the Lisbon Treaty, however, this was taken a step further, with Parliament given the capacity to 'request' formally that the President and/or members of the Executive Board come before its competent committees (namely, its Economic and Monetary Affairs Committee). In reciprocation, the ECB also gained the right be heard 'on its own initiative'.

European regulatory and other agencies

In 2007 there were 22 European agencies, as opposed to only five just over a decade earlier, plus three executive agencies, three CFSP agencies and three agencies created to promote cooperation in criminal matters. The increased number and proliferation of different organizational forms and institutional structures of agencies led Parliament in 2004 to call for an Interinstitutional Agreement on the operating framework of European Regulatory Agencies. The Commission produced a draft IIA in February 2005, but the Council deferred negotiations on concluding an agreement. In the meantime, in November 2005, the EP considered a motion for resolution regretting the Council's inaction and emphasizing that 'Parliament should exercise "*ex ante* scrutiny" in the form of hearings of candidate(s) for the office of director' of such agencies. Indeed, Parliament already had the right to choose two members of the management boards of leading agencies (such as the European Environment Agency, European Agency for the Evaluation of Medicinal Products, and the new European Chemicals Agency). As in the other appointment processes noted above, the EP has sought persistently to maximize its influence over appointments through procedural innovations. Thus, for example, in 2004 the Environment Committee held nomination hearings for candidates for the two posts on the Management Board of the European Centre for Disease Prevention and Control. In addition, the Committee also convened a hearing for the Executive Director of the Agency in January 2005. Subsequently, the Director of the newly created European Chemicals Agency and the EP's two nominees for its Board were also subject to a hearings process.

While the EP has sought to exercise '*ex ante* scrutiny' through the appointment processes it has also been anxious to exercise '*ex post* scrutiny'. This has taken various forms, including Parliament's requirement that its designated Board members should report back to the relevant parliamentary committees on developments within the agency; through the appointment by some EP committees of 'liaison members' responsible for maintaining contact with those agencies coming under their committee's purview; and through the 'discharge for the implementation of the budget and ongoing scrutiny of the agency's activities by its respective specialised committees' (PE 366.051 2005:3).

Power of scrutiny

> In the legislatures of the contemporary world . . . some methods of exerting pressure are relatively 'vague' and address themselves to a problem, normally without specifically suggesting a solution. (Blondel 1973:110)

Two of the most common methods in this regard are debates and questions. Undisputedly, the EP has sought to develop the classic parliamentary power to force the executive to be available to the Parliament and to compel its 'responsiveness to parliamentary questions, its participation in debate and its public defense of its position' (Mezey 1979:110–11). As with all other legislatures the EP has developed procedures to obtain information from the executive (Loewenberg and Patterson 1979:148–9). Yet the EP faces the peculiar difficulty of confronting a 'dual executive' – of Commission and Council, only half of which has any direct treaty-prescribed responsibilities to Parliament – and a series of other executive agencies and bodies (most significantly the European Central Bank) which have limited formal requirements to account to the EP. The growth of executive powers has only compounded the EP's difficulties; yet it has also simultaneously strengthened its resolve to extend the general parliamentary powers of oversight. Over time, therefore, the EP has developed a 'small arsenal of traditional parliamentary powers for scrutinising the activities of, and holding to account . . . Community institutions' (Westlake 1994a:174).

Questions

The right of Parliament to question the Commission was incorporated in the Treaty of Rome (Article 23). The Treaty provided for written and oral questions to the Commission. However, there was no provision for questions to the Council, though a convention developed after 1973 whereby Council agreed to answer MEPs questions. This undertaking to answer all parliamentary questions was confirmed by the Council in the 1983 Solemn Declaration (see Chapter 2). In 2002 the written question procedure was extended to the ECB.

Questions addressed to the Commission tend to elicit fuller and less circumspect replies than those put to the Council. In part, this is because of the difficulties encountered by the Council's Secretariat in drafting – and COREPER in agreeing – a response on behalf of all members of the Council (as well as encompassing the views of the Commission). To accommodate the amount of consultation required among Permanent Representatives, MEPs are required to give the Council at least three weeks' advance notice of a question for an oral answer with debate. The Commission on the other hand is expected to provide oral answers with only one week's notice. Replies from the Commission and Council to oral questions are followed by a debate and may prompt the adoption of a resolution. Given the limited time available at plenary sessions, considerable limitations have been placed upon the tabling of oral questions. Under Rule 108 (European Parliament 2007a) they may be tabled only by a committee, a political group, or at least 40 MEPs. The Conference of Presidents then decides whether the tabled questions should be placed on the agenda and in what order. Given these restrictions, relatively few oral questions with debate reach the agenda each year (see Table 7.1).

Questions for oral response may also be asked during a 60- to 90-minute period set aside respectively for the Commission and Council at designated times during plenary sessions. These sessions have become known as 'question time' after the procedure in the UK's House of Commons – from where the idea was borrowed after the first contingent of UK MEPs arrived in 1973. Since that date question time has become a permanent feature of plenary sessions. But 25 years later the EP's Working Party on Parliamentary Reform expressed concern that the 'current practice of Question Time is clearly unsatisfactory' (PE 392.600/CPT/GT 2007:11). In all but isolated instances the EP's question time lacks the excitement and political drama of some of the heated adversarial exchanges in the UK's House of Commons. Nonetheless, insiders are unwilling to dismiss the procedure out of hand, claiming instead that it remains 'a useful vehicle' (Corbett *et al.* 2007:284) primarily because it is 'one of the very few areas of Parliament's activities where the backbencher may enjoy direct, formal interaction and debate with a commissioner or minister' (Westlake 1994a:177). A total of 577 questions were answered at question time in 2004 (this was a low number occasioned by an election year), 1193 in 2005, 1091 in 2006, and 1074 in 2007 (see Table 7.1). In practice, however, such interaction is often stunted and perfunctory despite repeated attempts at enlivening question time. Other, more productive, 'mini' question times are now a common feature of several committees where Commissioners and their officials respond orally to questions from committee members.

Oral questions are far less numerous, however, than written ones. In 2004, 2005, 2006 and 2007 respectively 3633, 5036, 5876 and 6660 written questions were tabled (see Table 7.1). Rule 110 states that questions for written answer may be tabled by any Member and are forwarded to the institution concerned via the EP's President. Questions which do not require detailed research are expected to be answered within three weeks (and are deemed to be 'priority questions'). Each MEP may table one priority question each month. 'Non-priority questions' are to be answered within six weeks. All written questions and answers are published in the *Official Journal of the European Union*. Unanswered questions are also listed in the *Official Journal*. Often the Commission views the deadlines imposed by Parliament to be unrealistic, and leaves written questions unanswered beyond the deadlines stipulated by the EP. If the time limit is infringed the MEP tabling the question has the option, rarely used, of requesting that the issue be placed on the agenda of the appropriate committee at its next meeting. While the drafting of answers to written questions is a high priority of the Commission services, the Commission 'has strongly complained about the number of such questions and the administrative workload answering them imposes on its services' (PE 392.600/CPT/GT 2007:11).

The real value of written questions, as Raunio (1996b:362–3) points out, is that 'it forces the Commission to produce a reply, and members thereby receive an official statement from the Commission which they can afterwards use for their own purposes'. They also provide a means whereby MEPs can inform the Commission, and Council, of concerns and grievances experienced by their electorates or issues which they feel should receive greater attention by the EU's executive. In this way written questions serve the same purpose as other forms of questions and act as a two-way channel of communication between elected

Table 7.1 Type of question by year

Type of question	2004			2005			2006			2007		
	Comm.	Council	Total	Comm.	Council	Total	Comm.	Council	Total	Comm.	Council	Total
Oral with debate	53	37	90	80	37	117	87	45	132	59	23	82
Oral question time	369	208	577	740	453	1193	661	430	1091	665	409	1074
Written	3254	379	3633	4493	543	5036	5327	549	5876	6066	594	6660
Total	3676	624	4300	5313	1033	6346	6075	1024	7099	6790	1026	7816

Source: General Report of Activities of the European Union, 2004, 2005, 2006, 2007.

representatives and the EU's dual executive. That questions are of significance in symbolizing the responsibility of the Commission and Council to answer to Parliament is not in doubt. What is less certain, however, is how effective this channel is in practice (see Raunio 1997). Moreover, it should be noted that relatively few written questions originate directly and unambiguously from individual MEPs. Organized interests, corporate interests, lobbyists, citizens and national officials (and even Commission officials) have all been known to suggest the tabling of written questions by MEPs for the Commission and Council to answer. Yet this is also often a two-way process, with MEPs who are sympathetic to or interested in a particular case frequently asking those who are lobbying them to draft a written question. This can be to underscore parliamentary support and interest in an issue, or simply to extract information from the Commission or Council that might otherwise remain outside of the public domain.

Debates

Debate has been a classic function of legislatures through the ages. The term 'parliament' derives from the French verb *parler* meaning to speak. There is a strong tradition of legislative analysis which holds that, regardless of their legislative powers, parliaments are above all deliberative bodies. They act as forums within which executive policies and political issues can be discussed and assessed by elected representatives (see Judge 1999:29–30). In this manner, debate as a procedure is part of the 'vague' means of exerting influence identified by Blondel (see above). It is a very general part of the functions, identified in Chapter 1, of 'control' and 'administrative oversight' exercised by parliaments (see Packenham 1970:534; Mezey 1979:76–7). Indeed, for most commentators deliberation is not simply a 'function' of legislatures but is also conceived as a 'power' (see Westlake 1994a:181). In the case of the EP this power is enhanced by the fact that it controls its own agenda – unlike many national parliaments. This enables debates to be conducted on subjects of Parliament's own choosing and to a schedule of its own timing.

The EP has developed the procedure of debate, largely through informal and creative interpretation of its formal powers, to oblige the EU's dual executive to debate specific policies and wider matters of concern to representatives. Up until July 2002 Rule 50 (European Parliament 1999) allowed for a political group or at least 32 members to ask the President in writing for a debate to be held on a topical and urgent subject of major importance. Such debates became a part of the cathartic function of the EP – and served as a means of 'letting off steam on pressing matters' (Westlake 1994a:181). Despite the Commission and Council being actively involved in these debates, and frequently being pressed for action in resolutions adopted at the close of the debates, the practical impact of debate was extremely limited. Genuinely important topical and urgent questions have tended increasingly to be dealt with under Commission or Council statements (see below). In addition, matters on an 'urgent breach of human rights, democracy and the rule of law' (European Parliament 2007a:Rule 115) and 'extraordinary debates' (European Parliament 2007a:Rule 133) provide opportunities to consider issues which often attract widespread interest both within the EU and beyond. During its September 2007 plenary session, for example, Parliament debated Burma, Bangladesh and the financing of the Special Court for Sierra Leone under Rule 115, with all political groups – except the ID and ITS – tabling motions on each topic and with joint resolutions being adopted on each.

Since 2002, individual members have also been able, under Rule 144, to make a one-minute speech on a matter of political importance. In July 2007 the 30-minute plenary slot allocated for this purpose heard one-minute statements concerning, among other things, Hungarian–Slovak relations, EU policy on sports, CIA rendition flights, the position of the leader of the PSE group on Polish issues, safeguard clauses in the accession treaties, accidents in the workplace in Spain, and the use of plastic bags in supermarkets.

Rules 103 and 104 allow the Commission, Council and European Council to make statements. These are frequently requested by MEPs and the expectation is that the Commission will explain its actions in debate on a very regular basis. At the discretion of the EP's President the statement may be followed by a full debate or by 'thirty minutes of brief and concise questions from Members' (Rule 103), with motions for resolution usually tabled to conclude debate. Rule 104, initially introduced in 1999, seeks to ensure that the EP is informed as a priority (especially in advance of any press statement) of any significant Commission decisions.

In Chapter 6 the constraints imposed upon spontaneity and comprehension in debate by the simple practicalities of interpretation were noted. But the stuntedness of debate in plenary was further exacerbated by the EP's procedures and practices relating to debate. Various attempts have been made to address these procedural problems. Proposals to enliven plenary debates were included in a report produced by the EP's Vice-President, James Provan, in 2000. The issue was returned to in the 2004–2009 Parliament as part of a reform package proposed by the EP's President Josep Borrell. Leaders of the political groups agreed in September 2006 to a package which included an orientation debate on political priorities and an annual strategic debate to consider these priorities in the context of financial resources; but there was no commitment to move away from the established procedures for structuring debates in accordance with a predetermined order and strict timings. According to ALDE leader, Graham Watson, this was a missed opportunity to make the EP 'more relevant to the public' (see *European Voice* 5 October 2006). A further opportunity came, however, in February 2007 when a special Working Group on Parliamentary Reform, chaired by Dagmar Roth-Behrendt (PSE, Germany), was established by the Conference of Presidents. Part of the group's remit was to make plenary 'more lively and interesting', to consider the introduction of a 'State of the Union' debate as well as an annual debate on Parliament's priorities (European Parliament 2007b). Nonetheless, before the Working Group reported, a proposal – for eight 'micro-plenary sessions' to be added to the 2008 calendar, to be held in Brussels and to be scheduled after Commission meetings – was rejected by MEPs. The objective was to allow parliamentary debates to be held on major Commission proposals immediately upon their announcement and so bring a 'sense of immediacy' to deliberations and give the EP 'more prominence by making it the major platform where EU proposals were made public and debated' (*European Voice* 12 July 2007).

The Working Group's first interim report of September 2007 led to the adoption, by the Conference of Presidents on 25 October 2007, of a series of proposals designed to enhance the procedural efficiency and effectiveness, as well as the political profile, of debates within the EP. One proposal, designed to heighten the 'coherence and visibility of Parliament's priorities', was to programme debates on the Commission's Annual Policy Strategy and its Annual Legislative and Work Programme immediately after their publication. To assist the EP in its agenda-setting role, it was further proposed that, from January 2008, plenary sessions should be split into clearly defined time-slots; and that the Conference of Presidents would set out a rolling three-month programme for the scheduling of priority debates and a new form of 'current affairs' debates in the appropriate slots (European Parliament 2007d; PE 392.600/CPT/GT 2007:9). Moreover, additional time was to be allocated for 'spontaneous interventions and questions' by MEPs, with the extra time (up to one minute per speaker) to be distributed proportionally to political groups. Committee rapporteurs were also to be allocated additional time to introduce and conclude debates on legislative texts and to respond to points made in discussion. Similarly, Group spokespersons were to be allocated time at an early stage in debates and immediately before appropriate important votes.

These proposals were designed to secure the better management of debates and to redistribute time away from the 22 per cent spent in 2007 on non-legislative reports, and the 35 per cent on Council and Commission statements and oral questions, and to increase the time spent on legislative debates beyond 19 per cent and to maximize the 7 per cent of plenary devoted to Question Time (figures calculated by DG Presidency and reported in PE 392.600/CPG/GT 2007:10).

Hearings

The capacity of the EP to gain (and disseminate) information has been enhanced through the procedure of public hearings. Such hearings are convened by the EP's committees with the permission of the Bureau (European Parliament 2007a: Rule 183, interpretation). The purpose of hearings is to invite experts and interested organizations to provide evidence and engage in dialogue with committee members. Representatives of the Commission and Council attend the hearings, and the Commission is frequently invited to respond to the views expressed during the course of the hearing. Committee hearings have increased in number since 1999. In 2005, 71 public hearings, public seminars and symposia were convened, and 73 such public events were held in 2006 (excluding hearings of Commissioners-designate and directors of agencies). In 2007, 80 hearings and associated events were held and ranged across topics such as timeshare, security measures in the aviation sector, and the counterfeiting of medicines. Of this latter number, four were joint hearings of more than one committee and, in the case of one (on the rights of the child) a joint hearing of no less than seven committees was convened. Indeed, the number of hearings had nearly tripled from the 24 held in 2004.

The main advantages of public hearings are that they help committee members to familiarize themselves with a particular policy (either in terms of detail or the broader context). One dimension is that they provide a procedure whereby MEPs can engage in 'exploratory dialogue' and 'forward thinking' and so raise issues for consideration by the other EU institutions. Another dimension of hearings is that they provide MEPs with supplementary sources of advice and information from independent experts, organized interests and NGOs with which to assess the outcomes of the Commission's own pre-legislative consultations. One of the most dramatic examples of the range of advice and information made available to MEPs, as well of interest generated by hearings, came in January 2005 at a joint hearing convened by the Environment, Industry, and Internal Market Committees on the Commission's proposals pertaining to the Registration, Evaluation, Authorization and Restriction of Chemicals (REACH). Nearly 1000 people attended the two sessions to hear contributions from a range of representatives from manufacturing industries, commercial enterprises, consumers, trade unions, animal welfare organizations and national ministries, as well as scientific experts, 'downstream users' and representatives from the Commission. A 55-page verbatim report was produced along with a DVD of the proceedings. At the conclusion of the hearing Lena Ek (ALDE, rapporteur for the Industry Committee) observed: 'I want to thank all the participants who have put a lot of work into preparing documents and speeches and sitting here all day, listening and helping us as parliamentarians to get better results and decisions' (European Parliament 2005b:3–172).

Judicial review

Throughout its history the EP has instigated legal action both to advance and to defend its legislative role under the treaties (see Chapter 2). Litigation has been used by the EP to determine the choice of the correct legal basis for legislation, the right to be consulted, its institutional autonomy, and the clarification of parliamentary prerogatives. The Treaty of Nice extended the EP's prerogatives still further by enabling Parliament to bring court actions directly (on an equal footing with member states and the other EU institutions) without having to demonstrate specific concern. It also gained the power to ask the Court of Justice to provide an opinion on the compatibility of international agreements with the Treaty (Article 300(6); Article 218(11) TFEU). The significance of these amendments was judged by Yataganas (2001:278) to 'have given a massive boost to Parliament's role as a real codecision maker in the Community's decision making process'. One irony of this position as 'a real codecision maker' is that Parliament's traditional role is reversed. The EP becomes a co-defendant in cases brought to the Court as a result of legislation passed under the codecision procedure. In the case of the directive on advertising and sponsorship of tobacco products (Directive 98/43/EC), for example, the Council and the EP defended, unsuccessfully, their legislation in a case brought by the German government. The Court annulled the directive in October 2000 (Case C-376/98). However, an attempt by Germany to have Articles 3 and 4 of the revised directive (2003/33/EC) similarly annulled was dismissed by the Court in December 2006 (Case C380/03, Judgement 12 December 2006). The Commission may also bring actions against the co-legislators as it did, unsuccessfully, in seeking to annul Article 17(2) of the regulation concerning the monitoring of forests and environmental interactions in the Community (known as Forest Focus) (EC 2152/2003). The Court dismissed the action on 23 February 2006 (Case C-122/04).

Conclusion

In reviewing the formal powers of the EP it is apparent that it now wields enormously more powers than it did nearly three decades ago after the first direct elections in 1979. Chapter 2 charted the incre- ments of power over time, and this chapter has examined their cumulative standing in the first decade of the twenty-first century. What is apparent from this examination is that the EP now has the capacity to 'compel' the Council and Commission to take its views into account when processing most significant areas of EU legislation. Its role as co- legislator across virtually all areas of EU policy would find formal recognition in the Lisbon Treaty's specification of codecision as the 'ordinary legislative procedure' and in the enhanced role for the EP even across the so-called 'special legislative procedures'. Its budgetary powers, exercised jointly and equally with the Council, would, if the Lisbon Treaty was implemented, extend to all areas of EU expenditure, and its authorization powers would be enhanced in relation to the Commission – primarily through its 'election' of the Commission President. The consent of Parliament is generally required for international agreements, and even in the area of Common Foreign and Security Policy the EP has acquired a general right to be informed and consulted.

In this sense the EP has an array of 'constraints' which prevent the other EU institutions from taking unilateral policy decisions. In its formal capacity to modify and reject executive proposals the EP thus fulfils Mezey's requirements for categorization as a parliament with 'strong policy-making power' (Mezey 1979:26). It is now widely recognized as 'a force to be reckoned with across a wide range of policy domains' and its role has been 'transformed' since its initial marginal involvement in the EU's policy process (Wallace 2005:65). Not only do the formal powers of the EP enable it to be classified as a 'policy-making legislature' but as Auel and Rittberger (2006:125) point out, 'the European Parliament, in contrast to most national legislatures, actually uses its formal powers to their fullest possible extent'.

While such global assessments of formal power are increasingly apposite, they still need to be qualified, however, by the recognition that in certain important policy areas, particularly in areas such as agriculture and trade – but especially in the area of freedom, security and justice, or CFSP – the EP's ability to constrain the dual executive's actions remains limited, in relative terms. Even in the event of the Lisbon Treaty being implemented the EP's powers in these latter areas would still be limited. Moreover, even where the EP has the right of veto and the capacity to modify executive proposals (under codecision2), its use of these powers is contingent upon the ability to construct political majorities out of, often, divergent partisan and national perspectives and interests. These contingencies and limitations will be examined in Chapter 8.

Before then it is also necessary to note the limitations upon the exercise of the EP's formal powers to require the institutions of the dual executive to account publicly for their actions through deliberation and questioning. As noted above, too much should not be made of the exercise of these powers. On the one side, the procedures of debate and of oral and written questions suffer from many of the same limitations that are apparent in national legislatures (and recognition of this fact led to the creation of the Working Group on Parliamentary Reform in 2007). On the other, a decline in their appeal as instruments of control over the Commission and Council has also been identified (see Maurer 1999b:6). Indeed, Maurer (2007:99) makes the telling observation that the increase in the legislative powers and enhancement of the 'policy-making function' of the EP impacted upon its 'control function' to the extent that questions, initiatives and urgency resolutions have been downplayed. Nonetheless, these inquisitorial powers still embody the classic oversight and cathartic functions traditionally associated with legislatures (see Chapter 1).

In terms of budgetary powers, the EP has throughout its history been adroit in maximizing available procedures. From exercising only limited powers in the original treaties, the EP has incrementally enhanced its influence over the EU's budget through signing successive interinstitutional agreements and has reached the position where the Lisbon Treaty reiterates the joint responsibility of the EP and Council in the exercise of the EU's budgetary functions and, through the removal of the distinction between compulsory and non-compulsory expenditure, would, if implemented, ensure that all EU expenditure would be subject to the approval and control of the EP. For the first time since 1975, therefore, the annual budget procedure has been amended and may yet culminate in further enhancement of the EP's power over the budget (but still with limitations on the preparation of the annual budget imposed by the multiannual financial framework, which is nonetheless adopted only on the basis of the EP's consent).

In terms of the formal powers available to the EP in relation to the authorization, control and dismissal of the Commission, Parliament has made considerable strides. From having no direct input into the appointment process, Parliament has gradually secured the dual right to 'elect' the Commission President, and also to consent to the choice of the College of Commissioners as a whole. Moreover, the Council in proposing candidates for the Presidency of the Commission is required to take into account elections to the EP. In this sense, commentators refer to the 'parliamentarization' of the Commission or to the movement 'towards a parliamentary model'. Yet even if the Lisbon Treaty comes into effect, 'parliamentarization' of the Commission would remain an aspiration. As will be seen in Chapter 9, the EU still lacks several of the fundamental and interconnected characteristics normally associated with a parliamentary system.

Indeed, as Chapter 1 made clear, assessment of the EP as a 'parliament' and as part of a broader 'parliamentary system' requires recognition of the interconnected, interinstitutional and contextual elements of the exercise of formal powers. Chapter 8 moves beyond the specification of the EP's formal powers to examine the actual influence it wields in the early twenty-first century.

Chapter 8

Influence and Decision-Making

Despite the many and varied changes noted in earlier chapters of this book, the European Parliament still suffers an image problem. Some standard student texts on the EU, while acknowledging Parliament's increased powers in recent years, continue to argue that it remains 'a junior member in the EU decision-making system' and 'has a credibility problem' (McCormick 2005:94). The general lack of public awareness of Parliament's increased power was noted ruefully in 2004 by the then President of Parliament, Pat Cox: 'Parliament's role in law making is still poorly known and understood. Many still believe that governments inside the Council alone decide the contents of EU regulations and directives' (PE 287.644 2004:3). Yet, in contrast, specialist scholars of parliaments argue that 'the formal powers of the European Parliament allow us to qualify it as a policy-making legislature' (Auel and Rittberger 2006:124), and that comparative evaluations of the EP's influence have tended to rank the EP higher in terms of its legislative impact than many national parliaments (see Scully 2000a:235; Kreppel 2002:1; Scully 2007:179). Indeed, Hix *et al.* (2007:3) go so far as to argue that the EP is now 'one of the most powerful elected assemblies in the world'.

Given these divergent perceptions, this chapter reviews the evidence – both quantitative and qualitative – on the *legislative influence* of the EP. The chapter also examines the notion that the EP is able to wield legislative influence indirectly through the 'prior authorization' of the Commission's broad legislative programme as well as of specific policies. This form of indirect influence is often referred to as *influence over the executive* and is examined towards the end of this chapter.

This chapter reiterates the contention of Chapter 1 that any assessment of the EP's role (in this case its direct and indirect legislative influence) needs to be *interinstitutional* – to take account of the EP's relation with other institutions; *contextual* – to take account of the systemic context; and *interconnected* – to take account of Parliament's multifunctional nature.

Assessing legislative influence

While there is widespread agreement that the legislative role of the EP has increased significantly since the introduction of the cooperation procedure and, especially, since codecision, there still remain fundamental disputes about the exact extent of EP influence. A vital indicator of enhanced influence is the capacity of the EP to amend legislative proposals. For over twenty years the EP has been incrementally expanding its legislative influence, but public, and even academic, perceptions of its power have tended to lag far behind political reality.

Certainly, even over a decade ago, the cumulative totals of 'successful' parliamentary amendments under the cooperation procedure were striking. In comparison with national parliaments in the member states at that time the ability of the EP to amend legislation under cooperation was far greater, in quantitative terms at least. As the Commission itself recognized, soon after the introduction of the cooperation procedure, the volume of successful EP amendments was such that 'No national parliament has a comparable success rate in bending the executive to its will' (ISEC/23/94 Commission Press Release 15 December 1994, quoted in Earnshaw and Judge 1996:96). In the period 1987–97 the EP tabled 6008 amendments at first reading to 400 cooperation procedures. Of these amendments 54 per cent were accepted by the Commission and 41 per cent by the Council, and at second reading the respective percentages were 43 and 21. Clearly, therefore, the cooperation procedure was a 'significant event for the EP' (Tsebelis *et al.* 2001:578) and, as early as 1992, the EP's own Committee on Institutional Affairs concluded that the legislative role of the EP had been 'transformed' by the cooperation procedure (in Earnshaw and Judge 1995a:7). Maurer (1999b:39) was later to observe that 'the "success rate" of the European Parliament amendments . . . was impressive'. Yet still, it was widely recognized that the exact degree of transformation and the true significance of EP amendments under the cooperation procedure could not be determined by quantitative analysis alone.

Codecision1 procedure

After the introduction of the codecision1 procedure under the Maastricht Treaty the debate about the legislative influence of the EP intensified still further. While MEPs and most academic analysts believed that codecision1 was a considerable enhancement of the legislative powers of the European Parliament, a few strident, persistent and dissenting voices could be heard from political scientists working within rational choice/game theoretic frameworks. Despite their small numbers, their rational choice zealotry came to dominate the academic assessment of the new procedure. Consequently, much heat was generated by the claim that, from a 'theoretical point of view', the codecision1 procedure had the 'potential to actually reduce the legislative influence of the EP compared to the cooperation procedure' (Kreppel

2000b:8). This simple claim, based upon assumptions derived from rational choice/game theoretic models, effectively dominated and detoured the academic assessment of the legislative impact of the codecision1 procedure (see Tsebelis and Garrett 1996, 1997, 2000; Tsebelis *et al.* 2001:579; for a broader assessment of the impact of rational-choice studies of the EP's legislative influence see Judge 2008).

MEPs and parliamentary officials could only look on bemused as their 'reality' of increased legislative influence under the codecision1 procedure was challenged by the desiccated assumptions of a game theoretic model. As Richard Corbett (MEP, a former EP official and a leading analyst of the EP) noted, the conclusions based upon such models were 'the opposite of the opinion of almost every practitioner' (Corbett 2000:373). One reason why Corbett believed that the assessment of some rational choice scholars of the relative impact of the two legislative procedures was 'wrong' was because the 'statistics on the number of amendments accepted by the Commission and Council under each procedure . . . imply that Parliament's influence on legislation is greater under codecision than under cooperation'.

In the period 1 November 1993 to 30 April 1999 there were 165 completed codecision1 procedures with 40 per cent ($n = 66$) subject to conciliation under Article 189b of the Maastricht Treaty. Agreement was not reached in three of the 66 conciliation procedures. In the remaining 63 cases, 913 amendments were adopted by the EP at second reading. Overall some 27 per cent of the EP's second reading amendments were accepted unchanged. This represented an increase on the 21 per cent acceptance rate under the cooperation procedure. A further 36 per cent of amendments were accepted after the negotiation of compromises that were close to the EP's original position. Cumulatively, therefore, 63 per cent of amendments accepted at the conciliation stage reflected the EP's wishes closely, and 74 per cent of amendments in total were 'more or less' compatible with Parliament's position at second reading.

It should be acknowledged, however, that over the period 1993–9 there was a pronounced and increasing trend for successful amendments to represent compromises negotiated between the EP and Council in conciliation. In 1994, 26 per cent of amendments were accepted as compromises, whereas by 1999 the corresponding figure was 59 per cent. Similarly, in 1999 only 8 per cent of the EP's second reading amendments were accepted unchanged, whereas in 1994 the figure had been 44 per cent (PE 230.998 1999:11). This pattern emerged after a protracted struggle between the Council and Parliament with both parties eventually recognizing the advantages to be gained through negotiating strategies designed to secure compromise. Thus, for example, the EP sought to avoid reproducing amendments at second reading which already had been incorporated *de facto*, if not precisely, into the common position. On the Council's side, it moved from an initial bargaining strategy of offering the EP a single package which combined those amendments it was willing to accept along with those it rejected to one that distinguished between those amendments it could accept, those it could not, and those upon which a compromise might be found. In addition, the publication in the *Official Journal* of interpretative declarations, or statements of future legislative intent by the Commission or Council, became alternative means of resolving interinstitutional disputes over certain amendments.

Codecision2

In the 1999–2004 Parliament 403 legislative acts were adopted under codecision2. The innovation, introduced by the Amsterdam Treaty (see Chapter 7), which enabled an act to be adopted at first reading on the basis of the EP's position, was activated in 28 per cent of procedures ($n = 115$). A further 50 per cent of dossiers ($n = 200$) were concluded at second reading, and 22 per cent ($n = 84$) were adopted following conciliation, with two other procedures failing to gain approval by the plenary. Of the 115 dossiers concluded at first reading, 36 per cent were adopted without amendment to the Commission's proposal ($n = 42$) and 64 per cent ($n = 73$) were amended by Parliament. Of the 200 procedures concluded at second reading 50 per cent were adopted on the basis of the Council's common position without amendment, and 50 per cent were adopted following Council's approval of the EP's amendments. Of the 86 dossiers that proceeded to conciliation, consideration was given to 1344 amendments that had been adopted by Parliament at second reading (see Table 8.1). Of these, 307 (23 per cent) were adopted without change; 809 (60 per cent) were agreed after compromise; and 228 (17 per cent) were withdrawn during the course of conciliation (for details see PE 287.644 2004).

In the first half of the sixth parliament (July 2004 to December 2006) 169 legislative acts were adopted under codecision. Of these acts, 107 (63 per cent) were concluded at first reading, 51 (30 per cent) at second reading, and only 11 (7 per cent) progressed to conciliation. Of the 311 second reading amendments considered in conciliation, 24 per cent were adopted without change, 54 per cent were incorporated in some form in compromise amendments, and 21 per cent were withdrawn (European Parliament 2007e:10–13). Nearly 80 per cent of the EP's second reading amendments were thus accepted either in whole, in part, or 'in spirit' during the course of conciliation (see Table 8.1).

Table 8.1   Codecision2 1999–2006: the European Parliament in conciliation

	1999–2004		2004–2006	
Number of conciliation procedures	86		11	
Second reading amendments	*n*	*% accepted*	*n*	*% accepted*
Accepted unchanged	307	23	75	24
Accepted as compromise	809	60	171	54
Not accepted	228	17	65	21
Total amendments adopted at second reading	1344	100	311	100

Source: PE 287.644 2004; European Parliament (2007e).

Early agreements

What is notable is that, since the Amsterdam Treaty came into effect, there has been a marked shift toward 'early agreements' in the codecision procedure. Whereas in the first year after Amsterdam fewer than 20 per cent of dossiers were concluded at first reading, by the 2004–2009 Parliament nearly two-thirds of dossiers were concluded at this stage. A further innovation since 2004 has been the development of 'early' second reading agreements. Such agreements are reached after the EP has adopted its first reading position but before the Council reaches its common position. Although, technically, these are second-reading agreements they are political deals reached before the Council completes its first reading. What they entail are assurances, by the chair of the responsible parliamentary committee, that if Council incorporates in its common position the elements of the deal reached in negotiations, then the chair will recommend that that position be adopted without amendment in Parliament's second reading. In the first two sessions of the 2004–2009 Parliament some 15 per cent of all procedures were concluded at this early second reading stage.

The movement towards early agreements, as Farrell and Héritier (2007:296) observe, was 'unexpected' as such agreements were 'in no sense anticipated in the Maastricht provisions that introduced the codecision procedure'. The very ambiguities and complexities of the codecision1 procedure, and the procedural creativity of the EP (see Chapters 2 and 7), soon led to recognition by Council that Parliament's cooperation was essential for legislation to be processed efficiently. Under codecision1, however, interactions between Council and Parliament were mainly focused on third reading – with trialogues and other informal negotiations developed to lubricate the formal process of conciliation. At earlier stages in the procedure 'Parliament and Council effectively remained apart, each deciding its position without specific regard to the other' (Shackleton and Raunio 2003:173) and there was little attempt to avoid conciliation if divergent views emerged at first or second reading. In this sense, codecision was conceived initially as a sequential process with Council and the EP reacting in turn to each other's formal proposals up until the requirement for consensus at the conciliation stage. Nonetheless, to mitigate the cumbersome formal negotiating process in the Conciliation Committee, informal negotiations after second reading became 'normal practice' (Farrell and Héritier 2003a:588). In effect, the institutional innovation of informal trialogues constituted 'rules of engagement' in the opinion of at least one EP official – who also believed that they had been internalized to such a degree that 'by the end of the Maastricht era, they had become so self-evident that no one contested them' (quoted in Farrell and Héritier 2007:294). Significantly, as a precedent for the post-Amsterdam era, trialogues were also convened occasionally before second reading, especially on non-controversial, technical dossiers (Farrell and Héritier 2003a:588; Farrell and Héritier 2003b:24).

The experience of trying to make codecision1 work convinced the legislative institutions that any further extension of the scope of codecision in the Amsterdam Treaty would necessitate pragmatic responses as well as procedural reforms. In the months before the Treaty came into effect the Council, the Commission and the EP negotiated a Joint Declaration on the practical arrangements for the operation of codecision2 (OJ C 148, 28 May 1999:1). The Declaration urged that, in order 'to bring the legislative procedure to a conclusion as quickly as possible', 'appropriate contacts' should be established at second reading 'with a view to achieving a better understanding of the respective positions'. More innovatively, the Declaration anticipated that 'wherever possible acts can be adopted at first reading' if the institutions cooperated 'in good faith' in reconciling their differences. From such statements Shackleton and Raunio (2003:173) identified an acceptance of a new 'behavioural norm' that early agreements would be reached. Similarly, during the course of an interinstitutional seminar on the 'functioning of the codecision procedure after the treaty of Amsterdam' held in Brussels in November 2000, the development of 'a new legislative culture between the co-legislators' was further acknowledged.

Yet it was the Council, rather than the EP, which subscribed more wholeheartedly to these 'norms' and 'cultural values'. The reasons for this are fairly straightforward (for details see Shackleton and Raunio 2003; Farrell and Héritier 2004). First, the Council had limited staff resources and so would encounter workload problems if large numbers of contentious conciliations had to be processed simultaneously.

Second, as most contact with the EP over codecision is made by officials of the Council Presidency, the ability to accelerate proposals through the process at an early stage, and so to complete the dossier within the six-month term of the Presidency, is a powerful incentive to secure early agreement. So much so, that the general strategy now is 'to reach agreement as swiftly as possible whenever possible, thereby reducing the number of issues that end up in conciliation' (Hayes-Renshaw and Wallace 2006:212). In turn, this strategy impacted significantly on the Council's internal organization and work routines (see Hayes-Renshaw and Wallace 2006:210–20) with regular and significant interactions between the EP and Presidency officials, members of COREPER I, and the Council's Secretariat (especially those with *dorsale* responsibilities). The Council created a *dorsale*, a backbone, whose members coordinate codecision activities, attend various EP committee meetings and ensure, through the provision of centralized and coordinated information, that all member states' governments are kept abreast of the current stage of negotiations with Parliament.

However, Parliament was more hesitant in its normative, institutional and organizational responses to the move towards 'early agreements'. Persistent normative concerns have been expressed in the EP about the transparency of informal negotiations. As a general rule, as Shackleton and Raunio (2003:178) observe, 'the greater the volume of negotiation conducted earlier in the procedure the less transparent the proceedings'. Indeed, one of 'two manifest dangers' confronting Parliament in the move towards early agreements – identified by the three Vice-Presidents with responsibility for conciliation in 2001 – was that 'open and public debate in committee and plenary . . . would tend to be reduced in importance by informal negotiations taking place elsewhere' (European Parliament 2001). Concerns about transparency were also aired beyond the EP (see, for example, the UK's House of Commons European Scrutiny Committee, in HC 152 xxxiii 2002: 39–40).

A commitment to respect the principles of 'transparency, accountability and efficiency' was incorporated in the *Joint Declaration on practical arrangements for the Codecision Procedure,* of June 2007 (OJ C 145, 30 June 2007:5), as a reflection of the continuing concern about the secrecy surrounding early agreement negotiations. Even after the Joint Declaration, however, the worry still remained that the efficiency principle would continue to outweigh the transparency and accountability principles (see Bunyan 2007:9).

In terms of interinstitutional relations, the EP was also more hesitant than the Council in embracing early agreements. Indeed, within months of the Amsterdam Treaty coming into effect, reservations had been expressed in the EP about the advisability of developing too 'consensual' a relationship with Council at the early stages of codecision.

Thus, at the conclusion of the interinstitutional seminar in 2000 mentioned above, Dagmar Roth-Behrendt (leading Socialist MEP and, significantly, then PSE coordinator on the Environment Committee) voiced the opinion that the EP's political demands should continue to take precedence over and above any desire to reach early agreement with Council. The danger was that Council's intergovernmental mode of working would come to pervade the process of negotiation at the early stages of the codecision procedure. In which case, Parliament might 'find itself reduced to the role of the 16th Member State', and '[g]overnmental interests as expressed in the Council would tend to prevail more often' (European Parliament 2001). Parliament was thus very conscious of the risk of the procedure being 'undermined by a method of resolving differences of opinion which is essentially intergovernmental in nature' (European Parliament 2001a). In these circumstances Parliament maintained that in its working methods 'Council should be encouraged to become more like Parliament, not the other way around' (European Parliament 2001a).

The problem was however that Parliament did not have, at the time, consistent, structured organizational arrangements for reaching early agreements (see Shackleton and Raunio 2003:175–6). To some extent the debate within Parliament about the broader concerns surrounding early negotiations in codecision had tended to delay consideration of practical guidelines about their conduct. No standard operating procedures for early negotiations existed and even the requirement for MEPs to negotiate on the basis of a mandate and to keep the relevant committee informed was not codified. Indeed, different parliamentary committees adopted different procedures for opening negotiations with Council, ambiguous verbal agreements occasionally led to later misunderstandings, and there was little clarity about who should negotiate and on what basis (see European Parliament 2002a). Given these differences, the EP's Conference of Presidents approved guidelines, in November 2004, which were designed to regularize MEPs' working methods and interactions with the Commission and Council at first and second reading (European Parliament 2004c). In effect, the guidelines, although non-binding, established 'a yardstick against which the behaviour of negotiators, above all, their ability to keep the confidence of their colleagues, both inside and outside the committee, can be judged' (Rasmussen and Shackleton 2005: 20).

The 'worth' of informal negotiations 'at all stages of the codecision procedure' was confirmed in the Joint Declaration on the practical arrangements for the codecision procedure signed in June 2007 (OJ C 145, 30 June 2007:5). Indeed, there was a clear statement that such practices 'must continue to be encouraged'. The Joint Declaration built upon Parliament's 2004 guidelines and effectively conferred upon them the status of an interinstitutional agreement. Indeed, echoes of

Parliament's guidelines reverberated in the stipulation that, in advance of informal trialogues between the institutions, 'each institution . . . will designate its participants for each meeting, define its mandate for the negotiations and inform the other institutions of arrangements for the meetings in good time'.

The Joint Declaration went on to propose that trialogues, when taking place within the EP and Council, should 'be announced, where practicable'. This provision was aimed explicitly at enhancing transparency, as was the cautious concession by Council that the 'Council Presidency will endeavour to attend the meetings of the parliamentary committees' as well as considering carefully 'any requests it receives to provide information related to the Council position, as appropriate' (OJ C 145, 30 June 2007:6). Parliament had displayed a longstanding interest in promoting the position of committees in its dialogue with Council, but Council for its part had been 'extremely reluctant to accept that appearances in committee should become the main form of communication between it and Parliament' (Shackleton and Raunio 2003:180).

Overall, by mid-2007, not only had 'early agreements' at first and second reading become the norm but also the informal interinstitutional interactions of the initial years of codecision2 had become sufficiently formalized to constitute the basis of a new interinstitutional declaration. In this sense the declaration represented another example of the '*iterated* process of successive formal institutional change and informal institutional development' (Farrell and Héritier 2007:299, original emphasis; see also Chapter 2). A further example of this process came with the introduction, in early 2008, of a 'period of grace' or 'cooling-off period' between a committee's vote and plenary debate in order to allow for negotiations and to assure 'the necessary transparency among all stakeholders in the House' (PE 392.600/CPT/ GT 2007:12). Yet 'serious concerns' about first reading agreements and the 'potential lack of transparency and democratic legitimacy' persisted and were noted in a paper prepared for the Working Group on Parliamentary Reform (see Chapter 7). The Working Group's paper also concluded that early agreements did 'not increase Parliament's visibility in the public and the media who are looking for political confrontation along clear political lines and not for flat, "technocratic' debate"' (*European Voice* 17 January 2008).

Rejection

As noted in Chapter 1, Mezey (1979:25) maintains that a key variable in classifying the policy influence of legislatures is their ability to constrain the activities of executives: 'The most telling constraint that the legislature can place on the policy-making process is the veto. This means that the legislature can reject any proposal'. The significance of the cooperation procedure, which was introduced by the Single European Act (and eventually would be abolished in the Lisbon Treaty), was that it enabled the EP for the first time to say no to Commission proposals. Even then, however, the Council had the right to overturn Parliament's rejection of its common position by a unanimous vote and with the agreement of the Commission. With the introduction of the codecision1 procedure in the Maastricht Treaty, and certainly in its amended form under the Amsterdam Treaty, the EP obtained the right of legislative veto. Thereafter, a rejection of Council's common position by a majority of MEPs meant that the legislation fell. With this power the EP could 'no longer be accused of lacking teeth' (Corbett *et al.* 2007:216). Of course while it is one thing to have such formal powers, it is another entirely to use them. Thus, throughout the history of both the cooperation and codecision procedures, MEPs have been cautious in the deployment of the power of rejection.

Rejection under cooperation

When MEPs were asked why Parliament had exercised such restraint in rejecting Council's common positions under the cooperation procedure one leading MEP answered:

> Parliament doesn't like rejecting . . . It follows that the Parliament will always avoid rejection if it can. Parliament comes badly out of rejection if legislation is needed. It's better to have legislation that we regard as partially unsatisfactory or inadequate rather than no legislation at all. (Derek Prag, in Earnshaw and Judge 1995a:21)

Not surprisingly, in the light of this comment, Parliament used its power of rejection sparingly under the cooperation procedure. Only rarely did it seek to reject a common position and on only seven occasions did it succeed. The first rejection came as early as 1988 on a proposed directive on the protection of workers from benzene in the workplace (OJ C 290, 14 November 1988:36). The second came in May 1992 with the rejection of the common position on a proposal for a directive on artificial sweeteners (for details see Earnshaw and Judge 1993). The third rejection came on a proposal relating to energy consumption of household appliances in July 1992 (see Earnshaw and Judge 1996). In October 1993, on the basis of a recommendation by the Committee on Economic and Monetary Affairs, Parliament rejected a fourth common position on the speed, torque and maximum power of motorcycles (see Earnshaw and Judge 1996). The three other rejections concerned the incineration of dangerous waste, the limitation of emissions into the atmosphere from major combustion plants (both rejected in November 1994), and the dumping of dangerous waste (rejected in May 1996). In two of these cases the Commission withdrew its proposal while in the third (major combustion plant emissions) the final text adopted by Council included the provision which had prompted Parliament to reject the common position (PE 259.385/BUR 1997).

In essence, the rejections on sweeteners and on energy labelling revolved around constitutional, rather than policy, disputes between the EP and Council. In both cases parliamentary scrutiny of the proposals was redirected, on receipt of the common position, away from the policy substance of the proposal before it, to the issue of the constitutional propriety of the Council's actions. The EP's rejection of the sweeteners common position hinged upon the admission by the responsible Commissioner that Council was seeking to bypass Parliament's reconsultation. He went on to reveal (or at least to confirm on the formal record of proceedings) that unanimity would not prevail in Council should the EP reject the common position. The fact that the Commission took upon itself the withdrawal of its own proposal following the EP's rejection of the common position not only proved an important element in the EP's processing of this proposal but also caused constitutional reverberations (see Earnshaw and Judge 1993:113–4). In the case of energy labelling, the constitutional dispute arose over the issue of 'comitology' (see below) and the Council's incorporation of a Type IIIb regulatory committee into the proposal. This type of committee would have effectively undermined the Commission's implementation role. The Commission's attitude proved decisive in Parliament's decision to reject.

Indeed, so important is the issue of comitology to an understanding of the development of the legislative and oversight powers of the EP that it is advisable to take a slight detour in the discussion here to outline the interinstitutional dynamics and contestation associated with the procedure.

The European Parliament and comitology

Comitology (sometimes spelt 'commitology') is the term used to describe a complex and often bewildering array of committees which oversee, on behalf of the Council, the implementation powers exercised by the Commission (for details see Hix 2005:52–8; Christiansen and Vaccari 2006:9–16; Nugent 2006:176–80; Corbett *et al.* 2007: 293–303). What the system of 'comitology' provides for at the EU level, therefore, is a series of committees, composed of representatives from member states and chaired by the Commission, to supervise and regulate the implementing procedures of the Commission.

There are three main types of 'comitology committees': advisory (procedure I), management (procedure II), and regulatory (procedure III). Before 1999 Procedure II and III committees in turn each had two variants (IIa and IIb and IIIa and IIIb), but, after Council's Decision of 28 June 1999 (see below), the number of variants was reduced from two to one for each type of committee. As a basic guide, as Hix (2005:53) points out, 'as the number of the procedure rises, the autonomy of the Commission from national governments declines'. The three types of procedures were given formal status, standardized, and numbered I, II and III, by Council's earlier Decision of 13 July 1987. Although the comitology committees were standardized by the 1987 Decision (in the wake of the Single European Act), neither the SEA nor the Council Decision itself recognized an active role for the EP in the comitology process. Indeed, other than the general requirement pre-Lisbon, under Article 202, for Parliament to be consulted before the adoption of a decision setting out the 'principles and rules' for comitology, the EP had no participatory rights in the comitology process itself.

The EP has always been acutely aware, therefore, that extensive use of comitology procedures eroded its position in the legislative process. Thus, a protracted interinstitutional dispute followed the 1987 Decision. Initially, the EP mounted a formal legal challenge to the Decision in the European Court of Justice (C-302/87), but the Court ruled that the EP's application was inadmissible. Thereafter, the EP pursued a two-pronged strategy. First, it opposed the creation of regulatory committees, especially Type IIIb, which limited the discretion of the Commission (and so limited the Commission's accountability to Parliament) and, in the case of Type IIIb, even allowed for no decision to be reached. Second, it sought more transparency of the comitology process – more information on the composition, proceedings and materials sent to the committees.

Over the next two decades the EP campaigned to gain a more equal status with the Council in the comitology process. It did so by using both its formal budgetary and legislative powers (see Chapter 7), by seeking informal arrangements with the Commission, and through broader interinstitutional agreements with the Council and the Commission. In 1988, the then Presidents of the EP and the Commission agreed to the Plumb–Delors procedure. In 1993, the two institutions signed a code of conduct on the implementation of structural policies (the Klepsch–Millan agreement, this being replaced in turn by the Gil-Robles–Santer agreement in 1999). In 1994, after the entry into force of Maastricht and the introduction of the codecision procedure, a *Modus Vivendi* was agreed between Parliament, Commission and Council (for details on these agreements see Earnshaw and Judge 1996:116–7; Corbett *et al.* 2007:295–7; Kietz and Maurer 2007:28–35). In 1996, the *Modus Vivendi* was supplemented by a further agreement between the

Commission and Parliament (the Samland-Williamson agreement). The cumulative effect of these agreements and procedures was to increase the information available to the EP on the work of advisory, management and regulatory committees and to enhance the EP's capacity to express its views about the implementation procedures of the Commission.

In 1999 a new Council Decision superseded the 1988, 1994 and 1996 agreements, with the EP declaring them 'null and void' in its resolution of 17 February 2000. Under Article 7 of the 1999 Decision the EP was to 'be informed by the Commission of committee proceedings on a regular basis'. An agreement between the EP and the Commission was reached subsequently for putting the Council Decision into effect (PE 232.403 2000). And the 2000 Framework Agreement (see below) underlined the intention of both the EP and the Commission to 'ensure the strict implementation of this agreement' (European Parliament 2000: annex II).

Although the 1999 Council Decision has been hailed as 'a milestone in the evolution of comitology' (Christiansen and Vaccari 2006:10) it still did not advance Parliament's influence much beyond being able to call for reexamination of proposed measures on the grounds that the Commission had exceeded its implementing powers. In practice, therefore, the substance of measures considered in comitology remained beyond Parliament's reach. Indeed, while the 1999 Decision 'made comitology more transparent, it was hardly ideal from the Parliament's point of view' (European Parliament 2007e:17). In addition to the facts that the EP had neither the resources nor the expertise to scrutinize technical proposals fully (see Neuhold 2001a:18), and that in the first five years after the Decision came into effect the EP passed only six resolutions on the 10,000 or so implementing measures considered in comitology (Christiansen and Vaccari 2006:11), Parliament experienced difficulties in the practical arrangements for the provision of information about comitology procedures.

Amendment of the 1999 Decision was proposed by the Commission in 2002 and 2004. In the intervening period between these dates, the drafting of the Constitutional Treaty, the increased awareness by the EP of the potential for the insertion of 'sunset clauses' into legislative proposals (where expiry dates were placed on the delegation of implementing powers), and the embarrassment caused by the practical problems surrounding the transmission of texts, all conspired to raise the issue of comitology up the Council's agenda. In 2004 the Commission refocused its attention on the issue; and the UK Presidency in 2005, prompted by Parliament's rapporteur Richard Corbett, initiated a working group and subsequent interinstitutional discussions on the political and administrative aspects of comitology procedures. These discussions culminated in agreement on a new Council Decision that came into effect in July 2006 (OJ L 200, 22 July 2006, Decision 2006/512).

The three institutions agreed to amend the 1999 Decision to introduce a new procedure, the 'regulatory procedure with scrutiny', to apply to quasi-legislative 'measures of general scope designed to amend non-essential elements of a basic instrument' stemming from codecision acts. Under the 'regulatory procedure with scrutiny' Council and Parliament are placed essentially on an equal footing. Both institutions may object to comitology measures on the broad grounds that implementing powers are being exceeded, that the Commission is not respecting the aims or content of the basic instrument, or that subsidiarity or proportionality are being undermined. The new 'with scrutiny' procedure exists alongside the older comitology procedures with their associated parliamentary rights of scrutiny (see above). In fact, the new procedure may feature alongside the older comitology procedures within the provisions of a single legislative act.

For the first time, therefore, Parliament secured the right to block comitology measures. As Commission Vice-President Wallström noted, during Parliament's debate on the amended comitology decision, there had been 'a major breakthrough in terms of parliamentary control' (EP Debates 5 June 2006). She went on to confirm that under the new procedure, 'if Parliament were to object to the substance of an implementing measure, the Commission would be prevented from adopting it in that form'.

The logic of the 2006 Decision was also incorporated into the Lisbon Treaty in the form of the new concept of 'delegated legislation'. This was defined as 'non-legislative acts of general application to supplement or amend certain non-essential elements of the legislative act' (Article 290 TFEU). Such a definition was very close to that used as the basis for operation of the 2006 'regulatory procedure with scrutiny'. Both formulations – in the 2006 Decision and in the Lisbon Treaty – were, of course, inspired by the formulation agreed in the demised Constitutional Treaty. In addition, extending further on the new 'regulatory procedure with scrutiny', the Lisbon Treaty would confirm the possibility for Parliament (or Council) not only to 'call back' the Commission decision on delegated legislation to which it objected but also to revoke the delegation itself – and to do so on any grounds.

In enabling the EP to block implementing measures on quite broad grounds, the 2006 Decision, and the provision relating to 'delegated legislation' if the Lisbon Treaty is implemented, thus constitute further increments in Parliament's power. As Kietz and Maurer (2007:45) observe, 'The slow but gradual increase in the European Parliament's influence in comitology is a clear function of its increased power in decision making'. However, with increased parliamentary influence comes the attendant possibility of heightened friction with its co-legislator; in which case 'comitology provisions in future legislative procedures may become more rather than less controversial' (European Parliament 2007e:19).

Rejection under codecision1

Between 1 November 1993 and the end of Parliament's 1994–99 mandate, three legislative proposals were rejected by the EP – open network provision (ONP) in voice telephony 1994, biotechnology patenting 1995, and a measure to establish a Securities Committee in 1998. (In the case of ONP and biotechnology patenting new directives were subsequently agreed, respectively, in 1995 and 1998; for details see Earnshaw and Wood 1999; Rittberger 2000.) In two other cases Parliament adopted an intention to reject (engine power 1994 and European Capital of Culture 1999). The fact that there were so few rejections is noteworthy in itself. In essence, conflict replaced the normal processes of compromise on all of these proposals. Interinstitutional conflict, primarily over the issue of comitology, was at the heart of the EP's decisions to reject the ONP and transferable securities proposals (for details see Earnshaw and Judge 1996:122–3; Rittberger 2000:565–7; Judge and Earnshaw 2003:258–60). The rejection of the directive on legal protection of biotechnological inventions (commonly referred to as the biotechnology or gene patenting directive (COM(93)661)) resulted primarily from ideological division and party group contestation within the EP – which undermined the EP's majority voting requirements sufficiently to frustrate the successful completion of the codecision procedure. The directive is particularly notable for being the first legislative measure not to have been adopted after agreement had been reached in conciliation (for details see Earnshaw and Judge 1996; Earnshaw and Wood 1999; Judge and Earnshaw 2003:260–1).

Rejection under codecision2: Takeover Bids Directive 2001

As with the biotechnology patenting directive, the 'Takeover Bids' Directive (COM(95)655 1995) – or to give it its formal title, the 13th Directive on Company Law, Concerning Takeover Bids – was also rejected by plenary after agreement in the conciliation committee. But it was the first rejection of a joint text under the codecision2 procedure. What is also noteworthy is that the joint text was rejected after a tied plenary vote in July 2001 of 273 in favour 273 against and 22 abstentions. (Parliament's Rules of Procedure hold that if there is a tied vote then the text shall be deemed to be rejected). Indeed, the high level of participation in the vote – with 568 MEPs voting – was itself unique. Moreover, the directive also constituted the first codecision procedure during which a member state dissented openly and assertively from a previously agreed Council common position – and sought explicitly a parliamentary rejection. In June 2000 the German government, after reaching agreement in Council, subsequently withdrew its support in early 2001. The change of position came after intense lobbying of Chancellor Schröder by senior executives of German companies, especially VW and BASF, along with the head of the Mining, Chemical and Energy Workers' Union (*Financial Times* 6 July 2001). Once the German government had dissociated itself from the common position then the process of conciliation became complicated by the fact that:

> [t]he Council was then in the position of being unable to concede anything to Parliament by way of negotiation . . . Had it done so, all 14 Member States would have felt cheated, having already conceded much to achieve a common position. For one Member State to achieve something, having withdrawn from the common position, would have caused the Council great difficulty in future negotiations. (James Provan, EP Debates 3 July 2001)

In these circumstances the Council 'dug its heels in over the key issue in its common position, and was absolutely unwilling to budge a single centimetre' (Klaus-Heiner Lehne, EP Debates 3 July 2001). Conciliation was also complicated by deep divisions within the parliamentary delegation, and concerns were raised about the national composition of the EP's delegation, especially at the final meeting of the Conciliation Committee. In practice, who attended the meeting of the Conciliation Committee was important both for opponents of the directive (especially those from Germany) and for its supporters. The final vote in the conciliation delegation was controversial, with only a small majority in favour (eight for and six against). It would only have required one of the members in favour to have failed to make the journey to Luxembourg to vote, or a German substitute to have voted in his place, for the vote to have gone the other way. As it was, the substitute member concerned, from Germany, could only speak, not vote. Ultimately the basic division within Parliament's delegation to the Conciliation Committee was amplified in the third reading vote in plenary itself. This vote revealed that there was an almost exact bifurcation of Parliament. Indeed, the chairman of Parliament's delegation argued that in view of the fundamental divide within the delegation, 'it would have been wrong for half of the delegation to have rejected this directive late one night in Luxembourg, without the full Parliament having the opportunity of the third reading' (James Provan, EP Debates 3 July 2001).

After intense lobbying of German MEPs – by the German government, leading German companies and trade unions – they voted overwhelmingly as a single national bloc irrespective of EP party group. Similarly, MEPs from Italy's ruling coalition voted *en masse* against the measure. As the *Financial Times* noted (6 July 2001), 'In a rare display of unity, the German government and opposition, along with leading business associations and trade unions, all welcomed the vote'. Conversely, Frits Bolkestein, the Commissioner with responsibility for the 'Takeover' directive, had no doubts that the blame for failure rested 'squarely on Germany' (*Financial Times* 5 July 2001).

The rejection of the 'Takeover' directive thus provides an illustration of the continued salience of national factors in decision-making in the EP. A primary determinant of voting on the rejection of the 'Takeover' directive was clearly nationality, not party group (see Ringe 2005:742–3). Members' voting intentions were subject to intense scrutiny, and lobbying, not only by affected interests but also by national governments. The latters' attention to their respective national MEPs was in itself tacit acknowledgement of the influence exerted by the EP under codecision and the advantages to be gained from lobbying MEPs accordingly.

Rejection under codecision2: software patents 2005

The rejection of the software patent directive in July 2005 is of significance because it was the first instance when the EP used its power to reject Council's common position outright at second reading, and hence before the conciliation stage. As in the case of the rejection of the 'Takeover' directive, MEPs were almost evenly split over the issue. More importantly, as with the biotechnology patenting directive, what appeared at first sight to be a complex but limited technical issue became politicized and redefined into quasi-philosophical issues of freedom, democracy and respect for human knowledge. Equally of significance is the fact that consideration of the substantive dimensions of the proposal became entwined with conflictual interinstitutional dimensions. As the rapporteur, Michel Rocard, observed, Parliament felt 'collective anger throughout because of the way the Directive was handled by the Commission and Council' (European Parliament 2005c).

The Commission's proposal on software patents (COM(2002)92) sought to codify and harmonize European patent law relating to computer-implemented inventions (CII) (hence the proposal is sometimes referred to as the CII directive). As in the case of the biotechnology patenting directive, and the issue of the patenting of genes, the Commission underestimated the fundamental 'political' and ideational issues associated with its software proposal. At its most basic, the divide was between large companies, such as Microsoft and Nokia, which were supportive of intellectual property rights over computer-implemented inventions, and 'open-source' developers and campaigners whose primary objective was to keep software free from patents. Both sides identified the EP as a primary venue in which to promote their respective cases. The 'open-source' campaigners were particularly good at disseminating their views through electronic media and mobilizing mass support – with public demonstrations organized outside EP buildings and synchronized to coincide with key votes and discussions inside. Significantly, opponents of the measure not only contested the substantive policy issue but also were politically astute in exploiting procedural uncertainty and interinstitutional rivalry among the EU's institutions to advance their case.

The EP held its first reading debate on 23 September 2003. The vociferous opposition to the proposal was noted by both Parliament's rapporteur, Arlene McCarthy (PSE, UK) and Commissioner Bolkestein, both of whom drew attention respectively to the 'systematic campaign of misinformation being waged against the new legislation' (McCarthy, EP Debates 23 September), and the 'vocal and, at times, even personal campaign based on half-truths and misconceptions which play on legit-imate concerns over competitiveness, especially for smaller firms' (Bolkestein, EP Debates 23 September 2003).

Arlene McCarthy presented 28 amendments on behalf of the com-mittee responsible, the Legal Affairs and Internal Market Committee. A further 101 amendments were tabled by the political groups and other MEPs, vividly illustrating the absence of parliamentary consensus on this proposal. Indeed, as Council's interinstitutional file notes, concern was expressed by the Commission at the number of amend-ments tabled by the political groups and that 'Mr Bolkestein warned parliamentarians that a failure to reach an agreement on the Commission's proposal could imply that the relevant rules would instead be created and implemented through a renegotiation of the European Patent Convention, outside the reach of the Community leg-islator' (Council of the European Union 2003:2). This was taken to be a clear threat to Parliament.

Eventually 64 amendments to the proposal were adopted by plenary. The overall thrust of these amendments was to increase restrictions on patentability. At the final vote at first reading, 364 members voted in favour with 153 against and 33 abstentions. The large political groups split with, for example, only around a third of the Socialist Group following the (Socialist) rapporteur in supporting the Committee's amendments. The smaller groups tended to vote against the proposal.

Although the rapporteur argued, in a press release after first reading, that the EP had 'backed tighter limits on patents to provide protection, innovation and competition', the outcome was widely regarded as a victory for the campaigners against software patents. Certainly, the CEOs of Alcatel, Ericsson, Nokia and Siemens had no doubts about the outcome in their letter to the Commission of 7 November 2003 which noted that 'the vote in Parliament . . . has completely turned the Commission's original proposal around, removing effective patent pro-tection for much and in the case of telecommunications and consumer electronics, probably most – of our R&D investment. This would have devastating consequences for our companies' (eupat.ffii.org/log/03/telcos1107/index.en.html).

After the first reading, Council's Working Party on intellectual property (patents) reached a compromise in November 2003 on the Commission's proposal. This largely rejected Parliament's amendments. In fact the compromise reflected an earlier political agreement reached in Council in November 2002. In turn, the Commission accepted Council's evolving stance, and a common position was agreed informally by qualified majority in May 2004. While the Council claimed to have taken on board 'a number of amendments proposed by the EP', opponents of the proposal claimed that Council had 'reject[ed] all clarifying amendments made by the European Parliament . . . and instead pushe[d] for direct patentability of computer programs, data structures and process descriptions' (FFII 2004).

Although Council's formal adoption of the definitive common position was scheduled for November 2004, the European elections of June 2004 intervened. After the elections, the newly constituted EP sought to invoke its own rules of procedure and to argue that, because the legislative procedure had not been concluded, Parliament should be reconsulted on the CII directive and that a new first reading should be held. In February 2005 the EP's Legal Affairs Committee proposed just such a renewed consultation process – a proposal subsequently confirmed by Parliament's Conference of Presidents and later endorsed in Parliament's vote on the Commission's legislative and work programme for 2005 (OJ C 304E, 1 December 2005:387).

In the meantime the Council had been engaged in protracted internal negotiations, which had been made even more tortuous by the transitional QMV requirements resulting from enlargement. While the details of these negotiations need not detain us here, sufficient votes were mustered to adopt a common position in March 2005 and to transmit it formally to the EP in the following month. In so doing, Council ignored (with the exception of Poland) Parliament's attempt to win a renewed first reading and the Commission, in indicating its support of the common position, effectively sided with the Council.

Parliament was then left with no alternative other than to hold a second reading on the CII proposal. A new rapporteur, Michel Rocard, was appointed after the election. Rocard had served as the Culture Committee's draftsperson for the proposal before the election, and was deemed to be more in tune with Parliament's first reading position than Arlene McCarthy had been. Under Rocard's guidance the Legal Affairs Committee tabled 39 amendments to the common position, and a further 139 amendments were tabled by other members in plenary. In the event, in July 2005 all political groups voted to reject the proposal in its entirety, including the EPP-ED which had held out longest in favour of seeking agreement. For the Commission, Benita Ferrero Waldner had made it clear in advance of the vote to reject that 'should Parliament decide to reject the common position, the Commission would respect this and would not present a new proposal' (EP Debates 6 July 2005; significantly, the responsible Commissioner, Charlie McCreevy, was not present for the vote).

This was the first time under codecision that Parliament had used its power to reject the common position. Within the EP, rejection came to be viewed as the 'least worst option'. Thus, as Rocard pointed out, each of Parliament's political groups 'prefers to reject the text rather than to adopt the other's opinions' (EP Debates 6 July 2005). Also, of course, there was no identifiable absolute majority in Parliament. Although the final vote had been decisive – 648 votes to 14 with 18 abstentions – in fact the problem was that Parliament was 'split roughly 50/50, making the result totally unpredictable . . . and with a bilateral impossibility of achieving a qualified majority' (Rocard, EP Debates 6 July 2005). In these circumstances, with no cohesive and sustainable majority capable of modifying the common position (in either direction), all political groups sought rejection rather than amendment of the common position.

In an attempt to pin the blame on the other institutions, despite the EP's own inability to formulate a consistent position, the rapporteur recorded the 'collective and unanimous anger on the part of the entire Parliament' and lambasted the Council and Commission for their 'total and cynical contempt for the choices made by Parliament at first reading'. He also criticized the 'total absence of any consultation by the Commission in drafting the text for the second reading' (EP Debates 6 July 2005). While these criticisms provided a convenient interinstitutional rationale for rejection, they effectively sidestepped the manifest failure of MEPs to build absolute majority support around a position capable of amending the common position.

Codecision2: 'pushing out the frontier': first reading rejections

Not content with using, for the first time, the power of rejection at second reading stage, the EP also 'push[ed] out the frontier of existing rules' (Jacobs 2007:1) in its rejection of three Commission proposals at first reading stage. With customary creativity MEPs in the 2004–2009 Parliament effectively introduced an informal procedure to 'reject' at the first reading stage of codecision; even though the treaties do not confer such a formal right, nor do the EP's own rules of procedure explicitly countenance such a possibility. Yet it needs to be remembered that these 'rejections' were informal, as evidenced in the Commission's contestation of this procedural innovation. In effect the Commission sought to maintain its institutional and legal right to determine when and whether a proposal would be withdrawn. In the three cases examined below where Parliament has rejected the Commission's proposals at first reading – port services, rail freight, and humane trapping standards – the Commission only withdrew one proposal and left the others to await Council's further consideration.

Port services

The first case to be examined here is the rejection, in 2006, at first reading under codecision, of a Commission proposal on market access to port services that had originally been submitted in 2001 and had been rejected after conciliation by the EP in November 2003 (see PE 287.644 2004:48) The proposal had thus attained some earlier notoriety as only the second codecision2 dossier to fall after conciliation. The proposal rejected at first reading in January 2006 was little changed from the dossier rejected in 2003. Stephen Hughes (PSE, UK) reflected the views of many MEPs when he observed that it was 'an absolute insult to Parliament that it was brought back in virtually the same form within 18 months of its initial rejection' (EP Debates 17 January 2006).

Throughout its relatively short life the port services proposal encountered fierce opposition from dock workers across Europe. Dock workers were particularly concerned that attempts to liberalize port stevedoring and pilotage would impact adversely upon employment conditions and job security in European ports, increase the use of casual labour, and reduce health and safety standards. The aspect most objectionable to dock workers was the attempt to extend cargo handling to seafaring crew and to unregistered, land-based staff hired directly by shipowners. Not surprisingly, therefore, throughout the period that the proposals were being processed through the EU institutions, dockers staged a series of strikes and demonstrations across Europe. In February and March 2003 dockers from many EU states protested outside the EP in Brussels, and in January 2006 dockers from 17 EU states staged massive and often violent demonstrations in Strasbourg during Parliament's plenary session.

While protests were swirling outside, inside the EP the Transport and Tourism Committee reappointed Georg Jarzembowski (EPP-ED, Germany) as rapporteur. Jarzembowski had produced the report on the initial, rejected, proposal. During the course of its deliberations the Committee considered a working document which highlighted the controversial aspects of the new proposal. A public hearing was also convened, in June 2005, at which the major sectoral organizations gave evidence. The Director General of the Commission's DG for transport and energy, François Lamoureux, made a presentation at the hearing and answered questions from Committee members. On the basis of this detailed consideration, amendments to the Commission's proposal were made and voted on in Committee.

In the event, the Committee's vote held in November 2005 on amendments to the proposal proved to be exceptional and unprecedented. The outcome was that the report tabled to plenary by the Transport and Tourism Committee contained no amendments to the Commission's original proposal. This result was reached despite numerous compromise amendments having secured majority support at some stage in the voting proceedings. In a convoluted voting process, an amendment which sought to reject the Commission's proposal (supported by the PSE, GUE/NGL, Greens/EFA and IND/DEM groups, and British and Belgian EPP-ED members) was rejected by 26 votes to 22 with one abstention. Several compromise amendments (supported by EPP-ED and ALDE members) were then adopted by a majority; but, when the final vote was held on the report as amended, 23 members voted in favour and 24 voted against. This vote effectively nullified the rapporteur's compromise amendments that had already been adopted. But the legislative resolution – approving the Commission's proposal as amended – *was* adopted, by 26 votes to 24. For this reason the Committee's resolution contained no amendments. Thus plenary was confronted with three options: first, to consider only amendments tabled directly to plenary; second, to approve the initial proposal unamended; or, third, to reject it in its entirety. In support of the third option, the two opinion-giving committees (Internal Market and Employment and Social Affairs) had earlier both clearly, if not overwhelmingly, called on the Transport Committee to recommend rejection of the proposal (by 23 votes to 3, and by 18 votes to 10 with one abstention, respectively). In observing the plenary's predicament, Commissioner Jacques Barrot, noted:

> It is quite clear – and here we are faced with a paradox – that the Commissioner addressing you had hoped that you would reach a verdict on the text amended by your committee. The paradox is that you are going to have to reach a verdict on the initial text. Well, you will not criticise me for having faith in Parliament when I say that, in this area and with regard to this text, I believed that the improvements made by Parliament were excellent and in fact made it possible to respond to a number of valid criticisms. (EP Debates 17 January 2006)

In the wake of Parliament's vote to reject the proposal, by 532 votes to 120 with 25 abstentions, Commissioner Barrot declared his intention to consult the College of Commissioners and 'to propose that it accept the consequences' (which was construed by Parliament to signal Barrot's preference for the withdrawal of the proposal). Beyond the EP, the rejection was deplored by the main commercial organizations supporting the proposal – the European Sea Ports Organization (ESPO) and the European Community's Shipowners' Associations (ECSA) – and celebrated as a victory by the trade unions (see *Agence Europe* 20 January 2006).

In March 2006 the Commission decided to withdraw its port services proposal, pointing out not only that Parliament had rejected the proposal but also that in 'earlier Council discussions several Member States had expressed their reluctance on certain provisions'. By October 2007, however, the Commission had returned to the theme of dock labour liberalization within its Communication on European port policy. This time, however, the Commission stopped short of proposing a specific liberalizing measure and merely recorded that longstanding arrangements for dock work should not be used 'to impose, on employers, a workforce that they do not need, since this could under certain circumstances fall foul of the Treaty rules on the Internal Market, and in particular of Article 43 on freedom of establishment and Article 49 on freedom to provide services'.

Rail freight

In March 2004 the Commission adopted, as part of the third package of rail legislation, a proposal on rail freight services (COM(2004)144). In essence, the proposal sought to establish a compensation scheme which would have required railway freight operators to pay financial compensation for missed delivery deadlines in the case of goods carried by rail. After consideration of the proposal, Parliament's Transport and Tourism Committee voted by 31 votes to 12 to reject the proposal in April 2005. Members of the Committee argued that the legislation would not improve standards in the rail freight industry and would increase costs for rail freight services, distort competition compared with road transport; and that existing international legislation already imposed strict enough rules. In short, the Committee considered that competitiveness would not be promoted by this legislation. Moreover, the Committee's rapporteur, Roberts Zile (UEN, Latvia), who had been both finance minister and later transport minister in Latvia, maintained that the proposal did not take sufficient account of the special features of rail freight in the new member states. Given these conclusions the Committee's draft resolution to plenary simply recommended rejection of the proposal and its withdrawal by the Commission (PE 349.846 2005).

Plenary voted to reject the rail freight proposal on 28 September 2005. Having voted for rejection, Parliament then chose to refer the matter back to the Transport and Tourism Committee, under the procedure historically used to such significant effect under the consultation procedure (see Chapter 2). The clear intention was to 'elicit a position from the Commission, and to obtain the maximum amount of leverage before its final position' (Jacobs 2007:5). Before the final vote on the legislative resolution on 25 October, the Transport Council confirmed that it shared the EP's position (see *Agence Europe* 7 December 2005). The minutes of the sitting noted simply: 'In its vote, Parliament confirmed its rejection of the proposal for a regulation. The procedure was thereby brought to a close' (OJ C 272 E, 9 November 2006:28). If the Council had disagreed then the procedure would not have terminated there. Indeed, the Commission maintained formally that the proposal remained in existence, with Commission President Barroso writing shortly after Parliament's vote to the then Parliament President Borrell and the President of Council suggesting that the Commission would submit a further report within two years to justify its proposal (see *Agence Europe* 7 December 2005). No subsequent report appeared within this time frame and the concept of rail freight compensation did not appear in the Commission's communication on freight transport logistics published in October 2007.

'Humane' trapping standards

A third proposal rejected at first reading concerned the implementation by the EU of international agreements initially concluded in 1996 with Russia, the US and Canada on so-called 'humane trapping standards'. In July 2004 the Commission proposed a directive 'introducing humane trapping standards for certain animal species' (COM(2004) 532). The antecedents of the issue were long – and in fact the issue had resurfaced regularly as a subject of controversy in Parliament and, in particular, between the Environment Committee and the Commission and Council (and third-country governments and hunters). The initial legal instrument which underpinned the issue was the Council regulation prohibiting the use of leg-hold traps in Europe (Regulation 3254/91; OJ L 308, 9 November 1991:1–4). At the time, parliamentary activism played a key role advancing the cause of animal welfare. The leg-hold trap regulation required a listing of those countries (*de facto* the US, Canada and Russia) from which pelts and manufactured goods could be imported into the EU – as a result of their commitment to humane trapping standards – thereby avoiding the prospect of trade disputes between the EU and those countries. Yet Parliament had also adopted a resolution in 1998 rejecting the proposed agreement with those countries, arguing that the Commission and Council were putting the apparent requirements of WTO rules ahead of animal welfare (see OJ C 210, 6 July 1998:31).

When asked to consider the proposal in 2005, Karin Scheele (PSE, Austria), rapporteur for the Environment Committee, noted: 'The trapping standards laid down in the agreement essentially comprise those methods which trappers in the USA, Canada and Russia use, and these methods are described as humane' (PE 357.779 2005:6–7). In which case, she concluded that the proposal was 'unsatisfactory, and it is therefore difficult to improve [it] by means of amendments' (PE 357.779 2005:6–7) and proposed its rejection. This position was supported in Committee by 47 votes in favour, 3 against and 2 abstentions, and in plenary's rejection of the proposal on 17 November 2005. As with the rail freight rejection, Parliament used Rule 53 to refer the matter back to committee before a final vote. On 13 December the rejection was confirmed by 472 votes in favour with 32 against and 10 abstentions.

The Commission's perspective on the rejection was made clear by Commissioner Stavros Dimas:

> The rejection of the proposal will mean that the European Union will be left without any trapping standards in the immediate future and that the European Community will be unable to honour its international obligations . . . To close, I should like to stress that I shall take account of Parliament's opinion and I shall evaluate the positions formulated both in Parliament and in the Council. On this basis, the Commission will decide on possible action, including the possible withdrawal of the proposal. (EP Debates 16 November 2005)

However, the Commission did not withdraw the proposal. Indeed, the Commission's website in December 2007 still formally recorded the belief that the proposal 'needs to be adopted by the codecision procedure which gives the European Parliament the power to enact legislation jointly with the Council' (European Commission 2007b). On the other hand Council's General Secretariat, still in July 2007, deemed the proposal to be 'in limbo', and noted that Parliament had rejected the Commission's proposal and in so doing had asked Council not to adopt a common position and called for the Commission to withdraw its proposal (Council of the European Union 2007b).

In these three instances of rejection at first reading the EP has developed an informal procedure for terminating unwanted Commission proposals, where the Council is also sympathetic to such a course of action. This development conforms to Parliament's strategy of 'pushing out the frontier' of its formal powers through informal procedural innovations. In line with historical precedents, therefore, there is every prospect that 'any future revisiting of the codecision procedure should envisage the possibility of formal rejection of a proposal by Parliament or Council at first reading stage' (Jacobs 2007:6).

Legislative influence: case study

Variable legislative influence

The contingency of the EP's legislative influence is apparent in the case studies of rejection. In these cases the EP's influence was dependent upon the types of issue (institutional or substantive policy), the respective weightings of ideological and national interests and their respective configurations in the Council and the EP, and the legislative 'impatience' of the respective institutions. Beyond instances of rejection, Judge *et al.* (1994) made an early attempt to explain the differentials in the EP's legislative influence in terms of four major variables: first, the type of policy; second, the extent of intergovernmentalism; third, the nature of interinstitutional relations; and, fourth, institutional resources. A fifth variable was always implicit in Judge *et al.*'s analysis (1994:28) but not explicitly stated at the time. This was the nature of political group cohesion and coalition formation within the EP and the interlinked matrix relationship with national parties. The early work of Judge *et al.* has been extended and refined by Shackleton (2000) and Burns (2005).

Alongside these analytical advances, and the parsimonious insights provided by rational choice theorists, an impressive number of case studies have accumulated to reveal the variability of EP influence over EU legislation. In part, these case studies have been prompted by recognition of the fact that aggregate statistics on the adoption of amendments alone reveal little of the actual legislative impact of 'successful' parliamentary amendments. As Kreppel (1999:522) noted, 'Certainly not all amendments are created equal; some may have clear political significance while others are technical and non-controversial in nature'. For this reason, the more astute analysts of the EP's legislative influence have consistently argued in favour of, and engaged in, qualitative assessment of the relative degree of acceptance and the substantive significance of amendments (see Kreppel 1999; Tsebelis *et al.* 2001; Judge and Earnshaw 2003:252–4; 272–6; Maurer 2007:92–3). Thus, for example, Earnshaw and Judge provided initial analyses of over 20 cooperation procedures (Earnshaw and Judge 1993, 1995a, 1995b, 1996) and over 25 codecision procedures (Earnshaw and Judge, 1995b, 1996; Earnshaw and Wood 1999; Judge and Earnshaw, 2003) to provide qualitative data on the varying legislative impact of the EP. Other case studies have been provided by, for example,

Hubschmid and Moser (1997) who examined the directive on exhaust emission standards for small cars in order 'to analyse the extent of the EP's influence'; Tsebelis and Kalandrakis (1999) who presented a case study of the EP's contribution to legislative measures protecting the environment from dangerous chemicals; Shackleton (2000) who used the examples of the Auto Oil Package and the 5th Framework Programme for research and technology to reveal the substantial influence of the EP over EU legislation. Shackleton then offset these examples with those of the Programme for European Voluntary Service and the directive relating to the protection of personal data to reveal the limitations upon the EP's capacity to influence legislation. Rittberger (2000) has provided a detailed discussion of the directives on biotechnology and ONP, while Friedrich *et al.* (2000) have analysed the contribution of the EP to the Auto-Oil 1 Programme. Burns (2005) examined the Socrates, novel foods and biotechnology cases; and more recently Häge and Kaeding (2007) examined the 2006 directives on driving-time limits and the establishment of a Europe-wide driving licence.

In addition to these academic studies of the EP's legislative influence, Parliament itself produces – through the *Activity Reports of the Delegations to the Conciliation Committee* (1993–1999: PE 230.998 1999; 1999–2004: PE 287.644 2004; 2004–2006: European Parliament 2007e) – assessments of the impact made by the EP in the codecision procedure. These reports are especially valuable for present purposes because they make qualitative comments on the 'real impact' that the EP's amendments have had upon EU legislation. Thus the 1999–2004 report noted how the results of conciliation have had 'a tangible impact on the lives and livelihoods of all European citizens' and singled out for particular mention the achievement by Parliament of environmental improvement, better consumer protection, improved working conditions and employment opportunities, reinforced European competitiveness, and more ambitious Community programmes (PE 287.644 2004:14–17). In turn, the 2004–2006 report drew particular attention to the impact that the EP's amendments had had upon improving environmental standards relating to bathing water, mining waste, emissions of fluorinated gases, less environmentally harmful batteries, groundwater pollution, and in improving access to environmental information (European Parliament 2007e:5).

The first edition of this book examined the significant impact of the EP's amendments to the 'Tobacco' directive (COD 1999/0244). Through means of a detailed case study, the capacity of the EP to secure important substantive amendments on a variety of issues – including product descriptions, the size and message content of health warnings on cigarette packs, and the possible use of pictorial warnings – was revealed (Judge and Earnshaw 2003:271–6). In contrast, the processing of the EU's contribution to the Global Health Fund revealed the limitations of Parliament's influence on the final legislative outcome. However, both case studies illuminated the intricacies of both inter- and intra-institutional bargaining and the importance of the informal dimensions of influence alongside the formal, treaty-prescribed powers of the EP.

The next section, therefore, provides a further case study of significant legislative impact. Naturally, there are multitudinous examples that might have been selected. In particular, the significant contributions of the EP to the final form of the Services Directive (OJ L 376, 27 December 2006:36–68) and REACH (Registration, Evaluation and Authorization of Chemicals) Directive (OJ L 396, 30 December 2006:1–849) both provide classic, if remarkably convoluted, examples of Parliament's legislative impact. Indeed, German Chancellor Angela Merkel in addressing the EP, as the President-in-Office of the Council, drew specific attention to 'the recent work on the chemicals legislation REACH, the elaboration of the services directive . . . in which [the EP] constantly strove to set forward-looking priorities and managed to push them through, in tough negotiations with the Council and the Commission in some cases' (EP Debates 13 February 2007).

The case study provided here, however, has been chosen to reveal the intertwining of procedural, political and substantive policy considerations in determining the outcomes of the EP's processing of legislative dossiers. What becomes clear, very rapidly, from this study is that simple examination of plenary voting lists and scrutiny of adopted amendments reveal very little about the political and procedural complexities that are endemic to the exercise of legislative influence. Unlike the parsimony of rational choice models, the actual exercise of influence is complex and often seemingly 'irrational'.

Codecision2: significant influence: roaming charges

Evolution of the proposal

In 2007 there were over 470 million mobile telephone users in the EU, with mobile phone penetration already exceeding 100 per cent by 2006 (made possible by users taking out more than one mobile phone subscription). Mobile phone roaming charges were estimated to affect 147 million Europeans, of whom 110 million were estimated to be business users. When mobile users who subscribe to the services of a telephone operator in one member state use their phone abroad they are connected to the network of a foreign operator, and charged for 'roaming services'. The foreign operator then bills the home operator for what is known as a 'wholesale' service. In this sense there is no internal market in telecommunications as the service is purchased country by country. Until entry into force of the roaming charges regulation in 2007 (Regulation (EC) 717/2007), the average charge to customers for a roamed call in Europe was more than five times higher than the actual cost of providing the wholesale service and retail roaming charges were roughly four times higher than domestic tariffs (see European Commission 2005). In 2005 the International Telecommunications User Group, a lobby organization of, mainly, business users of telecommunications services, described mobile roaming as 'one of the most complex market abuses we have ever encountered, one that is slowly mutating, rather than disappearing . . . [and which] has proved remarkably resilient in the face of regulatory action' (Sutherland 2005).

The Commission's interest in acting against high roaming charges stretched back at least to 1998, when it launched an inquiry into the interconnection tariffs applied between fixed and mobile telecommunications operators within the EU (*Agence Europe* 11 February 1998). This was followed in 1999 by its announcement of a formal inquiry into the telecommunications sector, with roaming charges for mobile telephony specifically included (*Agence Europe* 25 September 1999). Based on EU competition rules, these early investigations were motivated in large part by the Commission's concern over the high tariffs charged for roaming services in Europe, and by the numerous complaints made to the Commission by consumer organizations across Europe. By 2001 competition Commissioner Mario Monti was already warning, following dawn raids of mobile phone operators by Commission competition policy officials, that 'we may need to take steps to ensure that roaming is regulated, and becomes cost-orientated – which it is manifestly not at the moment' (quoted in *Agence Europe* 14 September 2001). However, progress under the Commission's competition policy powers was slow, leading only in 2005 to T-Mobile and Vodafone being subject to a formal Commission 'statement of objections' over their charges for international roaming. Indeed, by 2005 the Commission's patience was growing thin. In that year, Viviane Reding, the Commissioner with responsibility for the Information Society and Media, announced that 'I am convinced that substantially more progress from the industry is both necessary and possible' (European Commission 2005). In the same year, in October, the Commission launched a dedicated web page to enable mobile subscribers to check sample mobile roaming charges.

Parliament's growing concern about roaming charges emerged in June 2000 when a proposal was made that the Commission should consider ways of reducing roaming charges to 'acceptable and transparent levels'. This proposal featured in a resolution on the Commission's communication on electronic communication which generally favoured 'avoid[ing] regulatory intervention in the mobile communications market, which has grown freely' (OJ C 67, 1 March 2001:54). The Commission was further urged to take action over roaming charges by several speakers in a second reading debate on a package of legislative proposals relating to electronic communication networks in December 2001 (see EP Debates 10 December 2001). At this time the EP reached a compromise with the Council and Commission that international roaming in national markets would be subject to review under the legislation, thus giving telephone operators notice that their tariffs would be monitored. However, Parliament's attempt to endow national telecommunications regulators with the power to introduce price controls on roaming charges was not accepted by the Council.

Despite this initial concern, roaming charges did not feature prominently on Parliament's agenda until after the 2004 European election. Moreover, the issue of roaming did not feature in the 2004 hearings of Commissioners-designate Kyprianou (consumer policy), McCreevy (internal market) or Kroes (competition). Importantly, however, Commissioner-designate Reding was asked about roaming charges at her hearing. As she later informed the UK's House of Lords European Union Committee:

> I will just tell you how [the issue of roaming charges] came to be on the table, because, in a political sense, that may be very interesting. You know that Commissioners go through a hearing at the European Parliament. At my hearing, the Parliament was very explicit that, 'You have to do something about roaming'. I did not know what I had to do, and so I promised the Parliament at that hearing that I would have a look at it. (HL 79-II 2007:48)

While the Commission was consulting the European Regulators' Group (Reding HL 79-II 2007:48) about roaming charges, the EP's newly established Internal Market and Consumer Protection Committee (IMCO), in association with Parliament's Industry Committee (ITRE), convened a public hearing on the issue in March 2005. The initiative for the hearing, *The Costs of International Roaming,* was taken by IMCO (and more particularly by its political group coordinators) shortly after the 2004 European elections. It focused explicitly on the high costs of roaming charges, and was the first parliamentary event to do so. Although responsibility for telecommunications within the EP rested firmly with the Industry Committee, IMCO managed through this hearing, and subsequently, to insert a pro-consumer voice into the intra-institutional deliberations on this issue. As Arlene McCarthy, who succeeded to the chair of IMCO after the death of its then chair Philip Whitehead, later noted, 'It was us [IMCO], it was this Committee, that actually raised the issue of high mobile phone roaming charges. It was our hearing that raised that issue for citizens and consumers' (European Parliament 2007f).

The March 2005 parliamentary hearing concluded that: roaming charges required sweeping reform, tariffs were excessive, and consumers were both badly informed and had no means of redress. Philip Whitehead (PSE, UK), the then chair of IMCO, called for an end to the 'real extortion' of roaming charges (*Agence Europe* 25 March 2005). This call was made in the face of arguments presented to the hearing by representatives from the mobile phone industry that commercial pressures would tend to reduce roaming charges, that competitive negotiations took place between mobile operators, and that regulation was unnecessary. In the industry's view, self-regulation was sufficient.

That many MEPs did not share the opinion of the mobile operators was evident on 30 November 2005 in the debate on the Industry Committee's report on the Commission's communication on 'European Electronic Communications Regulation and Markets 2004' (COM(2004)759). Although roaming charges were a relatively minor part of the Committee's draft resolution, and even though its main focus was upon broader aspects of electronic communications in Europe, successive speakers in the debate raised the issue of roaming charges. Thus, the rapporteur Patrizia Toia (ALDE, Italy) made it clear that: 'The question of roaming is crucial: we appreciate what the Commission and the European Regulators Group are doing but we ask for something more'. Similarly, Piia-Noora Kauppi (EPP-ED, Finland), draftsperson of the opinion of the Committee on Legal Affairs, urged the Commission 'to lower exorbitant international roaming charges'. In turn, Commissioner Reding used the opportunity to emphasize that the Commission was working with national telecommunications regulators to address roaming charges and also to point to the limits of what the Commission at that stage considered it was able to do. She stated: 'I have to make clear to you that the Commission is unable to impose prices itself, but it can push for a downward revision of prices. That is what we have done with the setting up of an Internet site for comparing prices in our Member States' (EP Debates 30 November 2005).

When adopted on 1 December 2005 the resolution welcomed the Commission's initiative on pricing transparency in the international roaming sector and urged the Council 'to instruct the Commission to draw up an action plan and timetable that will enable consumers to benefit from international roaming at the best possible cost and as soon as possible, throughout European territory, with continuity of service' (OJ C 285E, 22 November 2006:148).

A further joint IMCO-ITRE parliamentary hearing followed in May 2006. By the time of this hearing Commissioner Reding had announced (in February 2006) the Commission's intention to regulate roaming charges. This announcement was construed as the Commission's final warning to mobile phone operators – and prompt action thereafter might still have succeeded in allowing price caps to be avoided by the operators. Before the announcement, the operators had simply been encouraged to reduce charges, in part by having their roaming charges published by the Commission and, in part also through investigation – with a view to action under EU competition policy rules. By 2006, however, attention began to focus on regulation and questions were being asked about how regulatory measures might be used to reduce roaming charges and, more specifically, what kind of regulatory regime might be feasible? There were doubts at the time as to whether the treaties provided a sufficient legal basis for the EU to regulate roaming charges – as the operators did not hesitate to point out – and as Reding had acknowledged during Parliament's debate in December 2005. Nevertheless, there was a general acceptance that efforts to enhance price transparency had not had the effect of lowering prices.

The joint IMCO–ITRE public hearing – the second on the issue of roaming charges – was timed to correspond with the second phase of a two-phase, public consultation on the regulation of roaming charges sponsored by the Commission in early 2006. During the course of the hearing it became apparent that the representatives of industry had not adapted to the new context of concern about roaming charges. Indeed, they continued to advocate self-regulation, despite being unable to present specific proposals about what form that might take. If anything, therefore, the mobile operators succeeded only in confirming to parliamentarians that price caps were necessary; and ultimately in hastening action against themselves.

Mobile operators did eventually offer to reduce roaming charges, but this did not stall the adoption by the Commission of its proposal for a regulation on roaming on public mobile networks within the EU on 12 July 2006. Commissioner Reding was blunt in stating that the objective of the proposal, was in her view, 'to slash the unjustifiably high roaming charges within the European Union'. She also noted the intransigence of the mobile operators in the face of the Commission 'repeatedly urg[ing] mobile operators to lower the charges for using mobile phones abroad. But they stubbornly remained on average four times more expensive than domestic mobile phone calls' (Reding 2007). Significantly, Parliament's 2005 resolution featured among the justifications for the proposal and in the recitals of the proposal itself. Indeed, Parliament's hearings on roaming charges in March 2005 and May 2006, along with its resolution on electronic communications of

December 2005, and the growing scepticism in Parliament about mobile operators' charges, all combined to set an agenda in which a Commission proposal to set maximum retail price ceilings for private mobile phone operators became a realistic proposition. It should be remembered that establishing price controls over private operators was strongly out of step with the prevailing political atmosphere and, for that matter, the declared policy direction of the Barroso Commission. Yet the EP contributed to framing the issue in such a way that price controls came to be regarded as the course of action with the most potential for success. This is not to deny that other factors contributed to pressing the Commission into action. In the spring of 2006, for example, the European Council had also noted the importance of reducing roaming charges (but stopped short of proposing a mechanism through which this could be achieved); and Commissioner Reding was personally committed to act on the issue. Nonetheless, the EP had succeeded, notably through its hearings, in focusing attention on high roaming charges and, significantly, the operators' own failure to propose practical measures to alleviate the problem. Parliament had also demonstrated that it was supportive of action against high roaming charges and, furthermore, that it anticipated a Commission proposal to address the issue.

The EP's processing of the proposal

(i) In committee

The Commission's proposal (COM(2006)382) was founded on the 'European Home Market Approach'. This approach specified that common EU-wide maximum price limits would be established on the charges mobile operators levied for the wholesale provision of mobile roaming services made from and received within the EU, with safeguard price limits at the retail level set at 130 per cent of the applicable wholesale limit, and a maximum price limit also set. Price transparency requirements were also proposed. The Commission argued that its approach fulfilled the requirements of simplicity, effectiveness and timeliness and responded to the needs of European consumers. As the measure was proposed in the form of a Regulation no transposition delay would occur and there was no likelihood of differential implementation across the member states. National regulators were empowered by the proposal to enforce compliance with the Regulation.

The proposal was referred to Parliament's Industry Committee, with enhanced cooperation (see European Parliament 2007a:Rule 47) with IMCO. It was also sent to Parliament's Culture and Economic Committees for their opinions. Paul Rübig, the Industry Committee's

Austrian EPP-ED coordinator, was appointed rapporteur, and Joseph Muscat (PSE, Malta) became the draftsperson for IMCO. Manolis Mavrommatis (EPP-ED, Greece) was appointed draftsperson for the opinion of the Culture Committee and Andrea Losco (ALDE, Italy) draftsperson for the opinion of the Economic Committee.

From the start the proposal was regarded as a key legislative dossier in the EP. This was reflected in the attention it received in the various committees and in the number of amendments tabled. Indeed, the sheer number of amendments reflected, in turn, the intense lobbying conducted on the proposal within the EP – especially by mobile operators. Members of the Industry Committee tabled some 309 amendments, alongside 39 tabled by the rapporteur. In IMCO the draftsperson tabled 65 amendments and other members of the Committee tabled an additional 68 amendments. In the Culture Committee, 64 amendments were tabled in total, nine of which were tabled by the draftsperson, while in the Economic Committee the draftsperson tabled six amendments and other members tabled another 47. In total, therefore, nearly 600 amendments were tabled to the Commission's proposal in the committees.

The number of amendments is a partial indicator of the intricacies of the interactions of key MEPs within and between the respective committees, and the sheer complexity of the substantive policy issue itself. In substantive terms, parliamentary attention focused on: whether customers would be required to opt in or opt out of regulated price ceilings; the nature of wholesale price caps; the scope of transparency requirements; the duration of the legislation (the 'sunset' clause); and, of course, the levels of the retail price ceilings themselves.

Whereas the Commission had proposed that a retail price ceiling would be the default option for customers, Parliament's rapporteur proposed to the Industry Committee that the retail price ceiling (which he named the 'Euro-tariff') should be optional, with customers able to switch voluntarily to and from the tariff. Rübig argued that a 'price regulated standardised opt-in tariff . . . delivers protection to the consumer while leaving industry room to innovate' (PE 384.334 2007:14). Rübig initially stopped short of supporting specific retail price caps, but he did argue that no distinction should be made between calls made inside and outside visited networks and that incoming calls should be priced at no more than a third of outgoing calls. The Commission had proposed a retail price cap of €0.44 per minute for outgoing roaming calls, a cap of €0.30 for calls made inside a visited network and a €0.15 cap for incoming calls. Alongside the proposal for an opt-in system, the rapporteur also argued for a single wholesale charge rather than the dual system proposed by the Commission. In other words, no mobile operator could levy charges above a single wholesale rate from any other operator. He also proposed the innovation that all operators should provide a 'fair-use all inclusive monthly flat-rate to which no charge limits shall apply', and that this should cover data communications services as well as international voice roaming. The logic underpinning this proposal was that all operators should comply with a price-regulated standardized opt-in tariff, and so provide an all-inclusive flat rate. In return operators would be free to establish any other roaming tariff models they wanted, which would not be subject to regulation. Finally, Rübig also proposed that all elements of the eventual regulation should enter into force immediately; whereas the Commission had proposed a six-month transition period in which to implement the retail price ceiling.

Discussions within the IMCO tended to parallel those in the Industry Commitee. The draftsperson, Joseph Muscat, sought to increase flexibility while ensuring consumer protection by merging key aspects of the proposal – to establish operator-level average price caps at the retail level but combining these with maximum price caps at the individual call level. In line with Rübig, he also supported a single wholesale price cap and the immediate application of the Regulation. The main difference between the IMCO draftsperson and the rapporteur was Muscat's strong support for an opt-out system.

(ii) Committee votes

The votes on the draft Committee reports and the associated amendments proved to be highly eventful. The vote in IMCO witnessed a surprising defeat for Joseph Muscat's (and the Commission's) support for opting-out. This defeat was engineered by a coalition of EPP-ED and ALDE votes. Muscat commented at the time that this negative vote would 'not help protect the most vulnerable consumers' (*Agence Europe* 24 March 2007), and he wrote later that the vote was 'a parody of consumer protection . . . a committee in charge of consumer welfare should be more ambitious in its goals' (*European Voice* 19 April 2007). As a result of this unexpected outcome in IMCO, Muscat voted against adoption in committee of his own report. In doing so, he found support from BEUC, the European consumers' organization which 'applaud[ed] the decision of the rapporteur Mr Muscat (PSE) to vote against his own report after the Committee had watered it down' (BEUC 2007). In the end, the report was only narrowly adopted, by 22 votes to 19 with two abstentions.

Some weeks later the Industry Committee also voted against the position of its rapporteur, but on this occasion declared itself in support (by a three-fifths majority) of an opt-out system, and so voted in the opposite direction to the vote in IMCO. The Industry

Committee also supported price ceilings – of €0.40 for outgoing calls, €0.15 for incoming roaming calls and a wholesale cap of €0.23. These ceilings were slightly lower than those proposed in the Commission's July 2006 proposal, and those voted eventually by IMCO. In addition, the Industry Committee and IMCO both agreed that the Regulation should have immediate application and that it should be subject to a 'sunset' clause whereby it would expire after three years. On 12 April 2007, the Rübig report was adopted in the Industry Committee by 45 votes to three with one abstention.

(iii) Agreement at first reading via trialogues

The adoption of the Rübig report by the Industry Committee in April 2007 launched a process of informal negotiations in trialogues of Parliament, the Council and the Commission. Between mid-April and Parliament's plenary debate on 23 May four trialogues were convened. It was acknowledged by all three institutions that early agreement at first reading would allow entry into force of the regulation in time for the summer holiday season. The German Presidency of the Council also indicated that it sought to conclude an agreement during its term of office. As a result, the EP's plenary debate was delayed from the date initially scheduled, 9 May, until the 23 May to allow for negotiations with Council to be held. Parliament's key negotiators were Paul Rübig, Joseph Muscat, and the Chair of the Industry Committee, Angelika Niebler (EPP-ED, Germany). Negotiators for Council were led by President-in-Office Joachim Wuermeling, Germany's deputy economics minister, who, notably, had been a respected former EPP-ED MEP before being appointed to the German government at the end of 2005.

The first trialogue meeting, to some consternation among the EP's negotiators, was asked by the Council to examine suggestions for higher tariff ceilings than had previously been considered in Council. There was speculation at the time that these ceilings were proposed at the instigation of the UK, France and Spain as an initial negotiating ploy to help protect their national operators. Predictably, while no agreement was reached on this issue, consensus was reached at this first meeting on the time-limitation of the regulation to a maximum period of three years.

The second trialogue focused on the opt-out versus opt-in issue. While Parliament's rapporteur appeared ready to compromise with Council on an opt-in to the Euro-tariff (in line with his initial position in the Industry Committee but in contrast to the Committee's vote), it was reported that the Commission was standing by its proposal for an opt-out to apply. Indeed, 'opting-in' (except for new subscribers) was strongly supported by Council and mobile operators alike. A possible compromise was mooted, however, whereby opting-in might apply only for business users (*Agence Europe* 3 May 2007). For his part, the IMCO's draftsperson, Socialist Joseph Muscat, in advance of the second trialogue, had made it very clear that 'opting-out' was an essential precondition of PSE support for a first reading agreement. The prospect of the PSE denying its support for a first reading agreement led the German Presidency to propose a formula whereby customers would be given the opportunity to switch to the Euro-tariff within one month of the Regulation entering into force, but with customers having to respond during the first three months of the new regime. The new tariff would then come into effect as soon as customers made known their choice. In the end, this staggered formula was the basis of the final agreement. However, at this stage, member states and Parliament were unable to find much common ground on the tariffs themselves.

A final series of negotiations on 15 May found agreement. Yet as Joachim Wuermeling was later to observe, 'Agreement between the Council and Parliament was extremely difficult to achieve. There were tough negotiations; but it was a fair fight' (EP Debates 23 May 2007). The essence of the agreement was that tariff ceilings would decline over the three years the Regulation was in force from €0.49 per minute for roaming calls made, €0.24 for roaming calls received and €0.30 for wholesale tariffs in the first year to €0.46, €0.22 and €0.28 respectively in the second year, falling finally to €0.43, €0.19 and €0.26 respectively in the third year. While the Euro-tariff (named as such by Parliament) was to be higher than initially proposed by the Commission, Parliament had won on other scores. Single roaming retail and wholesale ceilings were agreed, rather than different caps depending on whether calls were made or received inside or outside a visited network. In line with the compromise on opting-out reached earlier in the trialogue negotiations, mobile phone operators would have one month in which to make a new offer to customers, with customers then having two months in which to accept or refuse the Euro-tariff offer. Customers who did not express a choice within that period would then be placed on the Euro-tariff. Nonetheless, Joseph Muscat hinted that the agreement might not win PSE support and believed that Parliament 'could have gone further'. He noted that 'For now, only one group has given the compromise its unconditional support . . . One cannot count on my group's support. I cannot commit myself on this package' (*Agence Europe* 16 May 2007).

By the time the final trialogue agreement was considered by the Industry Committee, on the eve of the plenary debate, any residual reservations had dissipated. Thus, the final compromise was accepted by 46 votes to nil with one abstention in the Committee. The Committee then submitted to plenary a single amendment which contained the entire trialogue compromise and replaced all of the amendments tabled in the original Rübig report (European Parliament 2007g).

In turn, the EP's plenary debate, although attracting wide media and public interest, was largely a formality and ended with a near unanimous vote (by a show of hands). Some 49 MEPs spoke during the debate – almost all of them welcomed the agreement, the only exceptions being the UKIP's Nigel Farage; Gunnar Hokmark, Swedish EPP-ED member and well known economic liberal; and two German MEPs, Alexander Alvaro (ALDE) and Herbert Reul (EPP-ED). All the dissidents shared a concern about the potentially *dirigiste* nature of the measure adopted.

Following Parliament's agreement at first reading on 23 May, the Telecommunications Council formally agreed to the deal on 7 June, and the Competitiveness Council adopted the measure without discussion on 25 June (OJ L 171, 29 June 2007:32). The Regulation entered into force on 30 June 2007.

Parliament's impact

In one respect, Parliament's influence may be perceived to have been limited – as the final Regulation largely reflected the substance of the Commission's initial proposal. Nonetheless, significant elements of the ensuing Regulation incorporated ideas propagated in the EP. Thus, the notion of a Euro-tariff was Parliament's creation, as was a system of single rates regardless of whether calls were made within or between networks. The 'sunset clause' was first mooted within the EP before gaining support in the Council. Equally, notwithstanding its internal differences of opinion, Parliament maintained, along with the Commission, a relatively firm 'opting-out' requirement, and managed to enhance transparency for consumers through requiring mobile operators to alert roaming customers automatically about charges and conditions when abroad. Far more critically perhaps, MEPs had contributed significantly to creating an environment within which the Commission could act to produce a proposal in the first place. Until the EP's hearing in March 2005 there was little appetite to regulate prices and even then it was far from clear whether the Commission would find the courage to take such a step or even if it was legally possible to do so.

Yet ultimately, Parliament, along with the personal resolve shown by Viviane Reding, managed to frame the problem of roaming charges in such a way as to make price regulation not only feasible and credible but also, more importantly, real. Indeed, the EP's significant contribution was acknowledged explicitly by Commissioner Reding in plenary debate (EP Debates 23 May 2007), and the rapidity with which the Regulation was processed was itself the source of some self-satisfaction among the institutions (see, for example, Karin Riis-Jørgensen, EP Debates 23 May 2007). Some months later, in November 2007, at a press conference following a jointly hosted IMCO-ITRE workshop, which was convened to assess the implementation of the roaming regulation, Commissioner Reding declared the regulation and its impact to have been 'a real success story'.

Influence over the executive

> The relationships between the legislature and the executive are the cornerstone of any parliamentary system: as parliaments are regarded as the main providers of legitimacy, executive authority must derive from, and be responsible to, the legislature. (Dehousse 1998:609)

In parliamentary systems, as noted in Chapter 1, there is a basic interconnectedness between the legislative and executive branches of government. This interconnectedness entails both *ex post* accountability and *ex ante* 'directedness' (in the sense of influencing future policy preferences). As noted in Chapter 7, the formal powers of dismissal and appointment extended beyond the choice of executive personnel to incorporate the EP's capacities to hold the Commission responsible for its collective and individual actions and also to influence its policy agenda. Of particular significance to the discussion here is the synchronization of the Commission's term of office with that of Parliament. After Maastricht the appointment of the President, and of the Commission as a whole, now broadly coincided with that of a new parliament. The intention was that the coterminous periods of office of the EP and the Commission not only would facilitate parliamentary scrutiny and control and increase the Commission's accountability to Parliament, but also would encourage the 'prior authorization' of the Commission's programme.

There are at least two major dimensions to the notion of 'prior authorization'. The first stems from the logic of 'control through selection'. The reasoning is simple in that it was believed not only that the post-Maastricht selection process would increase the EP's influence over who was appointed as President (and subsequently as Commissioners and to which specific portfolios) but also that it would enhance Parliament's impact on the Commission's policy agenda by securing the 'prior authorization' of the executive's programme. Paradoxically, the logic of maximized parliamentary control over the Commission's agenda rested in a further 'presidentialization' of the Commission itself under the treaties. Article 219 post-Amsterdam stated that the 'Commission shall work under the political guidance of its President'. In effect there are both positive and negative dimensions to such 'political guidance'. Perhaps, not surprisingly given the events surrounding the resignation of the Santer Commission (see Judge and Earnshaw 2002), the negative dimension of individual resignations and the individual responsibility of Commissioners tended to be the focus of attention. However, the positive dimension of presidential 'political guidance' was incorporated in a new right conferred by the Amsterdam Treaty on the President to agree or disagree (by 'common accord' (Article 214)) on member states' nominees for Commission posts. Furthermore, Declaration 32 to the Treaty also recorded that 'the President of the Commission must enjoy broad discretion in the allocation of tasks within the College, as well as in any reshuffling of those tasks during a Commission's term of office'. Lisbon developed this further by specifying that the Commission President shall 'lay down guidelines within which the Commission is to work . . . decide on the internal organization of the Commission' and ensure that it 'acts consistently, efficiently and as a collegiate body' (Article 17(6) TEU). After Lisbon, the President also had the capability to appoint, unilaterally, Vice-Presidents of the Commission. From the EP's perspective, such enhanced presidential authority contributed to a further incremental increase of parliamentary influence over the Commission. Thus Spence (2000:5–6), for example, identified the EP's ability to vote on the President as 'a way of influencing the Commission's agenda, as parliamentarians could make their ratification of a President conditional on his/her amenability to their programme'. In practice, however, as the appointments of the Prodi and Barroso Commissions illustrate, this 'conditionality' has remained limited.

A second dimension of 'prior authorization' is the acceptance of the Commission's policy programme by a parliamentary majority. In the case of the EU exactly what constitutes 'authorization' and what is being 'authorized' remain open to wide interpretation. Despite these ambiguities, the EP has become increasingly involved in helping the Commission to identify its priorities. A significant step in this direction was taken by Romano Prodi as President-designate, when he agreed to present to Parliament the Commission's 'policy perspectives for the next five years' (Prodi, Speech to the EP 14 September 1999). These 'perspectives' were formally outlined in the document *Strategic Objectives 2000–5 'Shaping the New Europe'* (European Commission 2000), submitted to the EP at its plenary of 15 February 2000. In plenary Mr Prodi was at pains to emphasize that the five-year programme 'is an extremely important undertaking', and likened the programme to 'a political manifesto' (EP Debates 15 February 2000). From Parliament's side Enrique Barón Crespo, as then leader of the PSE, particularly welcomed 'the first ever debate on the Commission's programme for government – the word President Prodi is so fond of; as

I am – for the whole legislature' (EP Debates 15 February 2000). In this respect he acknowledged that the five-year programme was 'breaking new ground'. However, he also recognized that the time-lapse of eleven months from Prodi's nomination to the presentation of the programme infringed the notion of 'prior authorization'. In which case he believed that, in future, 'it would be appropriate for the investiture of the next Commission to coincide with the presentation of a legislative programme'.

Nonetheless, Prodi 'perceived a broad consensus on the basic lines of our programme' within Parliament (EP Debates 15 February 2000) and from this base sought to effect a more ambitious scheme of policy management in the future. A first stage, in July 2000, was the incorporation of the five-year programme into a new Framework Agreement between the EP and the Commission (European Parliament 2000). The two institutions agreed that 'an incoming Commission shall present, as soon as possible, its political programme, containing all its proposed guidelines for its term of office, and shall establish a dialogue with the European Parliament' (for details of the Framework see Judge and Earnshaw 2002). The Commission also agreed to six-monthly reports on the implementation of the work programme and regular updates of any changed priorities occasioned by changing political circumstances.

A second stage came in January 2001 when the Commission presented its traditional work programme for the coming year (COM (2001)28) but stressed that its 'priority objectives' would now be pursued 'bearing in mind the guidelines laid down by the Commission when it came into office' (COM(2001)28:4). More radically, in February 2001, the Commission also adopted its first *Annual Policy Strategy*. This document set out the political priorities which required 'special attention in 2002'. It also defined actions stemming from those priorities and sought to allocate resources accordingly (COM(2001) 620 final:3). In turn, the introduction of the *Strategy* had knock-on effects for the presentation of the Commission's work programme to the EP. One immediate result was that the 2002 programme was presented in early December 2001, rather than, as in the past, at the beginning of the calendar year itself. A second consequence was that the work programme sought to assess progress in the current year, to identify the political and economic context for the forthcoming year, to identify the political priorities in light of the *Annual Policy Strategy*, and then to translate those priorities into practice in 2002 (COM (2001)620:3). In this sense it was identified as a 'genuine political programme' (Prodi, EP Debates 11 December 2001).

But the 2002 programme was accompanied by a third stage whereby future work programmes were to be based on 'a more structured dialogue' between the Commission and Parliament programme (Prodi, EP Debates 11 December 2001). Thus, the 2003 work programme was to

entail an initial presentation, in February 2002, of the political priorities approved by the Commission followed by the formal presentation
of the programme itself to the EP in November 2002. Yet for all the
talk of 'a more structured dialogue' there still remained manifest short-
comings in the eyes of MEPs (see Judge and Earnshaw 2003:289–90).

Concern with the presentation, timing and processing of the legislative and work programme led Parliament's Constitutional Affairs
Committee to recommend a revised timetable for its preparation and
for its consideration by the EP (PE 304.309 2002). The Committee's
starting-point was an acknowledgement that the annual legislative programme was 'an invaluable tool for the functioning of the European
institutions' but that the 'whole legislative cycle is opaque and quite
incomprehensible not only to the European Parliament, but also to the
citizens and the national parliaments' (PE 304.309 2002:11). By
changing the procedures surrounding the preparation of the legislative
and work programme the Committee sought to increase interinstitutional cooperation between the Commission and the EP and so
increase the influence of the latter in the legislative cycle and in the
identification of the priorities of the former institution.

From the outset the Barroso Commission emphasized the theme of
'partnership' with the EP in the identification of its strategic priorities
and in organizing its legislative programmes. Thus, on 26 January
2005, just two months after taking office, President Barroso presented
to Parliament the new Commission's five-year strategic objectives
(COM(2005)12), along with the annual legislative and work programmes for 2005 (COM(2005)15). In doing so he emphasized that:
'[t]his College and its President have been elected by a broad majority
in this House. As we put our proposals in front of you today, we want
to honour the confidence you have expressed in us. We have listened
to Parliament's views and we are ready to stand the test' (EP Debates
26 January 2005). In successive years Barroso repeated this theme
when introducing the Commission's annual work programme. Thus,
for example, the 2007 Work Programme was deemed to address 'many
of Parliament's concerns that have been conveyed to me and to the
Commission. This new Work Programme is more political. It is
focused on a smaller list of 21 strategic initiatives' (Barroso, EP
Debates 14 November 2006). In introducing the Commission's
Legislative and Work Programme for 2008, Barroso stated:

I would like to thank the European Parliament for its active
involvement in the work of developing this Programme. In particular the comprehensive summary report prepared by the
Conference of Committee Chairmen and endorsed by the
Conference of Presidents helped to shape our programme. Many

Commission proposals are a direct match to the priorities set out in your summary report. (EP Debates 13 November 2007)

Barroso's statement reflected the extensive discussions that had taken place since the Commission's *Annual Policy Strategy* had been presented to the EP in February 2007. A series of discussions had taken place between the EP's committees and relevant Commissioners on the content of the strategy before the summer break in July. Thereafter the Conference of Committee Chairs met with Commission Vice-President Wallström to discuss the summary report noted above. (While these discussions were taking place the Council also provided confidential comments on the *Annual Policy Strategy* to the Commission.) Clearly, while the Commission is more than willing to acknowledge the EP's contribution to determining its Work Programme, others are less convinced of the EP's impact. Thus, for example the UK's House of Commons Select Committee on European Scrutiny concluded that 'it is . . . not clear to what extent [the dialogue between the Commission and the EP] is a useful exercise' (HC 519-I 2007:7). In the Committee's view the value of the deliberations on the *Annual Policy Strategy* was often diminished by the vagueness of the proposals and the absence of clear links between proposals and wider budgetary considerations. Nonetheless, at least one MEP, Andrew Duff, was willing to defend the process: 'The Commission's Annual Policy Strategy for 2008 should be welcomed as a useful indicator. It is both clearer and more comprehensive than in previous years, and should assist all the institutions . . . in the better planning of their own work programmes' (Duff, HC 519-II:26).

Conclusion

From the evidence presented in this chapter there is little doubt, empirically, that the EP is a genuine co-legislator with the Council under the codecision2 procedure. This is so whether assessed quantitatively, in terms of the numbers of successful amendments, or qualitatively, in terms of the substantive changes effected to legislative proposals. What the detailed case studies examined above reveal is the contingency of EP influence. One theme of this book has been that the nature of interinstitutional bargaining, the systemic context (the nature of multi-level governance) within which those bargains are made, and the multi-functionality of the EP (as representative, legislative and oversight institution) all impact upon the capacity of Parliament to exert influence in the EU's policy process.

A further theme of this chapter, and of this book more generally, has been that the formal dimensions of influence have to be supplemented by recognition of the informal dimensions of the EP's contribution to the EU's decision-making processes. Other scholars have come to acknowledge the inextricable linkage of these formal and informal dimensions (see Farrell and Héritier 2002; Farrell and Héritier 2007), and of how the creative use of the EP's own rules of procedure, and interinstitutional innovations – such as trialogues, framework agreements and *modi vivendi* – serve to extend the EP's legislative influence beyond its treaty-prescribed powers. Not only is this a historical phenomenon, as revealed in Chapter 2, but it also constitutes a future strategy. Indeed, the elemental importance of this strategy was recognized by one Council Official:

> Parliament wants to be 'top-dog'. They are constantly building, piece by piece, brick by brick, and the trend has been over recent treaties to give them more powers, to give them a greater role . . . When you get an informal procedure established with Parliament, they want to concretize it in the Treaty, or in an inter-institutional agreement. (quoted in Farrell and Héritier 2002:15)

Simon Hix (2002:261) translated these established perspectives of the incremental advancement of the EP's powers (through small steps and qualitative leaps (see Chapter 2)) into a 'new theory of the development of the powers of the EP'. In so doing, Hix characterized the development of the EP's legislative powers as a transition from 'consultation to bicameralism' (2002: 261) and its powers over the appointment of the Commission as a transformation of the EU 'from international organization to parliamentary government' (2002:264). While Hix formulated these 'transitions' as mere statements, they are in fact contentions that need to be analysed. This we intend to do in Chapter 9, and in this regard, Hix's 'transitions' provide us with a neat pivot by which to turn from the specific focus of this chapter with legislative influence to the more general concern of the next chapter with the 'parliamentarization' of the EU.

Chapter 9

A Parliamentary Europe?

Introduction

An essential part of the analysis of this book has been to examine the extent to which the EP can be understood in terms of the universal roles ascribed to 'parliaments'. Established analyses of comparative legislatures have been used to assess the merits of arguments about whether the EP constitutes a 'true', 'proper' or 'normal' parliament; and discussions about whether the EU can be identified as a parliamentary system and the prospects for further 'parliamentarization' have been set within a broader examination of the notion of a 'parliamentary model' (see Chapter 1).

Manifestly the primary focus of this book has been the European Parliament itself. Yet, throughout the preceding chapters, the connections between the parliamentary processes at national level have intruded into the analysis of the supranational EP. Moreover, conceptions of what sort of political system the EU is – whether 'Type I governance' or 'Type II multilevel governance' (see Chapter 1) – have provided a subconscious structuring of the debate. That the sources of legitimation within the EU are multilevel is widely accepted, as is the idea of a 'dual legitimacy' rooted in representative parliaments at both national and EU levels. Indeed, as we will see below, the EU has consciously sought to develop dual legitimation in practice, through an acknowledgement that both national parliaments and the European Parliament have roles to play in providing authorization, representation and accountability in the Union. Thus, as we noted in Chapter 3, much of the political debate surrounding the future political order in Europe revolves around parliaments and further parliamentarization of the EU's political process.

Part of the purpose of this chapter, therefore, is to examine exactly what further 'parliamentarization' means and the forms that this process takes. A further purpose is to reveal the complexities and ambiguities entailed in that process. But, equally, this chapter also aims both to monitor the normative debate about the deepening of legitimation through parliamentary institutions and to examine the practical steps taken to enhance legitimation through coordination of the activities of national parliaments and the EP. If the 'future of Europe' is 'parliamentary', we need to understand what 'parliamentarization' entails and the extent to which the interinstitutional connections between national parliaments and the EP contribute to such a process.

A Europe of parliaments: the European Parliament and national parliaments

In Chapter 3 the concept of 'dual legitimation' was raised. This idea simultaneously grounded legitimacy, at one level, in the directly elected representative institutions of the member states and, at a second level, in the directly elected European Parliament. The prospective Lisbon Treaty confirmed the centrality of this concept in Title II (TEU), 'provisions on democratic principles':

> Citizens are directly represented at Union level in the European Parliament. Member States are represented in the European Council . . . and in the Council of Ministers by their governments, themselves democratically accountable either to their national parliaments, or to their citizens. (Article 10(2))

Yet, as noted in Chapter 3, the idea of dual legitimacy is replete with conceptual tensions; not the least of which is that increases in the legislative power of the EP, associated with the incremental extension of QMV in the Council, have been linked with decreases in the power of national parliaments and to notions of 'deparliamentarization' within member states (Benz 2004:882; Duina and Oliver 2005:173; Rittberger 2005:198–9). In this sense, attempts at linking the two levels of legitimation are seen not simply as processes of aggregation – of adding EU representative democracy onto existing national processes of representation – but, paradoxically, they are also seen to give rise to processes of disaggregation of legitimacy. Whereas the EP draws upon notions of a 'direct' transnational linkage of EU citizens to the EU's legislative processes, national parliaments invoke ideas of the 'indirect' authorization of EU legislative outputs through the negotiations of national ministers in the Council and their ultimate accountability to their own domestic parliaments. These 'direct' and 'indirect' legitimation claims do not necessarily sit easily alongside each other.

One response to this paradox has been to argue that there is no paradox: that the EP and national parliaments play distinct roles within the EU, yet both contribute to enhancing the democratic legitimacy of the Union (CONV 353/02 2002:2). This is the view traditionally advanced by the EP (see for example PE 221.698 1997:10–11; PE 304.302 2002:11–12) and repeated by Hans-Gert Pöttering (2007) on the fiftieth anniversary of the signing of the Treaty of Rome: 'The European Parliament and national parliaments are partners. Our work is complementary. Together we have the task of creating a democratic Europe'. Similarly most national parliaments have tended to conceive of their role in parallel, rather than in conflict, to that performed by the EP. Their primary focus has been upon the scrutiny, and subsequent holding to account, of the activities of their respective national ministers in the Council's legislative proceedings. This has led to the development of scrutiny systems, predominantly institutionalized in the form of European Affairs Committees, in all 27 national parliaments (see COSAC 2007b:7–9). Such scrutiny systems, whether document-based or procedurally based, are dependent for their effectiveness upon accessing information and processing such information at appropriate stages within the EU's legislative cycle (see CONV 353/02 2002:4–5). The EP, for its part, has traditionally acknowledged that the mode of scrutiny of EU policies employed by national parliaments is entirely a matter of national responsibility (PE 221.698 1997:7); it has maintained nonetheless that there were a series of measures which could be adopted at an EU level to facilitate national parliamentary scrutiny. Thus the EP supported the inclusion of the declarations on national parliaments in the Maastricht Treaty. There, for the first time, the role of national parliaments was acknowledged. A Declaration appended to the Treaty recognized that:

> it is important to encourage greater involvement of national Parliaments in the activities of the European Union. To this end, the exchange of information between national Parliaments and the European Parliament should be stepped up. In this context, the governments of the Member States will ensure, inter alia, that national Parliaments receive Commission proposals for legislation in good time for information or possible examination. (Treaty on European Union OJ C 161, 29 July 1992)

This commitment to the timeous provision of Commission proposals was restated in Protocol 20 of the Amsterdam Treaty. Modification of this Protocol was urged in the run-up to the Nice Treaty; and predictably the role of national parliaments resurfaced in the deliberations of the European Convention in 2002. In its working group on national parliaments, in its discussion papers (see, for example, CONV 67/02 2002), and in its plenary deliberations (see especially 6 and 7 June 2002, CONV 97/02 2002) the case for greater involvement of national parliaments in the EU's activities was explored. In its final report the working group proposed a number of measures to enhance access to EU documents by national parliaments (CONV 353/02 2002:6–9). These measures found reflection in the Protocol on the Role of National Parliaments of the Constitutional Treaty (OJ C 310, 16 December 2004:204–6) and in the first two Protocols of the prospective

Lisbon Treaty, on the role of national Parliaments in the EU, and on the application of the principles of subsidiarity and proportionality. The first stated that the Commission now had the responsibility for forwarding all draft European legislative acts, its consultative documents, its annual legislative programme, and 'any other instrument of legislative planning or policy' to national parliaments at the same time as they were sent to the EP and to Council. The second protocol, on the application of the principles of subsidiarity and proportionality, provided for national parliaments to be able to adopt a reasoned opinion on any draft measure within eight weeks of receipt of the draft legislative act. If the opinion of national parliaments was that the draft act did not comply with the principle of subsidiarity then account should be taken of the reasoned opinion. However, should a third of the votes of national parliaments record that the principle of subsidiarity had been transgressed, then the 'draft must be reviewed'. Furthermore, if for codecision legislation the Commission decided to maintain its draft, it was to provide a reasoned opinion explaining its decision, with the further safeguard that 55 per cent of members of the Council, or a simple majority in the EP, could overturn such an opinion. Some national parliaments expressed concern about this development and doubted whether an institutionalized dialogue between Commission and national parliaments was compatible with the EU's structure and balance of institutions (see COSAC 2007a:16).

Multilateral parliamentary networks

A second dimension of the relationship between the EP and national parliaments is the opportunity for institutional networking and institutional learning provided by formalized collaborative structures – most notably in the form of Conventions, the Conference of European Affairs Committees (COSAC), and in the more recent development of joint meetings of specialized parliamentary committees.

Conventions

If enacted the Lisbon Treaty (Title VI Article 48(3) TEU) provides for a Convention of representatives of national parliaments, Heads of State or Governments of the member states, of the European Parliament and of the Commission to be convened as part of the 'ordinary revision procedure' when considering future treaty reform. In developing the Convention model the Lisbon Treaty would allow the EP to propose treaty amendments as well as requiring the consent of the EP should the Council decide not to establish a Convention. In its assessment of this reform the EP's Constitutional Affairs Committee noted that: 'Parliament, which was the first to propose that the Convention method be used, cannot but welcome this change, which will help to make the revision procedure more transparent and democratic at the same time as making it more effective' (PE 347.119 2004:40).

Indeed, representatives from national parliaments and the EP had met together to consider treaty and institutional reform on three earlier occasions. In November 1990 a parliamentary 'assizes' (derived from a traditional French term) was held in Rome on the eve of the Maastricht IGC; in December 1999 an ad hoc 'convention' was established to draft the Charter of Fundamental Rights; and the post-Nice process witnessed the establishment of the Convention on the Future of Europe. The Declaration on the Future of the Union, annexed to the Treaty of Nice, had outlined a process of 'wide-ranging discussions with all interested parties'. For its part, the EP's Constitutional Affairs Committee maintained that such discussions should be conducted within 'a body such as the tried and tested Convention' (PE 304.302 2002:17). Thus, from expressing concern at any institutionalization of an assizes model a decade earlier, by 2002 the convention model was now largely accepted by the EP as 'tried and tested'. By 2007 Article 48 of the Lisbon Treaty (TEU) demonstrated the extent to which this 'innovation' had become an established part of the institutional thinking of the EU.

A second parliamentary chamber for Europe

In contrast, the Lisbon Treaty underlined the fact that the idea of a 'second chamber' or 'congress' of parliaments had not become an accepted part of the EU's institutional design. Certainly, the Convention on the Future of Europe had considered various possibilities for closer integration of the activities of national parliaments and the EP – including 'a second assembly at the European level' composed of representatives of national parliaments, or 'a second chamber representing national parliaments' as part of a bicameral European Parliament, or a 'Permanent Conference of Parliaments' (including representatives from the EP and national parliaments' (CONV 67/02 2002:13–14). Moreover, the President of the Convention, Valéry Giscard d'Estaing, explicitly favoured the creation of a second assembly. Ultimately, however, such a provision did not feature in the final draft of the Constitutional Treaty.

Historically, a recurring proposal for the 'parliamentarization' of the EU has been the creation of a second chamber of the European Parliament. As early as 1953 the Assembly of the ECSC, in its draft treaty for a European Political Community, included provision for a bicameral legislature. Alongside a Chamber of Peoples representing 'the peoples united in the Community' would have been a Senate to represent 'the people of each state' and with senators selected by national parliaments. These proposals fell with the failure of the draft treaties for the European Political and the European Defence Communities themselves (see Chapter 2). However, the early years of the twenty-first century witnessed a marked revival of interest in the notion of a bicameral European Parliament. In rapid succession leading politicians in France, Germany and the UK, alongside MEPs and individual EU Commissioners, advanced the case for a second chamber (for details see HL 48 2001:paras 13–16; HC 152-xxxiii 2002:paras 122–8; see also Kiiver 2005:127–8). A speech made by the UK's Prime Minister, Tony Blair, in Warsaw in October 2000, fuelled the debate about a second chamber in the EU. In the same year the German Minister for Foreign Affairs, Joschka Fischer, called for a bicameral European Parliament to reflect both 'a Europe of nation states and a Europe of citizens'. He suggested the second chamber could either draw its members equally from each member state in a small 'senate'; or, alternatively, have variable representation from each member state according to size. Nearly a year later, in April 2001, the German President, Johannes Rau, also called for a second chamber – but this time composed of ministers from the member states. Rau's proposal, in turn, echoed a scheme that had been articulated by the German Chancellor Gerhard Schröder in November 2000. Schröder proposed that the Council of Ministers should be transformed as a second legislative 'Chamber of States' to operate alongside the existing EP. A month later, in May 2001, the French Prime Minister, Lionel Jospin, suggested that a Congress of National Parliaments should be established to monitor the application of the principle of subsidiarity.

Generally the proponents of bicameralism believed that the existence of a nationally based second chamber would better connect European citizens to EU institutions and decision-making. Certainly, as the House of Lords EU Select Committee concluded, 'At the root of all the proposals for a second chamber there seems to lie a perception that there is a problem with the democratic legitimacy of the EU and its institutions' (HL 48 2001:para. 26).

For opponents, however, the practical difficulties involved in integrating second chamber scrutiny into the existing legislative procedures – of ensuring agreement as to the precise boundaries of the levels of competencies in the EU, or of identifying a discrete role that was not already performed by the EP or by national parliaments – seemed to outweigh many of the other potential benefits a second chamber might contribute to EU governance (see HL 48 2001:para. 54; HC 152-xxxiii 2002:para. 127). Overall, opponents found it difficult to see what 'added value' another chamber would contribute to the EU's decision-making processes. More pointedly, Andrew Duff MEP (ALDE, UK) stated that one could only speculate 'why it is that, just when a directly elected European Parliament is maturing steadily and its powers of codecision are settling down along come [proposals] to recreate alongside it, cuckoo style, its former, unelected predecessor' (HL 48 2001:memorandum by Andrew Duff, para. 3).

Conference of European Affairs Committees (COSAC)

COSAC is the French acronym for the Conference of European Affairs Committees. The Conference was established in 1989, following a French-led initiative to convene regular meetings of representatives of the respective European Affairs committees of national parliaments and representatives of the EP. At its first meeting in Paris in November 1989, COSAC agreed to increase the exchange of information among parliaments, and to meet twice a year in the country holding the Presidency of the Council to discuss issues of common concern. In 1991 specific rules of procedure were adopted to regulate COSAC meetings, and these were amended at the meetings in Athens and Rome in 1994, in Helsinki in 1999, and in Athens in 2003. In 2004 a COSAC secretariat, with initial funding for a two-year period, was established for the first time in Brussels. The continued funding of the Secretariat was agreed at COSAC's meeting in London in October 2005.

By mid-decade, therefore, COSAC – which had often been dismissed as a mere 'talking shop', or as a body that had 'largely squandered' its potential as a networking forum for national parliamentarians (see HL 48 2001:para. 73; HC 152-xxxiii 2002: para. 149: Kiiver 2005:114–5) – had, in the opinion of some national parliamentarians at least, 'completed a significant transformation' (Austrian Parliament 2004). This transformation was rooted in part in the Protocol on the Role of National Parliaments appended to the Amsterdam Treaty. This Protocol gave COSAC treaty status and empowered it to:

> make any contribution it deems appropriate for the attention of the EU institutions . . . examine any legislative proposal or initiative in relation to the establishment of an area of freedom, security and justice which might have a direct bearing on the rights and freedoms of individuals . . .

> address to the European Parliament, the Council and the Commission any contribution which it deems appropriate on the legislative activities of the Union, notably in relation to the application of the principle of subsidiarity, the area of freedom, security and justice as well as questions regarding fundamental rights. (Treaty of Amsterdam 1997)

In 2003, in recognition that the possibilities provided by the Amsterdam Protocol had 'not been fully utilised', COSAC adopted its new rules (COSAC 2003). Thus, for example, a change in voting rules was designed to enable 'contributions' (the 'conclusions' of COSAC meetings) to be adopted with a 75 per cent majority of votes cast or 50 per cent of votes, even though the expectation remained that contributions would be adopted by broad consensus. Alongside the rule changes there was a move towards greater professionalization of its organization in the acknowledgement of the need for better long-term planning of COSAC's meetings, the adoption of a new IT strategy and the creation of its own Secretariat. There was also confirmation that the core activities of COSAC were, in essence, the exchange of information, the dissemination of 'best practice', and the assistance offered to national parliaments to enhance their scrutiny processes. These core activities were deemed to be especially important in a period of significant enlargement and the integration of new national parliaments into the multinational network.

As a result of these rule changes, and of organizational refocusing, COSAC was well placed to structure deliberations of national parliaments upon the impact of the Constitutional Treaty generally and upon its subsidiarity and proportionality protocol more specifically. Thus, at its meeting in Dublin in May 2004 there was an intensive debate on how national parliaments might implement the subsidiarity 'early warning system'. This was followed in December 2004 by an agreement to undertake a 'pilot project' on a specific piece of legislation – the Commission's Third Railway Package – in order to assess how the 'early warning system' might work in practice. The project was conducted in a six-week period in spring 2005 by 31 of the 37 national chambers of EU-25 member states. COSAC's secretariat produced an overview of the assessments of national parliaments of this pilot, and on this basis COSAC declared that the project had been a 'useful experience' overall (COSAC 2005).

The intention to hold a second pilot was stalled, however, by the difficulties encountered in ratifying the Constitutional Treaty. COSAC decided that, rather than assume that the Treaty – and hence the early warning system – would come into force, it would examine instead how the scrutiny of subsidiarity might be improved and how national parliaments might maximize their impact through coordination of their scrutiny efforts. To this end two 'subsidiarity and proportionality checks', based upon the existing treaties and protocols, were subsequently conducted. Although these 'checks' were not intended as 'collective' exercises – as COSAC 'cannot determine how a national parliament should best scrutinise the actions of its government in relation to EU affairs' (COSAC 2007a:13) – the simultaneous scrutiny of Commission proposals was seen by a number of parliaments to be an 'added value' in itself. Overall, the conclusion was reached that 'concerted action of several parliaments may help to influence the outcomes of European Commission proposals' (COSAC 2007a:7).

When COSAC reviewed its experience of its 'checks' it found that 'almost all national parliaments point out that effective implementation of the subsidiarity control mechanism will encourage a greater cooperation between national parliaments, foster the exchange of best practice and even lead to greater coordination of their actions' (COSAC 2007b:23). In this regard COSAC was further encouraged by the European Council which invited national parliaments 'to strengthen cooperation within the framework of the Conference of European Affairs Committees (COSAC) when monitoring subsidiarity' (European Council 2006:14).

Nonetheless, despite this enhanced profile, COSAC's contribution to EU decision-making is limited by the following facts: the representatives of national parliaments do not generally have a mandate to speak for their respective parliaments; COSAC's 'contributions' are non-binding; and there is rarely a cohesive, coherent or unified 'parliamentary' perspective – given the different stages of institutional development among 27 European Affairs committees and the diversity of opinion within and between national parliaments upon further integration. Thus no matter how often their meetings or systematic their cooperation, the European Affairs committees of national parliaments – composed as they are of national parliamentarians with their own national priorities, national concerns and prejudices, and with no common institutional perspective – will find it difficult to reach collective outputs that extend much beyond a lowest common denominator. The sheer pace, depth, breadth, complexity and significance of EU decision-making limits the capacity of national parliamentarians to participate effectively in that process.

In the event of some COSAC members seeking to extend its role beyond its primary 'networking' functions, however, there will always be voices cautioning that the 'early warning mechanism' proposed in the Lisbon Treaty was not designed to change the institutional structure or the institutional balance within the EU. COSAC recognized this in noting that the subsidiarity and proportionality checks were not conducted 'collectively' and in affirming that there was 'no intent to establish COSAC as an additional body in the EU system' (COSAC 2007a:12–13). Similarly some members of the EP's Constitutional Affairs Committee have expressed reservations about any future development of direct links between the Commission and national parliaments. Maria Esteves MEP (EPP-ED, Portugal) contended, for example, that 'we have to remind national parliaments what their role actually is, namely interaction with the Council' (quoted in *EUobserver* 3 May 2006). This view was reiterated in Andrew Duff's statement that: 'We should encourage COSAC to focus on its true role – the scrutiny of national ministers for their performance in Brussels' (Andrew Duff quoted in *EUobserver* 3 May 2006). Despite a professed desire to work together, therefore, these statements may well point to a 'structural divergence in preferences, or a "natural competitive relationship" between the national parliaments and the European Parliament' (Kiiver 2005:122). There is always the danger that a more active role for national parliaments, and a heightened awareness of the implications of their domestic scrutiny, may exacerbate this competitive relationship. As Kiiver (2005:159) concludes, 'Good news for subsidiarity [and national parliamentary scrutiny] does . . . not necessarily mean good news for European parliamentarism'. Thus, while COSAC is undoubtedly of use in providing an educative and developmental forum and a networking locus for national parliamentarians its contribution to the wider 'parliamentarization' of the EU is inherently ambiguous.

Joint committee meetings

The EP has also extended its contacts with national parliaments through joint parliamentary meetings and joint committee meetings. In 2005 it was agreed that such meetings should be formalized, and subsequently joint parliamentary meetings have been co-convened by the EP and the national parliament of the state holding the EU presidency (Corbett *et al.* 2007:328). In addition, joint meetings of EP and national parliamentary committees have been held in the 2004–2009 Parliament. Although these do not constitute a comprehensive series of interactions between specialized parliamentary committees, they do point to the potentialities for future development. In this respect, one notable example of joint endeavour is the dialogue which has been established by the EP's Budgetary Control Committee and its counterparts in national parliaments. In October 2006 the EP's Budgetary Control Committee convened, in association with the Eduskunta (during Finland's EU Presidency), the first joint meeting to discuss the role of 'budgetary control committees in national parliaments with particular regard to the control of the Community budget' (PE 378.567 2006:3). The chairs or vice chairs of 23 national parliamentary budgetary and public finance committees attended this meeting. The stated objective of the Budgetary Control Committee in taking this initiative was to move beyond simple interparliamentary networking and information exchange and to address the practical issues of improving the financial management and accountability of the 80 per cent of the EU budget for which member states are responsible through the 'shared management' of EU spending. Indeed, the joint meeting was specifically asked to address innovations that had been proposed by the EP, in its discharge resolutions on the 2003 and 2004 budgets, for improving the control of EU spending nationally.

Several national MPs at this first meeting expressed their desire to have further discussions on matters of common interest. As a result, a second joint committee meeting was held in December 2007 to continue the dialogue. As with the first meeting the EP's Budgetary Control Committee produced a substantive agenda, this time continuing the discussion of the national management declarations and extending the debate to the implementation of structural fund spending. Taking account of the developments that had taken place since October 2006, the EP's rapporteur posed a series of questions about audit, control and accountability that 'the national parliamentarians might wish to comment on' (PE 398.310 2007:3). Two final questions asked for the identification of issues for consideration at possible future meetings and whether a national budgetary control committee would 'be interested in hosting a future meeting and thereby contribute significantly to the creation of a parliamentary network of budgetary control committees?' (PE 398.310 2007:10).

If the large proportion of EU funds committed and spent by member states provided obvious grounds for cooperation between budgetary control committees in national parliaments and the EP, then another area ripe for joint parliamentary scrutiny was the initiatives – under the Tampere and Hague Programmes – concerning freedom, justice and home affairs. In these areas both national parliaments and the European Parliament were at an equal disadvantage. In which case there was a commonality of interest in improving oversight on the part of the EP's Committee on Civil Liberties, Justice and Home Affairs (LIBE) and its counterpart committees in the member states. In November 2007, for example, a joint committee meeting of the EP's LIBE and the Committee on Constitutional Affairs, Rights, Liberties and Guarantees of the Portuguese Assembleia da Republica brought together national parliamentarians and MEPs during the Portuguese Presidency. The focus of the meeting was on the role of parliaments in relation to EU migration policy, terrorism, data security and passenger name records, and the relationships between European and national criminal law. This meeting followed an earlier joint meeting which had been convened in 2006 by LIBE in association with the Eduskunta during the Finnish EU Council Presidency. Both meetings were chaired jointly by the chair of the EP's LIBE Committee and the chair of the co-organizing national parliamentary committee.

Some of the broader issues of oversight, which confronted the 2006 and 2007 joint committee meetings, had been raised earlier in the more specific context of the democratic control of Europol. In 2002, for instance, the Commission noted (COM(2002)95) that, while parliaments did not normally have a direct influence on national police forces, the 'somewhat indirect form' of parliamentary control over Europol at both national and EU levels was a particular cause for concern. Attention was drawn to the role played by the EP's LIBE Committee in identifying and highlighting the accountability vacuum faced by Europol (COM(2002)95:4). Significantly, the Commission went on to recommend that the EU should '[e]stablish a formal mechanism for information exchange and co-ordination between national parliaments and the European Parliament . . . To this end a joint committee, consisting of members of both the Member States' and European Parliaments committees responsible for police matters could be established' (COM(2002)95:13).

Although this specific recommendation was not adopted it did highlight the potential for future interparliamentary cooperation through the medium of joint committees. As noted above, some of this potential has been realized in the areas of budgetary control and justice and home affairs.

Parliamentarization of the EU: executive–legislative roles

In outlining a 'parliamentary model' in Chapter 1 the fusion of executive and legislative roles was noted. In the EU there is certainly a fusion of executive and legislative roles but there is no corresponding unambiguous differentiation of executive and legislative institutions. In other words there are no clear and determinate institutional boundaries in the EU. Thus, whereas it is relatively easy to identify discrete executive and legislative institutions within each member state, in the EU 'institutions are profoundly and inescapably interdependent' (Peterson and Shackleton 2006:11). The best way of understanding the EU's institutions (specifically the EP in the case of this book), therefore, is in terms of their interinstitutional interactions. They are part of complex, interwoven and overlapping institutional networks. There are no singular institutional structures, only plural institutional forms. Thus, there is no single executive but rather a 'dual executive' of Commission and Council (see Hix 2005:69–71). Similarly there is no single legislature but an interconnected and interdependent 'Council-EP tandem' as well as a Council-Commission 'tandem' (Hayes-Renshaw and Wallace 2006:226,192) – and a 'Commission-EP tandem'. Manifestly the EP is a legislature but it also shares legislative functions with the Council and the Commission.

The significance of all of this for present purposes is that the initial conceptualization of interinstitutional relations in the EU affects the proposals that are subsequently made for the further 'parliamentarization' of the EU.

Parliamentarization of the Commission

Election of the Commission President

In national parliamentary systems, political executives normally depend upon a parliamentary majority for their authorization and continuance in office. There is thus a mediated linkage between parliamentary elections and the choice and sustenance of a government. In the EU, historically, there has been only the most tenuous linkage between EP elections and choice of the Commission. While the changes introduced under the Maastricht, Amsterdam, and Nice Treaties (and potentially Lisbon) have led some analysts to identify 'some movement towards the parliamentary model in the choice of the Commission President' (Hix *et al.* 2007:17), the extent of 'parliamentarization' remains limited. Despite the prospective Lisbon Treaty requiring the European Council to take into account the elections to the European Parliament when proposing a candidate for the Commission President, and confirming that the President was to be elected by the EP, the simple fact remains that the institutional framework of the EU still does not allow voters to determine who holds (or does not hold) executive office in the EU. To date, as Chapter 3 noted, EP elections have not been about who holds EU executive power and they continue to be dominated by national political issues, national parties, and the political standing of national governments at the time. Not surprisingly, therefore, one consistent proposal to simultaneously 'europeanize' EP elections and 'parliamentarize' the EU has been to provide a direct connection between EP elections and the choice of the Commission President.

Nearly two decades ago, David Martin MEP (1990:26) recognized that: '[a]t present, European elections are genuinely about electing a Parliament, but the effect of casting one's vote is less immediately perceptible to the voter. To allow the Parliament to elect the President of the Commission would go some way to rectifying that situation.' Support for the election of the Commission President was also evident in the 2002 Convention and in associated discussions on the Future of Europe. However, ideas about who would elect the President, and how, separated the proponents of election in the Convention. Those who favoured direct election were confronted with several choices. One was to hold separate elections for the President on the same day as the EP elections (see HC 252-xxxiii 2002:35; CONV 27/02 2002:36). A second was to elect some MEPs (possibly 60) on the basis of a transnational, cross-border electoral list, with the highest-placed candidate becoming Commission President (see HC 252-xxxiii 2002:Q117). Another proposal – which echoed an earlier suggestion of Jacques Delors – was that each main European transnational political family would designate a candidate for President of the Commission, with actual nomination secured on the basis of the outcome of the European election (Lamy and Pisani-Ferry 2002:78). This latter suggestion was echoed in further calls made for the 'parliamentarization' of the Commission nomination process by, among others, Smith (2004:56–7), Bogdanor (2007:12–13) and Hix *et al.* (2007:219–20).

In essence such proposals shared a belief that electors, national political parties and the media would treat EP elections more seriously if there was an apparent link between the outcomes of European elections and the composition and policy programme of the Commission. As Bogdanor (2007:13) speculated, '[i]f campaigns centred more clearly on presidential candidates, voters could see more clearly what consequences their vote would have. This might also lead citizens (and indeed national parties) to see EP elections as important events in their own right.' In this manner it was hoped that the 'second-order' nature of EP elections would be addressed (Smith 2004:44). Moreover, it was believed that such a linkage would enhance the accountability of the Commission President both to the EP, for the implementation of a programme based upon the 'mandate' provided by election, and ultimately to electors who would now have the opportunity to pass judgement on the President's performance in office at the next election. More broadly still, it was argued that a causal link between EP elections and the appointment of the Commission President would 'add a new "demos-enhancing" dimension to European elections' (Bogdanor 2007:12).

All of these perceived benefits would, according to their proponents, accrue without the need for further treaty reform (see Hix 2006:23; Bogdanor 2007:12). Treaty reform would be needed, however, if proposals for the direct election of the Commission President by the European Parliament were to be effected. Such a view found strong support at the time of the Convention from within the EP (see, for example, PE 232.758 2000:7; PSE 2002:8; Klaus Hänsch MEP HC 152-xxxiii 2002:Q157) and from without (see Hoffman 2002). A further proposal, designed to reflect the dual legitimation afforded by the EP and national parliaments, was for the convening of a congress of representatives from the EP and national parliaments to elect the President of the Commission (CONV 97/02 2002:10). Romano Prodi was reported to favour the nomination of his successors by MEPs and MPs but with the Council's formal approval (*Financial Times* 29 July 2002).

However, any direct linkage of the election of the Commission President to the EP (and national parliaments) would require a fundamental shift in the relationship between national and European parties, with the former relinquishing to the latter the choice of presidential candidates. Moreover, as Nickel observed over a decade ago, '[national] governments may not like the idea too' (1998:3). Clearly, this has proved to be an understatement. The very intensity of inter-governmental bargaining over the choice of Commission President and the allocation of Commission portfolios in 1999 and 2004 revealed the continuing dominance of national interests in the selection process and the jealous guarding of this pre-eminence by national governments. If anything, the increase in the significance of EU policy has increased the intensity of national bargaining and the tenacity with which member states seek to maintain their dominance. Without a seismic shift in the balance between national and EU party politics, and without the 'parti-sanization' and 'politicization' of the Commission through linkage of its political complexion with that of the EP, 'parliamentarization' in the sense of the electoral connection of the Presidency of the Commission to a parliamentary majority is likely to remain an aspiration rather than a practical reality. Indeed, there are some who argue that 'parliamentarization' in this sense *should* remain an aspiration, as there are manifest dangers in the politicization of executive–legislative relations in the EU. Not the least of these would be to 'add problems of political and partisan coordination to the already existing problems of institutional coordination' (Bartoloni 2006:40).

Responsibility of Commissioners to the EP

As noted in Chapter 7, the responsibility of the Commission to the EP remains embryonic in form. While Article 201 empowers the EP to force the collective resignation of the Commission there is no corresponding formal power to enforce the resignation of individual Commissioners. However, the revised Framework Agreement on Relations Between the European Parliament and the Commission, signed in 2005, included two important commitments under the heading 'political responsibility'. The first recognized that individual Commissioners had responsibility for the actions of their Directorates General, and the second acknowledged that if the EP expressed a lack of confidence in a Commissioner the President of the Commission would request the Commissioner to resign, or at least have to explain why no such request was to be made. In this way a parliamentary sanction could be wielded against an individual member of the Commission within the overarching and permissive collective control exerted by the Commission President.

Significantly, the new Framework Agreement brought into stark relief the potentially destabilizing effect that the increased 'parliamentarization' of the Commission might have upon the EU's existing institutional balance. Indeed, so great was the concern of the Council about the nature of the Agreement that it issued a formal statement noting that:

> several provisions of the new framework agreement seek to bring about, even more markedly than the framework agreement of 2000, a shift in the institutional balance resulting from the Treaties in force . . .

> The Council would point out in particular that under the EC Treaty (Article 201), a motion of censure on the activities of the Commission can only be tabled against all of the members of the Commission as a college, and not an individual member. Article 217 enshrines the principle of the collective responsibility for Commission action. (OJ C 161, 1 July 2005:1)

The Council was clearly apprehensive that the Framework Agreement, which did not require Council's approval or even involvement and which followed immediately after the Buttiglione episode, marked an important further step 'in the development of Commissioner's individual responsibility to Parliament' (Beukers 2006:53).

A two-way street: Commission–EP relations

While much of the debate about the 'parliamentarization' of the Commission has concentrated upon heightening the responsibility of the Commission to the EP, there is an obverse side to this debate. This side echoes Lijphart's (1984:72) observation that 'a logical corollary' of a legislature's power to dismiss an executive in a parliamentary system is the executive's right, in turn, to dissolve parliament and call new elections (see also Bergman *et al.* 2003:157–67). Not surprisingly, therefore, proposals for either the Commission or the Council to dissolve the EP have recurred in discussions on the institutional future of the EU. Thus, for example, in July 2000, Michel Barnier, the Commissioner responsible for the IGC, while sharing the EP's vision of a strong Commission presidency responsible to a strong Parliament, raised the prospect of institutional changes that would redirect the flow of accountabilities between executive and legislature. In this respect, Barnier (2000:10) argued that '[t]o balance the European Parliament's right to censure the Commission, provision should be made for the right to dissolve the assembly, either by the President of the Commission following approval by the European Council, or by the Council on the basis of a proposal by the President of the Commission.' A similar proposal also featured in the deliberations of the European Convention (Duff *et al.* 2002). The idea was taken further by Spanish Prime Minister José María Aznar, who proposed that the European Council should have the right to dissolve Parliament, on the basis of a proposal from the Commission (*Agence Europe* 22 May 2002). What united these proposals was that they tapped into a historic vein of parliamentarism and served as a reminder to the EP and commentators alike that the relationship between the executive and the legislature in a parliamentary system is interconnected and reciprocal. Moreover, they also served to underscore the political reality that any assertion of the parliamentary power of censure was likely to precipitate a counter-response by the executive institutions in the EU. Thus, a connected censure vote and dissolution procedure would ultimately constitute a 'doomsday device' (Strøm 2003:69–70) for Commission and Parliament alike.

The Council and bicameralism

In outlining schemes for a second parliamentary chamber in the EU (see above), the proposals for a transformation of the Council of Ministers into a second legislative 'Chamber of States' were briefly noted. But, for some, 'European bi-cameralism already exists, with the Parliament and the Council' (Michel Rocard, HL 48 2001:written evidence). Indeed, this is a view shared by many academics and other commentators. American academics Tsebelis and Money (1997) have been particularly persuasive in arguing that the Council should be treated as an upper chamber in a bicameral legislature, and that the conciliation procedure under codecision constitutes an approximation of the relations between the US House of Representatives and the Senate in the form of 'a conference committee of a bicameral parliament' (1997:203). Equally, Hix (2005:110) has stated his belief that 'the EU has evolved into something that would be familiar to observers of two-chamber parliaments in other democratic political systems' (see also Kreppel 2005:10; Shackleton 2005:132; Chryssochoou 2007: 362).

While there appears to be an emerging consensus, therefore, that there is 'movement towards a bicameral legislative authority' (Corbett *et al.* 2007:215) it is important to recognize that this 'movement' has ambivalent messages for the 'parliamentarization' of the EU. These messages diverge when a distinction is drawn between 'bicameralism' as a process of legislative decision-making and 'bicameralism' as an institutional form. Those who identify 'bicameralism' in the EU tend to conceive of the relationship between the EP and Council in terms of *legislative* processes and decision rules, whereas those who are sceptical of its empirical accuracy emphasize *institutional* relationships.

'Political negotiations' and 'conflict resolution' (Høyland and Hagemann 2007:5; Kønig *et al.* 2007:281) are at the centre of conceptions of bicameralism as decision-making modes. Rational choice scholars have been particularly attracted to such conceptions and have deployed various models and statistical techniques to investigate the contribution of the two chambers to legislative outcomes.

Bicameralism in the second sense as noted above, however, requires the Council to be identified in an 'institutional' sense as a 'legislature'. For most commentators this presents few problems. Thus, for example, Hix has little hesitation in identifying the Council as 'more like a normal legislature and less like an intergovernmental body than it used to' (2008:149). Yet there is little that is 'normal' about the institutional form of the Council. While the Council has a singular legal status, in practice it meets in different formations of national ministers depending on subject area. Since the Seville European Council in June 2002 the Council has worked through nine sectoral 'configurations' (European Council 2002:23). Moreover, the 'variable geometry' or 'differentiated integration' evident in the protocols and opt-outs of recent treaty amendments, complicates definitions of exactly what constitutes 'the Council' at any particular time. In practice, this means that it is often difficult to discern a single 'collective' institutional identity for the Council.

This institutional 'split personality' becomes even more pronounced, when the Council acts as an executive body. Unlike national second chambers, therefore, the Council not only is responsible for amending, authorizing and scrutinizing legislation but its members are also involved in the formulation and implementation of EU legislation, as well as in taking collective decisions on a range of policy issues not subject to EU regulations or directives. Indeed, since Maastricht there has been a 'spectacular growth in the executive role of the Council' (Hayes-Renshaw and Wallace 2006:325) in the areas of justice and home affairs, common foreign and security policy, and European security and defence policy. Moreover, the Council's *modus operandi* is bureaucratic. Thus, as Hayes-Renshaw and Wallace (2006:330) point out, the 'the majority of issues, including those with legislative impact, are in essence resolved by officials before being endorsed by ministers'. The 'executive credentials' of the Council are further reinforced in the routine involvement of the Commission in Council activities – to the extent that the Commission is often labelled the 'twenty-eighth member state'.

The cumulative effect is that it is often difficult 'to define in which mode the Council is acting' (Hayes-Renshaw and Wallace 2006:23).

This impacts upon the transparency of the Council. While it is generally accepted that the processes of intergovernmental bargaining and negotiation are eased by confidentiality in the Council when it acts in an executive capacity, there have been persistent calls for greater transparency and more open access when it acts as a legislative body (see PE 294.777 2001:9; CONV 97/02 2002:8–9). The force of this logic was acknowledged at the Seville European Council, where it was agreed that the debates of Council, when acting under codecision, would be open to the public during the initial stage of the procedure and during the final stage – of voting and explanations of voting (European Council 2002:25). Yet, other than allowing public access to the beginning and end stages of the codecision procedure, the routines of negotiation and bargaining at the intersections of the Council's executive and legislative roles have remained obscured from public view.

For those pressing for the Council to act formally as a second chamber, however, the need for transparency and for the separation of the executive and legislative functions of the Council is essential (see, for example, HL 48 2001:Q104; PE 294.777 2001:18). Former Commissioner Michel Barnier made the point forcefully that: '[i]f the Council of Ministers is to [be] recognised as a second chamber, a chamber of states ... then you have ... to separate the work of the Council between its executive work and its legislative tasks' (HL 48 2001:Q129; see also HC 152-xxxiii 2002:para. 105).

Yet exactly how, if at all, the two functions could be separated has constituted a considerable stumbling block to the conception of the Council as a second legislative institution. As presently constituted, the Council may be perceived as being 'the executive's executive', and, if anything, recent treaty reforms have resulted in executive processes in the EU being 'a whole order of magnitude more messy' than before (Lehmann and Schunz 2005:18). In these circumstances the Council of Ministers cannot simultaneously perform the legislative oversight functions normally ascribed to legislatures. If 'Parliaments are supposed to control the operation of the executive' (Dehousse 1998:598), then clearly the Council, constituted as a second chamber, would have the task of controlling itself.

Far from being 'a normal legislature', therefore, the Council is 'abnormal' in being at the core of the EU's executive and as such is involved in processes of formulation, bargaining and implementation normally beyond the legislative role ascribed to legislatures. In which case, as part of a dual executive, 'quite obviously the position of the Council of Ministers and the European Council impedes parliamentarisation of the EU' (Dann 2003:558). As part of the EU's executive, with major governmental tasks yet with no direct accountability to the elected European Parliament, the Council finds itself in a 'murky situation' (Dann 2003:574).

This institutional 'oddness' leads Dann (2003:572–4) to label the EU a 'semi-parliamentary democracy'. The characteristic features of such a system are: executive federalism based on executive cooperation and consensual decision-making; an institutional structure similar to that of the USA with separated institutions sharing power, where the executive is distinct from the legislature – but in the EU's case there is a 'negative power of appointment' of part of the executive in the form of the 'election' of the Commission's President (in this context the term 'semi-parliamentary European system' is also used by Magnette 2001:302; Magnette 2005:106).

Indeed, it is increasingly commonplace to use the US federal system and the US House of Representatives, rather than European national parliaments, as comparators for categorizing the EU polity and the EP (see for example Kreppel 2005:14; Shackleton 2005:137–8). The difficulty with such comparisons is that they require the characteristics of a presidential system (the USA) to be equated to the characteristics of what is at best a 'semi-parliamentary' system in the EU. Even if a 'semi-parliamentary' system is equated with a 'semi-presidential' system (and there are many who would argue that they should not be – see Elgie 1999:5–8) the institutional structure and relationship between executive and legislature in such systems, and their sources of electoral authorization, still remain markedly different from those in the US presidential system.

Post-parliamentarism: alternative conceptions of governance

While proposals for further 'parliamentarization' rest upon the normative assumption that the EU should institutionalize the values of representative democracy (see Chapters 2 and 3), there have been challenges – both normative and empirical – to such an assumption throughout the history of the EU. As we have seen in earlier chapters, notions of 'input legitimacy' derived from the procedural politics of elected representative institutions have been consistently challenged by ideas predicated upon 'output legitimacy' and non-majoritarian institutions designed to enhance 'problem-solving capacity', expertise and Pareto-improving policy outputs (see, for example, Bellamy and Castiglione 2003; Eriksen and Fossum 2004; Føllesdal 2004; Majone 2005; Offe and Preuss 2006). Such ideas have been matched by the identification of the EU as a 'network polity' characterized by non-hierarchical bargaining among networks of formal, public governing institutions and independent, private political actors and institutions in complex modes of multilevel governance (see Pollack 2005:36–46).

If anything, there is a belief that: 'governance by network may be becoming a steadily *more* important feature of the EU as evidenced by recent initiatives including . . . the use of interest groups or NGOs in the implementation of environmental or development policies, the Commission's emphasis on dialogue with civil society in its White Paper on Governance, and the increasing ubiquity of the so-called "Open Method of Coordination' (Peterson 2004:129).

These two specific developments will be examined in the next section, though they are symptomatic of wider tendencies towards the deployment of non-majoritarian institutions within EU governance in the various forms of regulatory agencies, 'high-level' consultative and advisory committees, and 'comitology' (see Chapter 8). Each of which pose their own challenges to 'parliamentarization'.

The Commission's White Paper on European Governance

In addressing the issue of 'reforming governance', in the period preceding the Nice European Council, the stated goal of the Commission's White Paper was 'to open up policy-making to make it more inclusive and accountable' (COM(2001)428 2001:8). The proposals were designed specifically to improve the Commission's processes of policy initiation and formulation and to ensure more effective policy execution. The emphasis upon consultation 'upstream' in the decision-making process was thus linked to a concern with effective implementation 'downstream'.

The White Paper was insistent that in order to achieve the delivery of better policies 'the Union must revitalise the Community method' (2001:29). In effect this was a plea to return to a simpler era where the 'Commission initiates and executes policy' and the 'Council and the European Parliament decide on legislation and budgets' (2001:29). Yet at its heart was the potential contradiction that some of the institutional provisions of the White Paper – especially increased use of the Open Method of Coordination (2001:21–2) – might pose a challenge to the Community method and to the very institutional balance that the Commission sought to preserve (see below). Equally, while the Commission maintained that its reforms were not 'exclusionary' as far as the European Parliament was concerned (2001:22) its proposals – for the creation of further autonomous EU regulatory agencies (2001:24); for enhanced and reinforced processes of consultation and dialogue with civil society organizations; for more extensive partnership arrangements; and for a more pro-active approach to working with networks – all, in their various ways, residualized the contribution of the EP.

Throughout the White Paper the Commission's conception of the EU policy process was pervaded by a technocratic ethos, with the need for 'better and faster regulation' (2001:20) often appearing to outweigh the need for democratic representation and accountability. In this sense, the emphasis was placed upon 'substantive legitimacy' or 'output legitimacy' (see Chapter 1; Lord and Beetham 2001:444).

Not surprisingly, however, this technocratic vision was challenged by the EP. In its resolution on the White Paper Parliament advised caution in the introduction of 'elements of participatory democracy' and counselled that the 'recognised principles of and structural elements of representative democracy' (OJ C 153E, 27 June 2002:316) should not be infringed. In 'reiterating its confidence in the Community method' and advocating the maintenance of 'the institutional balance' the EP assumed that the principles of parliamentarism would be paramount. Thus, in the EP's conception of 'method' and 'balance', democratic legitimacy was provided jointly by the EP and the parliaments of member states. The parliamentary vision of legitimacy:

> presupposes that the political will underpinning decisions is arrived at through parliamentary deliberation; this is a substantive and not merely a formal requirement . . .
>
> consultation of interested parties with the aim of improving draft legislation can only ever supplement and can never replace the procedures and decisions of legislative bodies which possess democratic legitimacy; only the Council and Parliament, as co-legislators, can take responsible decisions in the context of legislative procedures. (OJ C 153E, 27 June 2002:318)

In the EP's view, such participation and consultation based upon 'organized civil society' would 'inevitably' be 'sectoral'. Equally, the EP was anxious that the creation of expert and scientific groups, and increased delegation of decision-making powers to regulatory agencies, should not detract from the accountability and transparency requirements of representative democracy. Ultimately, in the face of such potential threats, the EP affirmed that the participation and consultation processes associated with the Commission's notion of governance could not serve as substitutes for the processes of democratic legitimation. Indeed, unlike parliamentary institutions, 'organized civil society' 'cannot be regarded as having its own democratic legitimacy, given that representatives are not elected by the people and therefore cannot be voted out by the people' (PE 304.289 2001:10). In this statement the EP reflected one strand of academic opinion (see Judge 1999:121–48, 176–7; Lord and Beetham 2001:453–8; Lord 2007:146–50).

In the light of the EP's reaction, and the responses of other organizations and individuals to the Commission's consultation on the White Paper, a Communication was issued in December 2002 on the *General principles and minimum standards for consultation of interested parties by the Commission* (COM(2002)704). Notably the Commission argued that 'there is no contradiction between wide consultation and the concept of representative democracy' but then went on to concede that 'it goes without saying that, first and foremost, the decision-making process in the EU is legitimised by the elected representatives of the European peoples' (COM(2002)704 2002:4). Nonetheless, the Communication stressed both the treaty obligation for the Commission to consult widely and also the functional benefits to be derived from consultation in ensuring that 'proposals are technically viable, practically workable and based on a bottom-up approach' (COM(2002)704 2001:4).

Ultimately, however, the significance of the exchange between the EP and the Commission over the White Paper was that the Constitutional Treaty and the Lisbon Treaty came to echo the divergent notions of democratic legitimation (see below).

Open Method of Coordination (OMC)

The Open Method of Coordination constitutes part of what Majone terms 'new governance' (2005:59) which moves away from the standard Community method, and its uniform EU-wide rules incorporated in 'hard law' of binding legislative and executive acts, and focuses upon procedural rather than substantive harmonization. This 'new' approach is characterized by 'flexibility, decentralized decision-making, nonbinding coordination, benchmarking, and policy-learning' (Majone 2005:59). The principle of the OMC was incorporated in the conclusions of the Lisbon summit in March 2000. The OMC is a strategy to disseminate legislative 'best practice' across member states through 'soft law' mechanisms and to promote the linkage of national policies with each other and to connect functionally different policies at EU level. It seeks to mobilize a wide range of state and non-state actors at multilevels and to foster cooperative practices and networking among such actors. In essence the OMC was intended to promote the new image of socio-economic development envisaged in the 'Lisbon strategy'. The policy areas incorporated in the strategy were broadly grouped under 'competitiveness fostering' or 'welfare fostering'. The latter included the politically sensitive areas of education, employment, pension reform and social inclusion policies. In these areas the OMC was seen as 'a convenient formula for placing issues high on the EU agenda while preserving national autonomy' (Borrás and Jacobsson 2004:190).

Not surprisingly the advent of the OMC has impacted upon the institutional balance in the EU. While the actual impact varies across policy areas, the general consensus is that the OMC has strengthened the European Council, though whether this has been unambiguously at the expense of the Commission is open to dispute (see, for example, the contrasting assessments of Borrás and Jacobsson 2004:190 and Majone 2005:60). What seems not to be in dispute, however, is that when a 'softer' OMC approach is adopted 'the EP is normally disadvantaged' (Nugent 2006:418; see also Borrás and Jacobsson 2004: 199). Indeed the Europa website openly acknowledges that the EP plays 'virtually no part in the OMC process' (europa.eu/scadplus/glossary/open_method_coordination_en.htm); and studies by Raunio (2005b:9) and Gornitzka (2006:19) reinforce the message of the marginalization of the EP in OMC processes. Equally, the OMC has impacted detrimentally upon the oversight capacity of national parliaments. National parliaments have encountered difficulties accessing documents, tracking informal negotiations, and generally 'getting a grip' on OMC processes (Duina and Raunio 2007:493). Overall, there is a suspicion that 'the OMC is developing as a mode of governance acting outside the traditional scrutinising structures of representative democracy' (Armstrong 2005:302). The crucial question also remains of whether or not parliaments at national and EU levels *should* be involved in these processes.

Lisbon Treaty: Provisions on Democratic Principles

As noted above, Title II of the Lisbon Treaty clearly states that the Union shall be 'founded on representative democracy' (Article 10(1)) and that both the EP and national parliaments – directly and indirectly – are essential to the good functioning of the Union. So far, so clear. However, in Article 11(2) it is apparent that the EU's institutions are expected to 'maintain an open, transparent and regular dialogue with representative associations and civil society', and specifically that the 'Commission shall carry out broad consultations'. New Article 152, under Title X Social Policy, clearly recognized and promoted 'the role of the social partners' at EU level, and the need to 'facilitate dialogue between the social partners'. In particular, a tripartite Social Summit for Growth and Employment was expected to make a special contribution to this dialogue.

Significantly Article 11 and Article 152 of the Lisbon Treaty had initially appeared in Title VI of the Constitutional Treaty under the General Heading 'The Democratic Life of the Union' and respectively under the subheadings 'The Principle of Participatory Democracy', and

'The Social Partners and Autonomous Social Dialogue'. In the Lisbon Treaty, however, the general heading was replaced by a new heading 'Provisions on Democratic Principles' and the subheadings were eliminated. Although the elimination of the headings proclaiming divergent 'principles', of 'representative democracy', 'participatory democracy' and 'social dialogue', were removed from the Lisbon Treaty, the potential contradiction between participatory and corporatist/associationalist modes of democracy on the one side and representative modes on the other remained intact. If anything these contradictions became further entangled in notions of 'direct democracy' in the provision for citizen's initiatives in Article 11(4). This Article enables initiatives, with the support of more than one million citizens 'who are nationals of a significant number of Member States', to be submitted to the Commission inviting it to make a proposal 'where citizens consider that a legal act of the Union is required'.

The fact that the Article on citizens' initiatives was added at the last minute to the Constitutional Treaty, and with little prior discussion in the Convention (see Smismans 2004:136; Smismans 2007:606) suggests that the potential conflicts between the principles of representative democracy and of participatory democracy either were considered not to be pressing or else were considered not to be problematic. Indeed, the very fact that initiatives were to be forwarded to the Commission rather than to the EP, and hence provide citizens with the same direct right as the EP to request the Commission to propose legislative action, suggests that the potential challenge to the implicit hierarchy of principles in the Lisbon Treaty – with the Articles on representative democracy placed above the Articles on participatory democracy – was not appreciated at the time.

Similarly the implicit assumption of the Lisbon Treaty that an EU model of participatory democracy – centred on organized civil society and grounded in functional representation – would 'harness and adapt participatory mechanisms with representative traditions' (Greenwood 2007b:356) was based on 'the *aspiration* that measures for participatory democracy can continue to develop without offending the mainstay principle of representative democracy' (Greenwood 2007b:336–7, emphasis added). But this is likely to remain an aspiration while the normative priority of the latter is challenged by the empirical reality of the former. Ultimately, a fundamental tension may be posited between these principles. In turn, this 'may explain the "schizophrenic nature" of the European normative and constitutional debate, where arguments on representative and participatory democracy have not met' (Smismans 2004:131). Significantly, these arguments continue not to meet in the Lisbon Treaty.

Parliamentarization: addressing post-parliamentarism in a semi-parliamentary system?

As we have seen above there is a widespread perception that, in the context of a decentred EU polity, 'conventional parliamentary approaches' (Shaw 1999:581) or 'classic parliamentary forms' are inapplicable (Magnette 2005:176). This view culminates in the characterization of the EU as a form of 'post-parliamentary governance' where 'post-parliamentary forms . . . tend to dominate and crowd out parliamentary influence in specialised areas of policy-making' (Andersen and Burns 1996:246). As we have also seen, this tendency has been identified particularly in relation to the structures of 'new governance' as exemplified in the Open Method of Coordination, stakeholder consultation, processes of 'agencification', and procedures surrounding comitology. In the face of these developments, further parliamentarization of the EU may already be doomed to failure.

Yet this is not the conclusion of this book. As we argued in Chapter 3, representative democracy still provides the normative frame within which debate about governance in the EU is conducted. At its simplest, politicians conceive of constitutional choices rooted in their existing experiences of parliamentary institutions (Kohler-Koch 2000:528; Rittberger 2005:204; Kohler-Koch and Rittberger 2007:21–2). At its most complex, 'a decentred polity seems unsuited to parliamentary politics; yet attempts to tailor post-parliamentary solutions to the EU's decentred polity presuppose the very parliamentary politics they are intended to replace' (Lord 2007:150). In other words, the outputs of multilevel network governance cannot be legitimated solely in terms of sectoral output efficiency and effectiveness; they depend in the 'last instance' upon authorization derived from electoral processes and the holistic character of parliamentary representation (see Judge 1999: 139–42). Even Andersen and Burns (1996:246) have to concede that networks are not 'particularly effective in legitimising the system of modern governance. Typically, the formal democratic arrangements, in particular parliament, still remain essential in this respect'.

Thus, if the European Parliament is 'essential' in this sense, then an understanding of how the EP operates and interacts with other institutions and actors in a multilevel EU polity is equally 'essential'. What this book has sought to do is to locate the EP within conceptions of the EU and within notions of what parliaments 'are' and 'do'. Manifestly there have been significant developments since the first edition of this book in terms both of the EP's formal powers and of its informal procedures. Ultimately, how these changes are assessed depends upon how the EU is conceived in the first place – as Type I or Type II governance.

It is perhaps fitting, therefore, to conclude with exactly the same words as in the first edition: 'In the study of the European Parliament, where you start from determines where you finish.'

References

Note: European Parliament committee reports appear in this bibliography with 'PE' as author and are listed numerically by PE number, rather than by year of publication.

Abromeit, H. (2002) 'Contours of a European Federation', *Regional and Federal Studies,* 12, 1, 1–20.

ALDE (2006) *Mid-Term Review European Parliament 2004–2006,* Alliance of Liberals and Democrats for Europe, available at www.alde.eu/fileadmin/files/Mid_Term_Review_2007/MID-TERM-EN-small.pdf

Andersen, S. S. and Burns, T. (1996) 'The European Union and the Erosion of Parliamentary Democracy: A Study of Post-Parliamentary Governance', in S. S. Andersen and K. A. Eliassen (eds), *The European Union: How Democratic Is It?,* London, Sage.

Armstrong, K. A. (2005) 'How Open is the United Kingdom to the OMC Process on Social Inclusion?', in J. Zeitlin and P. Pochet (eds), *The Open Method of Coordination In Action: The European Employment and Social Inclusion Strategies,* Brussels, Peter Lang.

Arter, D (2006) 'Conclusion. Questioning the "Mezey Question": An Interrogatory Framework for the Comparative Study of Legislatures', *Journal of Legislative Studies,* 12, 3/4, 462–82.

Attina, F. (1990) 'The Voting Behaviour of the European Parliament Members and the Problem of Europarties', *European Journal of Political Research,* 18, 3, 557–79.

Auel, K. and Rittberger, B. (2006) 'Fluctuant Nec Merguntur: The European Parliament, National Parliaments, and European Integration', in J. Richardson (ed.), *European Union: Power and Policy-Making,* 3rd edn, London, Routledge.

Auers, D. (2005) 'European Elections in Eight New EU Member States', *Electoral Studies,* 24, 4, 747–54.

Austrian Parliament (2004) *Conference of European Affairs Committee,* available at www.parlament.gv.at/portal/page?_pageid=1033,658148&_dad=portal&_schema=PORTAL

Bach, S. (1999) 'The Office of Speaker in Comparative Perspective', *Journal of Legislative Studies,* 5, 3/4, 209–54.

Bale, T. and Taggart, P. (2006a) 'The Newest of the New? Accession State MEPs: Who They Are and Who They Think They Are', paper presented to the Federal Trust Workshop on the European Parliament and the European Political Space, London, 30 March.

Bale, T. and Taggart, P. (2006b) 'First Timers Yes, Virgins No: The Roles and Backgrounds of New Members of the European Parliament, *SEI Working Paper* 89, Brighton, Sussex European Institute.

Bardi, L. (2006) 'EU Enlargement, European Parliament Elections and

Transnational Trends in European Parties, *European View*, 3, Brussels, Forum for European Studies.

Barnier, M. (2000) 'Europe's Future: Two Steps and Three Paths, A Personal Note', Brussels, European Commission.

Bartolini, S. (2006) 'Should the Union be "Politicised"? Prospects and Risks', *Policy Paper* no. 19, Paris, Notre Europe, available at www.notre-europe. eu/uploads/tx_publication/Policypaper19-en.pdf

Beach, D. (2005) *The Dynamics of European Integration: Why and When EU Institutions Matter*, Basingstoke, Palgrave Macmillan.

Beetham, D. and Lord, C. (1998) *Legitimacy and the European Union*, London, Longman.

Bellamy, R. and Castiglione, D. (2003) 'Legitimizing the Euro-Polity and Its Regime: The Normative Turn in EU Studies', *European Journal of Political Theory*, 2, 1, 7–34

Benedetto, G. (2005) 'Rapporteurs as Legislative Entrepreneurs: The Dynamics of the Codecision Procedure in Europe's Parliament', *Journal of European Public Policy*, 12, 1, 67–88.

Benz, A. (2004) 'Path-Dependent Institutions and Strategic Veto Players: National Parliaments in the European Union', *West European Politics*, 27, 5, 875–900.

Bergman, T. and Raunio, T. (2001) 'Parliaments and Policy Making in the European Union', in J. Richardson (ed.), *European Union: Power and Policy-Making*, 2nd edn, London, Routledge.

Bergman, T., Müller, W. C., Strøm, K. and Blomgren, M. (2003) 'Democratic Delegation and Accountability: Cross-national Patterns', in K. Strøm, W.C. Müller, T. Bergman (eds), *Delegation and Accountability in Parliamentary Democracies*, Oxford, Oxford University Press.

BEUC (2007), 'Roaming', Press Release, PR 007/2007, 22 March 2007, available at www.beuc.eu/Content/Default.asp?PageID=1468&LanguageCode =EN

Beukers, T. (2006) 'Enhancing Parliamentary Control Over The European Commission and the Member States: Constitutional Development Through Practice', *European Constitutional Law Review*, 2, 1, 21–53.

Blondel, J. (1970) 'Legislative Behaviour: Some Steps Towards a Cross-national Measurement', *Government and Opposition*, 5, 1, 67–85.

Blondel, J. (1973) *Comparative Legislatures*, Englewood Cliffs, NJ, Prentice-Hall.

Blondel, J., Sinnott, R. and Svensson, P. (1998) *People and Parliament in the European Union: Participation, Democracy and Legitimacy*, Oxford, Clarendon.

Bogdanor, V. (2007) *Legitimacy, Accountability and Democracy in the European Union*, Federal Trust Report, London, Federal Trust.

Bomberg, E. and Carter, N. (2007) 'The Greens in Brussels: Shaping or Shaped?', *European Journal of Political Research*, 45, Special Issue October, S99-S125.

Borrás, S. and Jacobsson, K. (2004) 'The Open Method of Co-ordination and New Governance Patterns in the EU', *Journal of European Public Policy*, 11, 2, 185–208.

Bowler, S. and Farrell, D. M. (1993) 'Legislator Shirking and Voter

Monitoring: Impacts of European Parliament Electoral Systems upon Legislator–Voter Relationships', *Journal of Common Market Studies*, 31, 1, 45–70.

Bowler, S. and Farrell, D. M. (1995) 'The Organizing of the European Parliament: Committees, Specialization and Co-ordination', *British Journal of Political Science*, 25, 2, 219–43.

Brzinski, J. B., Ginning, H., Haspel, M. and Saunders, K. (1998) 'Understanding Defection in the European Parliament', paper presented at the Annual Meeting of the American Political Science Association, September, Boston.

Bullen, R. and Pelly, G. (eds) (1986) *Documents on British Policy Overseas*, Series II, vol. 1, no. 114, London, HMSO.

Bunyan, T. (2007) 'Secret Trilogues and the Democratic Deficit', *Statewatch Analysis*, available at www.statewatch.org/news/2007/sep/ep-co-decision-secret-trilogues.pdf

Burgess, M. (2004) 'Federalism', in A. Wiener and T. Diez (eds), *European Integration Theory*, Oxford, Oxford University Press.

Burgess, M. (2007) 'Federalism and Federation', in M. Cini (ed.), *European Union Politics*, 2nd edn, Oxford, Oxford University Press.

Burns, C. (2005) 'Who Pays? Who Gains? How do Costs and Benefits Shape the Policy Influence of the European Parliament?', *Journal of Common Market Studies*, 43, 3, 485–505.

Caporaso, J. A., Marks, G., Moravcsik, A. and Pollack, M. A. (1997) 'Does the European Union Represent an *n* of 1?', *ECSA Review*, 3 (Fall), 1–5.

Capotorti, F., Hilf, M., Jacobs, F. and Jacqué, J. P. (1986) *The European Union Treaty: Commentary on the Draft Adopted by the European Parliament on 14 February 1984*, Oxford, Clarendon Press.

Carrubba, C. and Gabel, M. (1999) 'Roll Call Votes and Party Discipline in the European Parliament: Reconsidering MEP Voting Behaviour', paper presented at the Annual Meeting of the American Political Science Association, 2–5 September, Atlanta, Georgia.

Carrubba, C. J., Gabel, M., Murrah, L., Clough, R., Montgomery, E. and Schambach, R. (2006) 'Off the Record: Unrecorded Legislative Votes, Selection Bias and Roll-Call Analysis', *British Journal of Political Science*, 36, 4, 691–704.

CEPS (2007) *The Treaty of Lisbon: Implementing the Institutional Innovations*, Joint Study by Centre For European Policy Studies, EGMONT and European Policy Centre, November, Brussels, CEPS/EGMONT/EPC.

Chan, K. (2005) 'Central and Eastern Europe in the 2004 European Parliament Elections: A Not So European Event', *Sussex European Institute Working Paper* no. 81, Falmer, University of Sussex.

Childs, S., Lovenduski, J. and Campbell, R. (2005) *Women at the Top 2005: Changing Numbers, Changing Politics?*, London, Hansard Society.

Christiansen, T. and Vaccari, B. (2006) 'The 2006 Reform of Comitology: Problem Solved or Dispute Postponed?', *EIPASCOPE*, 3, 9–17.

Chryssochoou, D. N. (1994) 'Democracy and Symbiosis in the European Union: Towards a Confederal Consociation?', *West European Politics*, 4, 3, 1–14.

Chryssochoou, D. N. (1997) 'New Challenges to the Study of European

Integration: Implications for Theory Building', *Journal of Common Market Studies*, 35, 4, 521–42.

Chryssochoou, D. N. (2007) 'Democracy and the European Union', in M. Cini (ed.), *European Union Politics*, 2nd edn, Oxford, Oxford University Press.

Church, C. and Phinnemore, D. (2007) 'The Rise and Fall of the Constitutional Treaty', in M. Cini (ed.), *European Union Politics*, 2nd edn, Oxford, Oxford University Press.

Clegg, N. and van Hulten, M. (2003) *Reforming the European Parliament*, London, Foreign Policy Centre.

COD 1999/0244 *Directive on the Approximation of Laws, Regulations and Administrative Provisions of Member States Concerning the Manufacture, Presentation and Sale of Tobacco Products*, Brussels, Commission of the European Communities.

COM(93)661 (1993) *Proposal for a European Parliament and Council Directive on the Legal Protection of Biotechnological Inventions*, Brussels, Commission of the European Communities.

COM(95)655 (1995) *Proposal for a 13th European Parliament and Council Directive on Company Law Concerning Takeover Bids*, Brussels, Commission of the European Communities.

COM(97)510 final (1997) *Motor Insurance: Civil Liability, Fourth Directive (Amend. direct. 73/239/EEC, 88/357/EEC, 92/49/EEC)*, Brussels, Commission of the European Communities.

COM(2001)28 final (2001) *The Commission's Work Programme for 2001*, Brussels, Commission of the European Communities.

COM(2001)428 final (2001) *European Governance: A White Paper*, Brussels, Commission of the European Communities.

COM(2001)620 final (2001) *The Commission's Work Programme for 2002*, Brussels, Commission of the European Communities.

COM(2002)92 (2002) *Proposal for a Directive of the European Parliament and of the Council on the Patentability of Computer-Implemented Inventions*, Brussels, Commission of the European Communities.

COM(2002)95 (2002) *Democratic Control over Europol*, Communication from the Commission to the European Parliament and the Council, Brussels, Commission of the European Communities.

COM(2002)704 (2002) *Towards a Reinforced Culture of Consultation and Dialogue – General Principles and Minimum Standards for Consultation of Interested Parties by the Commission*, Communication from the Commission, Brussels, Commission of the European Communities.

COM(2004)144 (2004) *Proposal for a Regulation of the European Parliament and of the Council on Compensation in Cases of Non-compliance with Contractual Quality Requirements for Rail Freight Services*, Brussels, Commission of the European Communities.

COM(2004)532 (2004) *Proposal for a Directive of the European Parliament and of the Council Introducing Humane Trapping Standards for Certain Animal Species*, Brussels, Commission of the European Communities.

COM(2004)759 (2004) *European Electronic Communications Regulation and Markets 2004*, Communication from the Commission to the Council, the European Parliament, the European Economic and Social Committee and the Committee of the Regions, Brussels, Commission of the European Communities.

COM(2005)12 (2005) *Strategic Objectives 2005–2009. Europe 2010: A Partnership for European Renewal Prosperity, Solidarity and Security*, Communication from the President in Agreement with Vice-President Wallström, Brussels, Commission of the European Communities.

COM(2005)15 (2005) *Commission Work Programme for 2005*, Communication from the President in Agreement with Vice-President Wallström, Brussels, Commission of the European Communities.

COM(2006)194 (2006) *Green Paper: European Transparency Initiative*, Brussels, Commission of the European Communities.

COM(2006)382 (2006) *Proposal for a Regulation of the European Parliament and of the Council on Roaming on Public Mobile Networks within the Community and Amending Directive 2002/21/EC on a Common Regulatory Framework for Electronic Communications Networks and Services*, Brussels, Commission of the European Communities.

COM(2007)127 (2007) *Follow-up to the Green Paper 'European Transparency Initiative'*, Communication from the Commission, Brussels, Commission of the European Communities.

COM(2007)364 (2007) *Proposal for a Regulation of the European Parliament and of the Council Amending Regulation (EC) No. 2004/2003 on the Regulations Governing Political Parties at European Level and the Rules Regarding Their Funding*, Brussels, Commission of the European Communities.

Committee of Three (1979) *Report on European Institutions*, Luxembourg, European Council.

CONV 27/02 (2002) 'Contribution from Mr John Bruton, Member of the Convention', CONTRIB 10, Brussels, Secretariat, European Convention.

CONV 67/02 (2002) 'The Role of National Parliaments in the European Architecture', Information Note from Praesidium to Convention, Brussels, Secretariat, European Convention.

CONV 97/02 (2002) 'Note on the Plenary Meeting, 6 and 7 June', Brussels, Secretariat, European Convention.

CONV 353/02 (2002) 'Final Report of Working Group IV on the Role of National Parliaments', Brussels, Secretariat, European Convention.

Copeland, G. W. and Patterson, S. C. (1994) *Parliaments in the Modern World: Changing Institutions*, Ann Arbor, Michigan, University of Michigan Press.

Corbett, R. (1992) 'The Intergovernmental Conference on Political Union', *Journal of Common Market Studies*, 30, 3, 271–98.

Corbett, R. (1993a) *The Treaty of Maastricht, from Conception to Ratification: A Comprehensive Reference Guide*, London, Longman.

Corbett, R. (1993b) 'Governance and Institutional Development', in N. Nugent (ed.), *The European Union 1993: Annual Review of Activities*, Oxford, Blackwell.

Corbett, R. (1994) 'Representing the People', in A. Duff, J. Pinder and R. Pryce (eds), *Maastricht and Beyond*, London, Routledge.

Corbett, R. (1995) 'Governance and Institutional Developments', *Journal of Common Market Studies, Annual Review 1995*, 34, 29–42.

Corbett, R. (1998) *The European Parliament's Role in Closer European Integration*, London, Macmillan.

Corbett, R. (2000) 'Academic Modelling of the Codecision Procedure: A Practitioner's Puzzled Reaction', *European Union Politics*, 1, 3, 373–81.

Corbett, R. (2001) 'Evaluating Nice', Speech in the Committee on Constitutional Affairs, 9 January, European Parliament.

Corbett, R., Jacobs, F. and Shackleton, M. (2007) *The European Parliament*, 7th edn, London, John Harper.

Corporate Europe Observatory (2006) *Transparency Boost Needed for Cross-Party Groups'*, Corporate Europe Observatory, available at www.corporateeurope.org/crosspartygroups.pdf

COSAC (2003) *Contribution from the 28th COSAC*, Conference of Community and European Affairs Committees of Parliaments of the European Union, 27 January 2003, Brussels.

COSAC (2005) *Report on the Results of COSAC's Pilot Project on the 3rd Railway Package to Test the 'Subsidiary Early Warning Mechanism'*, Prepared by the COSAC Secretariat and presented to the 33rd Conference of Community and European Affairs Committees of Parliaments of the European Union, 17–18 May, Luxembourg.

COSAC (2007a) *Seventh Bi-Annual Report: Developments in the European Union: Procedures and Practices Relevant to Parliamentary Scrutiny*, presented to the 37th Conference of Community and European Affairs Committees of Parliaments of the European Union, 13–15 May, Berlin.

COSAC (2007b) *Eight Bi-Annual Report: Developments in the European Union: Procedures and Practices Relevant to Parliamentary Scrutiny*, presented to the 38th Conference of Community and European Affairs Committees of Parliaments of the European Union, 14–15 October, Estoril.

Cotta, M. (1974) 'A Structural-Functional Framework for the Analysis of Unicameral and Bicameral Parliaments', *European Journal of Political Research*, 2, 3, 201–24.

Cotta, M. and Best, H. (2000) 'Between Professionalization and Democratization: A Synoptic View on the Making of the European Representative', in M. Cotta and H. Best (eds), *Parliamentary Representation in Europe 1848–2000*, Oxford, Oxford University Press.

Council of the European Union (2003) *Proposal for a Directive of the European Parliament and of the Council on the Patentability of Computer-Implemented Inventions – Outcome of the European Parliament's First Reading*, 11503/03, Interinstitutional File 2002/0047 COD, General Secretariat, Brussels, Council of the European Union.

Council of the European Union (2007a) *Presidency Conclusions Brussels European Council 21/22 June 2007*, 11177/1 Rev1, Brussels, Council of the European Union.

Council of the European Union (2007b) 'Note for the Attention of the Members of COREPER I and II and the Spokespersons of The SCA: Codecision Dossiers – Portuguese Presidency', General Secretariat, Legal Services , Brussels, Council of the European Union, available at consilium. europa.eu/uedocs/cmsUpload/Codecisiondossiers_PortuguesePresidency.pdf

Cram, L. (2001) 'Integration Theory and the Study of the European Policy Process', in J. Richardson (ed.), *European Union: Power and Policy-Making*, 2nd edn, London, Routledge.

Crum, B. (2004) 'Politics and Power in the European Convention', *Politics*, 24, 1, 1–11.

Curtice, J., Fisher, S. and Steed, M. (2005) 'Appendix: An Analysis of the Results', in D. Butler and M. Westlake (eds), *British Politics and European Elections 2004*, London, Palgrave Macmillan.

Dann, P. (2003) 'European Parliament and Executive Federalism: Approaching a Parliament in a Semi-parliamentary Democracy', *European Law Journal*, 9, 5, 549–74.

de Haan, J. and Eijffinger, C. W. (2000) 'The Democratic Accountability of the European Central Bank', *Journal of Common Market Studies*, 38, 3, 393–408.

de Witte, B. (2002) 'The Closest Thing to a Constitutional Conversation in Europe: The Semi-Permanent Treaty Revision Process', in P. Beaumont, C. Lyons and N. Walker (eds), *Convergence and Divergence in European Public Law*, Oxford, Hart.

Dehousse, R. (1998) 'European Institutional Architecture After Amsterdam: Parliamentary System or Regulatory Structure?', *Common Market Law Review*, 35, 595–627.

Dinan, D. (1999) *An Ever Closer Union: An Introduction to the European Community*, 2nd edn, London, Macmillan.

Dinan, D. (2004) 'Reconstituting Europe', in M. Green Cowles and D. Dinan (eds), *Developments in the European* Union, 2nd edn, Basingstoke, Palgrave Macmillan.

Duff, A. (2001) 'The Treaty of Nice: From Left-Overs to Hangovers', http://www.andrewduffmep.org/Press%20Releases/newnice.rtf

Duff, A., Dini, L., Mclennan, L. and Severin, A. (2002) 'Suggestion For Amendment of Article 18a', Brussels, European Convention, available at european-convention.eu.int/Docs/Treaty/pdf/41899/18bisDuff%20EN.pdf

Duina, F. and Oliver, M. J. (2005) 'National Parliaments in the European Union: Are There Any Benefits to Integration?', *European Law Journal*, 11, 2, 173–95.

Duina, F. and Raunio, T. (2007) 'The Open Method of Co-ordination and National Parliaments: Further Marginalization or New Opportunities?, *Journal of European Public Policy*, 14, 4, 489–506.

Earnshaw, D. (1985) 'The European Parliament's Quest for a Single Seat', *Journal of European Integration/Revue d'Intégration Européenne*, 8, 1, 77–93.

Earnshaw, D. and Judge, D. (1993) 'The European Parliament and the Sweeteners Directive: From Footnote to Inter-Institutional Conflict', *Journal of Common Market Studies*, 31, 1, 103–16.

Earnshaw, D. and Judge, D. (1995a) 'Prelude to Codecision: A Qualitative Assessment of the Cooperation Procedure in the 1989–94 European Parliament', Political Series W11, Directorate General for Research, Luxembourg, European Parliament.

Earnshaw, D. and Judge, D. (1995b) 'Early Days: The European Parliament, Codecision and the European Union Legislative Process Post-Maastricht', *Journal of European Public Policy*, 2, 4, 624–49.

Earnshaw, D. and Judge, D. (1996) 'From Co-operation to Codecision: The European Parliament's Path to Legislative Power', in J. Richardson (ed.), *European Union: Power and Policy Making*, London, Routledge.

Earnshaw, D. and Wood, J. (1999) 'The European Parliament and

Biotechnology Patenting: Harbinger of the Future?', *Journal of Commercial Biotechnology*, 5, 4, 294–307.

Eco-Logica (2007) *European Parliament Two-Seat Operation: Environmmental Costs, Transport and Energy*, Report Produced for the Greens/European Free Alliance, Lancaster, Eco-Logica Ltd. Available at http://www.greens-efa.org/cms/topics/dokin/180/180441.eu_and_climate_change@en.pdf

Elazar, D. J. (1991) 'Introduction', in D. J. Elazar (ed.), *Federal Systems of the World: A Handbook of Federal, Confederal and Autonomy Arrangements*, London, Longman.

Electoral Commission (2004) *The 2004 European Parliamentary Elections in the United Kingdom: The Official Report*, London, Electoral Commission.

Elgie, R. (1999) *Semi-Presidentialism in Europe*, Oxford, Oxford University Press.

EPP-ED (2006) *Rules of Procedure of the Group of the European People's Party (Christian-Democrats) and European Democrats in the European Parliament*, December 2006, Brussels, EPP-ED

Eriksen, E. O. and Fossum, J. E. (2004) 'Europe in Search of Legitimacy: Strategies of Legitimation Assessed', *International Political Science Review*, 25, 4, 435–59.

Espíndola, R. and García, F. (2005) 'Spain', in J. Lodge (ed.), *The 2004 Elections to the European Parliament*, London, Palgrave Macmillan.

Eulau, H. and Karps, P. (1977) 'The Puzzle of Representation: Specifying Components and Responsiveness', *Legislative Studies Quarterly*, 2, 3, 233–54.

Eurobarometer (2004) *Post European Elections 2004 Survey*, Flash Eurobarometer 162, July, Brussels, European Commission.

European Commission (2000) *Strategic Objectives 2000–2005 'Shaping the New Europe'*, Brussels, Commission of the European Communities.

European Commission (2005) 'Commission Warns Consumers on Cost of Using Mobile Phone Abroad and Targets Lack of Price Transparency', Press Release, IP/05/901, 11 July 2005, Brussels, Commission of the European Communities.

European Commission (2006) *Impact Assessment of Policy Options in Relation to a Commission Proposal for a Regulation of the European Parliament and of the Council on Roaming on Public Mobile Networks within the Community*, COM(2006)382 final, 12 July 2006, Commission Staff Working-Paper, Brussels, Commission of the European Communities.

European Commission (2007a) *Financial Programming and Budget; EU Budget at a Glance*, available at www. ec.europa.eu/budget/budget_glance/where_from_en.htm

European Commission (2007b) 'Implementation of Humane Trapping Standard in the EU', DG Environment, Brussels, Commission of the European Communities, available at ec.europa.eu/environment/biodiversity/animal_welfare/hts/index_en.htm

European Council (2000a) *Presidency Conclusions: Nice European Council Meeting 7, 8 and 9 December 2000*, SN 400/00 Brussels, European Council.

European Council (2000b) *Treaty of Nice*, SN 533/1/00/REV1, Brussels, European Council.

European Council (2002) *Presidency Conclusions, Seville European Council, 21 and 22 June 2002*, SN 200/02, Brussels, European Council.

European Council (2006) *Presidency Conclusions: Brussels European Council 15–16 June*, 10633/06, Brussels, European Council.

European Parliament (1978) *Powers of the European Parliament*, London, Information Office of the European Parliament.

European Parliament (1979) *Rules of Procedure*, Brussels, European Parliament.

European Parliament (1981) *Rules of Procedure*, 2nd edn, Brussels, European Parliament

European Parliament (1987) *Rules of Procedure*, 4th edn, Brussels, European Parliament.

European Parliament (1993) *Rules of Procedure*, 8th edn, Brussels, European Parliament.

European Parliament (1994) *The European Parliament and Codecision: The Fourth Framework Programme*, Working Paper W-11, Directorate-General for Research, Luxembourg, European Parliament.

European Parliament (1997a) European Parliament Directorate-General for Committees and Delegations, Committee on Institutional Affairs, 'The European Parliament as It would be Affected by the Draft Treaty of Amsterdam of 19 June 1997', Brussels, European Parliament, http://www.europarl.eu.int/dg7/treaty/en/epchange.htm

European Parliament (1997b) General Secretariat Working Party Task Force on the Intergovernmental Conference: The Coordinator, *Note on The European Parliament's Priorities for the IGC and The New Amsterdam Treaty: Report and Initial Evaluation of the Results*, Brussels, European Parliament.

European Parliament (1999) *Rules of Procedure*, 14th edn, Brussels, European Parliament.

European Parliament (2000) *A Framework Agreement on Relations between the European Parliament and the Commission*, European Parliament Minutes, 5 July, C5–03498/2000, Brussels, European Parliament.

European Parliament (2001) *Improving the Working of the Codecision Procedure*, discussion document presented by Renzo Imbeni, James Provan and Ingo Friedrich, Brussels, European Parliament, available at www.statewatch.org/news/2001/mar/codecision.pdf

European Parliament (2001a) *Activity Report of the Delegations to the Conciliation Committee* 2000–2001, Delegations to the Conciliation Committee, Brussels, European Parliament.

European Parliament (2002) *Rules of Procedure*, Amended Text, provisional edition, July 2002, Brussels, European Parliament.

European Parliament (2002a) *Activity Report of the Delegations to the Conciliation Committee* 2001–2002, Delegations to the Conciliation Committee, Brussels, European Parliament.

European Parliament (2004) *Rules of Procedure*, 15th edn, Brussels, European Parliament.

European Parliament (2004a) *Conciliations and Codecision: A Guide to How Parliament Co-Legislates*, Brussels, European Parliament.

European Parliament (2004b) *Investiture Procedure of the 2004–2009*

Commission – Hearings of the Commissioners Designate, available at www.europarl.europa.eu/hearings/commission/2004_comm/structure_en. htm

European Parliament (2004c) *First and Second Agreements: Guidelines for Best Practice Within Parliament*, Brussels, European Parliament, available at www.europarl.europa.eu/code/information/guidelines_en.pdf

European Parliament (2005a*) Report on Budgetary and Financial Management, Financial Year 2005, Section I: European Parliament*, DV/614096EN, Committee of Budgetary Control, Brussels, European Parliament.

European Parliament (2005b) *Joint Public Hearing on the New REACH Legislation*, available at www.europarl.europa.eu/comparl/envi/reach/verbatim.pdf

European Parliament (2005c) 'Software Patents: The "Historic Vote" in the European Parliament Brings the Battle to an End', Press Service, Brussels, European Parliament, available at www.europarl.europa.eu/news/public/focus_page/057–1002–255–09–37–909–20050819FCS01001–12–09–2005–2005/default_p001c002_en.htm

European Parliament (2006) 'Budget Deal Reached for 2007–2013 – MEPs Give Their Views', European Parliament Press Service, available at www.europarl.europa.eu/news/public/story_page/034–7096–093–04–14–90 5–20060405STO07095–2006–03–04–2006/default_en.htm

European Parliament (2007) 'Information Note by the Three Parliamentary Representatives to the Intergovernmental Conference', 17 October 2007, Brussels, European Parliament.

European Parliament (2007a) *Rules of Procedure*, 16th edn, Brussels, European Parliament.

European Parliament (2007b) 'Improving the Public Perception and Efficiency of the Work of the European Parliament – Mandate for a Working Group on Reform of the Parliament', European Parliament Press Service, available at http://www.europarl.europa.eu/news/expert/infopress_page/008–3202–050–02–08–901–20070215IPR03201–19–02–2007–2007-false/default_en. htm.htm

European Parliament (2007c) 'Intergroups: MEPs Unite on Single Issues Across Party Lines', Press Service, 19 March 2007, Brussels, European Parliament, available at: available at www.europarl.europa.eu/news/public/story_page/008–4260–078–03–12–901–20070314STO04219–2007–19–03–2007/default_en.htm. European Parliament

European Parliament (2007d) *Reform of the European Parliament*, available at europarl.europa.eu/eplive/expert/multimedia/20071029MLT12549/media _20071029MLT12549.pdf.pdf

European Parliament (2007e) *Conciliations and Codecision Activity Report July 2004 to December 2006*, DV/651053, Delegations to the Conciliation Committee, Brussels, European Parliament.

European Parliament (2007f) 'Acceptance Speech by Mrs Arlene McCarthy on Her Re-election as Chair of the IMCO Committee, Brussels, 31 January 2007', IMCO-07–0033, Internal Market and Consumer Protection Committee, Brussels, European Parliament.

European Parliament (2007g) *Legislative Resolution of 23 May 2007 on the Proposal for a Regulation of the European Parliament and of the Council on Roaming on Public Mobile Networks Within the Community and Amending Directive 2002/21/EC on a Common Regulatory Framework for Electronic Communications Networks and Services*, available at www.europarl.europa.eu/sides/getDoc.do?type=TA&reference=P6-TA-2007-0199&language=EN&ring=A6-2007-0155#BKMD-3.

Evans, C. L. (1999) 'Legislative Structure: Rules, Precedents, and Jurisdictions', *Legislative Studies Quarterly*, 24, 4, 605–42.

Farrell, D. M. and Scully, R. (2007) *Representing Europe's Citizens: Electoral Institutions and the Failure of Parliamentary Representation*, Oxford, Oxford University Press.

Farrell, D. M., Hix, S., Johnson, M. and Scully, R. (2006), 'A Survey of MEPs in the 2004–2009 European Parliament', Paper Presented to the Annual Conference of the Political Studies Association Specialist Group on Elections, Public Opinion and Parties, Nottingham, September.

Farrell, H. and Héritier, A. (2002) 'Formal and Informal Institutions Under Codecision: Continuous Constitution Building in Europe's Parliament', *European Integration Online Papers*, 6, 3; http://eiop.or.at/texte/2002-003a.htm

Farrell, H. and Héritier, A. (2003a) 'Formal and Informal Institutions Under Codecision: Continuous Constitution-Building in Europe', *Governance*, 16, 4, 577–600.

Farrell, H. and Héritier, A. (2003b) 'The Invisible Transformation of Codecision: Problems of Democratic Legitimacy', Report No 7, Stockholm, Swedish Institute for European Policy Studies, available at www.sieps,su.se

Farrell, H. and Héritier, A. (2004) 'Interorganizational Cooperation and Intraorganizational Power: Early Agreements under Codecision and Their Impact in the Parliament and the Council, *Comparative Political Studies*, 37, 10, 1184–212.

Farrell, H. and Héritier, A. (2007) 'Codecision and Institutional Change', *West European Politics*, 30, 2, 285–300.

Featherstone, K. (1994) 'Jean Monnet and the "Democratic Deficit" in the European Union', *Journal of Common Market Studies*, 32, 2, 149–70.

FFII (2004) 'The Gloves Come Off for Round Two in the EU Fight Over Software Patents', Press Release, 2004/08/04, Foundation for Free Information Infrastructure, available at plone.ffii.org/pr/04/cons0408/index_html/view?searchterm=common%20position

Fieschi, C. (2000) 'European Institutions: The Far-Right and Illiberal Politics in a Liberal Context', *Parliamentary Affairs*, 53, 3, 517–31.

Fitzmaurice, J. (1975) *The Party Groups in the European Parliament*, Farnborough, Saxon House.

Fitzmaurice, J. (1988) 'An Analysis of the European Community's Co-operation Procedure', *Journal of Common Market Studies*, 26, 4, 389–400.

Fitzmaurice, J. (1994) 'The European Commission', in A. Duff, J. Pinder and R. Pryce (eds), *Maastricht and Beyond: Building the European Union*, London, Routledge.

Føllesdal, A. (2004) 'Legitimacy Theories of the European Union', *Arena Working Paper* no. 04/15, Oslo, European Centre for European Studies, available at www.arena.uio.no/publications/working-papers2004/papers/04_15.pdf

Føllesdal, A. and Hix, S. (2006) 'Why There is a Democratic Deficit in the EU: A Response to Majone and Moravcsik', *Journal of Common Market Studies*, 44, 3, 533–62.

Franklin, M. (2006) 'European Elections and the European Voter', in J. Richardson (ed.), *European Union: Power and Policy-Making*, 3rd edn, London, Routledge.

Freedman, J. (2002) 'Women in the European Parliament', *Parliamentary Affairs*, 55, 1, 179–88.

Friedrich, A., Tappe, M. and Wurzel, R. (2000) 'A New Approach to EU Environmental Policy-Making: the Auto-Oil 1 Programme', *Journal of European Public Policy*, 7, 4, 593–612.

Frognier, A. P. (2002) 'Identity and Electoral Participation: For a European Approach to European Elections', in P. Perrineau, G. Grunberg and C. Ysmal (eds), *Europe at the Polls: The European Elections, 1999*, New York, Palgrave Macmillan.

Gabel, M. and Carubba, C. J. (2004) 'The European Parliament and Transnational Political Representation: Party Groups and Political Conflict', *Europäische Politik*, Friedrich Ebert Stiftung.

Gabel, M. and Hix, S. (2002) 'The Ties that Bind: Partisanship and the Investiture Procedure for the EU Commission President', in M. Hosli, A. van Deemen and M. Widgrén (eds), *Institutional Challenges in the European Union*, London, Routledge.

Garman, J. and Hilditch, L. (1998) 'Behind the Scenes: An Examination of the Importance of the Informal Processes at Work in Conciliation', *Journal of European Public Policy*, 5, 2, 271–84.

Gornitzka, A. (2006) 'The Open Method of Coordination as Practice – A Watershed in European Policy', *Arena Working Paper* no. 16, Oslo, European Centre for European Studies, available at www.arena.uio.no/publications/working-papers2006/papers/wp06_16.pdf

GPC (2000) *All Change: The European Parliament One Year On*, Brussels, Government Policy Consultants.

Gray, M. and Stubb, A. (2001) 'Governance and Institutions 2000: Edging Towards Enlargement', in G. Edwards and G. Wiessala (eds), *The European Union: Annual Review of the EU 2000/2001*, Oxford, Blackwell.

Greens/EFA (2004) *A Green Contract for Europe*, available at www.greens-efa.org/cms/topics/dokbin/102/102762.a_green_contract_for_europe@en.pdf

Greenwood, J. (1997) *Representing Interests in the European Union*, London Macmillan.

Greenwood, J. (2007a) *Interest Representation in the European Union*, 2nd edn, Basingstoke, Palgrave Macmillan.

Greenwood, J. (2007b) 'Review Article: Organized Civil Society and Democratic Legitimacy in the European Union', *British Journal of Political Science*, 37, 3, 333–57.

GUE/NGL (1994) *Constituent Declaration*, The Confederal Group of the European United Left, available at www.guengl.org/showPage.jsp?ID=639

Guyomarch, A. (2000) 'The June 1999 European Parliament Elections', *West European Politics*, 23, 1, 161–74.

Häge, F. M. and Kaeding, M. (2007) 'Reconsidering the European Parliament's Legislative Influence: Formal vs. Informal Procedures', *Journal of European Integration*, 29, 3, 341–61.

Hallstein, W. (1972) *Europe in the Making,* London, Allen & Unwin.

Hausemer, P. (2006) 'Participation and Political Competition in Report Allocation: Under What Conditions do MEPs Represent Their Constituencies?', *European Union Politics,* 7, 4, 505–30.

Hayes-Renshaw, F. and Wallace, H. (2006) *The Council of Ministers,* 2nd edn, Basingstoke, Palgrave Macmillan.

HC 152 xxxiii (2002) *Democracy and Accountability in the EU and the Role of National Parliaments,* Thirty-third Report of the European Scrutiny Committee, London, Stationery Office.

HC 519-I (2007) *The European Commission's Annual Policy Strategy 2008,* Thirty-Second Report of the European Scrutiny Committee, Session 2006–07, London, The Stationery Office.

Henig, S. and Pinder, J. (1969) *European Political Parties,* London, George Allen & Unwin.

Herman, V. (1980) 'Direct Elections: The Historical Background', in V. Herman and M. Hagger (eds), *The Legislation of Direct Elections to the European Parliament,* Farnborough, Gower.

Herman, V. and Lodge, J. (1978) *The European Parliament and the European Community,* London, Macmillan.

Hibbing, J. R. and Patterson, S. C. (1986) 'Representing a Territory: Constituency Boundaries for the British House of Commons of the 1980s', *Journal of Politics,* 48, 992–1005.

Hix, S. (1997) 'Executive Selection in the European Union: Does the Commission President Investiture Procedure Reduce the Democratic Deficit?', *European Integration Online Papers,* 1, 21; http://eiop.or.at/eiop/texte/1997–021a.htm

Hix, S. (1998a) 'The Study of the European Union II: The "New Governance" Agenda and Its Rival', *Journal of European Public Policy,* 5, 1, 38–65.

Hix, S. (1998b) 'Elections, Parties and Institutional Design: A Comparative Perspective on European Union Democracy', *West European Politics,* 21, 3, 19–52.

Hix, S. (2001a) 'Legislative Behaviour and Party Competition in the Post-1999 European Parliament: An Application of NOMINATE to the EU', paper delivered at the One Europe or Several Programme Conference, April.

Hix, S. (2001b) 'Legislative Behaviour and Party Competition in the Post-1999 European Parliament: An Application of NOMINATE to the EU', *Journal of Common Market Studies,* 39, 4, 663–88.

Hix, S. (2002) 'Constitutional Agenda Setting Through Discretion in Rule Interpretation: Why the European Parliament Won at Amsterdam', *British Journal of Political Science,* 32, 2, 259–80.

Hix, S. (2002a) 'Parliamentary Behaviour with Two Principals: Preferences, Parties, and Voting in the European Parliament', *American Journal of Political Science,* 46, 3, 688–98.

Hix, S. (2005) *The Political System of the European Union,* 2nd edn, London, Palgrave Macmillan.

Hix, S. (2006) 'Why the EU Needs (Left–Right) Politics? Policy Reform and Accountability are Impossible Without It', *Policy Paper* no. 19, Paris, Notre Europe, available at www.notre-europe.eu/uploads/tx_publication/Policypaper 19-en.pdf

Hix, S. (2008) *What's Wrong With the European Union and How to Fix It*, Cambridge, Polity.

Hix, S. and Lord, C. (1996) 'The Making of a President: The European Parliament and the Confirmation of Jacques Santer as the President of the Commission', *Government and Opposition*, 31, 1, 62–76.

Hix, S. and Lord, C. (1997) *Political Parties in the European Union*, London, Macmillan.

Hix, S. and Marsh, M. (2005) 'Understanding European Parliament Elections: Punishment or Protest?', paper presented at the Conference on the 2004 European Elections, CEU Budapest, May 2005.

Hix, S. and Noury, A. (2006) 'After Enlargement: Voting Patterns in the Sixth European Parliament', Draft 2.0, paper originally presented to the Federal Trust Workshop, 'The European Parliament and the European Political Space', 30 March 2006, London: available at http://personal.lse.ac.uk/HIX/Working_Papers/Hix-Noury-After%20Enlargement-19April2006.pdf

Hix, S., Noury, A. and Roland, G. (2005) 'Power to the Parties: Cohesion and Competition in the European Parliament, 1979–2001', *British Journal of Political Science*, 35, 2, 209–34.

Hix, S., Noury, A. G. and Roland, G. (2007) *Democratic Politics in the European Parliament*, Cambridge, Cambridge University Press.

HL 48 (2001) *A Second Parliamentary Chamber for Europe: An Unreal Solution to Some Real Problems*, House of Lords Select Committee on European Union, Seventh Report, Session 2001–2, London, The Stationery Office.

HL 79-II (2007) *Mobile Phone Charges in the EU: Curbing the Excesses*, vol. II: Evidence, Seventeenth Report of the House of Lords European Union Committee, Session 2006–07, London, The Stationery Office.

Hoffman, L. (2002) 'Linking National Politics to Europe – an Opposing Argument', London, Federal Trust, available at www.fedtrust.co.uk

Holland, M. (1994) *European Integration: From Community to Union*, London, Pinter.

Hooghe, L. and Marks, G. (2001) 'Types of Multi-Level Governance', *European Integration Online Papers*, 1, 2; http://eiop.or.at/eiop/texte/2001–011a.htm

Hooghe, L. and Marks, G (2003) 'Unravelling the Central State, But How? Types of Multi-Level Governance', *American Political Science Review*, 97, 2, 233–43.

Höreth, M. (1999) 'No Way Out for The Beast? The Unsolved Legitimacy Problem of European Governance', *Journal of European Public Policy*, 6, 2, 249–68.

Høyland, B. (2006) 'Allocation of Codecision Reports in the Fifth European Parliament', *European Union Politics*, 7, 1, 30–50.

Høyland, B. K. (2005) 'Government-Opposition in Bicameral Negotiations: Decision-Making in European Union's Codecision Procedure', *EPRG Working Paper* no. 12, London, European Parliament Research Group, London School of Economics.

Høyland, B. and Hagemann, S. (2007) *Bicameral Politics in the European Union*, Arena Working Paper, 9, Oslo, Centre for European Studies available at www.arena.uio.no/publications/working-papers2007/papers/wp07_09.pdf

Hubschmid, C. and Moser, P. (1997) 'The Cooperation Procedure in the EU: Why Was the European Parliament Influential in the Decision on Car Emission Standards', *Journal of Common Market Studies*, 35, 2, 225–41.

Hug, S. (2006) 'Selection Effects in Roll Call Votes', *Centre For Comparative and International Studies Working Paper* no, 15, Zürich, Swiss Federal Institute of Technology.

Humphreys, J. (1997) *Negotiating in the European Union*, London, Random House.

Jachtenfuchs, M. and Kohler-Koch, B. (1997) 'The Transformation of Governance in the European Union', Mannheim, MZES Arbeitspapier AB III, Nr. 11, available at http://uscrpage.fu-berlin. de/-jfuchs/current/transfo. htm

Jacobs, F. B. (1999) 'Nominations and Appointments: An Evolving EU Model', paper presented to the ECSA Sixth Biennial Conference, June, Pittsburgh, PA.

Jacobs, F. (2007) 'Moving on Without the Constitution', paper Presented at the Tenth Biennial Conference of the European Union Studies Association, Montreal, 17–19 May.

Jewell, M. E. (1983) 'Legislator–Constituency Relations and the Representative Process', *Legislative Studies Quarterly*, 8, 303–37.

Judge, D. (1981) *Backbench Specialisation in the House of Commons*, London, Heinemann Educational Books.

Judge, D. (1993) '"Predestined to Save the Earth": The Environment Committee of the European Parliament', in D. Judge (ed.), *A Green Dimension for the European Community*, London, Frank Cass.

Judge, D. (1995) 'The Failure of National Parliaments', in J. Hayward (ed.), *The Crisis of Representation in Europe*, London, Frank Cass.

Judge, D. (1999) *Representation: Theory and Practice in Britain*, London, Routledge.

Judge, D. (2008) 'Parliaments and Parliamentary Systems', in W. A. Darity (ed.), *International Encyclopedia of the Social Sciences*, 2nd edn, Detroit, MI, Macmillan Reference USA.

Judge, D. and Earnshaw, D. (1994) 'Weak European Parliament Influence? A Study of the Environment Committee of the European Parliament', *Government and Opposition*, 29, 2, 262–76.

Judge, D. and Earnshaw, D. (1999) 'Locating the European Parliament', paper presented to the ECSA Sixth Biennial Conference, June, Pittsburgh, PA.

Judge, D. and Earnshaw, D. (2002) 'The European Parliament and the Commission Crisis: A New Assertiveness?', *Governance*, 15, 3, 345–74.

Judge, D. and Earnshaw, D. (2003) *The European Parliament*, Basingstoke, Palgrave Macmillan.

Judge, D. and Earnshaw, D. (2008) 'The European Parliament: Leadership and Followership', in J. Hayward (ed.), *Leaderless Europe*, Oxford, Oxford University Press.

Judge, D., Earnshaw, D. and Cowan, N. (1994) 'Ripples or Waves: The European Parliament in the European Policy Process', *Journal of European Public Policy*, 1, 1, 27–52.

Kaeding, M. (2004) 'Rapporteurship Allocation in the European Parliament: Information or Distribution?', *European Union Politics*, 5, 3, 353–71.

Kaeding, M. (2005) 'The World of Committee Reports: Rapporteurship Assignment in the European Parliament', *Journal of Legislative Studies*, 11, 1, 82–104.

Kallas, S. (2007) 'The European Transparency Initiative', speech made before Committee on Constitutional Affairs, SPEECH/07/491, 16 July, Brussels, European Parliament.

Katz, R. S. (1999) 'Role Orientations in Parliaments', in R. S. Katz and B. Wessels (eds), *The European Parliament, the National Parliaments, and European Integration*, Oxford, Oxford University Press.

Kietz, D. and Maurer, A. (2007) 'The European Parliament in Treaty Reform: Predefining IGCs through Interinstitutional Agreements', *European Law Journal*, 13, 1, 20–46.

Kiiver, P. (2005) *The National Parliaments in the European Union: A Critical View on EU Constitution-Building*, Maastricht, Universitaire Pers Maastricht.

Kirchner, E. and Williams, K. (1983) 'The Legal, Political and Institutional Implications of the Isoglucose Judgments 1980', *Journal of Common Market Studies*, 32, 2, 173–90.

Koepke, J. R. and Ringe, N. (2006) 'The Second-Order Election Model in an Enlarged Europe', *European Union Politics*, 7, 3, 321–46.

Kohler-Koch, B. (1997) 'Organised Interests and the European Parliament', *European Integration Online Papers*, 1, 9; http://eiop.or.at/eiop/texte/1997–009a.htm

Kohler-Koch, B. (2000) 'Framing: The Bottleneck of Constructing Legitimate Institutions', *Journal of European Public Policy*, 7, 4, 513–31.

Kohler-Koch, B. and Rittberger, B. (2007) 'Charting Crowded Territory: Debating the Democratic Legitimacy of the European Union', in B. Kohler-Koch and B. Rittberger (eds), *Debating the Democratic Legitimacy of the European Union*, Lanham, Rowman & Littlefield.

Kønig, T., Lindberg, B., Lechner, S. and Pohlmeier, W. (2007) 'Bicameral Conflict Resolution in the European Union: An Empirical Analysis of Conciliation Committee Bargains', *British Journal of Political Science*, 37, 2, 281–312.

Krehbiel, K. (1991) *Information and Legislative Organization*, Ann Arbor, University of Michigan Press.

Kreppel, A. (1999) 'The European Parliament's Influence Over EU Policy Outcomes', *Journal of Common Market Studies*, 37, 3, 521–38.

Kreppel, A. (2000a) 'Rules and Ideology and Coalition Formation in the European Parliament: Past, Present and Future', *European Union Politics*, 1, 3, 340–62.

Kreppel, A. (2000b) 'Procedure and Influence: An Empirical Analysis of EP Influence under the Codecision and Cooperation Procedures', paper presented to the Annual Meeting of the American Political Studies Association, Washington, DC.

Kreppel, A. (2002) *The European Parliament and the Supranational Party System: A Study in Institutional Development*, Cambridge, Cambridge University Press.

Kreppel, A. (2005) 'Understanding the European Parliament from a Federalist Perspective: The Legislatures of the USA and EU Compared', paper presented at European Union Studies Association Conference, 31 March–2 April, Austin, TX.

Kreppel, A. and Tsebelis, G. (1999) 'Coalition Formation in the European Parliament', *Comparative Political Studies*, 32, 8, 933–66.

Krook, M. L. (2005) 'Europeanizing Efforts to Promote Woman in Politics? Elections to the European Parliament, 1999–2004', paper presented at the Fourth European Consortium for Political Research Young Europeanization Meeting, Brussels, 28 January.

Krouwel, A. (2004) 'All Politics is National, but Policy is Supra-national: A Decisive Discrepancy', *Europäische Politik*, 03, Friedrich Ebert Stiftung.

Ladrech, R. (1996) 'Political Parties in the European Parliament', in J. Gaffney (ed.), *Political Parties in the European Union*, London, Routledge.

Laffan, B. (1992) *Integration and Co-operation in Europe*, London, Routledge.

Laffan, B. (1997) 'The IGC and Institutional Reform of the Union', in G. Edwards and A. Pijpers (eds), *The Politics of European Treaty Reform: The 1996 Intergovernmental Conference and Beyond*, London, Pinter.

Laffan, B. and Lindner, J. (2005) 'The Budget', in H. Wallace, W. Wallace and M. A. Pollack (eds), *Policy-Making in the European Union*, 5th edn, Oxford, Oxford University Press.

Lamy, P. and Pisani-Ferry, J. (2002) *L'Europe de nos volontés*, Les Notes de la Fondation Jean-Jaurès, 27, January, Paris, Fondation Jean-Jaurès.

Langdal, F. (2005) 'Sweden', in J. Lodge (ed.), *The 2004 Elections to the European Parliament*, London, Palgrave Macmillan.

Laursen, F. (1997) 'The Lessons of Maastricht', in G. Edwards and A. Pijpers (eds), *The Politics of European Treaty Reform: The 1996 Intergovernmental Conference and Beyond*, London, Pinter.

Lazar, M. (2002) 'The Communist and Extreme Left Galaxy', in P. Perrineau, G. Grunberg and C. Ysmal (eds), *The European Elections, 1999*, New York, Palgrave Macmillan.

Lehmann, W. and Schunz, S. (2005) 'Anticipating the European Constitution: Parliamentarization or Re-nationalization?', paper presented at European Union Studies Association Conference, 31 March-2 April, Austin, Texas.

Lightfoot, S. (2006) 'The Consolidation of Europarties? The "Party Regulation" and the Development of Political Parties in the European Union', *Representation*, 42, 4, 303–12.

Lijphart, A. (1984) *Democracies: Patterns of Majoritarian and Consensus Government in Twenty-one Countries*, New Haven, CT, Yale University Press.

Lijphart, A. (1991) 'Introduction', in A. Lijphart (ed.), *Parliamentary versus Presidential Government*, Oxford, Oxford University Press.

Lodge, J. (1982) 'The European Parliament After Direct Elections: Talking-Shop or Putative Legislature', *Journal of European Integration*, 5, 3, 259–84.

Lodge, J. (1983) 'The European Parliament', in J. Lodge (ed.), *Institutions and Policies of the EC*, London, Pinter.

Lodge, J. (1984) 'European Union and the First Elected European Parliament: The Spinelli Initiative', *Journal of Common Market Studies*, 22, 4, 377–402.

Lodge, J. (1989) 'The European Parliament from "Assembly" to Co-

Legislature: Changing the Institutional Dynamics', in J. Lodge (ed.), *The European Community and the Challenge of the Future*, London, Pinter.

Lodge, J. (1993) 'EC Policymaking: Institutional Dynamics', in J. Lodge (ed.), *The European Community and the Challenge of the Future*, 2nd edn, London, Pinter.

Lodge, J. (1994) 'The European Parliament and the Authority-Democracy Crises', *Annals of the American Academy of Political and Social Sciences*, 531, January, 69–83.

Loewenberg, G. and Patterson, S. C. (1979) *Comparing Legislatures*, Boston, MA, Brown.

Lord, C. (1998) *Democracy in the European Union*, Sheffield, UACES/ Sheffield Academic Press.

Lord, C. (2004) 'New Governance and Post-Parliamentarism', *POLIS Working Paper* no. 5, February, Leeds, School of Politics and International Studies.

Lord, C. (2007) 'Parliamentary Representation in a Decentred Polity', in B. Kohler-Koch and B. Rittberger (eds), *Debating the Democratic Legitimacy of the European Union*, Lanham, MD, Rowman & Littlefield.

Lord, C. and Beetham, D. (2001) 'Legitimizing the EU: Is There a "Post-Parliamentary Basis" for Its Legitimation?', *Journal of Common Market Studies*, 39, 3, 443–62.

Lovenduski, J. (2005) *Feminizing Politics*, Cambridge, Polity.

Magnette, P. (2001) 'Appointing and Censuring the European Commission: The Adaptation of Parliamentary Institutions to the Community Context', *European Law Journal*, 7, 3, 292–310.

Magnette, P. (2005) *What is the European Union? Nature and Prospects*, Basingstoke, Palgrave Macmillan.

Magnette, P. (2006) 'Lobbying in the European Policy Arena', available at www.europarl.europa.eu/eplive/expert/shotlist_page/20060523SHL08412/ default_en.htm

Magnette, P. and Nicolaïdis, K. (2004) 'The European Convention: Bargaining in the Shadow of Rhetoric', *West European Politics*, 27, 3, 381–404.

Majone, G. (2002) 'The European Commission: The Limits of Centralization and the Perils of Parliamentarization', *Governance*, 15, 3, 375–92.

Majone, G. (2005) *Dilemmas of European Integration: Ambiguities and Pitfalls of Integration by Stealth*, Oxford, Oxford University Press.

Malmström, C. (2007) *Why the One seat Campaign?*, Stockhom, Folkpartiet, available at www.folkpartiet.se/FPTemplates/PersonalContent_44296.aspx

Mamadouh, V. and Raunio, T. (2000) 'Committees in the European Parliament: The Distribution of Reports and Rapporteurships', paper presented at the Fourth Workshop of Parliamentary Scholars and Parliamentarians, Wroxton College, 5–6 August.

Mamadouh, V. and Raunio, T. (2003) 'The Committee System: Powers, Appointments and Report Allocation', *Journal of Common Market Studies*, 41, 2, 333–51.

Manin, B. (1997) *The Principles of Representative Government*, Cambridge, Cambridge University Press.

Manow, P. (2005) 'National Vote Intention and European Voting Behaviour, 1979–2004: Second Order Election Effects, Election Timing, Government

Approval and the Europeanization of European Elections', *MpIFfG Discussion Paper* 05/11, Cologne, Max Planck Institute for the Study of Societies.

Marks, G., Hooghe, L. and Blank, K. (1996) 'European Integration in the 1980s: State Centric v. Multi-level Governance', *Journal of Common Market Studies*, 34, 3, 341–78.

Marsh, M. (1998) 'Testing the Second-Order Election Model after Four European Elections', *British Journal of Political Science*, 28, 591–607.

Marsh, M. (2005) 'The Results of the 2004 European Parliament Elections and the Second-Order Model', in Niedermayer, O. and Schmitt, H. (eds), *Europawahl 2004*, Wiesbaden, Verlag für Sozialwissenschaften.

Marsh, M. (2006) 'Vote Switching in European Parliament Elections: Evidence from June 2004', paper presented at European Election Studies Group, Lisbon, 12–13 May.

Marsh, M. and Wessels, B. (1997) 'Territorial Representation', *European Journal of Political Research*, 32, 2, 185–210.

Martin, D. (1990) *European Union and the Democratic Deficit,* West Lothian, John Wheatley Centre.

Mather, J. (2001) 'The European Parliament – a Model of Representative Democracy?', *West European Politics*, 24, 1, 181–201.

Mather, J. D. (2005) 'European Parliamentary Electoral Law and the 2004 Elections: Towards Uniformity or Commonality?, in J. Lodge (ed.), *The 2004 Elections to the European Parliament*, London, Palgrave Macmillan.

Mather, J. (2007) *Legitimating the European Union*, Basingstoke, Palgrave Macmillan.

Maurer, A. (1999a) *What Next for the European Parliament?,* Federal Trust Series, Future of European Parliamentary Democracy 2, London, Federal Trust.

Maurer, A. (1999b) 'Co-Governing After Maastricht: The European Parliament's Institutional Performance 1994–99', Working Paper Political Series, POLL 104/rev.EN, Directorate-General for Research, Luxembourg, European Parliament.

Maurer, A. (2007) 'The European Parliament Between Policy-Making and Control', in B. Kohler-Koch and B. Rittberger (eds), *Debating the Democratic Legitimacy of the European Union*, Lanham, MD, Rowman & Littlefield.

Mazey, S. and Richardson, J. (2006) 'Interest Groups and EU Policy-Making: Organisational Logic and Venue Shopping', in J. Richardson (ed.), *European Union: Power and Policy-Making*, 3rd edn, London, Routledge.

McAllister, R. (1997) *From EC to EU*, London, Routledge.

McCarthy, A. (2003), 'Parliament Backs Tighter Limits on Patents to Provide Protection, Innovation and Competition for EU Industry', press release, available at eupat.ffii.org/log/03/plen0924/amccarthy-pr030924.html

McCormick, J. (2005) *Understanding the European Union: A Concise Introduction*, 3rd edn, Basingstoke, Palgrave Macmillan.

McElroy, G. (2002) 'Committees and Party Cohesion in the European Parliament', *European Parliament Research Group Working Paper* no. 8, available at http://www.lse.ac.uk/Depts/eprg/working-papers.htm

McElroy, G. (2006) 'Committee Representation in the European Parliament', *European Union Politics*, 7, 1, 5–29.

Melakopides, C. (2005) 'Cyprus', in J. Lodge (ed.), *The 2004 Elections to the European Parliament*, London, Palgrave Macmillan.

Mezey, M. (1979) *Comparative Legislatures*, Durham, NC, Duke University Press.

Mill, J. S. [1861] (1910) *Considerations on Representative Government*, London, Dent.

Milward, A. (1984) *The Reconstruction of Western Europe*, London, Methuen.

Monnet, J. (1978) *Memoirs*, New York, Doubleday.

Moravcsik, A. and Nicolaidis, K. (1998) 'Federal Ideas and Constitutional Realities in the Treaty of Amsterdam', in G. Edwards and G. Wiessala (eds), *European Union 1993: Annual Review of Activities*, Oxford, Blackwell.

Muntean, A. M. (2000) 'The European Parliament's Political Legitimacy and the Commission's "Misleading Management": Towards a Parliamentarian European Union?', *European Integration Online Papers*, 4, 5; http://eiop.or.at/texte/2000–005a.htm

Murray, A. (2005) *Three Cheers for EU Democracy*, CER Bulletin, Issue 39, December 2004/January 2005, London, Centre For European Reform, available at www.cer.org.uk/articles/39_murray.html

Neuhold, C. (2001) 'The "Legislative Backbone" Keeping the Institution Upright? The Role of European Parliament Committees in the EU Policy-Making Process', *European Integration Online Papers*, 5, 10; http://eiop.or.at/eiop/texte/2001–10a.htm

Neuhold, C. (2001a) '"Much Ado About Nothing?" Comitology as a Feature of EU Policy Implementation and Its Effects on the Democratic Arena', *Political Science Series*, 78, Vienna, Institute for Advanced Studies.

Neunreither, K. (1994) 'The Democratic Deficit of the European Union: Towards Closer Cooperation Between the European Parliament and the National Parliaments', *Government and Opposition*, 29, 299–314.

Neunreither, K. (2001) 'The European Union in Nice: A Minimalist Approach to a Historic Change', *Government and Opposition*, 36, 2, 184–208.

Nickel, D. (1998) 'The Amsterdam Treaty – a Shift in the Balance Between the Institutions!?', *Jean Monnet Papers*, 14, Cambridge, MA, Harvard Law School, http://www.law.harvard.edu/Programs/JeanMonnet/papers/98/9814.html

Nickel, D. (1999) 'Beyond Treaty Revision: Shifts in the Institutional Balance?', paper presented to the ECSA Sixth Biennial Conference, June, Pittsburgh, PA.

Nicolaïdis, K. (2003) 'Our European Demoi-cracy: Thoughts on the Constitutional Debate', in K. Nicolaïdis and S. Weatherill (eds), *Whose Europe? National Models and the Constitution of the European Union*, Oxford, European Studies at Oxford.

Nicolaïdis, K. (2004) 'We, the Peoples of Europe . . .', *Foreign Affairs*, 83, 6, 97–110.

Nicoll, W. (1994) 'The European Parliament's Post-Maastricht Rules of Procedure', *Journal of Common Market Studies*, 32, 3, 403–10.

Nicoll, W. and Salmon, T. C. (2001) *Understanding the European Union*, London, Longman.

Noël, E. (1989) 'The Single European Act', *Government and Opposition*, 24, 1, 1–14.

Norris, P. (1999) 'Recruitment into the European Parliament', in R. S. Katz and B. Wessels (eds), *The European Parliament, the National Parliaments, and European Integration*, Oxford, Oxford University Press.

Norris, P and Franklin, M. (1997) 'Social Representation', *European Journal of Political Research*, 32, 2, 185–210.

Norris, P and Lovenduski, J. (1995) *Political Representation: Gender, Race and Class in the British Parliament*, Cambridge, Cambridge University Press.

Norton, P. (1990) *Legislatures*, Oxford, Oxford University Press.

Norton, P and Wood, D. M. (1993) *Back From Westminster: British Members of Parliament and Their Constituents*, Lexington, University Press of Kentucky.

Nugent, N. (2006) *The Government and Politics of the European Union*, 6th edn, Basingstoke, Palgrave Macmillan.

Offe, C. and Preuss, U. K. (2006) 'The Problem of Legitimacy in the European Polity. Is Democratization the Answer?', *Constitutionalism Webpapers*, ConWEB No6/2006, available at www.qub.ac.uk/schools/SchoolofPolitics InternationalStudiesandPhilosophy/FileStore/ConWEBFiles/Filetoupload,522 16,en.pdf

Packenham, R. A. (1970) 'Legislatures and Political Development', in A. Kornberg and L. Musloff (eds), *Legislatures in Developmental Perspective*, Durham, NC, Duke University Press.

PE 155.236 (1992) *Notice to Members*, Committee on the Environment, Public Health and Consumer Protection, Brussels, European Parliament.

PE 167.189 (1997) *Institutional Aspects of Budgetary Control, Briefing Budgetary Affairs No. 2*, Directorate-General for Research, Luxembourg, European Parliament.

PE 221.698 (1997) *Report on Relations between European Parliament and the National Parliaments*, Committee on Institutional affairs, Brussels, European Parliament.

PE 226.077 (1998) *Report on Postponement of the Discharge to be Given to the Commission in Respect of the Implementation of the General Budget of the European Community for the 1996 Financial Year*, Committee on Budgetary Control, Brussels, European Parliament.

PE 229.204 (1999) *Report on the Amendments to be Made to the Rules of Procedure*, Committee on the Rules of Procedure, the Verification of Credentials and Immunities, Brussels, European Parliament.

PE 229.285 (1998) *Report on Giving Discharge to the Commission in Respect of the Implementation of the General Budget of the European Communities for the 1996 Financial Year*, Committee on Budgetary Control, Rapporteur James Elles, Brussels, European Parliament.

PE 230.998 (1999) *Activity Report of the Delegations to the Conciliation Committee, 1 November 1993 to 30 April 1999. From Entry into Force of the Treaty of Maastricht to Entry into Force of the Treaty of Amsterdam. Codecision Procedure Under Article 189b of the Treaty of Maastricht*, Delegations to the Conciliation Committee, Brussels, European Parliament.

PE 231.873 (1999) *Report on the Preparation for the Reform of the Treaties and the Next Intergovernmental Conference*, Committee on Constitutional Affairs, Brussels, European Parliament.

PE 232.403 (2000) *Report on the Agreement Between the European*

Parliament and the Commission on Procedures for Implementing the New Council Decision of 28 June 1999 – 'commitology' (1999/468/EC) (ACI 1999/2202), Committee on Constitutional Affairs, Brussels, European Parliament.

PE 232.649 (2000) *Report on the Convening of the Intergovernmental Conference*, Committee on Constitutional Affairs, Brussels, European Parliament.

PE 232.758 (2000) *Report on the European Parliament's Proposals for the Intergovernmental Conference*, Committee on Constitutional Affairs, Rapporteurs Giorgos Dimitrakopoulos and Jo Leinen, Brussels, European Parliament.

PE 232.762 (2000) *Report on Amendments to Parliament's Rules of Procedure to Ensure Balanced Rights Between Individual Members and Groups*, Committee on Constitutional Affairs, Rapporteur Richard Corbett, Brussels, European Parliament.

PE 259.385/BUR (1997) *Reply to Question 39/97 by Richard Corbett, Pursuant to Rule 28(2) of the Rules of Procedure, to the President: Rate of Acceptance of EP Amendments in Codecision Procedures*, Brussels, European Parliament.

PE 287.644 (2004) *Activity Report, 1 May to 30 April 2004*, Delegations to the Conciliation Committee, Brussels, European Parliament

PE 294.737 (2001) *Draft Treaty of Nice (Initial Analysis)*, Directorate-General for Committees and Delegations, Committee on Constitutional Affairs, Brussels, European Parliament.

PE 294.755 (2001) *Report on the Treaty of Nice and the Future of the European Union*, Committee on Constitutional Affairs, Rapporteurs Iñigo Méndez de Vigo and António José Seguro, Brussels, European Parliament.

PE 294.777 (2001) *Report on Reform of the Council*, Committee on Constitutional Affairs, Rapporteur Jacques F. Poos, Brussels, European Parliament.

PE 303.546 (2001) *Report on the Treaty of Nice and the Future of the European Union*, Committee on Constitutional Affairs, Brussels, European Parliament.

PE 304.283 (2002) *Report on the General Revision of the Rules of Procedure*, Committee on Constitutional Affairs, Rapporteur Richard Corbett, Brussels, European Parliament.

PE 304.289 (2001) *Report on the Commission White Paper on European Governance*, Committee on Constitutional Affairs, Rapporteur Sylvia-Yvonne Kaufmann, Brussels, European Parliament.

PE 304.302 (2002) *Report on Relations between the European Parliament and the National Parliaments in European Integration*, Committee on Constitutional Affairs, Rapporteur Giorgio Napolitano, Brussels, European Parliament.

PE 304.309 (2002) *Report on the European Commission's Legislative and Work Programme (Amendment of Rule 57 of Parliament's Rules of Procedure) (2001/2110(REG)*, Committee on Constitutional Affairs, Rapporteur Cecilia Malmström, Brussels, European Parliament.

PE 313.380 (2002) *Recommendation on the Draft Council Decision Amending the Act Concerning the Election of Representatives of the*

European Parliament by Direct Universal Suffrage, Annexed to Council Decision 76/787/ECSC, EEC, Euratom of 20 September 1976, Committee on Constitutional Affairs, Rapporteur José Maria Gil-Robles Gil-Delgado, Brussels, European Parliament.

PE 323.576 (2003) *Report on the Proposal for a European Parliament and Council Regulation on the Statute and Financing of European Political Parties*, Rapporteur Jo Leinen, Brussels, European Parliament.

PE 333.044 (2003) *Recommendation on the Appointment of Mr Jean-Claude Trichet as President of the European Central Bank*, Committee on Economic and Monetary Affairs, Rapporteur Christa Randzio-Plath, Brussels, European Parliament.

PE 338.978/BUR (2004) *Code of Conduct on Multilingulaism Adopted by the Bureau on 19 April 2004*, Brussels, European Parliament.

PE 347.119 (2004) *Report on the Treaty Establishing a Constitution for Europe*, Committee on Constitutional Affairs, Rapporteurs Richard Corbett and Íñigo Méndez de Vigo, Brussels, European Parliament.

PE 349.302/BUR/12 (2004) *Letter From Jean-Louis Bourlanges, Chairman of the Committee on Civil Liberties, Justice and Home Affairs, to Josep Borrell Fontelles*, President of the European Parliament, October, Brussels, European Parliament.

PE 349.846 (2005) *Report on the Proposal for a Regulation of the European Parliament and of the Council on Compensation in Cases of Non-compliance with Contractual Quality Requirements for Rail Freight Services* (COM(2004)0144 – C6–0004/2004 – 2004/0050(COD)), Committee on Transport and Tourism, Rapporteur Roberts Zile, Brussels, European Parliament.

PE 353.270 (2005) *Report on the Policy Challenges and Budgetary Means of the Enlarged Union 2007–2013*, Temporary Committee on Policy Challenges and Budgetary Means of the Enlarged Union 2007–2013, Rapporteur Reimer Böge, Brussels, European Parliament.

PE 355.359 (2005) *Report on Guidelines for the Approval of the European Commission, Committee on Constitutional Affairs*, Rapporteur Andrew Duff, Brussels, European Parliament.

PE 355.690 (2005) *Draft Report on the Revision of the Framework Agreement on the Relations Between the European Parliament and the European Commission*, Committee on Constitutional Affairs, Rapporteur Jo Leinen, Brussels, European Parliament.

PE 357.779 (2005) *Report on the Proposal for a Directive of the European Parliament and of the Council Introducing Humane Trapping Standards for Certain Animal Species*, Committee on the Environment, Public Health and Food Safety, Rapporteur Karin Scheele, Brussels, European Parliament.

PE 364.708 (2005) *Report on the Period of Reflection: The Structure, Subjects and Context or an Assessment of the Debate on the European Union*, Committee on Constitutional Affairs, Rapporteurs Johannes Voggenhuber and Andrew Duff, Brussels, European Parliament.

PE 366.051 (2005) *Motion for a Resolution on Winding up the Debate on the Question for Oral Answer to the Council on the Draft Interinstitutional Agreement Presented by the Commission on the Operating Framework for the European Regulatory Agencies*, Brussels, European Parliament.

PE 367.786 (2006) *Report on European Political Parties*, Committee on

Constitutional Affairs, Rapporteur Jo Leinen, Brussels, European Parliament.

PE 369.878 (2006) *Report on the European Court of Auditors' Special Report No 5/2005: Interpretation Expenditure Incurred by the Parliament, the Commission and the Council 2006/2001(INI)*, Committee on Budgetary Control, Rapporteur Alexander Stubb, Brussels, European Parliament.

PE 372.062 (2006) *Report on the Interinstitutional Agreement on Budgetary Discipline and Sound Financial Management*, Committee on Budgets, Rapporteur, Reimer Böge, Brussels, European Parliament.

PE 373.818 (2006) *Written Declaration on Holding Meetings of the European Council in Strasbourg*, by Richard Corbett, Alexander Alvaro, Christopher Heaton-Harris, Cecilia Malmström and Cem Özdemir, Brussels, European Parliament.

PE 378.567 (2006) *Draft Working Document on the on the Role of Budgetary Control Committees in National Parliaments with Particular Regard to the Control of the Community Budget. 'Redesigning Accountability Structures and Control Activities in the European Union'*, Committee on Budgetary Control, Rapporteur Jan Mulder, Brussels, European Parliament.

PE 380.576 (2006) *Report on Amendment of Rule 39 of Parliament's Rules of Procedure, Transitional Rules on Languages*, Committee on Constitutional Affairs, Rapporteur Ingo Friedrich, Brussels, European Parliament.

PE 384.334 (2007) *Draft Report on the Proposal for a Regulation of the European Parliament and of the Council on Roaming on Public Mobile Networks within the Community and Amending Directive 2002/21/EC on a Common Regulatory Framework for Electronic Communications Networks and Services (COM(2006)0382 – C6–0244/2006 – 2006/0133(COD))*, Committee on Industry, Research and Energy, Rapporteur Paul Rübig, Brussels, European Parliament.

PE 386.573 (2007) *Report on the Crisis of the Equitable Life Assurance Society (2006/2199(INI))*, Committee of Inquiry into the Crisis of the Equitable Life Assurance Society, Rapporteur Diana Wallis, Brussels, European Parliament.

PE 392.600/CPT/GT (2007) *The Plenary and the Calendar of Activities*, First Interim Report of the Working Party on Parliamentary Reform, Brussels, European Parliament.

PE 393.029 (2007) *Texts Adopted at the Sitting of 11 July 2007*, Brussels, European Parliament.

PE 396.489 (2007) *Report on the Nomination of David Bostock as a Member of the Court of Auditors*, Committee on Budgetary Control, Rapporteur Inés Ayala Sender, Brussels, European Parliament.

PE 398.310 (2007) *Working Document on the on the Role of Budgetary Control Committees in National Parliaments with Particular Regard to the Control of the Community Budget. Meeting with Budgetary Control Committees in National Parliaments on 18–19 December 2007*, Committee on Budgetary Control, Rapporteur Herbert Bösch, Brussels, European Parliament.

Pedersen, K. (2005) 'Denmark', in J. Lodge (ed.), *The 2004 Elections to the European Parliament*, London, Palgrave Macmillan.

Peterson, J. (1995) 'Decision-making in the European Union: Towards a Framework for Analysis', *Journal of European Public Policy*, 2, 1, 69–93.

Peterson, J. (2004) 'Policy Networks', in A. Wiener and T. Diez (eds), *European Integration Theory*, Oxford, Oxford University Press.

Peterson, J. and Bomberg, E. (1999) *Decision-Making in the European Union*, London, Macmillan.

Peterson, J. and Bomberg, E. (2000) 'The European Union after the 1990s: Explaining Continuity and Change', in M. Green Cowles and M. Smith, *The State of the European Union, vol. 5: Risks, Reform, Resistance, and Revival*, Oxford, Oxford University Press.

Peterson, J. and Shackleton, M. (2006) 'The EU's Institutions: An Overview', in J. Peterson and M. Shackleton (eds.), *The Institutions of the European Union*, 2nd edn, Oxford, Oxford University Press.

Pitkin, H. (1967) *The Concept of Representation*, Berkeley, University of California Press.

Pollack, M. A. (2005) 'Theorizing EU Policy-Making', in H. Wallace, W. Wallace, and M. A. Pollack (eds), *Policy-Making in the European Union*, 5th edn, Oxford, Oxford University Press.

Pöttering, H-G. (2007) *Address by the President of the European Parliament on the 50th Anniversary of the Signature of the Treaties of Rome*, available at www.eu2007.de/en/News/Speeches_Interviews/March/0325Poettering.html

Pridham, G. and Pridham, P. (1981) *Transnational Party Co-operation and European Integration: The Process towards Direct Elections*, London, Allen & Unwin.

Pryce, R. (1994) 'The Treaty Negotiations', in A. Duff, J. Pinder and R. Pryce (eds), *Maastricht and Beyond*, London, Routledge.

Pryce, R. and Wessels, W. (1987) 'The Search for An Ever Closer Union: A Framework for Analysis', in R. Pryce (ed.), *The Dynamics of European Union*, London, Croom Helm.

PSE (2002) 'A Successful Convention on the Future of Europe: Our Essentials', Brussels, Parliamentary Group of the Party of European Socialists.

Rasmussen, A. and Shackleton, M. (2005) 'The Scope for Action of European Parliament Negotiators in the Legislative Process: Lessons of the Past and for the Future', paper prepared for the Ninth Biennial International Conference of the European Union Studies Association, Austin, TX, March 2005.

Raunio, T. (1996a) *Party Group Behaviour in the European Parliament*, Tampere, University of Tampere.

Raunio, T. (1996b) 'Parliamentary Questions in the European Parliament: Representation, Information and Control', *Journal of Legislative Studies*, 2, 4, 356–82.

Raunio, T. (1997) *The European Perspective: Transnational Party Groups in the 1989–1994 European Parliament*, Aldershot, Ashgate.

Raunio, T. (1999) 'The Challenge of Diversity: Party Cohesion in the European Parliament', in S. Bowler, D. M. Farrell, and R. S. Katz (eds), *Party Discipline and Parliamentary Government*, Columbus, OH, State University Press.

Raunio, T. (2000) 'Losing Independence or Finally Gaining Recognition?', *Party Politics*, 6, 2, 211–23.

Raunio, T. (2005a) 'Finland', in J. Lodge (ed.), *The 2004 Elections to the European Parliament*, London, Palgrave Macmillan.

Raunio, T. (2005b) 'Much Ado About Nothing? National Legislatures in the EU Constitution', *European Integration Online Papers*, 9, 9, available at eiop.or.at/eiop/pdf/2005–009.pdf

Raunio, T. (2006) 'Political Interests: The European Parliament's Party Groups', in J. Peterson and M. Shackleton (eds), *The Institutions of the European Union*, 2nd edn, Oxford, Oxford University Press.

Reding V. (2007) 'Why this Website?', Brussels, Commission of the European Communities, available at ec.europa.eu/information_society/activities/roaming/why/index_en.htm

Reif, K. (1985) 'Ten Second-Order Elections', in K. Reif (ed.), *Ten European Elections: Campaigns and Results of the 1979/81 First Direct Elections to the European Parliament*, Aldershot, Gower.

Reif, K. and Schmitt, H. (1980) 'Nine Second-Order Elections: A Conceptual Framework for the Analysis of European Election Results', *European Journal of Political Research*, 8, 3–44.

Richardson, J. (2006) 'Policy-making in the EU: Interests, Ideas and Garbage Cans of Primeval Soup', in J. Richardson (ed.), *European Union: Power and Policy-Making*, 3rd edn, London, Routledge.

Ringe, N. (2005) 'Policy Preference Formation in Legislative Politics: Structures, Actors and Focal Points', *American Journal of Political Science*, 49, 4, 731–45.

Rittberger, B. (2000) 'Impatient Legislators and New Issue-Dimensions: A Critique of the Garrett-Tsebelis "Standard Version" of Legislative Politics', *Journal of European Public Policy*, 7, 4, 554–75.

Rittberger, B. (2005) *Building Europe's Parliament. Democratic Representation Beyond the Nation-State*, Oxford, Oxford University Press.

Rømer, H. (1993) Guidelines for the Application of the Rule Changes, Secretariat, Group of the European People's Party, Brussels, Group of the European People's Party.

Rosamond, B. (2000) *Theories of European Integration*, Basingstoke, Palgrave Macmillan.

Rosamond, B. (2007) 'New Theories of European Integration', in M. Cini (ed.), *European Union Politics*, 2nd edn, Oxford, Oxford University Press.

Rose, R. (2004) *Europe Expands, Turnout Falls: The Significance of the 2004 European Parliament Election*, Sweden, International Institute for Democracy and Electoral Assistance,

Schmitt, H. (2005) 'The European Parliament Elections of June 2004: Still Second Order?', *West European Politics*, 28, 3, 650–79.

Schönlau, J. (2006) 'European Party Statute: Filling the Half-Full Glass?', *European View*, 3, 143–52.

Schumpeter, J. A. [1943] (1976) *Capitalism, Socialism and Democracy*, 5th edn, London, Allen & Unwin.

Schwindt-Bayer, L. A. and Mishler, W. (2005) 'An Integrated Model of Woman's Representation', *Journal of Politics*, 67, 2, 407–28.

Scully, R. (2000a) 'Democracy, Legitimacy, and the European Parliament', in M. Green Cowles and M. Smith (eds), *The State of the European Union, vol. 5: Risks, Reform, Resistance, and Revival*, Oxford, Oxford University Press.

Scully, R. (2000b) 'Conditional Independence: Understanding MEP–National

Party Relations', paper presented to the Annual Meeting of the American Political Science Association, August, Washington, DC.

Scully, R. (2007) 'The European Parliament', in M. Cini (ed.), *European Union Politics*, 2nd edn, Oxford, Oxford University Press.

Scully, R. and Farrell, D. M. (2001) 'Understanding Constituency Representation in the European Parliament', paper presented at the Conference of the European Community Studies Association, Madison, Wisconsin, 31 May–2 June 2001.

Scully, R. and Farrell, D. M. (2003) 'MEPs as Representatives: Individual and Institutional Roles', *Journal of Common Market Studies*, 41, 2, 269–88.

Septembri. P. (2006) 'Is the European Parliament Competitive or Consensual . . ."and Why Bother"?', paper presented to the Federal Trust Workshop, 'The European Parliament and the European Political space', 30 March 2006, London: available at www.fedtrust.co.uk/admin/uploads/FedT_workshop_Settembri.pdf

Shackleton, M. (1998) 'The European Parliament's New Committees of Inquiry: Tiger or Paper Tiger?', *Journal of Common Market Studies*, 36, 1, 115–30.

Shackleton, M. (2000) 'The Politics of Codecision', *Journal of Common Market Studies*, 38, 2, 325–42.

Shackleton, M. (2005) 'Parliamentary Government or Division of Powers: Is the Destination Still Unknown?', in N. Jabko and C. Parsons (eds), *The State of the European Union, vol. 7: With or Against US? European Trends in American Perspective*, Oxford, Oxford University Press.

Shackleton, M. (2006) 'The European Parliament', in J. Peterson and M. Shackleton (eds), *The Institutions of the European Union*, 2nd edn, Oxford, Oxford University Press.

Shackleton, M. and Raunio, T. (2003) 'Codecision Since Amsterdam: A Laboratory for Institutional Change', *Journal of European Public Policy*, 10, 2, 171–187.

Shaw, J. (1999) 'Postnational Constitutionalism in the European Union', *Journal of European Public Policy*, 6, 4, 579–97.

Shephard, M. and Scully, R. (2002) 'The European Parliament: Of Barriers and Removed Citizens', in P. Norton (ed.), *Parliament and Citizens in Western Europe*, London, Frank Cass.

Smismans, S. (2004) 'The Constitutional Labelling of "The Democratic Life of the EU": Representative and Participatory Democracy', in A. Føllesdal and L. Dobson (eds), *Political Theory and the European Constitution*, London, Routledge.

Smismans, S. (2007) 'New Governance – The Solution for Active European Citizenship, or the End of Citizenship', *Columbia Journal of European Law*, 13, 3, 595–622.

Smith, J. (1999) *Europe's Elected Parliament*, Sheffield, UACES/ Sheffield Academic Press.

Smith, J. (2004) *Reinvigorating European Elections: The Implications of Electing the European Commission*, London, Royal Institute of International Affairs.

Spence, D. (1993) 'The Role of the National Civil Service in European Lobbying: The British Case', in S. Mazey and J. Richardson (eds), *Lobbying in the European Community,* Oxford, Oxford University Press.

Spence, D. (2000) 'Plus ça change, plus c'est la même chose? Attempting to Reform the European Commission', *Journal of European Public Policy,* 7, 1, 1–25.

Spierenburg, D. and Poidevin, R. (1994) *The History of the High Authority of the European Coal and Steel Community: Supranationality in Operation,* London, Weidenfeld and Nicolson.

Strøm, K. (1995) 'Parliamentary Government and Legislative Organisation', in H. Döring (ed.), *Parliaments and Majority Rule in Western Europe,* Frankfurt, Campus.

Strøm, K. (2003) 'Parliamentary Democracy and Delegation', in K. Strøm, W. C. Müller, T. Bergman (eds), *Delegation and Accountability in Parliamentary Democracies,* Oxford, Oxford University Press.

Sutherland, E. (2005) Speech prepared for a joint meeting of the Committee on Industry, Research and Energy (ITRE) and the Committee on Internal Market and Consumer Protection (IMCO) of the European Parliament on 16 March 2005, Executive Director, International Telecommunications Users Group available at www.europarl.europa.eu/comparl/imco/public_ hearings/050316_sutherland_speech_en.pdf

Thiem, J. (2006) 'Explaining Roll Call Request in the European Parliament', *Working Papers* 90, Mannheim, Mannheimer Zentrum für Europäische Sozialforschung.

Thomassen, J. and Schmitt, H. (1999) 'Partisan Structures in the European Parliament', in R. S. Katz and B. Wessels (eds), *The European Parliament, the National Parliaments, and European Integration,* Oxford, Oxford University Press.

Thomassen, J. and Schmitt, H. (2004) 'Democracy and Legitimacy in the European Union', *Tidsskrift for Samfunnsforskning,* 45, 1, 375–408.

Tindemans, L. (1976) 'European Union: Report to the European Council', *Bulletin of the European Communities,* supplement 1, no. 1, Bull. EC1–1976, Brussels, European Commission.

Treaty of Amsterdam (1997) Luxembourg, Office for Official Publications of the European Communities.

Treaty of Paris (1952) Luxembourg, Office for Official Publications of the European Communities.

Treaty of Rome (1957) Luxembourg, Office for Official Publications of the European Communities.

Treaty on European Union (1992) Luxembourg, Office for Official Publications of the European Communities.

Tsebelis, G. and Garrett, G. (1996) 'Agenda Setting Power, Power Indices and Decision Making in the European Union', *International Review of Law and Economics,* 16, 3, 345–61.

Tsebelis, G. and Garrett, G. (1997) 'Agenda Setting, Vetoes, and the European Union's Co-decision Procedure', *Journal of Legislative Studies,* 3, 3, 74–92.

Tsebelis, G. and Garrett, G. (2000) 'Legislative Politics in the European Union', *European Union Politics,* 1, 1, 9–36.

Tsebelis, G. and Kalandrakis, A. (1999) 'The European Parliament and Environmental Legislation: The Case of Chemicals', *European Journal of Political Research,* 36, 1, 119–54.

Tsebelis, G. and Money, J. (1997) *Bicameralism,* Cambridge, Cambridge University Press.

Tsebelis, G., Jensen, C. B., Kalandrakis, A. and Kreppel, A. (2001) 'Legislative Procedures in the European Union: An Empirical Analysis', *British Journal of Political Science,* 31, 3, 573–99.

Urwin, D. W. (1991) *The Community of Europe: A History of European Integration Since 1945,* London, Longman.

Van Orden, G. (2006) '"Very well, alone!": Why the UK's Tories Are Leaving the EPP-ED Group', *Europe's World,* Summer 2006, 108–12.

Verzichelli, L. and Edinger, M. (2005) 'A Critical Juncture? The 2004 European Elections and the Making of a Supranational Elite', *Journal of Legislative Studies,* 11, 2, 254–74.

Viola, D. M. (2000) *European Foreign Policy and the European Parliament in the 1990s,* Aldershot, Ashgate.

Vodafone (2006) 'Second Phase Consultation on Proposal for a Regulation of the European Parliament and Council on Mobile Roaming Services in the Single Market', Comments of Vodafone, 12 May 2006 available at ec.europa.eu/information_society/activities/roaming/docs/phase2/vodafone_group_services_limited.pdf

Wahlke, J. C., Eulau, H., Buchanan, W. and Ferguson, L. C. (1962) *The Legislative System,* New York, Wiley.

Wallace, H. (1993) 'European Governance in Turbulent Times', *Journal of Common Market Studies,* 31, 3, 293–304.

Wallace, H. (2005) 'An Institutional Anatomy and Five Policy Modes', in H. Wallace, W. Wallace and M. A. Pollack (eds), *Policy-Making in the European Union,* 5th edn, Oxford, Oxford University Press.

Wallace, W. (1996) 'Government Without Statehood: The Unstable Equilibrium', in H. Wallace and W. Wallace (eds), *Policy-Making in the European Union,* 3rd edn, Oxford, Oxford University Press.

Wallace, W. and Smith, J. (1995) 'Democracy or Technocracy? European Integration and the Problem of Popular Consent', in J. Hayward (ed.), *The Crisis of Representation in Europe,* London, Frank Cass.

Weiler, J. H. H. (1997) 'Legitimacy and Democracy of Union Governance', in G. Edwards and A. Pijpers (eds), *The Politics of European Treaty Reform: The 1996 Intergovernmental Conference and Beyond,* London, Pinter.

Weiler, J. H. H. (1999) *The Constitution of Europe,* Cambridge, Cambridge University Press.

Weiner. A. and Diez, T. (2004) *European Integration Theory,* Oxford, Oxford University Press.

Wessels, B. (1999) 'European Parliament and Interest Groups', in R. S. Katz and B. Wessels (eds), *The European Parliament, the National Parliaments, and European Integration,* Oxford, Oxford University Press.

Wessels, W. (1991) 'The Institutional Strategies Toward Political Union', in L. Hurwitz and C. Lequesne (eds), *The State of the European Community: Policies, Institutions and Debates in the Transition Years,* Boulder, CO, Lynne Rienner/Longman.

Wessels, W. (1996a) 'The Modern West European State and the European Union: Democratic Erosion or a New Kind of Polity', in S. S. Andersen and K. A. Eliassen (eds), *The European Union: How Democratic Is It?,* London, Sage.

Wessels, W. (1996b) 'Institutions of the EU System: Models of Explanation', in D. Rometsch and W. Wessels (eds), *The European Union and Member States,* Manchester, Manchester University Press.

Wessels, W. (1997) 'An Ever Closer Fusion? A Dynamic Macropolitical View on Integration Processes', *Journal of Common Market Studies,* 35, 2, 267–99.

Wessels, W. (2001) 'Nice Results: The Millennium IGC and the EU's Evolution', *Journal of Common Market Studies,* 39, 2, 197–220.

Wessels, W. and Diedrichs, U. (1997) 'A New Kind of Legitimacy for a New Kind of Parliament – the Evolution of the European Parliament', *European Integration Online Papers,* 1, 6; http://eiop.or.at/eiop/texte/1997–006a.htm

Wessels, W. and Diedrichs, U. (1999) 'The European Parliament and EU Legitimacy', in T. Banchoff and M. P. Smith (eds), *Legitimacy and the European Union: The Contested Polity,* London, Routledge.

Wessels, W. and Rometsch, D. (1996) 'Conclusion: European Union and National Institutions', in D. Rometsch and W. Wessels (eds), *The European Union and Member States,* Manchester, Manchester University Press.

Westlake, M. (1994a) *A Modern Guide to the European Parliament,* London, Pinter.

Westlake, M. (1994b) 'The Commission and Parliament', in G. Edwards and D. Spence (eds), *The European Commission,* London, Cartermill.

Westlake, M. (1995) 'The European Parliament, the National Parliaments and the 1996 Intergovernmental Conference', *Political Quarterly,* 66, 1, 59–73.

Westlake, M. (1998) 'The European Union's "Blind Watchmakers": The Process of Constitutional Change', in M. Westlake (ed.), *The European Union Beyond Amsterdam: New Concepts of European Integration,* London, Routledge.

Westlake, M. (2007) 'A Paradoxical Parliament?', *European Political Science,* 6, 4, 341–51.

Wurzel, R. (1999) 'The Role of the European Parliament: Interview with Ken Collins MEP', *Journal of Legislative Studies,* 5, 2, 1–23.

Yataganas, X. A. (2001) 'The Treaty of Nice: The Sharing of Power and the Institutional Balance in the European Union – a Continental Perspective', *European Law Journal,* 7, 3, 242–91.

Index

Key: **bold** = extended discussion; b = box; f = figure; n = note; t = table.

abortion 144, 175
Abromeit, H. 19
accession treaties
   ratification 45
   safeguard clauses 222
accidents
   traffic (settlement of claims) 196
   workplace 222
accountability 9, 44, 81, 84, 87, 183, 189,
   207–8, 211, 215, 235, 240, 267, 273, 283,
   286, 289, 292, 294
*Activity Reports of Delegations to Conciliation
   Committee* 255, 309, 320, 321
age 92, 112
Agence Europe 134, 155, 252, 257
'agencification' 298
agora 179
Agreement Index (Hix *et al.*, 2007) **138–9**
agriculture 61, 65, 92, 189, 193, 199, 226
AKEL (Cyprus) 131
Albertini, G. 94
Alcatel 246–7
Alleanza Nazionale (Italy) 122, 130
Alliance of Independent Democrats in Europe
   119
Alliance for Lobbying Transparency and Ethics
   Regulation (Alter-EU) 106
Alliance of Liberal and Democrats for Europe
   (ALDE) 94, 122, 141–2, 162, 169t,
   173–5, 181, 208–9, 211, 223, 225, 250,
   259, 262–3, 266, 279
   composition (2008) 125t, **128–9**
   ideological diversity 139
'allocation responsiveness' (Eulau and Karps)
   100
Alvaro, A. 266
Amato, G. 122
'amounts deemed necessary' 49
Amsterdam Treaty (1997): articles
   Article 2 51
   Article 34 193
   Article 189 52
   Article 190 52
   Article 214 (appointment of Commissioners)
      268
   Article 219 ('presidentialization' of
      Commission) 267–8
   Declaration 32 (allocation of tasks within
      Commission) 268

protocol (EP plenary sessions) 185
Protocol on Institutions 51
Protocol 20 (role of national parliaments)
   275, 279–80
Amsterdam Treaty (1997): general **51–3**
   adoption of an act at first reading in EP
      232
   'early agreements' 233–5
   implementation (1999) 16
   'leftovers' 53
   'normal legislative procedure' 189
   provisions relating to EP **52–3**
Andersen, S. S. 22, 298
Andersson, J. 169t
animal experimentation 197
Annual Policy Strategy (European Commission,
   2001–) 269, 271
anti-semitism 133
appointments **212–17**
Arter, D. 12
artificial sweeteners 238, 239
Assembleia da Republica (Portugal):
   Committee on Constitutional Affairs
   283
assent (legislative procedure) 49, 57, 168,
   170t, **194–5**
Athens 279
Attina, F. 136
attitudinal explanations **78–9**
auditing 117–18, 152, 201–2, 212, **213–14**,
   283
Auel, K. 226
Austria 70, 71t, 76, 94, 96t, 99t, 121, 125t,
   133, 152, 169t, 253, 262
'authorization' concept 10, 16, 273
Auto Oil Package 255
Ayala Sender, I. 214
Aznar, J. M. 289

Bach, S. 159, 160–1
Bachelot, R. 93
backbenchers 219
Balfe, R. 162
ballot structure 71t
Bangladesh 222
Bardi, L. 119
Barnier, M. 288–9, 291
Barón Crespo, E. 160, 174–5, 268–9
Barroso, J. M. D. 8, 136, 161, 205, 252

Barroso Commission (2004–) 129, 140, 196, 210–11, 261
  appointment **206–9**
  'partnership' with EP 270
  strategic objectives 270, 304
Barrot, J. 250–1
BASF 244
Basque language 158
Bayrou, F. 128
Bayrouistes 129
Beach, D. 58
Beetham, D. 22, 80, 87, 294, 295
Belgium 58, 69, 70, 71t, 79, 93, 96t, 98, 99t, 125t, 206, 250
Bellamy, R. 293
Benedetto, G. 178
Berès, P. 169t, 174, 176
Bergman, T. 86
best practice 280, 295
BEUC (consumers' organization) 263, 301
Beukers, T. 208, 209, 211
bibliography xi, **300–329**
bicameralism **289–92**
  types 290
biotechnology 243, 245, 255
bivariate analysis 78
Blair, A. C. L. ('Tony') 135, 278
Blomgren, M. 301
Blondel, J. 13, 17, 188, 204, 221
Bogdanor, V. 286
Böge, R. 169t, 180, 200–201
Bolkestein, F. 245, 246
Bomberg, E. 21–2, 130
Bonde, J.-P. 122, 132, 152, 160
Bonino, E. 93, 120
border controls 99
Borrás, S. 296
Borrell, J. 128, 152, 174–5, 179, 222, 252
Bösch, H. 169t
Bourlanges, J.-L. 126, 174
Bowis, J. xii
Bowler, S. 101, 172
Brazil 11
'British effect' (Farrell and Scully) 101
Brok, E. 53, 54, 62, 173–4
Brussels 2, 52, 102, 106–7, 123, 149, 152, 181, 185, 282
  buildings 9, 150, 153, 249
  demonstrations 249
  EP committee meetings 148, 150
  EP micro-plenary sessions 149, 223
  EP plenary sessions 148
  seminar on codecision procedure (2000) 234, 236
BSE crisis (1997) 179, 180, 210
Buchanan, W. 328
budgetary authority 43, 201
budgetary control 36, 37, 284
budgetary discipline
  interinstitutional agreement (2006) 42

budgetary resources (EP temporary committee) 179
Buitenen, P. van 131
Bulgaria xi, 1, 99t, 125t, 127–8, 131–2, 154
Bullen, R. 28, 34
Bunyan, T. 235
Burgess, M. 19
Burma 222
Burns, C. 254, 255
Burns, T. 22, 298
business associations 102, 245
Busquin, P. 93, 206
Buttiglione, R. 207, 208, 211, 288

cabinet 16
Calvinist Christian Union (Netherlands) 132
Cameron, D.
  promise to withdraw Conservative Party from EPP-ED 127
Campaign for EP Reform (2006–) 151–2, 152–3
Campbell, R. 302
Canada 252, 253
Canary Islands 94
cancer research 184
candidate selection 70, 72, 137, 145
car insurance 196
Carrubba, C. J. 143–4, 145
Carrubba, C. J., *et al.* (2006) 143–5, 302
Carter, N. 130
Castiglione, D. 293
Catalan language 158
Catalonia 83
Cavada, J-M. 169t
censure power 33
Central Europe 46, 73, 93
Centre for European Policy Studies (CEPS) 65, 302
Cercas, A. 135
Cervical Cancer Interest Group (CCIG) 184
Chamber of Peoples (proposed, 1953) 278
'Chamber of States' (Schrder) 278, 289
Chan, K. 73
Charter of Fundamental Human Rights 53, 59, 277
Charter of Members' Assistants 163
Chasse, Pêche, Nature, Traditions (France) 132
chef de cabinet 166
chemicals 217, 224–5, 255, 256, 309
Chichester, G. 173, 174
children 224
Chile 165
Christian Democrats 109, 114, 124, 126, 127, 140, 206
Christian values 133
Christiansen, T. 239
Christlich-Demokratische Union (CDU, Germany) 126
'Christian Democrats' (Germany) 173, 180

Chryssochoou, D. N.   289
Church, C.   58
CIA rendition flights   179, 222
Cioroianu, A.   93
'citizen interest associations'   102
citizens' initiatives   61, 297
citizenship/civic duty   79, 82, 270, 278
Civil Democrat Party (ODS/CR) 127
civil servants   103, 166
civil society   12, 55, 72, 179, 293–4, 296
Clarke, F.   xii
class   92, 112
'classic parliamentary forms'   298
Clegg, N.   85–6
Clercq, W. de   175
climate change
  combustion-plant emissions   238–9
  EP's multiple seat   153
  EP temporary committee   179
  exhaust emission standards   255
Clough, R.   302
coalitions   115, **140–1**, 146
codecision (legislative procedure)   48–9, 243
  debates of Council (publication)   291
  renamed 'ordinary legislative procedure'
    (2004)   61
  version one (post-Maastricht Treaty)   189,
    230–2, 233–4, 238
  version two (post-Amsterdam Treaty)
    188–93, 226, **233–7**, **248–54**, **256–67**,
    271, 307
codecision (second version)
  'behavioural norms' and 'cultural values'
    234
  exit-points   190–2
  first reading rejections   **248–54**
  'pushing out frontier'   **248–54**
  rejection by EP   **243–54**
  significant EP legislative influence (roaming
    charges)   **256–67**, 307
Cohesion Fund, 57, 194
Cohn-Bendit, D.   122
Cold War   74, 115
Collins, Sir Ken   xii, 107, 175, 177
Colombo, E.   42, 46
comitology   45, 49, 52, 61, **239–42**, 243, 293,
  298, 311
comitology committees
  advisory (procedure I)   239, 241
  management (procedure IIa, IIb)   239–40,
    241
  regulatory (procedure IIIa, IIIb), 239–40,
    241
commitology
  same as 'comitology'   239
Committee of Permanent Representatives
  (COREPER)   36, 218, 235
Committee of Regions   106
Common Assembly *see* 'ECSC: Common
  Assembly'

Common Foreign and Security Policy (CFSP)
  51, 60, 226, 290
  'CFSP agencies'   216
  'CFSP High Representative'   161
  'foreign policy'   44, 201
'communications strategy'   2
communists   122, 131
competition   193, 257, 258, 260
competitive party government   86, 109
competitiveness   246, 255
Competitiveness Council   266
'competitiveness fostering'   296
complexity management   147
compromise   231, 232
compulsory voting   76 79
computer-implemented inventions (CII)   245,
  247
'conciliation'   **36–7**, 41, 231–5, 289, 321
Conciliation Committee   36–7, 192, 234, 243–4
  activity reports   255, 309, 320, 321
  codecision2 procedure   191f
Conciliations Secretariat   182
confederal consociationalism   20
Confederal Group of European Left/Nordic
  Green Left (EUL/NGL or GUE/NGL,
  1995–)   ix–x, 122, 94, 160, 169t, 173,
  174, 181, 209, 250
  composition   125t, **131**
  Constituent Declaration (1994)   131
  'Group of European United Left (GUE)'   ix,
    114, 130, 175
  opposed Barroso Commission   207
  'Party of European Left'   119
confederalism   20, 31
confederations   19
Conference of European Affairs Committees
  (COSAC, 1989–)   162, 275–6, **279–82**,
  305
  'checks'   280–1
  rules (2003)   280
  secretariat (Brussels, 2004–)   278, 280
confirmation hearings   **205–9**, **212–16**, 258
'conflict resolution'   289
Congress of National Parliaments (Jospin)
  278
consensus   97, 136, 146, 164, 193, 235, 246,
  269, 292
'consent' (previously 'assent')   194
Conservative Party   120, 126, 127, 134, 173
  'invisible and toothless' (van Orden)   127
constituency
  hybrid   98
  problem of definition   98
constituency size   98, 99t, 101
constitutional courts   19, 20
constitutional review principle   51
consultation   168, 170t, **193**, 294–6
consumer protection   168, 255, 258
  see also roaming charges
'control'   17, 221

'controlled full multiculturalism' 155
'conventional parliamentary approaches'
    (Shaw) 298
conventions **276–9**
cooperation (legislative procedure) 52, 168,
    170n, 229–30, 254
  abolished in Lisbon Treaty 238
  EP's power of rejection of European Councils
    common positions **238–9**
  introduced by SEA 238
Copeland, G. W. 11, 12, 14
Copp, A. 30
Corbett, R. xii, 46, 48, 49, 55, 124, 183, 205,
    231, 241, **304–5**
Corporate Europe Observatory 185, 305
Costa, P. 94, 169t
Costs of International Roaming 258
Cot, J.-P. 154, 167
Cotta, M. 11
Council of Europe: Parliamentary Assembly
    (Strasbourg) 149
counterfeit medicines 224
Council of Ministers 19–20, 59, 60, 81, 108,
    189, 274, 278, 289, 292
  'abnormal' legislature 292
  'ambiguous relationship' with EP 61
  appointment of European Commission
    President 285
  author 306–7
  bicameralism **289–92**
  budget (draft) rejected by EP (1979, 1982,
    1984) 199
  budgetary powers 198–201, 226
  co-legislator with EP 271, 294
  codecision1 231–2
  codecision2 191f, 232, **243–54**
  comitology **239–42**
  'common position' 238–9, 243–5, 247, 253
  'compelled' to take EP's views into account
    226
  directive on advertising 225
  early agreements **233–7**
  European Commission tandem 284
  European Parliament tandem 284–5
  as executive body 290
  executive credentials 291
  executive versus legislative roles 291
  'executive's executive' 291
  financial framework 62
  identified as 'legislature' 290
  influence of EP on decisions 40
  informal conciliations and trialogues 48–9
  initiation of legislation 195
  institutional form 290
  majority voting 44, 47
  merger (1965) 35
  modus operandi 'bureaucratic' 290
  parliamentary debates **221–4**
  parliamentary questions **218–21**
  'period of reflection' (2005) 62
  problem of definition 290
  QMV 55, 56–7, 189
  retained control over EP size and national
    membership 56
  roaming charges 258–61, 265–6
  as 'second chamber' **289–92**
  secretariat 218, 235, 253
  software patents directive (2005) **245–8**
  'split personality' 290
  'strengthened' by OMC 296
  statements 223
  successful EP amendments 230, 231
  takeover bids 243–4
  transparency 291
  unanimous voting 53
  weighting of votes 53, 54
  working party on intellectual property 247
Council of Ministers: Decisions
  1987 (comitology) 240
  1999 (comitology) 240, 241–2
  2002 (preferential list voting) 70
  2006 (comitology) 241–2
Court of Auditors (1975–) 117–18, 152, 201–2
  appointment 212, **213–14**
  'quasi-parliamentary' institution 212
Court of First Instance 116, 120
Cowan, N. 313–14
Cox, P. 160, 229
crime and criminal justice 65, 180, 192, 216
Croatia 165
Crocodile Club (1980–) 43
Crowley, B. 122
Crum, B. 58
Cyprus 70, 71t, 75, 79, 94, 96t, 99t, 125t,
    128–9, 131, 214
Czech Republic 70, 71t, 96t, 99t, 125t, 127,
    131, 133, 169t, 175

D'Alema, M. 93
d'Hondt system 70, 71t, 133–4, 173–4
Dann, P. 292
Dansk Folkeparti 130
Daul, J. 122, 152, 173
Davies, C. xii
de Haan, J. 216
debates 217–18, **221–4**, 227, 235, 237
Debré, M. 34
'decentred polity' 298
decisional procedures
  'dual legitimation, dual deficit' **86–7**
  legitimacy **84–8**
  'multiple *demoi*, multiple legitimation'
    87–8
  'state-based' model **84–6**
decision-makers 6, 102, 111, 113
decision-making
  COSAC contribution 'limited' 281
  indirect 80
  joint 23
  legislative influence and **229–72**

decision-making – *continued*
  miscellaneous   6–7, 16, 20, 88, 103, 147,
      158, 190, 290, 292
  'policy-making'   19, 238, 298
  polycentric and multilogic pattern   20
  practical locus   185
  'salience of national factors'   245
  structure   113
decision-making efficiency   47, 56
decision-making function   3, 5, 11, 12, 17,
      18–19, 21, 22,
decision-making power   11, 293
decision-making process   29, 44, 54, 134, 141,
      187, 215, 225, 278–8, 295
'decisions'   61, 65
Declaration on Future of EU (European
      Council, 2000)   55, 57
Dehaene, J.-L.   55
Dehousse, B.   30
Dehousse, R.   53, 84
Del Turco, O.   174
'delegated legislation' (Lisbon Treaty)   242
'delegated regulations'   61
Delors, J.   44, 286
Delors I Package   (EU finances)   199
Delors II Package (EP temporary committee)
      179
democracy   80–1
  corporatist   297
  representative   60–1, 64, 68–9, 80, 82, 89,
      292, 294–8
  'normative frame'   298
  parliamentary   16
  participatory   61, 294, 297–8
Democracy in EU (Lord, 1998)   83
democratic deficit   21, 47, 77, 80–1, 85, 318,
      319
democratic principles
  Lisbon Treaty   274, **296–8**
democratic theories   4
Democratic Unionist Party   134
democratization   25, 38, 46, 53, 84, 87
Democrazia è Libertà - La Margherita   128
'demoicracy' (Nicolaidis)   83, 89, 319
demos   6, 20, 21, 68, 90, 286
'*demos*' versus '*demoi*'   82–4
'*demos, demoi*, and EU governance'   84–8
'multiple *demoi*'   83–4, 87–8
Denmark   60, 70, 71t, 96t, 99t, 122, 125t,
      129, 131–2
'deparliamentarization'   274
diabetes   197
Diamandouros, N.   213
Diedrichs, U., 17, 51, 87–8
  fusion model   23–4
Diez, T.   18
'differentiated integration'   290
diffuse support   15
Dimas, Commissioner   208, 209, 253
Dimitrakopoulos, G.   53

Dinan, D.   26, 38, 44, 48, 57
diplomatic and consular protection   193
'direct legitimacy'   81
'directive'   65
directives on tobacco advertising (1998, 2003)
      225
directors of agencies   224
dirigisme   266
discharge procedure   170t
discrimination   65
dock labour, 150, 249
dorsale 235
double majority voting system   59
Draft Treaty on European Union (1984)
      42–4, 45, 58, 302
  preamble   43, 46
  Article 36   43
  Article 38   44
  Article 76   44
driving licence (Europe-wide)   255
driving-time limits   255
Droop electoral formula   71t
drug trafficking   180
dual executive   4, 148, 188, 217, 221, 226,
      284, 292
dual legitimacy   20, 54, 273
dual legitimation   60, 274, 287
dual legitimation, dual deficit   **86–7**
dual mandate   72, 92
Dublin   280
Duff, A.   55, 271, 279, 282
Duisenberg, W.   215
duopoly   164
Dutch language   154

early agreements   **233–7**
Earnshaw, D.   41, 58, 118, 149, 195, 203–4,
      210, 230, 238–40, 243, 254–6, 268–70
East Europe   46, 73, 93, 108
ECHELON (communications interception
      system)   179
ECOFIN   214
ECOFIN Council   215
economic development   100
economic growth   199, 200
economic and monetary union (EMU)   46, 51
  cooperation procedure   52
economic recovery (EP temporary committee)
      179
Economic and Social Committee   106
Edinburgh   151, 200
education   92, 296
Eduskunta   282, 283
efficiency   44, 47, 56, 89, 114, 235
Eijffinger, C. W.   216
Ek, L.   225
Elazar, D. J.   19
election cycles/electoral cycles   74–5
elections   28, 30
  campaigns   72–3, 81

elections – *continued*
democracy and legitimacy **80–1**
first-order' 73–4, 76
'head' versus 'heart' 74
linkage and legitimacy **68–89**
local 79
national 75, 76, 79–80, 82, 85, 98, 109
parliamentary 285
'second-order' **73–6**, 77–9, 87, 286, 318, 325
simultaneity 76, 79–80
see also EP: elections
Electoral Commission 79, 307
electoral districts and preferential voting **69–70**
electoral formula 71t
electoral procedures **69**, 71t
electoral system/s 79, 90
majoritarian 97
electoral system effect 101
electorate 15–16, 73, 78, 81, 82, 91, 109, 111, 219
power to dismiss government 84
electronic communications 261
electronic voting 143
Elgie, R. 292
elites 11, 15, 98, 100, 137
elitist technocratic model **27–8**
'emergency brake' 65
empiricism 14
bicameralism 290
decision to call RCV 144
EP 'genuine co-legislator' 271
European Commission President (appointment) 136
MEP voting patterns 146
representative democracy 292
sources of legitimation 88
employment 179, 255, 296
Enabling Act (Germany, 1933) 134
energy consumption 238, 239
energy sector (fiscal measures) 65
English language 156, 157
engrenage (locking-in) 29
environment 44, 100, 115, **130–1**, 255
fiscal aspects 193
liability regime for damage 195–6
Equitable Life 180
Ericsson 246–7
Eriksen, E. O. 293
Espndola, R. 73
Esteves, M. 282
Estonia 70, 71t, 93, 96t, 99t, 125t, 139
Eulau, H. 100, 328
EUobserver 282
Euratom 32, 167, 213
Euratom Commission 35
Euratom Treaty 32, 33, 58
Eurlings, C. 93
Euro-gap 76

Eurobarometer 78
'Euromed' Parliamentary Assembly 165
Europa website 296
Europe
Cold War divide transcended 74
democratic unification 46
integrationist project 66
post-parliamentary **22–3**
Europe of Democracies and Diversities (EDD, 1999–2004) 131–2
'Europe of parliaments' **274–84**
Europe by Satellite (EbS) 208
European Agency for Evaluation of Medicinal Products 217
European Assembly (1957–62) 40
direct elections **33–4**
formal powers **32–3**
formal and informal roles of parliamentarians 33
'marginal enhancement of powers' (1957) 32
'parliamentary participation in policy process' principle 32–3
powers of censure and dismissal 33
renamed European Parliament (30 March 1962) 35
right of initiative 33
European Capital of Culture 243
European Central Bank (ECB) 82, 190, 194, 217
'European System of Central Banks' 51, 190, 194
parliamentary questions 218
precursor 215
'quasi-executive' institution 212
European Central Bank: President 49, 185, 186, **214–16**
appointment 212, **214–16**
European Centre for Disease Prevention and Control 217
European Chemicals Agency 217
European Coal and Steel Community (ECSC) 26, 27, 28
audit body 213
executive power 29
European Coal and Steel Community: Common Assembly **28–30**
committees 167
elections subcommittee 30
location in ECSC **29–30**
members, integrationist aspirations, and interinstitutional relations **30–1**
powers 28–9, 69
proposals for direct elections 69
rules of procedure 30, 183
secretariat 149
European Coal and Steel Community: Council 28, 29, 31, 149
European Coal and Steel Community: High Authority 27–32, 35, 149

European Coal and Steel Community: Treaty 33, 183
European Commission (or 'Commission of the European Communities')
1999–2004   93
2004–9   1, 93
2009–14 (forthcoming)   64
amendments to proposals (in EP)   103–4
annual report   33
appointment   54, **204–6**
appointment: Barroso Commission   **206–9**
appointment: EP involvement   48, 49
Assembly power to force resignation   33
authorization, control, dismissal   227
budgetary discharge   **201–3**, 320
budgetary powers   199–201
censure and dismissal   **209–12**
code of conduct (1990)   45
codecision1   231–2
codecision2   191f, 232
codecision2 (rejection by EP at first reading)   **248–54**
comitology   239–42
common position   248
'compelled' to take EP's views into account   226
composition   53, 286
consultation   296
consultation 'upstream' and implementation 'downstream'   293
conventions   276
crisis (1999)   124
direct links with national parliaments   282
enforcement of resignation   287
EP influence   **267–71**
EP rejection under cooperation procedure   238–9
EP relations 'two-way street'   **287—8**
EP tandem   284–5
EP written declarations   197
EP's refusal to grant discharge (1984)   202
financial irregularities   131
'Forest Focus'   225
'guardian of the Treaty'   32
implementation of budget   202
informal conciliations and trialogues   48–9
'institutional lobbyist' of EP   **107–8**
interaction with EP   236
involvement in European Council activities   291
joint hearings   195
legislative programme   276
legislative proposals   281
legitimacy   85
merger (1965)   35
nomination process   184
'opinions'   50–1
origins   32
parliamentarization   227, **285–9**
parliamentary debates   **221–4**

parliamentary questions   **218–21**
parliamentary questions (written)   219
'partisanization' and 'politicization'   287
policy agenda   267, 268
policy initiation and formulation, 293
'policy perspectives' (Prodi, 1999)   268
policy programme   286
political dependence on EP   39–40
'political guidance' of president   267–8
'political programme'   268, 269
political-party funding   120–1
power to formulate recommendations for legislative action   41
'presidentialization'   267–8
proposals: EP's right of rejection   238
proposals: tabled under first pillar   189
REACH proposals   224
reports   170n
right of initiative   33, 189
roaming charges **256–67**
size   59–60
software patents directive (2005) **245–8**, 303
subject to vote of EP confidence (proposal dropped)   56
successful EP amendments   230, 231
synchronization of term of office with that of EP   267
timeous provision of proposals   275
'twenty-eighth member-state'   291
website   253
White Paper on governance (2001)   **293–5**, 303
work programmes   223, **269–71**, 303–4, 321
European Commission: Annual Legislative and Work Programme   223
European Commission: Annual Policy Strategy   223
European Commission: Directive 86/609 (animal experimentation)   197
European Commission: Directorate-General for Transport and Energy   250
European Commission: Directorates-General   287
European Commission: documents   7, **303–4**
COM(93)661 (biotechnological inventions)   243, 303
COM(95)655 (takeover bids)   **243–5**, 303
COM(97)510 final (motor insurance)   196, 303
COM(2001)28 (work programme for 2001)   269, 303
COM(2001)428 (European governance)   **293–5**, 303
COM(2001)620 (work programme for 2002)   269, 303
COM(2002)704 (consultation of interested parties)   295, 303
COM(2002)92 (software patents)   245, 303

European Commission: documents – *continued*
COM(2002)95 (democratic control over
Europol) 284, 303
COM(2004)144 (rail freight services) 251,
303, 322
COM(2004)532 (trapping standards) 252,
303
COM(2004)759 (electronic communications)
259, 303
COM(2005)12 (Barroso Commission's
strategic objectives) 270, 304
COM(2005)15 (work programme for 2005)
270, 304
COM(2006)194 (transparency) 106, 304
COM(2006)382 (roaming charges) 261,
304
COM(2007)364 (political party funding)
120–1, 304
European Commission: President 2, 50, 52,
54, 60, 161, 211, 227, 240, 288, 289
appointment 62, 85–6, 136, 204, 267
appointment procedure 55–6
direct election (option) 286
'election' 64, 226, **285–7**, 292
election by EP on proposal from European
Council 47
intergovernmental bargaining 287
European Commission: Statements 223
European Commission: Vice-Presidents 59,
268
European Commissioners (specific)
Energy 208, 209
External Relations 206
Information Society and Media 257
Taxation and Customs 209
European Commissioners (general)
appointment **85–6**, 267
collective responsibility 288
'College of Commissioners' 204, 210, 227,
251, 268, 270, 288
confirmation hearings 205–6, 207
enforcement of individual resignation
287–8
failed EP attempt to secure right of individual
dismissal 210–11
intergovernmental bargaining 286
'political responsibility' 211
resignations and individual responsibility
268
responsibility to EP **287–8**
European Commissioners-designate 205–9,
224
Financial Programming and Budget 207
Justice, Freedom, and Security 207
European Communities (1951–) 31, 35
financial regulation 202
'first pillar' 51
European Community (EC) 30, 44, 49, 77,
149, 188
constitutional blueprint 35

extension of competences 47
identity 42–3
'intergovernmental association' (Debr, 1960)
34
legislation 40
legislative procedure 48
legitimacy 81
'own resources' (1970–) 198
procedural reform and expansion of
competences 46
'European Community Treaty' 227
Article 19 70
Article 217 288
Article 201 286, 288
Article 202 240
Article 272 198
Article 289 54
Article 300(3) 194
Article 319(2–3) 201
see also Rome Treaty (1957)
European Community's Shipowners'
Associations (ECSA) 251
European Constitutional Treaty or Treaty
Establishing Constitution for Europe
(Rome, 2004): **57–62**
Article I-8 59
Article I-20 64
Article I-24(6) 59
Article 1–27 62, 85
Article I-27(3) 60
Article I-33 61
Article I-36 61
Article I-37 61
Article I-46 60
Article I-47 60–1, 151–2
Article I-60 60
Article 8c 59
Article 10 60
Protocol on Role of National Parliaments 275
European Constitutional Treaty: general
citizen's initiatives 297
'Democratic Life of Union' 297
'difficulties in ratifying' 280
drafting 57–8
EP: specific institutional issues 60–2
IGC 62
overview **59–60**
'Principle of Participatory Democracy' 297
'Social Partners Autonomous Social
Dialogue' 297
European Convention (CONV, 2002–) 57–8,
59, 65, 275, 277, 285–6, 304
European Council: meetings
1992 (Edinburgh) 151, 200
1996 (Turin) 50
2001 (Nice) 293
2002 (Seville) 290, 291
2004 (Brussels) 58
2006 (Austria) 152
2006 (Finland) 152

European Council: meetings – *continued*
　2007 (Brussels)　63
　2008 (Brussels)　8
European Council: Presidency　59, 235, 237,
　241, 256, 264, 279, 282–3
executive versus legislative tasks　291
European Court of Justice (ECJ)　20, 34, 43,
　51, 52, 56, 200, 213, 225
　Case C-230/81　150
　Case C-108/83　150
　Case 294/83　117
　Case C-258/85　150
　Case C-302/87 (comitology)　240
　Case C-213/88　150
　Case C-39/89　150
　Case C-345/95　151
　Case C-376.98　225
　Case C-380/03　225
　Case C-122/04　225
　Case C-338/05　120
　Isoglucose ruling (1980)　38–9
European Court of Justice: Statute　190
European courts (various)　21, 49, 51, 82
European Defence Community (EDC)　31,
　278
European Democratic Alliance　124
European Democratic Party (EDP)　119, 128,
　129
European Economic Community (EEC)
　annual budget (power of EP to reject)　36
　audit body　213
　budget　33
　budgetary provisions (treaty reforms, 1970,
　　1975)　36
　committees　167
　conciliation　36–7
　democratic dynamic　33–4
　enlargement (1973)　34
　establishment　31–4
　expenditure 36
　formal structures and informal changes
　　(1957–79)　35–7
　intergovernmentalism　36
　interinstitutional dynamic　35
　see also 'Rome Treaty (1957)'
European Economic Community: Commission
　35
European Economic Community: Council　32
European Economic Community: Economic
　and Social Committee　32
'European electorate'　81
European Environment Agency　212, 217
European External Action service　193
'European Home Market Approach'　261
European integration　63, 82, **99–100**, 126,
　127, 129, 131, 135, 140, 167
'European issue'　74
European Liberal, Democrat and Reform Party
　(ELDR)　ix, 72, 119, 128–9, 140, 142
　'constitutive agreement' with EPP-ED　160

European Medicines Agency　212
European Monetary Institute　215
European Ombudsman　**212–13**
European Parliament (EP, 1962–)
　accorded formal role in IGC (1996)　50
　accounts (approval delayed by Budgetary
　　Control Committee, 2004)　152
　action as representative body　**90–112**
　agenda　110, 160, 161b, 165, 221, 223
　agreement on budgetary matters (1988)　41
　allocation of seats per member-state　56
　amendments　190, 194, 232, 233t, 246–8,
　　250, 262, 265–6, 271
　amendments: codecision2　191f
　amendments: qualitative assessment　254
　amendments: 'real impact'　255
　amendments: translation　158
　appointment and dismissal　**203–12, 212–17**
　armoury: 'nuclear weapon' versus 'smart
　　bomb'　210, 211–12
　assent procedure　45
　assessment　3
　assessment factors　5
　attitudinal change　**38–9**
　author　37, 52, 181, 196, 236, **308–10**
　bargaining power　50
　budget　163b, 163
　buildings　2, 153
　comitology　**239–42**
　composition　56
　conception of 'method' and 'balance'　294
　constraints　226
　control of debates　161
　control over finance　47
　coordination of committee decisions with
　　group positions　123
　costs of linguistic services　**157–8**
　council conciliation delegations　161b
　debates　110, 222–3
　demonstrations outside　246, 249
　dimensions (interinstitutional, contextual,
　　interconnected)　6
　direct elections principle　28, 30, 31
　direct representative capacity　24
　early agreements　**233–7**
　effectiveness　53
　'essential'　298–9
　first reading　49–50
　formal organization　**167–86**
　formal parliamentary leadership　**158–9**
　formal powers　**188–228**, 299
　formal powers: consolidation　49
　formal powers: limitations　227
　formal treaty reforms　**42–6**
　functional efficiency　114
　'fundamental paradox'　2
　fundamental questions　4
　future　7
　historical evolution　6, 25, **26–67**
　image problem　229

European Parliament – *continued*
  increasing power, increasing number of
    women MEPs 97
  incremental advances 38
  influence: formal versus informal 6–7
  influence over executive branch 267–71
  informal conciliations and trialogues 48–9
  informal procedures/strategies 7, 35, 37,
    40, 41, 272, 299
  inquisitory role 40
  institutional design and organizational
    adaptation 186–7
  institutional issues (Constitutional Treaty,
    2004) 60–2
  institutional status 1
  interconnectedness 229
  interinstitutional context 229
  interinstitutional dialogue 45–6
  internal workings 6
  internal 'institutionalization' process 56
  internal organization 147–87
  intra-group bargaining 136–7
  intra-group cohesion 138–9
  joint hearings 195
  judicial review 225
  known as 'European Assembly' (until 1962)
    35
  leadership roles 186
  'leading role in European dialogue' (2005)
    62–3
  legal powers 56
  legislative activity 86
  legislative influence and decision-making
    229–72
  legislative initiative 41, 47, 49, 51, 52–3
  legislative power/competence 36, 40, 44–5,
    51, 57, 66, 240, 272, 274
  legislative procedure/process 46, 48
  legislative role 134, 146
  as legislature 9–12
  location 9–25, 54
  location 'changed over time' 66
  location within EU's system of governance
    xi, 3–4, 5, 6–7, 17–24, 299
  marginalization in OMC processes 296
  microcosmic representation 91, 92–4
  multi-functionality 24–5, 271–2
  multiple seat 148–54, 197
  multiple seat: costs 153–4
  and national parliaments 274–84
  national party delegations 134–5
  new institutional balance (1982) 43
  'no simple answers' 9
  non-attached members 133–4
  notions of what parliaments 'are' 299
  office accommodation 153
  official languages 154–8
  'opinions' 50–1
  'part-sessions' 185
  part-sessions: agenda 164b

party groups 113–46
policy agenda 137
policy influence maximization 200
power 36, 167, 230
power to enforce resignation of European
    Commissioners 55
power of rejection 237–54
power of scrutiny 217–25
power of veto 192, 226
prerogatives 49
procedural precedent 37
procedures 6, 40, 147
'proper' parliament (or not) 5
provisions of Amsterdam Treaty 52–3
psychological turning point 40
readings: codecision2 procedure 191f
reports 46
representation of women 94–8
revenue-raising versus expenditure powers
    198
right to block comitology measures 242
right of legislative veto (Maastricht Treaty)
    238
right to propose treaty amendments 276
'right to use one's own language' 154,
    158
role: appointment of members of European
    Commission 52
role: public perception 48
rule changes and procedural innovation
    39–40
second chamber (under discussion) 277–9
size (number of MEPs) 2, 51–2, 54, 56, 60,
    64, 126, 168
status (upward mobility) 66
Strasbourg and Brussels locations 52
sui generis issue/uniqueness 10, 148
'system development' role 51
threat of delay 39–40
'transition from consultation to
    bicameralism' (Hix) 272
website 100, 186, 197, 208
'winner' in Amsterdam Treaty 53
working patterns 41
see also plenary sessions
European Parliament (1979–2004 sessions)
    138–9
European Parliament (1989–94 session) 140,
    142, 160, 167
European Parliament (1994–9 session) 111,
    129, 140–2, 160, 243
European Parliament (1999–2004 session)
    110, 128–32, 139, 141–2, 160, 162, 168,
    171, 197, 206, 232–3, 255
  voting decisions 138
European Parliament (2004–9 session) 110,
    114, 119, 130–2, 136, 139, 141–2, 148,
    151, 156, 160, 162, 171, 173, 181,
    184, 197, 206, 232, 233t, 248–9, 255,
    282

European Parliament: Agriculture and Rural Affairs Committee 168, 169–70t, 173, 174
European Parliament: Budgetary Control Committee 152, 169–70t, 171–2, 174–5, 202–3, 213–14, 282–3
European Parliament: budgetary powers/competence **198–203**
discharge **201–3**, 320
draft budgets 199, 201
miscellaneous 51, 57, 61–2, 226–7, 240
qualitative aspects 201
resolution (8 June 2005) 200
European Parliament: Budgets Committee 121, 128, 169–70t, 171, 173, 174, 176, 200,
European Parliament: Bureau 152, 154–5, 159, 162, **163**, 164b, 204, 224
functions 163b
membership 163
European Parliament: Civil Liberties, Justice, and Home Affairs Committee (LIBE) x, 169–70t, 171, 174, 208, 283–4
European Parliament: Code of Conduct on Multilingualism (2004 revision) 155
European Parliament: College of Quaestors 159
European Parliament: committee bureaux **172–6**
European Parliament: committees **167–78**
appointment of European Commissioners (hearings) 205
budgetary procedure reports 170t, 171
debates merely minuted 186
group coordinators **176–8**
hearings **205–9**, **212–16**, **224–5**, 258
inter-institutional agreement reports 170t, 171
'liaison members' 217
meetings 150, 185
membership 169t, **171–2**
mid-term review of leadership 174, 175
miscellaneous 6, 49–50, 110, 137, 147–8, 157–8, 164b, 185, 190, 197, 235–7, 271
own initiative reports 170t, 171
reports 7, 170t, **176–8**
review (1999) 167–8
review (2004) **167–71**
structure **167**
'substitute' members 171
votes 143
workload 168, 171
European Parliament: committees of inquiry 47, 49, **179–80**
European Parliament: Conference of Committee Chairs 159, 164, **165–6**, 270
European Parliament: Conference of Delegation Chairs 159, **165–6**

European Parliament: Conference of Presidents **163–4**
duties 164b
inter-institutional relations 164b
membership 164
minutes 164
European Parliament: Constitutional Affairs Committee 53, 57–8, 61–2, 116, 120, 151, 156, 169–70t, 174, 270, 276–6, 281–2
European Parliament: Culture Committee 247
European Parliament: Culture and Education Committee 156, 169–70t, 174, 262
European Parliament: Development Committee 166, 169–70t, 174–5
European Parliament: Directorate-General (translation) 157
European Parliament: documents 7
PE 221.698/1997 (democratic legitimacy/national parliaments) 274, 275
PE 226.077/1998 (budgetary discharge) 202, 320
PE 232.403/2000 (comitology) 241, 321
PE 232.758/2000 (constitutional affairs) 286, 321
PE 287.644/2004 (conciliation committee/port services) 232, 249, 321
PE 294.777/2001 (Council reform) 291, 321
PE 304.289/2001 (European governance) **294–5**, 321
PE 304.302/2002 (democratic legitimacy) 274, 321
PE 304.309/2002 (European Commission's work programme) 270, 321
PE 323.576/2003 (party funding) 119, 322
PE 353.270/2005 (budgetary means of EU-25) 200, 322
PE 357.779/2005 (trapping standards) 253, 322
PE 367.786/2006 (political parties) 120, 323
PE 372.062/2006 (budgetary discipline) 200, 323
PE 392.600/CPT/GT/2007 (parliamentary reform) 218, 223–4, 323
European Parliament: Economic and Monetary Affairs (ECON) Committee 169–70t, 171, 174, 176, 186, **215–16**, 238, 262
European Parliament: elections
(1979) 9, 37, 38, 42, 74
(1979–87) 38–42
(1979–94) 74–5
(1989) 46
(1999) 76–7, 81, 124, 128, 160
(2007, Romania) 133
(2009 forthcoming) xi, 64, 67, 204

European Parliament: election (2004) xi, 1,
  69–76, 77, 118, 122, 128, 131, 133, 247,
  258
  constituencies 71t
  date 70
  electoral districts and preferential voting
    69–70
  electoral procedures **69,** 71t
  electoral systems and turnout 71t
  'second-order' elections **73–6**
  transnational party groups **72–3**
  turnout 69, 70, 71t
  voting rights and eligibility **70, 72**
European Parliament: elections (general)
  68–9
  campaigns 117
  candidates 91
  Europeanization 285
  impact 38
  minimum age to stand for election 70
  pointers to subsequent general elections
    75
  proportional representation 69
  reasons for not voting 78
  right to stand as candidates 70
  'second-order national contests' (Reif and
    Schmitt) **73–6,** 77, 78, 79, 286, 318,
    325
  uniform procedures 194
  uniformity principle ceded (Amsterdam
    Treaty) 69
  voting rights and eligibility **70, 72**
  wider political context 76
European Parliament: Employment and Social
  Affairs Committee 170t, 175, 250
European Parliament: Environment Committee
  103–4, 107, 168
European Parliament: Environment, Public
  Health, and Food Safety Committee
  168–71, 173–5, 177, 179, 197, 217, 224,
  236, 252–3
European Parliament: External Economic
  Relations Committee 175
European Parliament: Fisheries Committee
  168, 169–70t
European Parliament: Foreign Affairs
  Committee 166, 169–70t, 171, 173–5
European Parliament: Health and Consumer
  Intergroup 184
European Parliament: Human Rights sub-
  committee 174
European Parliament: Industry Committee
  103–4, 168, 206
European Parliament: Industry, Research, and
  Energy Committee (ITRE) 168, 169–70t,
  173–4, 208, 224–5, 258, 260, 262–5, 267
European Parliament: Information Offices
  100
European Parliament: Institutional Affairs
  Committee (1981–) 43, 46, 230

European Parliament: Internal Market and
  Consumer Protection Committee (IMCO,
  2004–) 168, 169–70t, 171, 174, 224,
  250, **258–60,** 262–4, 267
European Parliament: International Trade
  Committee (2004–) 168, 169–70t, 174–5
European Parliament: Legal Affairs Committee
  168–71, 173, 175, 177, 247–8, 259
European Parliament: Legal Affairs and Internal
  Market Committee 246
European Parliament: neutralized committees
  177
European Parliament: Petitions Committee
  169–70t, 171–2, 212–13
European Parliament: Political Affairs
  Committee 150
European Parliament: President **159–61**
  elections **160–1**
  frequency of election 160
  functions **160–1,** 161b
  inter-institutional role 161b, 161
  official visits within and outside EU 161b,
    161
  present at Heads of Government Meetings
    58
European Parliament: Quaestors 163b, 163
European Parliament: Regional Development
  Committee (2004–) 168, 169–70t, 173
European Parliament: Regional and Transport
  Committee 168
European Parliament: Research, Technological
  Development, and Energy Committee
  (1994–9) 177
European Parliament: resolutions 7, 46, 197
  6 July 1982 43
  17 May 1995 51
  13 April 2000 54
  31 May 2001 57–8
  8 June 2005 (budgetary powers) 200
European Parliament: Rules Committee 107
European Parliament: Rules of Procedure
  182–4
  changes (1979–2002) 183
  miscellaneous 1, 6, 37, 39, 62, 85, 147,
    154, 161b, 161, 170t, 186–7, 196–7,
    206, 212, 248–9, 272
  overhaul (1999) 115
  'philosophy' 183
  tied votes 243
European Parliament: Rules of Procedure
  (specific)
  'Annex 1' 107
  Annex 9(2.1) 106, 309
  Rule 9(1) 106
  Rule 9(2), later Rule 9(4) 105–6
  Rule 19 134
  Rule 22 163b
  Rule 22(a) 37
  Rule 23(3) 164
  Rule 24 164b

European Parliament: Rules of Procedure –
  continued
  Rule 25   162
  Rule 26   165
  Rule 29(1)   115–16, 133
  Rule 29(2)   115
  Rule 31, 134
  Rule 32   50, 204
  Rule 33 (later Rule 99)   204
  Rule 35 (1981)   39
  Rule 36 (1981)   39
  Rule 41 (1986)   45
  Rule 45   195
  Rule 50   221
  Rule 53   253
  Rule 57(1)   155
  Rule 59   177
  Rule 64   181
  Rule 103   222
  Rule 104 (1999–)   222
  Rule 108   218
  Rule 110 (written questions)   219
  Rule 113   195
  Rule 115   222
  Rule 133   222
  Rule 138   156
  Rule 138(1)   155
  Rule 138(2) 155–6
  Rule 139(1) (amendment, 2006)   156
  Rule 144 (2002–)   222
  Rule 150(6)   155
  Rule 175   179
  Rule 177   171
  Rule 183   224
European Parliament: Secretariat   52, 148,
  150, 157, **166–7**
European Parliament: Tabling Office   155
European Parliament: temporary committees
  178–9, 200
European Parliament: Transport and Tourism
  Committee (2004–)   168–71, 249–50,
  251–2
European Parliament: Vice-Presidents   110,
  159, **162**, 163, 181, 222, 235
European Parliament: Women's Rights
  Committee   144, 168
European Parliament: Women's Rights and
  Gender Equality Committee   168,
  169–70t, 173, 175–6
European Parliament: Working Party on
  Parliamentary Reform   218, 323
European Parliament-Latin American
  Parliamentary Assembly (2006–)   165
European Parliamentary Group on Breast
  Cancer (EPGBC)   184
European Parliamentary Labour Party (EPLP)
  135
European party statute
  progress towards   **118–21**
European Patent Convention   246

European People's Party and European
  Democrats (EPP-ED, 1999–)
  composition   **124–7**
  'ED'   166
  'EPP'   72, 94, 140, 160, 166, 176, 206
  favoured Barroso Commission   207
  ideological diversity   **126–7**
  rules (2006)   127
'European policy'   99
European Political Community (EPC)   31,
  277–8
  draft treaty (1953)   31
European Political Union (EPU)   46, 47
European Public Affairs Directory (2006)
  102
European Public Prosecutor's Office
  'possible creation'   65
European Regulators Group   259
European research   61
European Sea Ports Organization (ESPO)   251
European Transparency Initiative (2006)   106,
  304
European Union (1993–)   49, 83
  budget   65, 120, 161b, 213, 283
  budgetary functions   64
  competences   60, 61, 66, 74, 118, 278
  competences 'conferred by member-states'
    59
  conceptualization   83–4
  constitutional blueprint   35
  coordination of economic and employment
    policies   60
  democratic and legitimacy deficits   15
  dual executive   84–5
  finances   49
  governance   4, 7, 15, **17–24**
  'government'   68
  'has federal characteristics but is not federal
    state'   20
  institutional architecture   66
  institutional capacity   50
  institutional matrix   56
  interinstitutional structures   183–4
  international status   53
  legislative process   113, 178
  military and defence provisions   66
  national permanent representation   107–8
  normative and constitutional debate
    ('schizophrenic nature')   298
  opposition to superstate   133
  as 'parliamentary government'   272
  pillar structure abandoned   59
  policy-making   50, 180
  political system   15, 17, **19–21**
  principle of change   51
  'semi-parliamentary democracy' (Dann)   292
  'semi-permanent treaty-revision process'   55
  single legal personality   59
  symbols   59
  treaty amendment process   65–6

European Union (EU-15, 1995–2004)   1, 50, 75, 92–5, 115
    turnout   76
European Union (EU-25, 2004–6)   1, 53, 69, 76, 92–4, 99t, 128, 130–1, 155–6, 168, 174, 179, 214, 247, 280
    new member states   80
European Union (EU-27, 2007–)   1, 50, 53, 87, 93, 99t, 111–12, 114–15, 128, 131–2, 136, 154,156, 281
European Union: Charter on Fundamental Rights   57
European Union: Conciliation Committee **181–2**
European Union: Foreign Affairs Council   59
European Union: High Representative for Foreign Affairs and Security Policy   64
European Union: Minister of Foreign Affairs 59, 60, 62
European Union bodies
    appointments   **212–17**
European Union Democrats (party, 2005–) 119–20
European Union enlargement   51, 53, 55–6, 114, 115, 128, 130
    institutional issues   58
European Union expenditure   2, 199, 283
    classification   200
    'compulsory' versus 'non-compulsory'   62, 198, 199, 201, 227
European Union institutions   18, 20, 225–6
    good administrative conduct   196
    interdependence   4
European Voice   124, 133, 174, 176, 223
Europeanization   79, 97
Europol   284, 303
Euroscepticism/Eurosceptics   75, 79, 81, 126–9, 132, 133–4
eurosclerosis (1970s/1980s)   42
'Euro-tariff'   262, 265, 266
eurozone states   200
Evans, C. L.   194
ever-closer union   **26–67**
ex ante 'directedness'   267
ex ante scrutiny   216–17
executive branch   14, 15–16, 19–23, 84–6, 189, 203–4, 217–19, 230, 237–8, 285, 292
    EP influence   229, **267–71**
    formal and informal constraints   17
    influence over   229
    right to dissolve parliament and call new elections   288–9
    and call new elections   288–9
executive federalism   292
'executive measures'   61
executives   12, 14
ex post accountability   217, 267
'extraordinary debates'   222

'Fair Chair' campaign (2006)   160

family   65, 133
Farage, N.   122, 132, 266
Farrell, D. M.   **100–1**, 110–11, 172, 301–2
Farrell, H.   233, 234, 272, **310**
fascism   180
Fatherland and Freedom Party (Latvia) 130
Fazakas, S.   162, 174
Featherstone, K.   27
federal lists (Germany)   70
federal model   **28–30**
federalism   18, **19–21**, 23, 31, 43–4, 47, 58, 87–8, 126, 128–9
    constitutional blueprints   66
    cooperative model   19
federalist democratic vision   27
Federation of European Nurses in Diabetes 197
Federazione dei Verdi (Italy)   122
Fenzi, E.   xii
Ferguson, L. C.   328
Ferrero Waldner, B.   248
Fianna Fáil   122, 129–30
Fieschi, C.   129
Fifth Framework Programme for Research and Technology (1998)   182, 255
Financial Framework   201
Financial Perspective/Interinstitutional Agreement (FP/IIA)   200–201
Financial Regulation (1605/2002)/amendment (1524/2007)   121
financial regulations   57
financial services   180
Financial Times   244–5
Finland   70, 71t, 76, 92–3, 96t, 99t, 103, 125t, 129, 131, 259, 282–3
first pillar   51, 57, 189, 190, 194
first reading   49–50, 230, 232–4, 236–7, 246–7, **264–6**
    rejection of European Commission proposals **248–54**
first-past-the-post   69
Fischer, J.   278
Fisher, S.   306
fisheries   61
Fitzmaurice, J.   126, 205–6
Flautre, H.   174
Florenz, K.-H.   xii, 173, 174, 179
Føllesdal, A.   85, 293
Fontaine, N.   54, 160, 166
Fontelles, J. B.   121, 160, 169t
foot-and-mouth crisis (EP temporary committee)   179
For Human Rights in United Latvia (Party) 130
Ford, G.   107
'Forest Focus'   225
Forza Europa   115
Forza Italia   115, 126
Fossum, J. E.   293

Framework Agreements   1, 272
  comitology   (2000) 241
  Relations between EP and European
      Commission (2000)   42, 211, 269,
      308
  Relations between EP and European
      Commission (2005)   196, 211, 287–8
'framework laws'   61, 65
France   1, 26, 50, 69–70, 71t, 77, 93–8, 99t,
      122, 124, 125t, 131, 161–2, 169t, 174,
      206, 214, 264, 278–9
  anti-Maastricht MEPs   129
  referendum (2005)   62
France: National Assembly   31
Franklin, M.   72, 80, 95, 110,
Frassoni, M.   122, 124, 152
Fratini, F.   209
Freedman, J.   95[-]97
freedom   61, 226, 245, 279–80, 283
Freedom Party (Austria)   132
Freie Demokratische Partei (FDP)   129
French government   150–1, 152
French language   154, 156, 157
French Socialist Party   128
Friedrich, A., *et al.* (2000)   255, 311
  Tappe, M.   311
  Wurzel, R.   311
Friedrich, I.   162
Front National (France)   116, 120, 122,
      132–4
functional differentiation   22
functional groups   90, **101–8**
functionalists   11
fusion model (Wessels and Diedrichs)   **23–4**,
      87–8
Future of Europe   285–6

Gabel, M.   143–4, 145, 302
Gahler, M.   175
Galeote, G.   169t
game theory   230–1
Garca, F.   73
Gargani, G.   169t
Garman, J.   182
Garrett, G.   231, 327
Gaullism   124, 126
Gebhardt, E.   97
gene patenting   243, 245
general public   24, 63
genetically modified organisms   196
Genscher, H-D.   42
Genscher–Colombo proposals (1981)   **42–3**
German language   154, 156, 157
German reunification   46
  EP temporary committee)   179
Germany   1, 26, 44, 69–70, 71t, 77, 93, 96t,
      97–8, 99t, 121, 125t, 131, 160, 169t,
      174–5, 204, 206, 209, 223, 225, **243–5**,
      249, 264, 278
  takeover bids   243–4

Gil-Robles, J. M.   126, 160
Gil-Robles–Santer agreement (1999)   240
Giscard d'Estaing, V.   277
'giving of assent'   10
Global Health Fund   256
Gollnisch, B.   122, 133
Gornitzka, A.   311
governance
  alternative conceptions   **292–8**
  demos, demoi and   **84–8**
  multilevel network   298
  'new, non-territorial form'   21
  parliamentary model   54
  'post-parliamentary'   102, **298–9**
  two models   5
  Type I (federal analogy)   18, **19–21**, 87,
      273, 299
  Type II (multilevel)   18–19, 21–5, 68, 87,
      271, 273, 293, 299
government   88
  layers   20
  versus 'governance'   22
  versus 'opposition'   80, 109, 140, 145, 186
  representative   80, 84, 86
  systems   15
  see also national governments
Government Policy Consultants (GPC)   126,
      311
government spending   199
Gray, M.   54
Greater Romania Party   132, 133
Greece   70, 71t, 79, 93–4, 96t, 99t, 125t, 131,
      162, 169t, 214, 262
Green, P.   124
Green Group   94, 114, 121, 173
  opposed Barroso Commission   207
Green Group v. *European Parliament*
      (judgement   23 April 1986)   117
Green Papers   106, 170n, 171, 195, 304
  see also 'European Commission:
      documents'
Green parties   75, 109
  Die Grnen (Germany)   122, 130
  Les Verts (France)   130
Greens   209
Greens/European Free Alliance (EFA) Group
      94, 122, 141, 153, 160, 162, 181, 250
  composition   125t, **130–1**
  'European Free Alliance' (1981–)   119,
      130–1
  'European Green Party'   119
Greenwood, J.   102, 106
'group weeks'   123, 134
Grybauskait, D.   207

Häge, F. M.   255
Hagenbach–Bischoff electoral formula   71t
Hague Programme   283
Hannan, D.   120, 134
Hänsch, K. 166, 286

Hare electoral formula 71t
Hare–Niemeyer formula 70, 71t
Harkin, M. 129
Harley, D. 122, 166
Harvey, O. 28
Hatzidakis, K. 93
Hausemer, P. 178
Hayes-Renshaw, F. 235, 290–1
Hayter, W. 34
Heads of State and Government 44, 51, 54,
    55, 58, 64, 161b, 161, 276
Helmer, R. 120, 133–4
Helsinki 279
Herczog, E. xii
Héritier, A. 233, 234, 272, **310**
High Authority (ECSC) 27–32, 35, 149
Hilditch, L. 182
Hilf, M. 302
history 73
Hitler, A. 134
Hix, S. 2, 22, 49, 50, 72, 75, 78, 85–6, 114,
    123, 136, 210, 239, 284, 289, 310,
    312–13
  'transitions' 272
Hix, S., *et al.* (2005) 138
  Noury, A. 313
  Roland, G. 313
Hix, S., *et al.* (2007) 112, **137–9, 141–2,** 146,
    229, 286, 313
  Noury, A. 313
  Roland, G. 313
  critics **143–5**
  validity of data used **143–5**
Hoffman, L. 286
Hokmark, G. 266
Holland, M. 27
Holstein, W. 81
home affairs 190, 283, 284, 290
homosexuality/gay rights 175, 208
Honeyball, M. 175–6
Hooghe, L. 18
Hoon, G. 93
Høreth, M. 22, 25, 89
Hortefeux, B. 93
household appliances
  energy consumption 238, 239
Høyland, B. K. 86, 178, 313–14
Hubschmid, C. 255
Hug, S. 144
Hulten, M. van 85–6
human genetics 179
human knowledge 245
human rights 59, 194, 222
Humphreys, J. 108
Hungarian language 156
Hungary 70, 71t, 76, 96t, 99t, 125t, 129, 222

identity 81
  concentric circles 83
  ethno-cultural 83
    European 73, 82, 83
    linguistic 154
identity cards 65, 193
Identity, Tradition, and Sovereignty Group
    (ITS, 2007) 122, 124, **132–3,** 222
ideology 73, 114, 126–7, 129–30, 133, 136,
    139, 141, 160, 167, 176, 243, 254
  'moderation for legislative influence'
    (Kreppel) 141
  predictor of how often groups will vote
    together 142
Ilves, T. 93, 175
image 78, 105, 154, 229
'imperfect d'Hondt' system 121
Independence and Democracy Group (ID,
    2004–) 94, 121–2, 129–30, 160, 210,
    222, 250
  composition 125t, **131–2**
  ideology 132
indirect taxation 193
individuals 100–1, 210–11, 279, 287–8
industrial policy 193
inflation rates 199
influence 11
  'vague' (Blondel) 188, 221
'informal conciliations' 37, 48–9
informal networks 22
information 117, 224, 241, 275, 279–80,
    283–4
  'interinstitutional' 104
  supply and demand 104
  transmission, translation, timing **103–4**
information deficiencies 103
information overload 147
information technology (IT) 280
'input legitimacy' 88, 292
institutional balance (EU) 296
institutional boundaries 284
institutional explanations 77, **79–80**
institutional fusion 24
institutional reform 44
institutional resources
  effect on EP's legislative influence 254
institutions 27
  communautaire 30
  formal 22
  national 24
  non-majoritarian 293
  supranational 29
integration theories 4
integrationist aspirations 6, **30–1,** 46, 55
intellectual property 245, 247
interconnectedness 4, **16–17**
interdependence 4, 284
interest groups **101–8,** 184, 221, 293
'interest representation' 102, 112
  transmission, translation, timing (of
    information) **103–4**
Intergovernmental Conferences (IGCs) 1, 44,
    48, 56–9, 65, 149, 151, 161b, 211

Intergovernmental Conferences (IGCs) –
    continued
  (1996) **50–1**, 54
  (2000) **53–4**, 118, 288–9
  (2004) **55**, 63
  (2007) **63–4**, 67
  EMU 46, 47
  EPU 47
  Maastricht 277
  mode of treaty reform 58
intergovernmentalism 20–1, 23
  effect on EP's legislative influence 254
'intergroups' (of MEPs) **184–5**
Interinstitutional Agreements 1, 36–7, **41–2**,
    49, 66, 180, 198, 210, 227, 236, 240, 272
  budgetary discipline (1988–) 199
  budgetary powers (1993, 1999) 200
  budgetary powers (2006) 201
  financial matters (1999, 2006) 42
  regulatory agencies (2005 draft) 216
interinstitutional bargaining 141, 271
interinstitutional bodies 181
interinstitutional committee 47
interinstitutional conflict 243
interinstitutional cooperation 188
interinstitutional declarations 237
interinstitutional dialogue **45–6**
interinstitutional interactions 4, 284
interinstitutional networks (informal) 5
interinstitutional relations 3, **30–1**
  effect on EP's legislative influence 254
interinstitutional rivalry 245–6
interinstitutional structures 187
internal market 44, 45, 257, 258
  harmonization of national provisions 193
  treaty rules (Articles 43 and 49) 251
internal organization (EP) **147–87**
international agreements 226
International Diabetes Federation: Europe
    Region 197
International Telecommunications User Group
    257
internet 259
interparliamentary delegations 165
interpretation **154–8**
interpreters 155, 156, 157
interviews xii, 107–8, 177
inter-war era 26
Iraq 128
Ireland 60, 69–70, 71t, 76–7, 92–4, 96t,
    98–100, 122, 125t, 129, 131
  referendum (12 June 2008) 8
Irish language 154, 156
Isoglucose ruling (ECJ 1980) 38–9
'issues of particular interest' 104
Italian constitution 79
Italian language 154, 156
Italy 1, 42, 44, 64, 69–70, 71t, 76, 93–5, 96t,
    98, 99t, 116, 122, 125t, 126, 129, 131,
    133, 162, 169t, 174, 214, 244, 259, 262

Jackson, C.   xii, 107–8, 124
Jacobs, F.   xii, 302, 305
Jacobsson, K.   296
Jarzembowski, G.   249
Jewell, M. E.   98
joint committee meetings
  EP and national parliaments **282–4**
Joint Declaration (1975) 36, 41
Joint Declaration (codecision2, 1999) 234
Joint Declaration on Practical Arrangements for
    Codecision Procedure (2007) 235, 236–7
joint parliamentary committees (JPCs) 165
Jospin, L.   278
Judge, D.   14, 22, 41, 47, 58, 80, 90–1, 98,
    102, 111, 118, 172, 195, 203–4, 210, 221,
    230–1, 238–40, 243, 254–6, 268–70, 295,
    298, **306**, **313–14**
judicial cooperation 60
judicial institutions 22
judicial review **225**
June List (Sweden) 132
JuniBevaegelsen/June Movement (Denmark)
    122, 132
justice 61, 226, 279–80, 283–4, 290

Kaeding, M.   178, 255
Kalandrakis, A.   255, 328
Kallas, S.   106
Karmios, C.   214
Karps, P.   100
Katz, R. S.   110, 111
Kauppi, P-N.   259
Kennedy, S.   i, xii
Kerstens, P.   xii
Kietz, D.   240, 242
Kiiver, P.   278, 279, 282
Kirchner, E.   38–9
Klepsch, E.   160
Klepsch–Millan agreement (1993)   240
Klich, B.   93
Koepke, J. R.   75, 315
Kohler-Koch, B.   22, 89, 103
Kratsa-Tsagaropoulou, R.   162, 181
Krehbiel, K.   147
Kreppel, A.   141, 143, 144, 146, 184, 229,
    254, 289, 292, **315–16**, 328
Krook, M. L.   95, 97–8
Kudrycka, B.   93

Labour Party 128, 136
Labour Party: National Executive   135
Laeken Declaration (2001)   58
Laffan, B.   19, 199, 200
Lamfalussy, A., Baron   215
Lamoureux, F.   250
Land lists (Germany)   70
Langdal, F.   73
language 2, 73, 113, 124, 148, **154–8**,
    186
'language profiles'   155

LAOS (Greek Orthodox traditionalist party) 132
Latvia 70, 71t, 76, 96t, 99t, 125t, 128, 130–1, 139, 209, 251
Latvian language 156
Law and Justice Party (Poland) 130
law and law-making 10–11, 61, 65, 92
lawyer-linguists 155, 182
Lazar, M. 131
League of Polish Families 130, 132, 134
left–right politics **141–2**, 144, 146
Lega Nord (Italy) 129, 130, 132
legal instruments
  'simplified into six types' 61
legal personality 119
Legal Protection of Biotechnological Inventions (directive) 243
legislation 3, 91, 189
legislative branch 19–20, 22, 203–4, 292
legislative cycle 103, 275
legislative influence 188
  assessment **229–37**
  codecision2 (roaming charges) **256–67**
  complexities 256
  and decision-making **229–72**
  variable **254–6**
legislative initiative **41**, 45, 189
legislative organization 147–8
legislative powers (EP) **188–97**
  assent procedure **194–5**
  'codecision2' (second version of codecision) **188–93**
  consultation 193
  initiation of legislation **195–6**
  written declarations **196–7**
legislative process 168, 188, 240, 290
legislative proposals 186, 279
  capacity to amend 230
  draft 276
  'emergency brake' system 192–3
  final votes 185
  'sunset clauses' 241
legislatures
  bicameral 19–20
  'central organizational questions' 6, 147
  characteristic features **10–12**
  comparative analysis 273
  constraints (Blondel) 14
  formal and informal constraints 17
  functions 3
  legislative influence categories 40
  location 148
  Mezey's typology **41**, 66
  normal role 292
  Norton's typology **41**, 66
  organization 158–9
  'policy-making' 66, 226, 229
  'policy-making' versus 'policy-influencing' **12–14**, 14f
  power 221

power to initiate legislation 14
role and functions 5
role of presiding officers 159, 160–1
theories **5**, 25
'universal' functions **12–15**
veto power 238
see also parliaments
legitimacy 6, 9, 20, 24, 34, **68–89**, 90–1
  'democratic legitimacy' 20, 28, 29, 39, 55, 278, 294–5
  disaggregation processes 274
  elections and democracy **80–1**
legitimacy crisis 21
legitimation 10, 29, 73, 80, 90–1, 273
  multiple **87–8**
  normative debate 273, 296
  political debate versus academic debate 89
legitimation function 3–6, 11–12, **15**, 16–17, 18, 25
Leinen, J, 53, 120, 169t, 174, 323
Lewandowski, J. 173
liberal democracy 22, 82, 86, 102, 112, 117
Liberal Democrat Party (UK) 122, 129
Liberal Democrats (Lithuania) 130
Liberals/liberals 109, 114, 122, 162
Libicki, M. 169t
Lightfoot, S. 117, 119
Lijphart, A. 288
Lindner, J. 198, 200
linguistic equality principle 154–5
linguistic services 166
linguistic sovereignty 154
linkage function 3–6, 11, 12, **14**, 16–17, 18, 25
linkages 113
  elections and legitimacy **68–89**
  representation and MEPs **90–112**
Lisbon strategy (2000–) 296
Lisbon Summit (2000) 295
Lisbon Treaty (Reform Treaty, 2007): general
  abolition of cooperation procedure 238
  assent procedure 194
  assent procedure: became 'consent' 65
  budgetary functions 227
  budgetary powers 198, 200
  budgetary procedure 201
  change of wording from Constitutional Treaty 297
  comitology 242
  'consultation' 193
  cooperation procedure: abolition 65
  'delegated legislation' 242
  'early warning' mechanism 281
  ECB-EP relations 216
  initiation of legislation 196
  national parliaments 275–6
  objective 8
  opt-outs, opt-ins, derogations 65
  'ordinary legislative procedure' 189, 226

Lisbon Treaty – *continued*
  parliamentarization of Commission 'remains
      aspiration'   227
  'pillar structure was collapsed'   65, 190
  'pre-Lisbon article 202'   240
  provisions on democratic principles   **296–8**
  'Provisions on Democratic Principles'   297
  referencing   7–8
  referendum (Ireland, 2008)   8
  'slight detour'   **62–6**
Lisbon Treaty (2007): Treaty on European
      Union (TEU)   64
  Article 10(2)   274
  Article 11(2)   296–7
  Article 11(4) (citizens' initiatives) 297
  Article 14(1)   (legislative and budgetary
      functions)   64
  Article 17(7)   (appointment of Commission
      President)   64, 85, 206
  Article 27   193
  Article 48   193, 194, 196, 277
  Article 49   194
  Title II   274, 296
Lisbon Treaty (2007): Treaty on Functioning of
      European Union (TFEU)
  Article 23   193
  Article 48   192–3
  Article 76   190
  Article 77   193
  Article 81   192, 193
  Article 82   65, 192–3
  Article 83   65
  Article 87   193
  Article 121   185
  Article 129   190
  Article 218(11)   225
  Article 234   209
  Article 257   190
  Article 281   190
  Article 284   185
  Article 286   213
  Article 287(4)   213
  Article 289   65
  Article 289(3)   65
  Article 294   192
  Article 312   194
  Article 314   65, 201
  Article 319(2–3)   202
  Article 341   148
  Title X, Article 152 (Social Policy)   296–7
  Part Three   66
list system 69
Lista Emma Bonino   116, 120, 128,
Lithuania   70, 71t, 93, 96t, 99t, 125t, 130
Lithuanian language   156
lobbying   22, **102–8**, 184–5, 207, 244–5, 257,
      262
  'problem' and regulation   **105–7**
  transmission, translation, timing (of
      information)   **103–4**

lobbyists   112, 221
  code of conduct   106
  effective definition   105
  good, 'vital source of information' for MEPs
      103–4
  'institutional'   **107–8**
  public register (1996–)   105–6
  self-regulation   105–6
Lodge, J.   39, 41–2, 46, 48, **316–17**
Loewenberg, G.   11, 16, 17, 68, 88, 90, 98,
London   279
Lord, C.   22, 49, 72, 80, 83, 87, 89, 114, 123,
      210, 294–5
Losco, A.   262
Lovenduski, J.   95, 302
Lulling, A.   162
Luxembourg   70, 71t, 76–7, 79, 92–4, 96t,
      98, 99t, 125t
Luxembourg City   52, 106–7, 149, 244
  EP: occasional plenary sessions 150
  EP: General Secretariat   9, 148
  Konrad Adenauer Building   153
  Plateau du Kirchberg   150
Luxembourg government   150

Maastricht Treaty (Treaty on European
      Union/TEU, 1991): articles
  Article 7   57
  Article 8   82
  Article 189b   231
  Article 191   118
  'Article 192 (then 138b)'   196
  Article N   50, 51
Maastricht Treaty (1991): general   **47–51**
  appointment of Commission President
      204–5
  appointment of European Commission   267
  appointment of European Commissioners
      205–6
  assent procedure   194
  auditing of EU accounts   202
  codecision procedure   230, 233, 238, 240
  comitology   240
  'conciliation' procedure   231
  'disappointed EP'   48
  ECB appointments   214, 215
  executive role of European Council   290
  functioning   51
  initiation of legislation   **195–6**
  introduction of Ombudsman   212
  national parliaments   275
  pillars (first, second, third)   57
  provided legal base for EP Committees of
      Inquiry   180
  ratification process   135
Macedonia   165
Macintyre, F.   xii
macroeconomic indicators   199
Magnette, P. 58, 136, 292, 317
Majone, G.   293, 295–6

majority voting 23, 44, 47, 243
'making a success of Single Act' (EP temporary committee, 1987) 179
Malmström, C. 93, 152, 153–4
Malta 69–70, 71t, 75, 79, 94, 96t, 99t, 125t, 262
Maltese language 156
Mamadouh, V. 172, 177, 178
Manin, B. 80
Markov, H. 169t, 175
Marks, G. 18, 19, 302
Marsh, M. 74–6, 78, 99–100
Martens, W. 81
Martin, D. 46, 85, 285
Martin, F. 94
Martin reports 46–7
Martínez Martínez, M. A. 162
Mather, J. 72, 98
Matsakis, M. 129
Maurer, A. 210, 227, 230, 240, 242, 254
Mauro, M. 162
Mavrommatis, M. 262
Mazey, S. 104
McAvan, L. 121–2
McAllister, R. 46, 318
McCarthy, A. 169t, 246–7, 259
McElroy, G. 171, 172
McMillan-Scott, E. 162
media 179–80, 205, 208, 237, 245, 266–7, 286
Medina Ortega, M. 180
member-states 8, 59–60, 64, 69–70, 119, 154, 243–4, 274–4, 283–4, 295
  budgetary contributions to EU 198
Members of European Parliament (MEPs)
  ability of constituents to contact 100
  'act on behalf' of electors 98
  appointment to national governments 93
  constituency office 101
  continuous service since 1979 94
  declaration of 'interests' 106–7, 185
  determinants of re-selection 117
  'European list' versus 'national list' 54
  Eurosceptic 120
  expenses and fees 162
  'few assistants' 103
  former ministers 92–3
  former regional and local politicians 93–4
  Gaullist 124
  independents 129
  lack 'truly European mandate' 81
  linkage and representation 90–112
  'no control over where EP sits' 148
  non-affiliated 125t, 184
  number 2, 51–2, 54, 56, 60, 64, 126, 168
  rarely voted against national parties (1979–2004) 137
  re-elected 94
  representation of individual interests 100–1
  representative style 111
  role orientation 110
  single European-wide constituency 54
  socialist 124, 140
  socio-economic background 92, 112
  territorial representation 98–101
  transnational, cross-border electoral list (option) 286
  web pages 107
  working methods (regularization, 2004) 236
Members' Statute (1999) 108
MEPs against Cancer (MAC) 184
Merger Treaty (1965) 32, 35
  'Article 4' 35
  effective from 1967 35
Merkel, A. 174, 256
Mexico 165
Mezey, M.
  notion of constraints 14, 40, 204
  policy-making strength of legislatures 12–13, 14f, 25, 28, 41, 226, 237–8
  support accruing to representative institutions 15
'micro-plenaries' (EP) 149
Microsoft 245
Milan 94
Milan summit (1985) 44
Mill, J. S. 105
Mining, Chemical, and Energy Workers' Union (Germany) 244
ministers 219, 275, 282
Mishler, W. 97
'Mixed Group' 116
mixed polity 24, 24
mobile operators 260–5
mobile telephone users 256
'modernizers' (Labour Party) 128
modi vivendi 272
Modus Vivendi (1994) 240–1
Molnar, J. 214
Money, J. 289
Monnet, J. 29, 34
  'ambiguous institutional legacy' 26–8
  Memoirs (Monnet, 1978) 28
Monnet Plan (France, 1946–) 27
Montgomery, E. 302
Monti, M. 257
Moravcsik, A. 53, 302
Morgantini, L. 174
Morillon, P. 169t
Moser, P. 255
Mote, A. 132
Mulder, J. 162
multilateral parliamentary networks 276–84
  conventions 276–9
  COSAC 279–82
  joint committee meetings 282–4
  second parliamentary chamber (EU) 277–9
multiple *demoi* (Weiler and Nicoladis) 88
Murrah, L. 302

Muscardini, C.   122
Muscat, J.   **262–5**
Mussolini, A.   133
Mussolini, B.   132

nation-state   20–2, 29, 82–3, 117, 278
national delegations   123, 136
'national electorate'   82
national governments   3, 20, 29, 85, 93, 138,
     148, 229, 245, 274, 287
   choice and sustenance   285
   'institutional lobbyist' of EP   **107–8**
   socialist   75
   third-country   121
national interests   29, 244–5, 254, 287
national parliaments
   budgetary and public finance committees
        282–3
   committees   282–3
   constituency size   98
   EP and   **274–84**
   European Affairs committees   47, 275
   female representatives (2003–7)   96t
   MPs   90, 111
   role in budgetary affairs   198
   scrutiny process/role   280–4
   see also COSAC
national sovereignty   126
nationalism   115
nationality   124, 176, 178
neo-federalism   19, 20
neo-functionalism   27
Netherlands   70, 71t, 76, 93–4, 96t, 99t, 125t,
     131
   referendum (2005)   62
'network polity'   293
networks   298
Neuhold, C.   171, 241
Neunreither, K.   87
'neutralized committees'   171–2
new governance thesis   24, 295
'new institutionalism'   147
Nice Treaty (2001)   **53–7**
   Article 214   55
   Article 214(2)   204
   Article 300(6)   225
   assent procedure   194
   'disappointment'   58
   EP: power to bring court actions   225
   institutional issues 'unresolved'   58
   national parliaments   275
   outcomes versus aspirations   **55–7**
   pillars   57
Nice Treaty annex (Convention on Future of
     Europe)   277
Nicholson of Winterbourne, Baroness   175
Nicholson, J.   162
Nickel, D.   194–5, 287
Nicoladis, K.   53, 58, 83, 88
Nicoll, W.   31, 38, 50,

Niebler, A.   169t, 174, 264
no-confidence votes   203
'no taxation without representation'   198
Noël, E.   44
Nokia   245, 246–7
non-governmental organizations (NGOs)   22,
     224, 293
non-legislative reports   223
non-legislative resolutions   145
Nordic countries   129
Nordic Green Left   *see* Confederal Group of
     European Left
'normal legislative procedure'   189
Norris, P.   91, 95
Northern Ireland   69, 71t, 131, 134
Norton, P.   **10–11**, 12, **13–14**, 14f, 28, 41, 66,
     98
Noury, A.   138, 139, 142, 313
nuclear energy   193
nuclear materials   180
Nugent, N.   i, xii, 34, 58, 239, 296

O'Leary, D.   xii
Offe, C.   293
Official Journal of the European Union (OJ)
     C-series   7, 120, 186, 219, 232, 253
Ombudsman   49, 194, 196
O'Neill, N.   xii
Onesta, G.   162
Onyszkiewicz, J.   175
Open Method of Coordination (OMC)
     293–4, **295–6**, 298
open network provision (ONP)   243, 255
open-list systems   101
'open-source' campaigners   245–6
'opinions'   61
'optimal form of government'   24
opt-outs   290
'oral question with debate'   197
Orden, G. van   127, 175
'ordinary legislative procedure' (Lisbon Treaty)
     48, 64–6, 189, 190, 193, 226
'organized civil society'   294–5, 297
'output legitimacy'   22–3, 29, 88, 293–4
Ouzký, M.   169t, 174
'own resources' (1970–)   36, 198–9
own-initiative reports   195, 197

Packenham, R. A.   **11**, 221
Palacio, L. de   206
Pareto-improving policy output   293
Paris   34, 279
Paris Treaty (1951)   26–7, 31, 35
   Article 20: repeated in Rome Treaty (1957,
        Article 137)   32
   Articles 20–25   28
   Article 21   28, 30
   Article 25   30
Paris Treaty (1952)   31
Parish, N.   169t, 174

'parliament' (etymology) 221
Parliament Magazine 140
parliamentarism 142
parliamentarization 4, 7, 16, 19, 89, 145,
    227, 272, **273–99**
  European Commission **285–9**
  executive-legislative roles **284–92**
Parliamentary Assembly of African, Caribbean
    and Pacific regions and EU (ACP-EU)
    165
parliamentary committees 159
Parliamentary Cooperation Committees 165
'parliamentary Europe' model 19, 25
'parliamentary model' 4, **15–17**, 273, 284
parliamentary representation
  minimum thresholds 70
parliamentary system of government 15–16,
    17, 88, 203, 228, 267, 273
  characteristics 'lacking in EU' 227–8
parliaments **274–84**
  definition 14
  legislative output 182–3
  legislative powers 221
  'main providers of legitimacy' 84
  national sovereignty 29
  regional 119
  representative 273
  role within political system 15
  second chambers 290
  universal roles 273
  see also legislatures; national parliaments
Partido Popular (Portugal) 127
Partito Pensionati (Italy) 127
party candidates (unalterable lists) 70
Party of European Socialists (PSE Group)
  author 286, 324
  coalition with EPP **140–1**
  composition 125t, **128**
  ideological coherence 128
  opposed Barroso Commission 207
party federations
  transnational 109–10, 117
party funding
legal challenges 120
'party government' 109, 110, 111, 145
party group coordinators 181, 258
party group leaders 121, 124, 144, 145, 162
  bargaining over EP committee leadership
    176
party group meetings **123–4**
party groups **113–46**
  activities 184
  budgetary matters 164b
  bureaux 121–2, 123
  cohesion 144, 145–6
  cohesion: effect on EP's legislative influence
    254
  committee leadership 173, 174, 175
  competitiveness versus cooperativeness 142
  composition **124–34**

cooperation 146
  'duopoly' versus 'oligopoly' 114, 140
  formal versus informal procedures 122
  formation of intergroups 185
  funding **117–21**
  group meetings **123–4**
  inter-group coalitions and competition
    140–1
  left–right politics **141–2**
  parliamentary-specific activities **116–24**
  rapporteurships 178
  representation on EP committees 172
  role 6
  rules on size and formation **115–16**
  size 121, 134, 138–9, 173
  small 184
  structures and staffing **121–3**
  support staff 124
  transcended by nationality 244–5
  transnational **72–3, 113–15**
  see also political parties
party loyalty (departures from) 135–6
party manifestos 72–3, 109, 117
'party representation' 112
party systems 112
  EU paradox 110
'party whips' 176
Pascu, I. 175
passports 65, 193
patents 247
Paterson, W. E. i, xii
Patjin Report 34
Patten, C. 206
Patterson, S. C. 11, 12, 14, 16, 17, 68, 88,
    90, 98
PDS (Germany) 131
peace 130
Peasants and New Democratic Party
    (Lithuania) 130
Pedersen, K. 73
Pelly, G. 28, 34
pension reform 296
'people', the 68, 80, 88, 91, 113
  demos 87
  territorially defined 82
People's Party (Poland) 130
perception 61, 229, 230, 278
Permanent Conference of Parliaments (mooted)
    277
Peterle, A. 174
Peterson, J. 4, 21–2
'*petits pas*' versus 'qualitative leaps' 38, 42,
    46, 66, 272
Phinnemore, D. 58
Pielbags, A. 209
Pitkin, H. 90, 91
Plaid Cymru (PC) 130
plenary sessions **185–6**
  agenda 165
  EP (Luxembourg City, 1986) 149

plenary sessions – *continued*
  EP (Strasbourg)   123, 150
  European Convention   275
  number of days   151
  occasional   150
  votes by show of hands   143
  see also European Parliament
Pleven Report   34
Plumb–Delors procedure (1988)   240
'pluralistic citizenship' (Wessels and Diedrichs)
    88, 89
Podesta, G.   154–5
Poland   1, 69–70, 71t, 76, 93–4, 96t, 98, 99t,
    107, 125t, 130, 133, 169t, 174–5, 222
policing   65, 190, 193, 284, 303
'policy advocacy'   98–100
policy influence   12–14
'policy responsiveness'   98–100
policy segmentation   22
policy type
  effect on EP's legislative influence   254
Polish language   156
'political affinities'   116
political community   11
political convention   40
political foundations   120
'political negotiations'   290
political parties   22, 54, 90, 159
  centre-right   115
  cohesion (national parties versus European
      party groups)   135–9
  competitive system   110
  definition   119
  delegations (national)   134–5, 138
  disciplined (EP)   206
  European   72, 81
  funding   56, 117–21, 304
  governing   75, 135
  leaders (national)   121
  national   74, 117, 137, 145, 254, 285–6
  representation in EP   108–10
  right-wing   126
  selection of candidates for EP   137, 145
  small   74, 75, 120
  social democratic left   115
  transnational   3, 6, 72–3, 85–6
  see also party groups
'political responsibility'   211
political spectrum (left–right)   141–2, 144, 146
  left   115, 131
  left-of-centre   206
  centre-left   128, 129
  centre-right   115, 126, 129
  right   126, 130, 132, 160
  far-right   132, 133
political systems   15, 21, 25, 80, 87, 88, 273
political will   294
Pollack, M. A.   18, 293, 302
pooling of sovereignties   20
population   59

port services   249–51
Portugal   70, 71t, 92–3, 96t, 99t, 125t, 129,
    131, 206, 214, 282, 283
post-communist states   76
post-parliamentarism   22–3, 24, 102, 292–8,
    298–9
post-war era   149
postal voting   79
Pöttering, H.-G.   63, 122, 126, 134, 152,
    160–1, 166, 174, 274
power   95, 97, 159, 195, 205, 221
  hierarchies   22
power asymmetry   105
preferential voting   69–70
presidential system   15–16, 292
Preuss, U. K.   292
price ceilings   262–5
Pridham, G.   126
Pridham, P.   126
Priestley, J.   166
primates (use in experiments)   197
principal–agent relationship   137
'prior authorization' principle   204, 229,
    267–9
problem-solving   29, 293
procedural harmonization   295
Prodi, R.   136, 268–9, 287
Prodi Commission (1999–)   206, 211
professional associations   102
Programme for European Voluntary Service
    255
proportional list system   97
proportional representation   69, 97
proportionalists   91, 112
proportionality principle   276, 280, 281
Protection of Personal Data directive   255
Provan, J.   222, 244
Pryce, R.   27, 47
PSE Group   *see* Party of European Socialists
public administration   92
public affairs consultancies   102
public hearings   224–5, 249–50, 258–61, 266

Quaestors   162–3
qualified majority voting (QMV)   52, 55–6,
    61–2, 65–6, 189, 192, 204, 247, 274
'qualified supranationalism'   123,
'question time'   218–19, 220t, 224
questionnaires   206, 207, 215
questions (parliamentary)   40, 217, 218–21,
    222
  oral response   218–19, 220t, 227
  'priority' versus 'non-priority'   219
  written   219–21, 227

race and racism   112, 133, 180
Radicals (Italy)   116
rail freight   253
  codecision2 (rejection at first reading)   249,
      251–2, 303, 322

rapporteurs   43, 45–6, 53, 104, 108, 110, 150, 171, **176–8**, 179–81, 183, 200, 203, 214, 223, 241, 245–7, 249–51, 259, 262–3, 283, 321
  bidding system   177
Rasmussen, P. N.   122
rational choice   230–1, 254, 256, 290
Rau, J.   278
Raunio, T.   73, 86, 110, 134, 146, 172, 177–8, 234–6, 296, 317
  written parliamentary questions   219, 221
'recommendations'   61, 65
red tape   201
Reding, V.   93, **257–61**, 266–7
referendum campaigns   121
France/Netherlands (2005)   1
Reform Treaty   63
reformism   132
regional associations   102
regional constituencies   69, 98, 101
regional policy   44
regional and social funds   82
regionalism/regionalists   109, 115
Register of Financial Interests   106
Registration, Evaluation, Authorization, and Restriction of Chemicals (REACH)   224–5, 309
  REACH Directive (2006)   256
regulation ('better and faster')   294
Regulation on Statute and Financing of European Political Parties (proposed 2003, effective 2004) 118, **119–20**, 322
'regulations'   61, 65
regulatory agencies   293, 294
  appointment   **216–17**
regulatory committees: Type IIIb   239, 240
'regulatory procedure with scrutiny' (2006)   242
Reif, K.   73
rejection   **237–54**
  under codecision1   **243**
  under codecision2: software patents (2005)   **245–8**, 303
  under codecision2: takeover bids (2001)   **243–5**, 303
  under 'cooperation'   **238–9**
Report and Initial Evaluation of Results (of IGC and Amsterdam Treaty)   (EP 1997) 52,
representation   **68, 90–112**, 273
  four foci   90
  literature   90
  microcosmic   **90–8**
  national processes   87
  style   **111**
representative assemblies
  linkage between 'composition' and 'action'   91
research and development   44, 247
residence permits   193

Resolution on Breast Cancer in Enlarged EU (2006)   184
Reul, H.   266
Richardson, J.   22, 104
Riis-Jörgensen, K.   267
Ringe, N.   75, 245
Rittberger, B.   22, 28–9, 89, 226, 243, 255
roaming charges (mobile telephone)   **256–67**, 307
  agreement at first reading via trialogues   **264–6**
  EP committee   **261–3**
  EP committee votes   **263–4**
  EP's impact   **266–7**
  EP's processing of proposal   **261–6**
  evolution of proposal   **256–61**
  opt-in system   264–5
  opt-out system   263, 264–5, 266
roaming charges regulation (2007)   257, 266–7
'roaming services'   257
Rocard, M.   245, 247–8
Rodríguez Zapatero, J. L.   135
roll-call votes (RCVs)   138, 142, **143–5**
  'not a random sample'   144
Romania   xi, 1, 93, 99t, 125t,127–8, 131–3, 154, 175,
Rome: Conference of Parliaments of Community ('Assizes', 1990)   47, 277
Rome: Treating Establishing a Constitution for Europe
  signed (29 October 2004)   58
Rome Declaration (1990)   47
Rome Treaties (1957)   35
  institutional arrangements   31–2
Rome Treaty (EEC Treaty, 1957): articles
  Article 23   218
  Article 43(2)   39
  Article 137   32
  Article 138   69
  Article 140   40
  Article 144   33
  Article 145   32
  Article 155   32, 41
  Article 203   33
Rome Treaty (EEC Treaty, 1957): general
  establishment of European Economic Community   **31–4**
  fiftieth anniversary (2007)   274–5
  right of legislature to question Commission   218
  'Treaty Establishing European Community'   8
  see also 'European Community Treaty'
Rømer, H.   166
Rometsch, D.   23, 24
Rosamond, B.   18, 27
Roth-Behrendt, D.   223, 236
Rothe, M.   181
Roucek, L.   175

RPFIE   129
Rübig, P.   **262–4**, 266
rule of law   59, 222
Russia   131, 252, 253
Rutelli, F.   128

Sainte-Lagüe electoral formula   71t
Salmon, T. C.   31, 38
Samland–Williamson agreement (1996)
  240–1
Santer, J.   136, 204
Santer Commission   205
  resignation (1999)   203, 209–10, 211, 268
Sarkozy, N.   153, 161
Sartori, A.   94
Saryusz-Wolski, J.   169t, 174
Schambach, R.   302
Scheele, K.   253
Schmitt, H.   73, 76, 80, 108, 110
Schönlau, J.   118
Schörder, G.   244, 278
Schulz, M.   121, 122, 133
Schuman, R.   26
Schuman Group   126
Schuman Plan   26–7
Schwindt-Bayer, L. A.   97
Scotland   83
Scottish National Party (SNP)   130
scrutiny   **217–25**, 275
Scully, R.   15, 86, 110, 111, 135, 136–7,
  100–1, 229, 310, **325–6**
second reading   192, 196, 231–4, 236–7, 248,
  258
  'early' agreements   233
secrecy   235
Securities Committee   243
security   61, 226, 279–80
selection bias   144
'semi-parliamentary European system'
  (Magnette)   292
semi-parliamentary system   **298–9**
semi-presidential system   292, 307
Senate (proposed, 1953)   278
separation of powers   16, 19
Septembri, P.   145
'service responsiveness'   98, **100**
Services Directive (2006)   256
Shackleton, M.   xii, 4, 142, 180, 234, 235,
  236, 254, 255, 289, 292, 305, **326**
Shaw, J.   298
Shephard, M.   100
Siemens   246–7
Sierra Leone   222
Sifunakis, N.   169t, 174
Silaghi, O. I.   93
'sincere cooperation' principle   59
single currency   99
Single European Act (SEA, 1986)   35, 41,
  44–5, 183, 188, 240
  Articles 8 and 9   194

'cooperation procedure'   45
'deficiencies'   **46–7**
  effective (1987–)   38
single market (1992–)   44
single national constituency   69, 98
single transferable vote (STV)   69, 101
  'STV–Droop electoral formula'   71t
'sinister interests' (Mill)   105, 112
Sinn Féin   131
Skinner, P.   xii
Slovakia   70, 71t, 75–6, 96t, 99t, 125t, 133,
  169t, 174, 175, 214, 222
Slovakian language   156
Slovene language   156
Slovenia   70, 71t, 76, 94, 96t, 99t, 125t, 139,
  184
Smismans, S.   297
Smith, J.   30, 81, 85–6, 198, 286
Social Democrats (Germany)   128
social dialogue   297
social groupings   90
social inclusion   296
social justice   130
social partners   296–7
Social Summit for Growth and Employment
  296–7
Socialist Group (EP)   121–2, 246
Socialist Party (Spain)   135, 136
Socialist People's Party (Denmark)   130–1
Socialist Unity for Europe (Italy)   134
Socialists   109, 114, 115, 206, 236
'Socrates'   255
Socrates, J.   161
Söderman, J.   213
'soft law' mechanisms   295
software patents directive (2005)   **245–8**, 303
Solana, J.   161
Solemn Declaration on European Union (1983)
  40, 42–3, 218
SOS Democracy   120
sovereign state   19
Soviet Union   165
Sozialdemokratische Partei Deutschlands (SPD)
  122
Spain   1, 70, 71t, 75, 83, 94, 96t, 99t, 125t,
  131, 135, 160, 162, 169t, 174, 222, 264,
  289
Spanish language   156, 157
Spanish Socialist Party   128
'special legislative procedure'   61, 65, 66,
  193
Special Report 13/2000 (Court of Auditors)
  117
Spence, D.   107, 268
Spinelli, A.   43
Staff Regulations of Officials of the European
  Communities   166
'standard legislative procedure'   189
Staszak, S.   xii
'State of Union' debate   223

Statute of European System of Central Banks
190
Steed, M.   306
Strani, L.   xii
Strasbourg
Common Assembly (ECSC, 1952–)   30
demonstrations outside EP   249
EP budget session   148
EP overcharged on rent   152
EP plenary sessions   148, 150
EP seat   149
European Council meetings (offer to French
Government)   152
French Government inflexibility   153
normal venue for EP's monthly part-sessions
151
speech by Barroso (18 June 2008)   8
'spirit and memory of Europe'   149, 151
Strasbourg complex: Churchill, Madariaga,
Weiss Buildings   9, 153
*Strategic Objectives 2000–5: 'Shaping New
Europe'* (2000)   268–9, 307
Strategy Documents   170n, 171
Structural Funds   57, 194, 199, 283
Stubb, A.   xii, 54, 103, 158
subsidiarity 'early warning system'   280
subsidiarity principle   43, 47, 49, 64, 276,
279–82
'substantive legitimacy'   293
'sunset' clauses   241, 262, 266
support **15**
Svensson, P.   301
Sweden   70, 71t, 75–6, 92–4, 96t, 99t, 125t,
131, 132, 169t, 266
systemic context   271

T-Mobile   257
Tajani A.   93
'Takeover Bids' Directive (2001)   **243–5**, 303
Tampere Programme   283
Taylor, S.   2
Technical Group of Independent Members
(TDI)   116
technical groups   184
technocracy   29, 88, 237, 294
telecommunications   247
'no internal market'   257
Telecommunications Council   266
territorial representation   90, **98–101**
Treaty on European Union (TEU)   8
see also Lisbon Treaty; Maastricht Treaty
Treaty on Functioning of European Union
(TFEU)   8, 63
see also Lisbon Treaty
Theato, D.   175,
Thiem, J.   143, 144
third pillar   57, 190, 193
Third Railway Package (European
Commission)   280
third reading   233–4, 244

Thomassen, J.   108, 110
time   3, 25, 82, 103, 158, 186, 190, 197, 218,
223–4, 226
time effect   **79–80**
Tindemans, L.   77
Titley, G.   xii
tobacco   195, 255–6
Toia, P.   259
Toma, A.   xii
Tomlinson, J.   180
tourists   196
trade   65, 189, 226
trade associations   102
trade unions   245
transit regime 180
transition states   46
translation   **103–4, 154–8**
transmission, translation, timing (three Ts) (of
information)   **103–4**
transparency   48–9, 55, 105, 121, 235,
237, 240–1, 260–2, 266, 291, 294,
296
Transport Council   252
trapping standards   249, **252–4**, 303, 322
travel costs   153
Treaty Amending Certain Budgetary Provisions
of Treaties (Luxembourg, 1970)   36
trialogues   48–9, 182, 200, 233–4, 237,
272
Trichet, J.-C.   215–16
'truly European mandate' (Hallstein)   81
'trustee' role   111
Tsatsos, D.   54
Tsebelis, G.   143, 231, 255, 289
Turkey   165
turnout   71t, 73, 74, 76–80, 81
attitudinal explanations   77, **78–9**
European elections (2004)   71t
institutional explanations   77, **79–80**
reasons for concern   77

Ulster Unionists   127
Union for Europe of Nations (UEN, 1999–)
94, 119, 121–2, 132, 141, 169t, 173, 181,
211, 251
composition   125t, 129–30
ideological diversity   130
Union pour la Démocratie Française   (UDF)
128–9
Union pour un Mouvement Populaire (UMP)
122
'Union of Peoples'   53
United Kingdom   34, 50, 55, 60, 64, 70, 71t,
75–7, 79, 83, 92–101, 124–6, 133, 162,
169t, 174, 209, 218–19, 250, 259, 264,
278–9
European elections (electoral system)   69
Government   107–8, 180
permanent representation in Brussels
107

United Kingdom Independence Party (UKIP) 122, 132, 266
United States of America (USA) 216, 252–3
  federal system 292
  institutional structure 292
  US House of Representatives 289, 292
  US Senate 289
United States of Europe model 19–20, 23
universal suffrage 28
Urwin, D. W. 26, 31

Vaccari, B. 239
'variable geometry' 290
VAT 198
Veneto 94
Venice 94
Venstre (Denmark) 129
Verhofstadt, G. 206
Vidal-Quadras, A. 162, 181
viscosity concept (Blondel) 14
Vitorino, A. 93
Vits, M. de 162
Vlaams Belang (Belgium) 132
Vodafone 257
Voggenhuber, J. 121
voting rights and eligibility 70, 72
voting systems 59
VVD (Netherlands) 129
VW 244

Wallace, H. 235, 290–1
Wallace, W. 19, 30
Walloons 206
Wallström, M. 207–8, 242, 271
Warsaw 278
Washington, DC 102
waste
  civil liability for damage 195
  dangerous 238–9
  incineration 238
Watson, G. 122, 129, 223
Weiler, J. 82–3, 84, 88
Weiner, A. 18, 19
'welfare fostering' 296
welfare state 83
Welle, K. 166

Wessels, B. 99–100, 318, 328
Wessels, W. 17, 20, 27, 46, 51, 87–8, 324, 328–9
  fusion model 23–4
West Europe 73
West Germany 42
Westlake, M. xii, 28, 31, 35, 39, 44, 47, 142, 143, 145, 212, 215, 221, 329
Westminster Parliament 98
  House of Commons 218–19, 278–9, 286
  House of Commons: European Scrutiny Committee 235, 271, 312
  House of Lords 92, 278–9, 291, 313
  House of Lords: EU Select Committee 258, 278–9
'whips' 137
Whitehead, P. xii, 174, 259
'wholesale' service (mobile telephones) 257
Wieczorek-Zeul, H. 93
Williams, K. 39
women 168, 208
  'European effect' 95
  representation in EP 94–8
Wood, D. M. 98
Wood, J. 243, 254
workers 92, 238
working conditions 255
Working Group on Parliamentary Reform (2007) 223, 227, 237
working time directive (2005) 135
workload 168, 171, 234
written declarations 196–7
  lapsed 197
  written declaration 40/2007 (use of primates in experiments) 197
WTO rules 253
Wuermeling, J. 93, 264, 265
Wurtz, F. 122, 160
Wurzel, R. 311
Wynn, T. xii, 128

Yataganas, X. A. 54, 56, 225

Záborská, A. 169t, 175–6
Zagari, M. 150
Zile, R. 251